BEVERLY HILLS PUBLIC LIBRARY

3 5048 00476 7354

D0793482

WITHDRAWN

APR 1 5 2000
DATE DUE

THE SWEETNESS OF LIFE

By the same author

'Actio' and Persuasion: Dramatic Performance in
Eighteenth-Century France

The Complete Lover: Eros, Nature and Artifice in the
Eighteenth-Century French Novel

ADULT
92
VIGEE-LEBRUN
Louise-Elisabeth

THE SWEETNESS OF LIFE

A Biography of Elisabeth Louise Vigée Le Brun

ANGELICA GOODDEN

ANDRE DEUTSCH

Beverly Hills Public Library
444 North Rexford Drive
Beverly Hills, California 90210

WITHDRAWN

First published in 1997 by
André Deutsch Limited
A subsidiary of VCI plc
106 Great Russell Street
London WC1B 3LJ

Copyright © Angelica Goodden 1997
All rights reserved

The author has asserted her moral rights

A catalogue record for this title is available
from the British Library
ISBN 0 233 99021 6

Typeset by Falcon Oast Graphic Art
Printed in Great Britain by
WBC, Bridgend

CONTENTS

ILLUSTRATIONS

Self-portrait (1781)
Charles-Alexandre de Calonne (1785)
Hyacinthe-Gabrielle Roland, later Marchioness of Wellesley (1791)
Countess Golovina (1797–1800)
Louise, Queen of Prussia (1801)
Giuseppina Grassini in the role of Zaïre (1804)
Mont Blanc (1807)
Madame de Staël as Corinne at Cape Miseno (1808)

The artist's brother (Etienne Vigée: 1773)
The Vicomte de Vaudreuil (1784)
Bacchante (1785)
Self-portrait (1782)
Madame Grand (1783)
The Marquise de Pezay and the Marquise de Rouget with her two
    children (1787)
Self-portrait with Julie Le Brun (1789)
The Duchesse de Polignac (1783)
Madame du Barry (1782?)
Marie-Antoinette 'à la rose' (1783)
Marie-Antoinette and her three children (1787)
After 'Countess Skavronskaya' (1790)
Lord Hervey, the Bishop of Derry (1791)
Head of a young woman ('Lady Hamilton': c. 1790)
Emma Hamilton as sibyl (1791–2)

Giovanni Paisiello (1791)
Hubert Robert (1788)
Grand-Duchess Elizabeth (*c.* 1795)
Stanislas Augustus II, King of Poland (1797)
Julie Le Brun (1798)
Varvara Ivanovna Narishkin, *née* Ladomirsky (1800)
The Alphirtenfest at Unspunnen (1808)
Mrs William Chinnery (1803)

ACKNOWLEDGEMENTS

I have incurred many debts of gratitude in the course of writing this biography. St Hilda's College allowed me two terms of sabbatical leave during which I was able to study, look at pictures and draft chapters; the Faculty of Medieval and Modern Languages at Oxford gave me generous grants that helped support me during long periods abroad, and provided me with secretarial assistance at a crucial time; and the Churchill Foundation, which elected me to a Fellowship in 1994, made possible travel to the further-flung places associated with Madame Vigée Le Brun. Libraries, librarians, custodians of collections, experts and *amateurs* in the most literal sense of the word, in Oxford, London, Paris, Rouen, Versailles, Vienna, Rome, St Petersburg, New York and Washington, supported my efforts in innumerable ways, whether by offering me precious facilities for study, talking to me or corresponding with me. I owe much too to the hospitality of the many institutions in Europe and America which provided me with bed and often board, and to the friends who welcomed me in all the cities associated with Madame Vigée Le Brun. Different parts of the book were written in different places, but nowhere made a more stimulating and yet soothing background to work than the library of the Taylor Institution in Oxford.

All translations are my own.

INTRODUCTION

'Madame Le Brun was the idol of her century,' the playwright Brifaut wrote over 150 years ago. In her time Elisabeth Louise Vigée Le Brun was seen as a figure of exceptional glamour and chic, though she was also attacked – for being prettier than other women, she says, or for being fashionable, or for selling her pictures expensively. Being a remarkably accomplished painter and self-publicist, as well as a favourite of Marie-Antoinette and an impenitent supporter of the French monarchy, she naturally inspired envy and attracted gossip. As she reveals in her *Souvenirs*, the memoirs she wrote in the 1830s, she felt that celebrity could be particularly painful for women. She worked unremittingly hard, bringing up her daughter single-handed after her emigration in 1789, and even helped to support an apparently spendthrift husband. But she was rewarded with the accusation that she painted too much to paint well.

She is the subject of several biographies dating from the early twentieth century, but none has been written for seventy-five years. Joseph Baillio's catalogue to the Kimbell Art Museum exhibition of 1982 was the first scholarly evaluation of her *oeuvre* since André Blum's monograph of 1920, and Baillio's forthcoming *catalogue raisonné* will be a landmark in Vigée Le Brun studies. Since there can be no denying the intrinsic interest of her life and work, or the significance of her position as a highly successful woman painter at the end of the *ancien régime*, the decades of neglect seem surprising. It may be that the very approachability of her art has served her ill. She has a colour-sense that often puts one in mind of Nattier and Allan Ramsay; she paints ravishing pictures of aristocratic women (less frequently men), and they are naturally easy on the eye. For many years it has been fashionable for 'serious' art to be more difficult of access, more intellectually demanding, and perhaps more dissenting. Elisabeth Louise Vigée Le Brun, who lived too long and remained too firmly wedded to the ways of the *ancien régime*, seems suspiciously uncomplicated: if there is something rather endearing about her obvious

1

flattery of her female clients, perhaps there is also something slightly troubling about her facility. She is, one might have thought, too technically accomplished to be called second-rate, but her achievements are still standardly belittled as the merely decorative products of a bankrupt court, or the shamelessly feminine whitewash of a decadent world.

Attacking a woman's work because it lacks 'manly' seriousness is nothing new, of course: the contemporary artist Angelica Kauffman, for instance, who was much admired by Vigée Le Brun, was often criticised for the rococo prettiness and consequent effeteness of her portraits. But with or without a male solidity to their performance, both women were international celebrities in their day. Contemporaries evidently saw in their work qualities which, at least in Vigée Le Brun's case, subsequent generations have been more reluctant to acknowledge. She lived on to the mid-nineteenth century, still painting, but had become unfashionable well before she died. To the Victorian English and the post-Restoration French she seemed frivolous, and the moral neutrality of her work (except insofar as painting portraits of voluptuous women and courtesans was morally charged) made her distasteful to a more pious age. She refused to embrace the new principles of political liberalism or to celebrate the benefits of economic materialism, except when these dated from the *ancien régime*, preferring to depict the court of an absolute monarch and the offspring of old, landed money; and so she seemed both provokingly snobbish and out of step with the reigning ideology. Her feminism was not of a kind to appeal to the early twentieth century, because it was too limited: she exalted no self-made women but herself, and seemed happier to paint members of her own sex as idle sybarites than to show them as women of achievement. Her technique was held to be as suspect as her person, a polished art that covered life with a layer of enamel, both over-precise and under-practised (because she never had the chance to study drawing academically). The verdict passed on her in 1804 by an English connoisseur – 'that *imitative* kind of painting resemble[s] waxwork'[1] – dogged her for decades after, and her technical weaknesses were as mercilessly dissected as Kauffman's. Until a few decades ago she seemed to many lovers of painting beside the point, charming and seductive but shallow and politically incorrect.

Perhaps the tide is beginning to turn, at least in France. There is now a Vigée Le Brun room at the Louvre, where the artist presides over Greuze, Vincent, a clutch of male historical painters and her female contemporaries Madame Labille-Guiard (a portraitist) and Madame Vallayer-Coster (a still-life painter). *Ancien régime* art no longer suffers from the blanket disfavour that has dogged it for decades. But the remarkable scale of Elisabeth Louise Vigée Le Brun's achievements deserves more attention than it has been paid, and the attributes of her painting which have often attracted criticism need to be seen, unashamedly, as their strength. Because she drew almost all her subjects from a highly distinctive, cosmopolitan social world – a crumbling world after 1789, but one she tried to preserve on canvas – her existence as a painter, too, has to be set against the polite society of the courts and salons she frequented. In her, life and art are inextricably bound together.

She was witness to an age of change in more ways than one. She never supported the political upheavals, at least until the Bourbon restoration, and escaped France for the more hospitable climate of other European countries after the fall of the Bastille. Other changes were more welcome, if not radical enough for her taste. Like Adélaïde Labille-Guiard, she fought the male-dominated artistic establishment, challenging the virtual exclusion of women from membership of the Académie royale de peinture et de sculpture and contesting the assumption that women artists should confine themselves to the minor and decorative modes of painting. Vigée Le Brun passionately wanted the regard that accompanied the title of history painter (something which the more versatile Kauffman managed to win for herself), but had in the end to acknowledge that portraiture was her forte. She could comfort herself with the reflection that it was better paid and offered greater chances of social mobility.

She refused to accept other prevailing assumptions about the proper activities of her sex. Though she was married for nearly twenty years, she would not let her status as wife and mother impede her progress as an artist. (Nor would she let the fact that her husband was a picture-dealer be made legitimate grounds for her exclusion from the Académie, though according to the statutes it should have been.) She knew other female painters whose careers were held back by marriage – her early painting-companion Rosalie Boquet, or her own pupil Marie-Guilhelmine de Laville Leroulx, the future Madame Benoist – but she herself determined to live as independently as possible. She was good at selling herself too, trailing her most successful portraits all over Europe, and settling where she knew she could find clients – Rome, Naples, Vienna, St Petersburg, Moscow, Berlin and London. She may or may not have been personally threatened by the events of the Revolution. But she sensed the imminent loss of her wealthy native clientele, and so moved elsewhere.

Because she was a trend-setter, she attracted attention wherever she went: her female sitters wanted to be painted as she saw them, dashingly, sentimentally, invitingly or merely tactfully, in costumes that were either *le dernier cri* or timeless in their understated elegance and simplicity. Given her public persona, it naturally followed that she should be the subject of gossip. It was claimed that her portraits were really painted by men, that she knowingly used her contacts, sexually and otherwise, to procure advancement, and so on. But women artists, at least from Artemisia Gentileschi onwards, were used to such accusations.

Vigée Le Brun was perhaps more hurt by assertions that she, whose origins were relatively humble, was a social climber, and that the King himself deprecated her familiarity with Marie-Antoinette. But on balance, and despite occasional denials in the memoirs she wrote at the end of her life, she probably found it pleasant to be newsworthy: the range of superior clients she could attract was adequate compensation for slander and backbiting. As the familiar of the Queens of France, Naples and Prussia, of the Empress of Russia and the Prince of Wales, she could afford to smile at petty malice. She even allowed herself to feel a degree of superiority to some of her female clients – Napoleon's upstart sister Caroline Murat, for instance, or the voluptuous sibyl of the demi-monde, Emma Hamilton.

Over the length of her career, she amassed enough social and cultural capital to ensure widespread acceptance in her chosen milieu. Sufficiently adroit to achieve most of what she wanted most of the time, she enjoyed phenomenal success and a corresponding degree of adulation. She triumphed over institutional prejudice against women, and turned both her sex and her talent to best account. She understood the nature of the contract between herself and her clients, and was pragmatic about its implications. There was an unspoken agreement that she would make her sitters appear attractive, alluring, dignified, charming or otherwise fascinating, and be appropriately rewarded; and she rarely met with objections to such methods.

In short, Talleyrand's *douceur de vivre* and Vigée Le Brun's art perfectly illustrate each other: both are nostalgic evocations of a lost world whose imperfections must not be closely examined. Politician and artist alike preferred an unclouded vision, choosing to view France in the 1780s as a paradise of decorum and harmony rather than the background to mass suffering and destitution. Their partiality, unsurprisingly, has laid them open to the criticism of later ages. The untranslatable word *doux* occurs often in Vigée Le Brun's *Souvenirs*. A monarchist who tirelessly proclaimed her apolitical nature, yet carefully avoided republican governments during her twelve-year exile from France after 1789, she enjoyed the 'gentleness' of courtly life wherever she settled. She loftily proclaimed the contentedness of beggars in Italy, peasants in Austria and serfs in Russia, and in her portraits adroitly concealed the blemishes of their social superiors. She improved her own life story too, exalting her phenomenal rise from *petite bourgeoise* to intimate of Marie-Antoinette and the Empress of Russia, and papering over the cracks of her other life as part-time wife and mother of a spoiled but neglected daughter. She wrote her memoirs to vindicate herself in the face of slanderous accusations, she claims, and meant her admiring self-portraits with her daughter Julie to be a testimony to moral as well as technical excellence. But the life, like the art, calls for closer attention than it has often been given. '*Douceur*' is only half the story.

Louise, as I shall call her,[2] refused to listen to history as it was being made. She ignored all the news about France after her emigration, initially because she dreaded hearing about the *ancien régime*'s collapse, and she was never abreast of current affairs. She failed to understand why the monarchy needed to be toppled, detested Napoleon and most of the parvenus created by his Empire, unreservedly welcomed the Restoration of 1814 and was mystified by the overthrow of the Bourbon monarchy in the July Revolution of 1830. She never mentions the citizen-king Louis-Philippe who succeeded to the throne, no doubt because the concept of a citizen-king was anathema to her. Yet she was herself a bourgeois parvenue, and despite her loathing of post-Revolutionary capitalism she was as money-conscious as any of Balzac's businessmen and bankers. In the course of her life she periodically regretted the urge to accumulate beyond rationality or purpose, because the unappeasable hunger for *more* resulted in her producing second-rate work; but still she painted as busily as ever. Though she refers to painting as her 'dearest distraction',[3] she obviously took a thoroughly pragmatic view of it too, charging enormous prices for her work all over Europe. When she lived in Russia and England some of the natives called her a grasping *arriviste*, and jealously or snobbishly ignored her. But she was perhaps no more than adept, and much more skilful at moving with the times than it suited her to admit.

Beyond question, and quite apart from her achievement as a successful female artist in a male-dominated world, she was a superb painter. She remains puzzlingly unknown to a British public despite the number of works by her in state and private collections, or is perhaps known as a feminist (which she would have disliked) rather than as a portraitist. Sometimes she suffers the indignity of being confused with her husband's uncle, the seventeenth-century historical painter Charles Le Brun, which retrospectively confirms the justice of her suspicions about marriage: she was reluctant to give up the name Vigée when she became Jean-Baptiste-Pierre Le Brun's wife at the age of twenty, because she was already well known in her own right. Sometimes she is known without being recognised: her 1782 self-portrait in a straw hat in London's National Gallery, for instance, has appeared on innumerable calendars and notebook-covers, but shoppers are probably better acquainted with the image than with the identity of the subject. The fact that she is relatively unknown in

Britain is even more surprising in view of the fact that she lived and worked in England for over two years. But Angelica Kauffman, who spent much longer in London, left considerably more work behind and was an official member of the English artistic establishment, is hardly more familiar. Perhaps the artists' sex is still an unacknowledged barrier. Louise was no David, it is true, and does not deserve his celebrity: her draughts-manship (like Kauffman's) is often inferior, and she was not an artistic revolutionary. Yet her restrained classicism – a matter of a loose chemise rather than a stiff court dress, or a coiffure *à la Titus* rather than a styled and powdered wig – was by its very nature more appealing to many con-temporaries than the stern rectilinearity of David's works. Like Kauffman, Louise painted for her time, not ahead of it.

But her time was carefully selected, and she was unrepentant about the fact. She preserved the *douceur* until it began to seem rather quaint and old-womanish, and even then continued – but with touches of the new Romanticism – to mine the same vein. Yet she is the author of several magnificent portraits, and deserves far better than the sardonic dismissal which otherwise enlightened modern critics still give her.[4] Her achieve-ment, in an age more famous for its women painters than any before or since, deserves a full reappraisal.

CHAPTER ONE

THE BEGINNINGS : 'I was always remarked upon'

In the course of her extraordinary career Louise would live in some of the grandest parts of Europe's grandest cities – opposite the Winter Palace in St Petersburg, in the heart of Vienna's imposing *Innenstadt* and in the best streets and squares of London's West End. But none of this splendour was foretold in her beginnings. She was born on 16 April 1755 in the rue Coquillière, in a street in the first *arrondissement* of Paris which was neither remarkable nor particularly distinguished. Today it offers a mix of shabby cafés, restaurants and banks, growing smarter at its eastern end as it nears the church of Saint-Eustache (where Louise was christened), the Forum des Halles and the Centre Georges Pompidou. Some members of the *monde* lived there in the eighteenth century, it is true, preserving the cachet the street must have had in the seventeenth century, when the aristocratic novelist Madame de Lafayette was a resident.[1] But it had a varied population at the time of Louise's birth, and was certainly less chic than its closeness to the Louvre, Palais-Royal and rue Saint-Honoré might seem to suggest.

Yet her start was propitious, even if she had far to rise. Like other celebrated women painters – most notably Artemisia Gentileschi (1597–c. 1651) and Angelica Kauffman (1741–1807) – she was born of artist stock. As the daughter of the portraitist Louis Vigée and his wife Jeanne (née Maissin), a former hairdresser from Lorraine, she certainly used her father's artistic contacts to further her own progress as a painter. The early pages of her memoirs are peppered with the names of artists who befriended her: Davesne, who taught her how to load a palette, Joseph Vernet, and the celebrated history painter Doyen, whose consoling visits after her father's early death helped to start her painting again. She plainly adored her father, though she seems to have suspected her mother of preferring her good-looking younger brother to herself. In later life she would pride herself on her closeness to her own daughter, but it was evidently limited: Julie had to fit in with her mother's painting commissions, was farmed out on willing acquaintances of whom Louise then became suspicious, and according to Louise ended up falling into bad company which prevented mother and daughter from living together. She died young, one of Paris's paupers, despite the fact that Louise was a wealthy mother and could 'refuse her nothing'. Perhaps it was better to be the daughter of an apparently cool Jeanne Vigée.

Louis Vigée was a talented pastellist – a portrait of the actor Biancoletti which he did at the age of fifteen suggests that he was as precociously gifted as his daughter – and Louise calls some of his portraits worthy of La Tour.[2] Like her, he was a conservative, and mistrustful of anything that heralded a new order. When he spent an evening with the *philosophes* Diderot, Helvétius and d'Alembert, he became convinced by their talk (Diderot was a particularly voluble and explosive talker) that the whole world would soon be upside-down.[3] He was a good conversationalist himself, and people often sat to him just to hear him speak, but he steered clear of radical topics, as his daughter would do in her pre- and post-Revolutionary salons. Both undoubtedly felt that the old ways served them and their art well, especially as they drew most of their clients from the moneyed bourgeoisie, aristocracy and court.

The Vigée family lived unextravagantly and unostentatiously, and throughout her life Louise preferred simplicity and even austerity to the sumptuousness of the *ancien régime* – perhaps the result of an instinctive liking for naturalness, but possibly a consequence of her upbringing. Since Louis Vigée was First Portraitist to Madame de Pompadour, a post to which he had been named in preference to famous artists like La Tour, Boucher, Drouais and Carle Vanloo, it must be assumed that the family was comfortably off. (At one point in her memoirs Louise mentions that they had a cottage in what was then the village of Neuilly, where she often went when she was very young.) But in fact Louis Vigée never achieved the status his daughter won, and cannot have commanded the prices she was able to charge as a result of her courtly connections and her membership of the prestigious Académie royale de peinture et de sculpture. He was an assistant professor at the Académie de Saint-Luc (the guild which Louise briefly joined before its dissolution in 1776), and remained a lifelong member. This comparative lack of status must have affected the prices he could charge for his portraits as well as the range of sitters he could attract. If the guild was the poor sister of the prestigious royal academy, it was also regarded by the latter with mistrust, seen as detracting from its glory with periodic exhibitions of its members' work, diluting that glory by creating independently of royal commission and edict, and – worst of all – treating painting as a trade rather than a liberal art. Louis Vigée had been dead for several years when the Director of the King's Paintings, the comte d'Angiviller, had the Académie de Saint-Luc closed down.[4] But perhaps he would have taken a perverse pleasure, convinced monarchist as he was, in this particular assertion of absolutist power.

It was, then, a relatively workaday household. If Louis Vigée was the main breadwinner, he did not spend all his time painting. Louise readily forgives in him the mild womanising she will later bitterly criticise in her own husband, and tells her reader without rancour what he did every New Year's Day: 'It was a holiday for him,' she writes,

> and he walked all over Paris, not to pay anyone a visit, but simply in order to kiss all the young girls he met, on the pretext of wishing them a happy New Year.[5]

But it was because he was a sociable man that Louise had the opportunity to meet other artists at such a young age. If they did not come to the family home just to hear Louis Vigée talk, they might be attracted by the prospect of a better meal than they were likely to have at their own home.[6] Davesne, witty enough to be a valued guest at the Vigée suppers, was also poverty-stricken, perhaps because of the mediocrity Louise detected in both his verse and his painting. He invited Louise to his house in turn, and her visits became regular. But she was shocked, when she once stayed on for dinner, to discover how frugally he and his wife ate. Later, in her years of fame, Louise took a certain pride in dining off a boiled egg in Prince Kaunitz's Vienna, or providing the fabled *souper grec* for a mere fifteen francs. But the soup and boiled potatoes which made up the Davesne meal seemed to her pitifully inadequate. An exact contemporary of Brillat-Savarin, she knew good food when she was presented with it, even if she was never a *gourmande*. When she went to the Louvre (where many royal academicians lodged) for drawing lessons with the painter Briard, she bought succulent *boeuf à la mode* from the concierge at one of the gates to sustain her, and never forgot how good it had tasted.[7] An edict later prohibited artists living in the Louvre from taking female students, incidentally, so closing one of the few avenues to professional training that were open to women.

Louise's informal artistic education began when she was eleven or twelve years old. Up to that time her upbringing had been ordinary enough for a girl born into the Parisian *petite bourgeoisie*. At the age of three months she was sent to board on a farm at Epernon, near Chartres, not because her mother disliked infant children – at least, not as far as we know – but because it was standard practice in all but the poorest French families to put children with wet-nurses for the first few years of their lives.[8] Perhaps Louise's feeling that her mother was less fond of her than she might have been stemmed from this early abandonment, but it seems unlikely: Jeanne Vigée was simply being conventional. At the end of the century only five per cent of babies were being fed by their own mothers,[9] despite the huge influence of Rousseau and his various diatribes against the use of *nourrices*.

Louise's parents kept her at the farm until she was five, then a fairly normal age for a child to leave its nurse. D'Alembert, the brilliant mathematician and encyclopaedist whose talk so upset Louis Vigée, lived with his own nurse until he was fifty, which suggests that she was kindlier and more caring than many. Having been abandoned by his mother, the novelist Madame de Tencin, on the steps of a Paris church, he was lucky to have survived infancy at all: the majority of foundlings died for lack of a *nourrice*. Almost as soon as Louise returned home to the rue Coquillière she was sent away again, this time to board at the Couvent de la Trinité on the rue de Charonne, in the faubourg Saint-Antoine. Perhaps – although she never mentions it – this was because her mother was still working as a hairdresser. The faubourg Saint-Antoine was only half a mile from the family home; but Louise, like most children away from home, missed her family, and treasured the periods of release when she could return to her parents. 'I suffered greatly from ill-health at the convent,' she writes, 'which meant that my father and mother often came to fetch me to spend a few days at home with them, and that delighted me in every way.'[10] It may be significant that she herself never put her daughter *en pension*, preferring to take her with her on her travels all over Europe, and hiring private teachers for her in Italy, Austria and Russia. But Louise was a curious combination of the over-protective and the lax where Julie was concerned, and seems to have valued her as much as a drawing-room ornament as a being in her own right. To judge by her references to Julie's linguistic, musical and artistic skills, she did buy her a better education than she had received herself. Louise remained obstinately monoglot throughout her career (though she was no doubt right to assume that French would be the *lingua franca* wherever she travelled in civilised Europe), and her enemies sometimes remarked on her ignorance.

Most convents did little but teach *la morale* and the social graces, which is why that great eighteenth-century victim of *ennui*, Madame du Deffand, so mourned the shallowness of the education they had given her. 'You know nothing,' she wrote to Voltaire a year or two before Louise left the Couvent de la Trinité for good, '. . . of the condition of those who think and are reflective, who have a certain energy, but are without talent, passion, occupation or distraction.'[11] The novelist Laclos wrote dismissively about women's schooling at about the time he published his scandalous *Les Liaisons dangereuses* (1782), which itself demonstrates the dangers already highlighted by Diderot and d'Alembert's *Encyclopédie* (1751–72). According to one article in the *Encyclopédie,*

> Women who have renounced the world before learning to know it are charged with inculcating principles in those who are to live in it. It is thence that a girl is often led to the altar to assume duties of which she knows nothing, and to unite herself to a man she has never seen. More frequently still she is recalled to her family for a second education which reverses all the ideas she acquired in the first, and which focus[es] more on manners than on morals . . .[12]

Perhaps belonging to the bourgeoisie – whose morals were traditionally the foil to aristocratic excess – provided Louise with some protection. But she seems never to have been as startlingly innocent as her later client the duchesse de Chartres (married to one of the most infamous roués of the day, the future Philippe-Egalité), of whom she writes, 'Some time after her marriage, as she was standing by the window, one of her attendants, seeing some kept women go by, said: "Look, there are some *filles.*" "How do you know they are not married?" asked the duchess in her candid ignorance.'[13] Louise was the child of a working family brought up in a capital city, and her convent education had in no sense left her an *ingénue.*

When she left the convent in 1767 she was only eleven years old. Perhaps her parents thought that she had been educated enough for a girl: typically for the age, her brother's schooling seems to have been taken altogether more seriously. The eighteenth century did boast a number of *femmes savantes* – Diderot's lover Sophie Volland, Voltaire's Emile du Châtelet and d'Alembert's presumed mistress Julie de Lespinasse, once Madame du Deffand's protégée but later her rival as a *salonnière* – but Louise would never have wanted to emulate them intellectually, even if she had been able to. Besides, future portraitists did not have to be learned, though historical painters needed a solid grounding in the classics as well as in ancient and modern history. When Louise herself opened a salon, it was more an occasion for music-making and light conversation than one for serious discussion. The only *salonnière* of comparably modest educational background was Madame Geoffrin (whose portrait as an elderly woman had been done by Louis Vigée), but she was far keener to entertain philosophers and men of letters than courtiers and ornaments of society: Sainte-Beuve called her salon on the rue Saint-Honoré the best organised and best conducted of its time, a veritable institution of the eighteenth century.[14] Madame Geoffrin did actually once pay Louise a visit. 'Having heard of me,' Louise writes, 'she came to see me one morning, and said the most flattering things to me about my person and my

11

talent.'[15] But her education would have been a different matter.

In 1767 the Vigées may simply have decided to let her follow her artistic bent – very wisely, as it turned out, because the money she was able to earn was soon needed. Whether or not her convent was one of the establishments where drawing was taught, Louise had always sketched as though her life depended on it.

> I doodled constantly and everywhere; my exercise-books, and even those of my companions, were filled in the margins with little heads full-face or in profile; on the dormitory walls I sketched figures and landscapes in charcoal, which, as you may imagine, meant that I was often in disgrace. Then at break-time, I would draw everything that entered my head on the sand. I remember at the age of seven or eight drawing by lamplight a bearded man, which I have always kept. I showed it to my father, who exclaimed in transports of joy, 'You are to be a painter, my child, if ever there was one.'[16]

So her calling was acknowledged, and the older Louise describes it in suitably reverential terms as an innate passion which never dimmed, but actually increased with time. Not even her father can have imagined the scale of her future success in all the courts of Europe, or the ease with which she would enter the smartest drawing-rooms of Paris, Rome, St Petersburg, Moscow, Berlin and London. But he did all he could to help her, allowing her into his studio and introducing her to artist friends who in turn instructed her, which makes Louise's later claim that she had no master seem decidedly suspect. Undoubtedly, she wanted to glorify her achievement in the *Souvenirs* by over-emphasising the part her innate talent had played in her professional success. Even her mother, beautiful but strict, joined in the educational effort, allowing Louise to paint her semi-nude in a picture now known only from a photograph, but which was previously misattributed to Watteau.[17] Despite her uprightness, this concession to her daughter's talents is not so surprising. Since Louise was debarred from attending life-drawing classes at the Académie royale schools, she had to use her own family as models. As a hairdresser by training, the former Jeanne Maissin presumably knew what support would-be female professionals needed.

But the year which marked Louise's release from the convent was to become a year of great sadness. During a dinner at home Louis Vigée swallowed a fishbone which lodged in his gullet, and neither the attentions of the best surgeon in Paris nor the ministrations of his family could save his life. He had been less clever about money than his daughter would later prove to be (she amassed a fortune despite supporting an allegedly spendthrift husband and losing large sums in the collapse of banks and the upheavals of revolution), and his estate[18] was insufficient to cover the household expenses and the cost of Etienne Vigée's education. Whether or not her mother had been working – and Bachaumont says that she was a *celebrated* hairdresser[19] – there is no suggestion that she was earning now. Nor, says Louise, could her own earnings as a twelve-year-old artist – whatever they may have been – yet make up the shortfall, and in any case she was immobilised by grief at her father's death. So within a few months, in January 1768, Jeanne Vigée contracted a marriage of convenience to a forty-four-year-old jeweller, Jean-François Le Sèvre, who had smart premises in the rue Saint-Honoré.

Before Louis Vigée's death the family had moved to the rue de Cléry, an unremarkable street in the second *arrondissement* off the rue Montmartre. Exchanging it for the vicinity of the Palais-Royal meant moving into the *monde*, and that must have been gratifying to someone of Louise's ambitions. Quite how her penetration of this world began is unclear: she simply remarks in her memoirs that the duchesse de Chartres was an early patron and that she brought other commissions in her train. Louise's astounding youthful talent must have excited the same admiration as Angelica Kauffman's had, and won her the same rewards. Her father's courtly connections probably gained her limited acceptance in the world of high society, and perhaps Le Sèvre's aristocratic and wealthy clientele helped too. Friends like Joseph Vernet, the painter of landscapes and seascapes, provided her with introductions, and the charm for which she would become known no doubt helped her further them. But her first sales, both before and after her mother's remarriage, were highly irregular, since she was working as a professional without the all-important membership of a guild (a position she would rectify a few years later). Eventually her studio would be shut down and her effects confiscated as a result of this irregularity.

Her growing fame was gratifying, but Louise saw little or nothing of the money she was earning. At least, so she claims in the *Souvenirs*: her miserly stepfather was pocketing it all, she says, and she was too worried about causing her mother distress to object. Joseph Vernet was furious with her for allowing this to happen, telling her to pay for her keep and save the rest. But her future husband's 'life' of Louise tells a different story. According to Le Brun, the household was quite wealthy enough for Louise to be able to keep her earnings, and so she began saving young. This meant she never needed the so-called immoral earnings she was later slanderously accused of amassing as the mistress of the finance minister Calonne.[20] Le Brun's story is surely the more plausible (though of course his motive for telling it may have been connected with the fact that *he* would later be accused of living off Louise, and spending her fortune on women): Louise resented her mother's remarriage, and saw every reason to blacken her stepfather's name. Nothing but her conscience could have dictated the course of supporting this Harpagon-like creature, and Louise would always be markedly unsentimental where money matters were at issue. Later on, as Le Brun's wife, she would be obliged to hand over her income, because the law required all married women except *marchandes* to do that; but she was under no such obligation to Le Sèvre.

So this episode in the *Souvenirs* really tells us little more than that Louise loathed Le Sèvre, and was probably jealous of him. 'I hated this man,' she wrote,

> the more so since he had taken possession of my father's wardrobe, and wore his clothes exactly as they were, without adjusting them to fit his figure. You will readily understand, dear friend, the sad impression this made on me![21]

Louise's list of pictures done between 1768 and 1772 includes one of Le Sèvre 'in a nightcap and wearing a dressing gown', a painting now lost but which may have illustrated this disreputable penchant for appropriation. On the other hand, the clothes could well have been his own. Louise's artistic licence is as apparent in her memoirs as in the more flattering of her portraits.

The episode also illustrates a recurrent theme of the *Souvenirs* and of the career they record: obsessiveness about money, sometimes mild but more often acute. Throughout her life she saw herself, both grudgingly and proudly, as the provider. She seems to have enjoyed taunting Le Brun – the famous and distinguished connoisseur-dealer – with his improvidence, and acting the part of the traditional male as well as the conventional female. The over-productiveness she would later accuse herself of, the desperate accumulation of ever more money, the defiant pose of single mother first bringing up her daughter away from home and then losing her in the freezing wastes of Russia to an unworthy male, were expressions of a complex neurosis. She was worth any man, she seemed to say, and could exceed any male's earning-power (she certainly charged more than almost any contemporary male painter). No more than Julie Le Brun needed the feeble Gaétan Nigris had Jeanne Vigée needed the Molièresque Le Sèvre: Louise could have done for both of them. In 1768, as she saw it, she was the only replacement necessary for her adored father, though she does also acknowledge that at the age of twelve she was hardly earning enough to perform such a function. All her future obsession seems to have its origin in a young girl's rivalry and misplaced sense of guilt.

If there were distinct advantages to the family's new circumstances, Louise barely admits them. Perhaps her silence about the exact origins of her rise in the *monde* is connected with her unwillingness to thank Le Sèvre for anything, least of all for his having provided an environment propitious to the flourishing of her career as a society portraitist. The most she will say about her new home is that it made it easy for her to take walks in the pleasant gardens of the Palais-Royal when she was not working. But such freedom could have its dangers, and Le Sèvre soon stopped her from promenading there. He tried to make amends by providing the family with a country retreat, but Louise was unimpressed.

> My stepfather took a shabby little house at Chaillot, and we would go and stay there on Saturdays, returning to Paris on Monday morning. Lord! what a country property! My dear, imagine a tiny garden like a priest's; no trees, no shade from the sun apart from a small arbour where my stepfather had planted beans and nasturtiums which did not grow. Besides, we only had a quarter of this charming garden; it was divided into four with little stakes, and the three other parts were rented out to shop-boys, who every Sunday came to enjoy themselves pot-shotting at birds.[22]

According to Louise, it was jealousy that had made Le Sèvre prohibit her walks in the Palais-Royal, but he may simply have been acting as any father or stepfather would. The western avenue of the gardens, the allée de Foy, was said by Louis-Sébastien Mercier to be closed to the chaste, and in his dialogue *Le Neveu de Rameau* Diderot describes watching the sport of debauchees and their prey there:

> Fair weather or foul, it is my custom to walk in the Palais-Royal at five o'clock in the evening. I am the person one sees sitting on the d'Argenson seat, always alone and dreaming. I talk to myself of politics, love, taste or philosophy. I put no check on my mind's libertinage: I let it follow the first idea which presents itself, wise or mad, just as one sees dissolute young men in the allée de Foy tailing a courtesan, with her breezy looks, smiling face, lively eyes and retroussé nose, and abandoning her for another, attacking all of them and attaching themselves to none. *My* harlots are my thoughts.[23]

In the 1780s the duchesse de Chartres's husband, now the duc d'Orléans, built arcades and shops in the gardens, which reduced their extent. But they still remained a pleasant place to take the air in, planted with lime and chestnut trees and closed to carriages, and the younger Louise greatly resented her stepfather's intervention.

She had obviously already become extremely pretty, which is how she depicts herself in her mature portraits, but she claims to have acquired her radiance late. Perhaps she simply wants to tell a dramatic story, emphasising crucial turning-points and imposing a mythic structure on her life. 'I forgot to tell you, dear friend,' she writes to her friend Natalya Kurakina in the second of the letters which preface her memoirs,

> that I had undergone a metamorphosis and grown pretty . . . my mother became appreciative of my face and figure, for I had regained my plumpness and so acquired the freshness of youth.[24]

When she left the convent she had still been an ugly duckling, and her younger brother the angel of beauty. 'At this time of my life,' she notes unsparingly,

> I was ugly. I had an enormous forehead, very deep-set eyes; my nose was the only pretty feature in my thin, pale face. In addition, I had grown so fast that it was impossible for me to stand upright; I drooped like a bent reed. All these imperfections distressed my mother; it seemed to me that she preferred my brother, for she spoiled him and readily forgave him his youthful peccadilloes, whereas she was very strict with me.[25]

But she had the consolation of her prodigious talent. It is nowhere better shown than in the picture (dated 1773 but probably done four years earlier, when she was fourteen) of her brother *en écolier*, clutching the school equipment her artistic skills had perhaps helped to buy. Here he looks a typical schoolboy, perky and mischievous, but he evidently underwent a change in later life: his nickname then was 'Figé', fossilised or set in his ways, and he had the reputation for being an insufferable pedant. It was claimed that he had been lecturing from his mother's womb,[26] and his original wit was entirely smothered by the pomposity of the *Lumpenprofessoriat*. He was elected to a chair in declamation at the Athénée, and liked giving readings of his own rather indifferent poetry as well as other people's works. His plays are cold, pretentious, weak in plot and unoriginal; his extravagant eulogies of Napoleon Bonaparte won him no favours under Consulate or Empire; but on the succession of Louis

XVIII he was, despite his earlier enthusiasm for the republican cause, given the post of royal reader, at which he was generally agreed to excel, and awarded the Cross of the Légion d'honneur. The best that could be said of him as a writer was that he was versatile. Just as he praised every political regime he lived under, so in his literary work he flitted from the school of Dorat to that of the elegant Gresset, from the satire of Boileau to the caustic wit of Piron. Unlike his sister, he was by nature lazy, and owed much of his worldly success to the entrée which her patronage gave him to high society.

The early portrait foretells none of his stuffiness and pretentiousness. The picture of Etienne clutching pen and portfolio was obviously influenced by the work of Drouais, Chardin, Greuze and others who painted boys studying or writing, and confirms the views on the distinctive nature of childhood expounded in Rousseau's novel *Emile* (1762). 'People always look for the man in the child,' Rousseau had complained,

> without considering what he is before becoming a man . . . [But] nature wants children to be children before being men. If we try to pervert this order we shall produce forced fruits which have neither ripeness nor flavour, and which will soon rot: we shall have young doctors and old children.[27]

Etienne Vigée en écolier is fully in the spirit of the eighteenth-century cult of childhood. It was a cult Louise would continue in her many adoring portraits of her daughter Julie and the other child pictures she did. If not worshipping, the picture of Etienne is painted with obvious affection, and confirms the good looks Louise felt Jeanne Vigée preferred her son for.

Work like this certainly helped to get Louise noticed in the world. Joseph Vernet, she writes, was impressed enough to offer her some fatherly advice. 'My child,' he said,

> Do not follow the system of any school. Simply learn from the works of the great Italian and Flemish masters; but above all, paint as much as you can from nature: nature is the first of all masters. If you study it carefully, it will prevent you from ever adopting a 'manner'.[28]

To have won such a man's attention was certainly a coup. To be told by an established artist that she should rely on her inborn gifts rather than the tricks of routine was also reassuring to someone whose sex meant that formal academic training would always be denied her. But what did Vernet mean by 'manner', and did Louise in fact succeed in avoiding it? According to Diderot's review of the 1767 Salon, manneredness was a vice common to all the fine arts, a quality seductive to the young and the multitude, but more abhorrent to the man of taste than ugliness. Ugliness at least was natural.

> It seems to me that *manneredness*, in mores, speech or the arts, is first of all a vice of polite society ... Mores grow depraved ... speech becomes epigrammatic, ingenious, laconic, sententious; the arts become corrupted by refinement ... people become singular, bizarre, *mannered*; from which it appears that *manneredness* is a vice of polite society in which good taste tends towards decadence. ... The word *manner* can be interpreted positively or negatively; but almost always negatively when it is alone. One says: To have a *manner*, to be *mannered*, and that is a vice; but one also says: His *manner* is grand; it is the *manner* of Poussin, Le Sueur, Guido Reni, Raphael, the Carracci.[29]

Manneredness, in other words, is an affectation that runs counter to the rule of nature. Yet as Diderot also observes, art can never be a perfect imitation: 'The sun of art is not the same as the sun of nature, nor the painter's light that of the sky . . .'[30] All art must select and interpret, but in so doing it should still avoid deliberate falsification. Rousseau's attack on the perverted values of civilisation, or Laclos's glorifying of natural woman in his essay *Des femmes et de leur éducation*,[31] may come to mind in this connection. Emile is to be made to run with the deer and antelopes, not pose and posture with society dancing-masters. The most famous of them, Marcel, provokes Diderot's wrath:

> I have said somewhere that the famous Marcel *mannered* his pupils, and I stand by my statement. The supple, gracious, delicate movements he gave to the limbs separated the animal from the simple, real actions of nature, for which he substituted conventional attitudes, which he understood better than anyone in the world. But Marcel knew nothing of the frank gait of the savage.[32]

The rigorous imitation of nature, Diderot concludes, may make art poor, petty and mean, but never false or mannered.

Throughout her career Louise sought the natural effect – the casual coiffure, the loose flowing dress, the simple 'antique' style, the spontaneous-seeming attitude. But for all that, there is artifice in her naturalness. In the Schillerian sense of the word, she was sentimental.[33] Schiller's sentimental creature has left the naïvety of primitive nature or childhood behind, and can only contemplate it from the distant vantage-point of civilisation and maturity. Marie-Antoinette might play at being a shepherdess in the hamlet of the Trianon, but it would never be more than play (and Louise, perhaps to her credit, refused the Queen's request to paint her in shepherdess costume). The eighteenth century, which thought that it had 'discovered' nature, was none the less still wedded to culture.

Vernet's reference, in any case, was to 'the natural' rather than to 'the world of nature'. He never intended to deflect Louise from portraiture to landscape painting, his own forte. For the artist who aspired to be natural, freedom from the prescriptions of standard training could be an advantage. Again, Diderot stands witness. He quotes Chardin on the thankless rule-governed dressage forced on to young (male) artists, the imposition of methods inadequate to convey truth to life:

> Chardin seemed to doubt that any education was longer and more painful than that of the painter, not even the doctor's, lawyer's or Sorbonne academic's. 'We are given our pencil-case at the age of seven or eight,' he said. 'We start drawing from a model, eyes, mouths, noses, ears, then feet, hands. We have long been bent over our portfolio when we are placed before Hercules or the torso; and you have no idea of the tears which this satyr, this gladiator, this Venus de' Medici, this Antinous made us shed. . . . After languishing for days and spending nights by lamplight over immobile, dead nature, we are presented with living nature; and suddenly the work of all the previous years seems to reduce to nothing: we were no more embarrassed the first time we picked up a pencil. You have to learn to see nature with your own eyes; and how many people have never seen it and never will see it! It is the torment of our lives. We had been confined to the model for five or six years, then suddenly we were left to consult our own genius, if we had any.'[34]

Louise's sex, in other words, may have saved her as many difficulties en route to becoming an acknowledged artist as it caused her. True, she had not developed her talents wholly independently of academic doctrine: Briard had given her drawing lessons and lent her antique busts as well as examples of his own work. But in comparison with contemporaries like David and Vincent, she had been informally taught. Diderot wrote with sympathy as well as asperity of the natural consequences of auto-didacticism in women. The 1767 Salon congratulates Anna Therbusch on a painting of a man – 'It's not without merit for a woman; three-quarters of the [male] Académie artists could not do as well'[35] – which revealed a fearless attitude to the truth. The artist has broken the rules of propriety and painted a nude male from life: 'She had the courage to summon nature and look at it.' In a letter to the sculptor Falconet of May 1768 Diderot pursues the theme. Therbusch's painting of a satyr surprising Antiope showed the artist rising above prejudice:

> She said to herself: I want to be a painter, I will do all I have to do to become one; I will call upon nature, without whom one can do nothing; and she boldly had the model undressed. She looked at the naked man. You may imagine how the gossips of both sexes prattled.[36]

Women were not admitted to life classes given under the auspices of the Académie royale or London's Royal Academy. In Zoffany's famous picture of the English Royal Academicians, the male academicians are gathered round a male nude, but the two female members, Angelica Kauffman and Mary Moser, are present only as portraits on the wall. Such institutional prejudice mattered inasmuch as life-drawing was the basis of historical painting, the highest genre in the pictorial hierarchy, and one to which ambitious women aspired. Despite having been received as a history painter by the Royal Academy, Kauffman was often criticised for painting feeble, effeminate men, perhaps because the real-life model was denied her. (Women's standard confinement to the 'lesser' modes of portraiture and still life was partly in consequence of this exclusion.) Diderot was struck by the fact that Anna Therbusch's Antiope had obviously been modelled on her chambermaid or inn servant – 'The arms, the thighs, the legs are flesh, but flesh which is so soft, so flaccid, but so flaccid, so soft, that in Jupiter's place I'd have regretted taking the trouble to metamorphose myself'[37] – but does not draw the obvious conclusion that women artists generally *had* to make use of non-professional models if they wanted to practise from life. He himself served as a model for another picture by Anna Therbusch, a bust portrait for which he nonetheless completely undressed. 'I should not have dared to suggest it to you,' she said, 'but you have done well, and I thank you.'[38] Louise, on the other hand, had used her own mother as a semi-nude model, and possibly other members of her family too; and during Louis Vigée's lifetime she had probably even been able unofficially to attend his classes at the Académie de Saint-Luc.

Several years after their conversation, Louise painted Joseph Vernet himself – fully clothed, in velvet frock-coat, lace jabot and wig. It is an unnatural picture in the sense that Vernet, who holds a palette in his left hand and a brush in his right, would never have worn such a costume for painting, any more than Louise herself would have worn the décolleté dress and wide-brimmed straw hat she is wearing in the immensely stylish self-portrait in the National Gallery, her palette cradled in her arm like a bouquet of flowers. But in other respects the Vernet portrait of 1778 *is* natural, and underlines Louise's ability to paint male sitters in a warmly unfussy way. In many of her female portraits, by contrast, she tries to flatter, and the polish of the features seems to emphasise her impulse to 'improve'.

Vernet's other piece of advice, that Louise should learn from the works of the great Italian and Flemish masters, was also heeded. After Louis Vigée's death, her mother decided that looking at pictures would help cheer Louise up, and took her to see the paintings in the Luxembourg Palace. Perhaps she felt that the stimulus would start her daughter painting again, and so help the family finances, or perhaps her concern was disinterested. Louise would later be much affected by her exposure to Rubens during a tour of Flanders with her husband in 1781, but seeing his Marie de' Medici cycle in the Luxembourg Palace was eye-opening.

There was plenty of other painting to be seen in eighteenth-century Paris – royal galleries, the *cabinets* of private connoisseurs – but Louise actually thought the Palais-Royal collection of the duc d'Orléans the most impressive. Like the young Kauffman in the galleries of Milan, Florence and Rome, she was granted permission to make copies of some of the paintings, and never forgot what they taught her.

> The minute I went into one of these rich galleries, I was just like a bee, forever storing away bits of knowledge and memories useful to my art, and intoxicating myself with the delight of contemplating great masters. In addition, to fortify myself, I copied some pictures by Rubens, some heads by Rembrandt, Van Dyck, and several heads of girls by Greuze, for they taught me important lessons about the half-tones in delicate complexions; Van Dyck taught me the same thing, but more subtly.[39]

Even moralists like Diderot admired Greuze's 'stunners', the young women with come-hither looks that appealed so greatly to Sir Richard Wallace. Louise imitated their liquid eyes and ingratiating attractiveness in many female portraits.

Nowhere were Louise's credentials as a portraitist of beautiful society women more emphatically confirmed than in the three lost pictures of the ravishing adventuress and double agent Madame de Bonneuil done in 1773, when she was eighteen.[40] The *Souvenirs* are uninformative about how

Louise depicted her, but the subject seemed to call for treatment as exotic as she would later give to Nelson's paramour Emma Hamilton. (Roslin, who was dazzled by Madame de Bonneuil's looks, painted her in African dress, veiled like the natives of the île Bourbon.) Her liaison with the obese financier Beaujon, who later sat to Louise, was well known, as was the one with the debauched duc de Chartres. She rose effortlessly in the Versailles firmament, which helped her equally pretty daughter to marry well. Connections with high society and statesmen made her an effective 'letterbox' in the correspondence between Parisian royalists and émigrés after the Revolution, and she was involved in the activities of the anti-Bonapartist and pro-monarchist faction in England in the years before the Restoration of 1814.

Society was not peopled only by the beautiful, though Louise's work sometimes seems to suggest otherwise. One evening, at a dinner given by the sculptor Lemoyne, she met the famously ugly actor Lekain, who said nothing – perhaps as a respite from hours of declamation on stage – but ate enormously.[41] On this occasion his frightful looks simply enhanced the beauty of Madame de Bonneuil, who was also present, but when he was acting Lekain could make an audience forget his physical repellence.

> The costume of a knight, for instance, softened the severe and repulsive expression of a face without a single regular feature, so that you could bear to look at him when he was playing Tancred; but in the rôle of Orosman, which I once saw him in when I was sitting very close to the stage, the turban made him so hideous, though I admired his fine, noble manner, that I was afraid.[42]

The portrait she painted of him in 1778 or thereabouts must considerably 'improve' his looks, since his famous facial puffiness has become no more than heaviness around the jowls, and his over-emphatic, threatening eyebrows have been refined. She does, though, keep Lekain's long face and sensual lips.

However keen she was to cultivate an elegant and moneyed clientele – and the *Souvenirs* list increasing numbers of them from her late teens onwards – Louise insisted on tempering sociability for the sake of her painting. Although she took a real delight in company, and adored the nobility, she knew that her real business was portraiture. So after one painful occasion when she ruined a white satin dress by sitting on a loaded palette, she accepted only evening invitations – that is, to supper rather than dinner, which was then generally eaten in the early or mid-afternoon – when the painting for the day would be over and her equipment safely stored away.

She obviously knew that the whole of the faubourg Saint-Germain, as well as the court, was fascinated by her. Her social rise had been astonishing, like Angelica Kauffman's (Kauffman too was of humble birth). Also like Kauffman, she seems to have been modest and respectful at the same time as sure of her talent, and to have known instinctively how free she could allow herself to be in elevated company. The court of Louis XVI was still etiquette-bound, though the King himself was a man of simple tastes and his wife Marie-Antoinette had a liking for informality. Louise was careful to keep her place, and cannot have forgotten that to courtiers she remained a member of the third estate, attractive and phenomenally gifted, but socially inferior. However much Louis XVI desired to be the people's king, it was in the nature of the court to be exclusive: exclusivity maintained prestige and fostered deference. Too easy a mingling with the lower classes would fatally temper the authority invested in majesty.

It would be different, of course, when the commoner's position had been sanctioned by royal favour. Louise would become Marie-Antoinette's favourite portraitist and enjoy all the favour such a position entailed. But until that time she had to behave with circumspection. Privilege could assert its claims brusquely, and sometimes she was snubbed. Once, in 1779 or 1780, when she was visibly pregnant, the old princesse de Conti would call her 'Mademoiselle' to remind her of her rank; and Louis XVI may indeed have told his wife to see her less often, as was rumoured. But as a painter – particularly a portrait-painter – she also commanded respect, in the way a high-class *couturier* or *couturière* might do, because her profession dealt with enhancing the glory of the court through the flattering presentation of its denizens: her talent was welcomed, and she with it, on account of its power to elevate and transcend. Her status was assured too because she was a practitioner of a liberal art, and one which had had its own royal academy in France for over a century (a hundred years before a similar body was established in England).

But if courtly snobbishness towards her was rare, there were other respects in which she found the *monde* less polite than its reputation. She did not read Richardson's vast letter-novel *Clarissa* until after her marriage (perhaps believing, with her beloved Rousseau, that 'never did a chaste girl read a novel about love',[43] and that to give such books to the young in the hope that edification would ensue was like setting fire to a house to test the fire-fighting equipment).[44] But in her teens she was already aware of the dangers represented by real-life Lovelaces, particularly noble ones. She seems, as a result, to have known how to look after herself. The debauched duc de Chartres caught sight of her one evening after a concert at the Colisée, a pleasure-dome in the middle of Paris. He was, Louise writes, with an equally dissolute companion, the marquis de Genlis, and the poor women who passed before their eyes were spared none of their infamous sarcasm. – 'Ah! as for this one,' the Duke said very loudly as he pointed at me, 'there's nothing to be said about *her*.' This remark, which several people besides me heard, caused me such satisfaction that I remember it even today with a certain pleasure.[45]

As well she might, for Louise was glamorous and successful enough to be a natural subject of gossip. Her devout mother had taught her a strict moral code, it is true, but perhaps it was *savoir-vivre* as much as genuine innocence that preserved her general reputation for virtue in society – until, that is, some particularly scurrilous attacks on her and her friend Calonne, the Comptroller-General of Finance, did her serious damage in the late 1780s. But she could defend herself against unwelcome advances when she wanted to. She had to admit, she writes in her second letter to Natalya Kurakina,

> that I was always remarked upon on walks and at the theatre, with people actually flocking around me, and you may easily imagine that several admirers of my face made me paint theirs, in the hope of winning my affection; but I was so taken up with my art that there was no distracting me from it . . . as soon as I noticed that [these men] were giving me the glad eye, I painted them *gazing into space*, which means that one cannot look at the painter. Then, at the first flicker of their pupil towards me, I said to them: *I am just doing the eyes*; that provoked them a little, as you can imagine, and my mother, who never left my side, and whom I had let into my confidence, chuckled quietly.[46]

Since Louise's self-portraits as well as her memoirs show a well-developed awareness – verging on the coquettish – of her attractions, we may occasionally feel that she protests her purity too insistently to be altogether credible. She was, after all, surrounded by aristocratic women who deceived their husbands, even if they refrained from flaunting the fact. There is no reason to believe that Louise, who remained bourgeois at heart, availed herself of the same sexual licence as her elevated clients. But women, as Laclos's infamous marquise de Merteuil complains, have never enjoyed the male's freedom to publicise their love affairs, for a sexual double standard operates. One thinks of Louise's good looks and the hordes of admirers, and one cannot help wondering.

CHAPTER TWO

TOWARDS THE ACADÉMIE:
'Finally I was admitted'

The deliberately naïve account presented by Louise's memoirs suggests that it was an unspecific *douceur* in late eighteenth-century life that captivated her as she advanced through courtly society, not the momentary intoxications of particular passions. If the reign of Louis XVI saw a reaction against the hedonism of the rococo and what was often seen as the shameless self-indulgence of Louis XV's age, the salons and the sophisticated feminine *monde* of Paris still demanded lightness and grace of the kind which Louise's talents seemed supremely fitted to reflect. Pre-Revolutionary society in the capital was in many ways the most cultivated in modern Europe, and the premium on intelligence, polish and manners was high.

Louise herself, for all her championing of artlessness, was a self-aware and astute operator. The elevated world which became her own demanded tact and social skill, a degree of reticence and an affectation of entertaining lightness. Louise's concerns might be deadly serious, but they must not be presented as such. In her memoirs, therefore, she describes the success that came to her in the mid-1770s as something unbidden, delightful but surprising. In fact she cultivated her public with great promotional flair, and set about advertising herself in a discreet but effective fashion.

One entrepreneurial coup is described to Natalya Kurakina in provokingly *faux-naïf* terms.

> I have often said to you, dear friend, that my girlhood was like no other; not only did my talent, however feeble it seemed to me when I thought of the great masters, make me welcome and sought-after in every drawing-room, but I sometimes received proof of a goodwill which I can only call public and which, I frankly admit to you, gave me great joy.[1]

For example, she disingenuously continues, she did portraits of the cleric-statesman Cardinal Fleury and the moralist La Bruyère, which she based

25

on engravings, and in 1775 offered them in homage to the Académie Française. This was a clever and calculated move. The pictures won her considerable publicity, and she was granted free entry to every one of the institution's public sessions in thanks. Her long tradition of association with academies all over Europe – in Italy, Austria, Russia and Prussia as well as in France – had begun.

The perpetual secretary of the Académie, d'Alembert, paid Louise a personal visit to express the members' gratitude. She did not quite know what to make of his person, partly because he lacked easy social grace and seemed disdainful and intransigent. He was, after all, known as a *philosophe* who believed that the chief enemies of progress were the nobility, the powerful, and the patrons of the arts, which could scarcely recommend him to Louise. The unpublished diary of police inspector d'Hémery describes d'Alembert about twenty years before this occasion as a man with a smooth, ruddy face, small of stature and of average girth, but distinguished by great vanity and presumption,[2] but his moral character seems to have grown more refined with age. Louise was struck by his bloodlessness and frigidity, but was also impressed by his exquisite politeness.[3] Despite the fact that d'Alembert never liked society much, as sociable a creature as Madame du Deffand was dazzled by him. She admired his straightforwardness, a quality she was proud to possess herself, as well as his towering genius: 'He is the most honest of men, the best boy in the world, and no one could have more wit.'[4]

The moody, uncouth outsider, as is well known, went on to become an habitué of the most refined salon in Paris. But he remained to many a shadowy figure, and certainly an austere one. In the words of Madame du Deffand's portrait, 'He has all the essential qualities without having all those demanded by society; he lacks a certain gentleness and the charm that should attend it.'[5] Notwithstanding these deficiencies, she set about having him installed as a member of the Académie Française. Having secured his election after three failed attempts, she can only have been mortified by his defection from her salon to the rival one of her niece and one-time protégée Julie de Lespinasse, whom she had driven from her own house in a fit of jealousy. D'Alembert undoubtedly loved the orphan Julie, and those who did not believe him impotent assumed that she was his mistress.

Julie died prematurely in 1776 when she was only forty-four, her 'machine' worn out by torrid love affairs and terminally damaged by neurosis. D'Alembert's visit to the celebrated young artist must have preceded her death by only a few months. The story of the most famous salon rivalry in eighteenth-century France is nowhere mentioned in the *Souvenirs*, and Julie de Lespinasse's febrile brilliance, intellectual sharpness and intensely passionate nature might well have been antipathetic to the considerably younger Louise. Besides, Julie had an *âme citoyenne*, hungry for reforms and freedom, and Louise was suspicious of any attempt to upset her decorous world. Her own salon, in the early days of marriage and later, would be the reverse of *philosophe*.

When Louise and her family moved to the rue de Cléry after Le Sèvre's retirement in 1775, it was too early to think about a salon. She was only twenty, and still had some way to go before she could be regarded, either socially or artistically, as an established figure. Additionally, she was still single. Julie de Lespinasse might be a spinster, but *salonnières* were generally married women – even if they were widowed or separated – of a certain age.

We do not know what Louise thought of exchanging an apartment on the rue Saint-Honoré for a home in the second *arrondissement*. It may be assumed that Le Sèvre, no longer having clients to impress, was keen to save money, and was happy enough to swap chic for something cheaper. On the other hand, he may still have been pocketing the profits from Louise's painting; if so, it was presumably in his interests to maintain an establishment in which the rich and well-born would be happy to sit for their portraits. It was unusual for any portrait-painter to work away from his or her studio, though obviously exceptions were made in the case of royalty (and Louise would later paint the obese Beaujon in his exquisite town house, now the Elysée Palace, because he was incapable of moving). So it mattered that the premises had style.

The rue de Cléry must have offered a very different appearance in the 1770s from its present one. It is now in a crumbling, seedy and mildly threatening commercial *quartier* of the Paris clothes district, with the warehouses of fabric wholesalers and the headquarters of latter-day Rose Bertins (Bertin was *modiste* to Marie-Antoinette). It has few remaining buildings of any architectural distinction, and it is hard to imagine Louise's elevated clients and friends – duchesses, *maréchaux de France*, Calonne, the Grand Falconer and social butterfly Vaudreuil – paying court to her there. But then it offered a much smarter appearance, and undoubtedly they did.

In the seventeenth century the street had been poor and relatively unprepossessing, periodically infected by putrid fumes wafting across from the rubbish dumps at the Butte-aux-Gravois. Some of its eighteenth-century residents were prosperous. The future Madame de Pompadour was born in one of the houses, and her father – whom Voltaire mischievously called a former butcher – was a rich entrepreneur; the painter Francesco Casanova (brother of Casanova de Seingalt), who according to the *Souvenirs* had made and spent a lot of money, lived there; and so did the very wealthy finance minister Necker and his daughter Germaine, later to become Madame de Staël and a client of Louise's. Other residents were less well-off, like the poet André Chénier, who had two rooms at number 97. The category into which Louise's future husband Jean-Baptiste-Pierre Le Brun fitted is uncertain: Jeanne Le Sèvre thought him 'very rich', perhaps because of the stupendous Old Masters displayed in his gallery, but her daughter soon came to believe otherwise.

Le Brun had the head tenancy of numbers 19 to 21, though Louise wrongly describes him as having just become the owner when she and her family moved into an apartment there in 1775. In fact he did not get full possession of the buildings until 1778, for a price of 200,000 *livres* (but he seems to have paid no more than half the sum).[6] The property, of which only part is still standing, was owned at the end of the seventeenth century by Robert Poquelin, a brother of Molière's, who sold it in 1700 to Louis Lubert. It was Lubert's heirs who rented the *hôtel* to Le Brun in 1775. The part occupied by Le Sèvre and his family was presumably the now-demolished number 21, for the modest plaque on the façade of the present number 19, flanked by other signs for *prêt à porter* and *tissus*, has the date of Louise's residence there as 1778–89. (In fact she married Le Brun, and moved into his part of the building, in 1776.) The largest of the hôtel de Lubert's apartments were occupied by the marquis de Pezay, a libertine and courtier expert in political intrigue whose widow Louise would subsequently paint together with the marquise de Rougé, and the painter Ménageot. Ménageot, who later put Louise up at the French Academy in Rome when he was director there, became a close friend. Almost inevitably, their friendship led to rumours that he actually painted her pictures for her, accusations Louise indignantly rebutted.[7]

The initial relationship with Le Brun himself was businesslike. According to Louise, the real attraction for her was the fact of his being a picture-dealer:

> as soon as we were settled in, I went to see the magnificent pictures of every school that filled his apartment. I was delighted to have a neighbour whose profession enabled me to inspect the great paintings of the masters. Monsieur Le Brun was infinitely obliging and lent me extremely beautiful and very valuable pictures to copy.[8]

It is even possible that Louise dabbled in the production of fakes there. The *Lady in a Blue Hat*, once thought to be by Vermeer (Le Brun's great rediscovery as an art dealer and connoisseur),[9] has such an eighteenth-century air about it that it is tempting to view it as a pastiche done by Louise in Le Brun's gallery.[10]

Le Brun's neighbourliness, of course, was not quite what it appeared. 'I had become indebted to him for the most important lessons I could have learned, when at the end of six months he asked me to marry him.'[11] She does not sound enthusiastic. Why should she? There was no particular advantage for her in marriage. As she says, 'I was twenty years old and I had no worries about my future, since I was earning a great deal of money.' Louise was not one of those girls brought back from the convent to live at home and, in the words of the Encyclopédie article 'Femme', 'wait impatiently in a state of constraint and boredom for a change of name to transport them to independence and pleasure.' Socially she already lived a varied life, while her profession, which brought her her greatest pleasure, had earned her a degree of independence. Part of her dowry – which amounted to over 15,000 livres – consisted of unspecified 'savings from painting', and she knew that her talent and social skills guaranteed her an income for the future.

The independence that could be expected from marriage was, of course, relative. Her earnings would legally become her husband's, and as Louise puts it,

> his frenzied passion for women of easy virtue, combined with his passion for gambling, caused the ruin of his fortune and my own, of which he had entire possession; to the extent that in 1789, when I left France, I had not twenty francs to my name, after having personally earned over a million. He had run through it all.[12]

(In fact, as she later admits, she had rather more than twenty francs when she left France, since she had just been paid for a portrait.)

But given the age in which she lived, she did not necessarily have to fear other losses from marriage, and she maintained either a semi-detached or a completely detached relationship with Le Brun throughout the period when they were legally man and wife. It is thus less surprising than it might at first appear that when she returned from her twelve-year exile abroad, during which time Le Brun had divorced her, she still chose to move into their joint home: she had, after all, partly paid for it, and had never lived particularly intimately with him there even during their married life. But it must have been a fairly amicable relationship as well as a convenient marriage – convenient in that Le Brun seems never to have attempted to make Louise into a 'proper' wife, one who would have been constantly by him, decorously and obediently helping his picture-dealing business as a more conventional woman might have done. Instead she painted in her studio and welcomed her own guests in her apartment, while he continued his trade and – according to Louise – his philandering, which she involuntarily subsidised.

Of course the truth is slightly more complicated. Louise may not have supported him morally as an adoring partner, but she drew clients his way: some of her wealthy patrons undoubtedly also did business with him, either buying from him direct, commissioning him to buy for them, or employing him to dispose of their pictures as necessary. (Le Brun held many sales both before and after the Revolution, and was often asked to auction the magnificent aristocratic collections he had helped build.) For her part, Louise continued to benefit from the accessibility of the great works of art assembled in Le Brun's gallery. Perhaps it was a convenient marriage in other ways too. Le Brun seems to have seen the practical advantages of having a wife 'in the trade' before he ever thought of proposing to Louise: according to her, he was engaged to a Dutch picture-dealer's daughter at the very time when Louise herself accepted him, and begged Louise not to reveal their own wedding plans until he had finished doing some lucrative dealing with the Dutchman. Perhaps he was truly smitten with her, but he still maintained his head for business. And since he made the claims of his profession clear so early on, Louise no doubt felt licensed to maintain her own priorities too. She never let marriage (or motherhood) interfere with her work as a painter.

Louise was entirely unsentimental about the transaction. Eighteenth-century wedlock, in the words of the Goncourts, was less an institution or sacrament than a contract, entailing neither constancy in the man nor fidelity in the woman. Each demanded tolerance of the other, and felt entitled to receive it.[13] Louise's own union, in keeping with this mood, was one entered into without illusion and apparently without love. One wonders why she accepted Le Brun when she had conquered the court, and herself possessed such glamour. She mentions another proposal at one point in the *Souvenirs*,[14] but gives no hint of the social class of her suitor. After her marriage she was rumoured to be having affairs with high-ranking courtiers, but affairs were quite another matter; and perhaps she never received a proposal from an aristocrat. She clearly liked Le Brun, and probably had no idea that he was a womaniser and spendthrift. She was, she says, 'driven above all by the desire to escape the torment of living with my stepfather, whose bad temper had been increasing daily since he had nothing to do'.[15] She may, too, have wanted to please her mother, who was eager for her daughter to make what she regarded as a good match. But to judge by Louise's own, probably biased account – for a disillusioned wife is a tendentious source – the advantages were more clearly to be seen on Le Brun's side.

Yet he deserves a higher regard than the *Souvenirs* accord him. His person, as even Louise admits, was agreeable, and he had a pleasant face.

'It is not that Monsieur Le Brun was a wicked man: his character presented a mixture of gentleness and liveliness; he was highly obliging towards everyone, and in a word he was amiable enough.' Another witness paints a more detailed physical and moral portrait of him.

> He was of average height, about five feet two inches tall. He had a good figure. His hair, eyebrows and eyes were black. His gaze was piercing, full of intelligence and life. His brow was lofty, his nose straight and delicate, his mouth medium-sized and finely shaped. The upper lip indicated finesse, and the lower one, which was a little pronounced, foretold an ardent, sensual life. He had very fine hands. . . . He was a very skilful businessman, and through his contact with the *monde* had acquired great polish in his language and bearing. His appearance was always exquisite. At home, in the summer, he usually wore white bombasine ribbed frock-coats, waistcoats also of white bombasine, either wrapover or with wide lapels, breeches of Indian nankin, white silk stockings and shoes with gold buckles. In other seasons he dressed very grandly. He powdered his hair and wore it in a little pigtail which bobbed about and looked neat, and which always astonished and charmed his little niece. Le Brun earned several million at picture-dealing, but died none the richer for it, since he had mistresses for whom he rented or bought love-nests, to whom he gave coaches and four, and to whom he paid large allowances; they squandered and dissipated his fortune so effectively that when he died his daughter inherited almost nothing, and his executors were unable to pay his niece a pension of 4,000 francs he had bequeathed to her.[16]

However impressed she may have been by his pictures, and however pressing the need to escape Le Sèvre, Louise remained unconvinced that she should be marrying him:

> I felt so little inclined to sacrifice my liberty that on the way to the church I was still debating with myself: Shall I say yes? Shall I say no? Alas! I said yes, and exchanged one set of woes for another.[17]

Her feelings were not improved when, too late, she was warned off the marriage by various friends who were unaware that it had already taken place.[18] Subsequently, in the light of Le Brun's spendthrift ways, Louise tried to secure her financial position by petitioning for a 'separation of property', the best legal redress available at a time when divorce was not

31

possible. With a dowry of 15,000 *livres* and her regular earnings from painting, she claimed, she had hoped to live peacefully and free from worries over money; but her husband's speculations had resulted in crippling debt.[19] Her application was unsuccessful, but in September 1792 divorce did become legal on the grounds of straightforward incompatibility, by mutual agreement or for other unspecified reasons. Yet it was Le Brun himself who finally obtained a divorce in 1794, worried that his association with the then *émigrée* Louise would result in the confiscation of his property.

Whatever moral defects he may have possessed, Le Brun was a very distinguished connoisseur and dealer.[20] He was himself the son of a dealer, Pierre Le Brun, but seems not to have inherited the talents of his great-uncle Charles Le Brun – his most impressive artistic production, characteristically enough, seems to have been the frontispiece to a sale catalogue.[21] But there was nothing mediocre about his eye when it came to matters of taste. His main interests lay in dealing in Old Masters and building up private collections, though he also helped increase the general public's knowledge of the Northern masters by publishing the important *Galerie des peintres flamands, hollandais et allemands* in 1792. He was more adaptable politically than the staunchly monarchist Louise, and became Keeper of Pictures to both the duc d'Orléans – the future Philippe-Egalité – and the comte d'Artois, later Charles X. Under the republican regime he became a 'commissioner-expert' in recognition of his extensive knowledge of the arts: this made him indispensable in the 1790s to those who were then engaged in building up a national museum. In this capacity he inventoried various *émigré* collections and put aside for the nation many of the priceless pictures he had previously sold to private collectors. But the establishment decided that he was a political opportunist and denied him the responsibilities he felt he deserved; so he reverted to art-dealing.

The hôtel de Lubert had a magnificent gallery where Le Brun held his picture sales, and where young artists also exhibited. During the Terror of 1793–4 it was used for secret masses, and later still for concerts.[22] Given the splendour of these surroundings, Louise may have been surprised at being confined to cramped quarters herself when she became Le Brun's wife. She had, she says, 'a small antechamber and bedroom which served as drawing-room, hung with wallpaper like the toile de Jouy of my bed-curtains'.[23] (Throughout the eighteenth century, bedrooms retained their function as reception rooms.) This was certainly far less grand than the famous buttercup-yellow watered silk decorated with flame bows that adorned the walls of Madame de Deffand's drawing-room; but the cotton prints of Jouy are among the most charming expressions of the furnishing taste of the period, and Louise's bedroom was probably smarter than she admits. She observes that her furniture, compared with the very rich decoration of Le Brun's apartment, was 'perhaps too simple', given that she entertained court and town every day. It was still claimed by Champcenetz, an elegant and libertine member of the *jeunesse dorée* who circulated widely in polite society, that 'Madame Le Brun had gilt panelling, lit her fire with banknotes, and burned only aloe-wood'.[24] But *maréchaux de France* still had to sit on the floor if all the available chairs had been taken, and when they were as fat as the maréchal de Noailles sometimes had the greatest difficulty getting up again.

Louise is at pains – perhaps too great pains – to emphasise the frugality of her own tastes and her lack of interest in money, despite her evident resentment at Le Brun's appropriation and squandering of her earnings. The scandal-mongering about banknotes is presumably related to the rumours about Louise's involvement with Calonne and the pilfering from the Treasury it allegedly involved. Louise, of course, is all injured innocence. When she painted the Comptroller-General in 1784, she writes,

> people peddled countless absurd stories about how the portrait had been paid for; some claimed that the Comptroller-General had given me a quantity of those sweets called 'papillottes' wrapped in banknotes; others, that I had received in a pie a sum large enough to bankrupt the Treasury; in short, a thousand versions each more ridiculous than the last. The fact is that Monsieur de Calonne had sent me 4,000 francs in notes, inside a box valued at twenty *louis*. Some of the people who were with me at the time I received the box are still alive and can vouch for the fact. There was even some surprise at the moderateness of the sum; for shortly before, Monsieur de Beaujon, whom I had just painted in the same dimensions, had sent me 8,000 francs, without anyone thinking this amount excessive.[25]

Was Louise Calonne's mistress? The scandal-sheets insisted that she was,[26] and later – inaccurately – claimed that she had gone to London to join him when she escaped from Paris in 1789, whereas in fact she went to Italy. When Louise's portrait of him was exhibited, the ill-disposed said that it showed her to be truly a *mistress* of her subject. Le Brun, anxious to preserve his wife's good name, maintained that the portrait sittings lasted as long as they did only because the minister was too busy to come often.[27] (All he said to Louise, however, was that he would demonstrate her financial independence of Calonne after her death by listing her portraits on a funerary monument to be erected in his garden, which cannot have

reassured her much; and in any case she outlived him by thirty years.)
More damagingly, Louise's carriage was once seen stationed outside
Calonne's official residence all night; but this, she alleged, was because she
had foolishly lent it to a woman, the comtesse de Cérès, who *was* actually
having an affair with him.[28]

Perhaps Louise was genuinely innocent – she would surely never have
been so maladroit as to advertise a liaison in such a way – but protesta-
tions like this scarcely inspire confidence:

> Monsieur de Calonne always seemed unseductive to me, because
> he wore a 'fiscal wig'. A wig! Imagine me, with my love of the
> picturesque, ever accustoming myself to a wig! I have always
> detested them, to the extent that I once refused a rich husband
> because the man in question wore a wig; and I painted other men
> who did likewise only with reluctance.[29]

But Calonne's power was seductive. He certainly regarded himself as a
man who could make things happen. When Marie-Antoinette asked a
favour of him, he famously responded that if it was possible, it was already
done, and if impossible, *would* be done.[30] He did not much interfere
with her or the rest of the court's expensive pleasures, and enjoyed the
privileges of his position. In Louise's portrait – whose three-quarter
length inspired the witty actress Sophie Arnould to remark that Louise
had cut off his legs to keep him by her[31] – he seems unabashed by the fact
that his desk bears the charter of the *Caisse d'Amortissement*, a fund
intended to reduce the principal of the huge national debt which would
eventually cause the downfall of the Comptroller-General himself. He
looks preeningly self-satisfied, and is impressively dressed: delicate French
needle-lace, a glossy black taffeta coat from Vanzut and Dosogne (the
most expensive outfitters in Paris), and the blue moiré ribbon and glittering star of the order of the Saint-Esprit, the grandest French court order.[32]
He knows that he appears a man of substance, the owner of two châteaux
and a Paris house with a priceless picture collection. Since a heavily curled
lawyer's wig is a part of his official costume, Louise has had to paint him
in it despite her aesthetic objections.

Calonne had a European reputation as an art collector. He accumulated
a number of drawings and pictures, many of them extremely valuable,
while he was Comptroller-General, and later during his exile in England
and wanderings over Europe. But from the time of his disgrace – he was
driven from office in 1787 after being forced to admit to the state's huge
deficit – he was under pressure from his creditors, and began to sell off
some of them. Later, his generosity towards the brothers of Louis XVI

obliged him to dispose of his entire collection. There were auctions in Paris in 1788, and in London in 1793, 1794, 1795 and finally in 1803, eight months after his death: the Paris sale, which included a Van Dyck Saint Sebastian, a Murillo Holy Family and a Joseph Vernet storm scene, was supervised by Jean-Baptiste-Pierre Le Brun, at that time Keeper of Pictures to the comte d'Artois and the duc d'Orléans. The first London auction was more spectacular still, with what seemed like a whole gallery of Old Masters on offer – fourteen pictures by Rubens, ten Poussins, ten Titians, eight Van Dycks, seven Rembrandts, six Tintorettos, five Claudes, three Veroneses, three Giorgiones, and a Salvator Rosa, Raphael, Leonardo and Correggio apiece. Talleyrand described Calonne as

> a big man with a fine enough figure, a sprightly air, his face not disagreeable, his features mobile and changing expression from one moment to the next, a shrewd, piercing look, but one which betrayed and inspired mistrust; a laugh less gay than malicious and caustic.

The prince de Bénévent's memoirs convey a similar view. 'He was ugly, big, sprightly, a fine figure of a man; he had a witty aspect and an agreeable tone of voice.'[33]

It was generally agreed that he had considerable powers of attraction, as ugly men often do. Louise's portrait suggests all his seductiveness, but none of his ugliness: her Calonne has a positively agreeable face, if a markedly smug one. Whether or not he was sexually involved with her, Calonne was clearly a ladies' man. Women flooded to his receptions, but he too cultivated their company, fully understanding what Madame de Staël's mother Suzanne Necker meant when she said in a moment of uncharacteristic wit that 'women fill the hours of conversation and life like those bits of padding one puts inside chests of china: you count them for nothing, but everything would break without them'.[34] Louise's salon became important to him, and the *hôtel* of Yolande de Polignac, Marie-Antoinette's favourite, was also a focal point.

The rumour that Calonne was paying for the extension to the hôtel de Lubert which Le Brun was having built across the courtyard, facing on to the rue du Gros-Chenet, added to the gossip about his so-called relationship with Louise. As she protests, she and her husband were quite wealthy enough to be able to afford it themselves.[35] She knew what the work she did could fetch, though when it suited her to do so she affected complete ignorance of financial matters. Perhaps this was because she still wanted to present herself as a 'natural' artist who painted for love, not pecuniary reward, or perhaps she liked at times to appear a typically ignorant woman. But for someone who was evidently well aware of the market value of her pictures, and who – whether advised by her husband or not – came to charge spectacularly high prices for them, she is strangely reluctant to admit any acquaintance with the world of hard cash. 'I was so unconcerned about money,' she writes airily,

> that I barely knew the value of it: the comtesse de Guiche, who is still alive, can confirm that when she once came to my house to ask me to paint her portrait, and told me she could only afford a thousand *écus*, I replied that Monsieur Le Brun did not wish me to do any for less than a hundred *louis*. This mistake in arithmetic was very disadvantageous to me during my last trip to London; I constantly forgot that a guinea was worth more than a *louis*, and I did my sums for my portraits, including the one of Mrs Canning which I painted in 1803, as though I were in Paris.[36]

What Louise says about her quarters in the hôtel de Lubert – 'The things which made my house agreeable did not demand any luxury; I have always lived very modestly'[37] – is in keeping with this image of simplicity and unworldliness. So, too, are her undoubtedly genuine remarks about her taste in costume. This wife of a dandy dressed so plainly that, she rather unpersuasively claims, she could never have attracted so gorgeously clad a man as Calonne. 'I spent extremely little on my toilet,' she observes,

> and people even reproached me for looking too casual, since I wore nothing but white muslin or lawn dresses, and I only had richly-trimmed robes made for my sessions at Versailles. Doing my hair cost me nothing, I arranged it myself, and usually just twisted a muslin scarf around my head, as can be seen in the self-portraits in Florence, St Petersburg and in Monsieur Laborde's collection in Paris. I have always painted myself like this in my self-portraits, except the one hanging in the Ministry of the Interior where I am dressed in Greek style.

Greek costume – tunics, flowing drapery, a pure line and a generally un-fitted look – did not simply reflect the revival of the antique which had begun in mid-century with the excavations at Herculaneum and Pompeii, and influenced painting, architecture and the decorative arts as well as costume. It also expressed the cult of nature, a reaction against sophistication and luxury associated with writers like Rousseau and Diderot. Of course it was like other such forms of nostalgia in that it was championed by the culturally sophisticated: only those who could really afford to keep themselves warm dressed in the flimsiest of materials irrespective of season, and consequently ran the risk of catching pneumonia. One had to be a Madame du Barry, the former mistress of Louis XV who lived in a jewel-box of a château at Louveciennes, to choose to wear nothing but lightweight chemise dresses and take a cold bath every day.

The Louise who professed to dislike luxury similarly made her living practising what could be thought of as a luxury art, only affordable to people living in palaces and mansions whose walls they wished to see agreeably adorned. As Diderot remarks in the 1767 *Salon*, 'The fine arts owe their birth to money.'[38] The eighteenth century's ambivalence about luxury stemmed partly from the perception that it represented both social refinement and its corruption; after all, 'sophisticated' means 'adulterated' as well as 'cultured and discriminating'. In Diderot's words,

> People have seen that the same cause which produced [the fine arts], fortified them and led to their perfection ultimately degraded them, debased them and destroyed them; and they have put themselves in different camps as a result. One lot have told us how the fine arts were created, perfected and made marvellous, and have used this as a means of defending that luxury which the other lot have attacked by pointing to the debasement, degradation, impoverishment and cheapening of the same fine arts.

Luxury was tainted, according to Diderot, when it shored up the lives of those who were themselves corrupt, holders of venal posts who needed to be seen to live in the style they thought appropriate to their borrowed grandeur, or when it was paid for by sovereigns only at the price of bankrupting their people. (He seems almost to be anticipating the reign of Calonne and the minister's much-criticised support of Marie-Antoinette's extravagance.) But in themselves the luxury arts could generate wealth and trade, which made them socially desirable.

Louise had little taste for abstract philosophical speculation, and would no doubt have disliked Diderot's socialist fervour. When she allows herself to express any regrets about her art, they have to do with the loss of artistic quality entailed by rapid production as well as with the money-grubbing urge which partly lay behind her enormous productiveness; and of course the two phenomena are linked. Besides, she was too deeply imbued with the values of a conservative monarchy to want to question the glories and splendours which surrounded it and maintained its prestige. Court society, she knew, depended on show;[39] and since she wanted court society to continue, pursuing it all over Europe when it seemed terminally threatened in France, she had to continue promoting the show.

Her upholding of courtly values and her taste for luxuriating in simplicity are in no way incompatible: minimalism may be the reflection of a very artful intelligence or a very cultivated world. Nor is it surprising that a thoroughly minimalist event which she engineered should have been one of the most celebrated social 'happenings' of the 1780s. The *souper grec* of 1788, an occasion which the credulous or ill-willed represented as one of opulence and shameless luxury, had actually been conceived in a spirit of almost archaic simplicity. This celebration of Attic purity and *cuisine minceur* was prompted, Louise writes, by a reading from Barthélemy's neo-Hellenic novel *Les Voyages du jeune Anacharsis en Grèce*. Etienne Vigée was the reader.

When he arrived at the passage where, describing a Greek dinner, the author explains how various sauces are made, he said that we must sample them that evening. I instantly summoned my cook and told her the plan; and we agreed that she would make one kind of sauce for the fatted chicken, and another for the eel. As I was expecting some extremely pretty women, I conceived the idea of our all dressing in Greek style to surprise Monsieur de Vaudreuil and Monsieur Boutin, who were not due to arrive until ten. My studio, full of everything I used to drape my models in, would supply me with enough clothes, and the comte de Parois, who lodged in my house in the rue de Cléry, had a superb collection of Etruscan vases. As luck would have it he came up to my apartment that very day at about four o'clock. I told him of my plan, as a result of which he brought me a quantity of goblets and vases to choose from. I cleaned all these objects myself and put them on a mahogany table, set without a tablecloth. When that had been done, I placed behind the chairs a huge screen, which I took care to hide by covering it with drapery gathered up at each end, as one sees in Poussin's paintings. A suspended lamp shed a strong light on the table; in short, all was prepared, even my costumes, when Joseph Vernet's daughter, the charming Madame Chalgrin, arrived first. I immediately did her hair and dressed her. Then came Madame de Bonneuil, so remarkable for her beauty; Madame Vigée, my sister-in-law, who, without being so pretty, had the loveliest eyes in the world; and all three were instantly transformed into veritable Athenian women. Le Brun-Pindare entered; we unpowdered him and smoothed his side-curls out, and I set on his head a laurel wreath in which I had just painted young Prince Hendryk Lubomirski as the Love of Glory . . . The comte de Parois luckily had a great purple cloak which served to drape my poet in, and in the twinkling of an eye I had made him into Pindar, Anacreon. Then came the marquis de Cubières. While someone went to fetch from his house a guitar he had made into a golden lyre, I dressed him: I also dressed Monsieur Rivière (my sister-in-law's brother), Guinguené and Chaudet, the famous sculptor.

The time was getting on; I barely had a moment to think about myself; but as I always wore those white dresses in the shape of tunics which are at present called smocks, I needed to do no more than put a veil and a crown of flowers on my head. I mainly attended to my daughter, a charming child, and Mademoiselle de Bonneuil, today Madame Regnault-d'Angély, who was as beautiful as an angel. Both were ravishing to look at, carrying very light antique vases and preparing to pour us out wine.

At half-past nine the preparations were concluded, and as soon as we had all grouped ourselves we each got up in turn to go and look at those who were seated, so new and picturesque was the effect of this table arrangement.

At ten o'clock we heard the comte de Vaudreuil and Boutin's coach enter, and when these two gentlemen arrived at the double door of the dining-room, which I had had opened wide, they found us singing Gluck's chorus 'The God of Paphos and Cnidos', which Monsieur de Cubières accompanied on his lyre.

I have never in all my days seen two such astonished, thunderstruck faces as those of Monsieur de Vaudreuil and his companion.[40]

Brillat-Savarin or the very wealthy Monsieur de Sainte-James, whose lavish feasts in his *hôtel* on the Place Vendôme Louise found over-facing, might not have been impressed by the supper, which apart from the chicken, eel and accompanying sauces consisted of a honey-and-raisin cake and two dishes of vegetables washed down with a single bottle of old Cyprus wine. But its fame spread, thanks to Vaudreuil's and Boutin's reports. Some ladies of the court asked Louise for a repeat performance, which for unspecified reasons she refused. They were stung at the refusal.

Soon the rumour spread in the *monde* that this supper had cost me 20,000 francs. The King spoke of it with displeasure to the marquis de Cubières, who most fortunately had been one of the guests, and so could convince His Majesty of the idiocy of such a claim. None the less, what was held down to the modest price of

20,000 francs at Versailles was upped to 40,000 in Rome; in Vienna, the Baroness Stroganova informed me that I had spent 60,000 francs on my Greek supper. You know that in St Petersburg the sum was finally fixed at 80,000, and the plain truth is that this supper cost me roughly fifteen francs.[41]

Louise loved charades, of which this occasion was an elaborate version: the meal was far less important than the dressing-up and play-acting. The antiquity she liked was the 'amiable', almost rococo antiquity of the painter Vien, not the stern, geometrical universe of David. Her enthusiasm was for modishness rather than scholarship; and Barthélemy's immense book struck a chord with a society which, like her, wanted its antiquity presented in an appetising form. There may seem nothing very alluring about the work to a modern reader, who finds in it little trace of the author's biting wit (though much evidence of his great learning); but it enchanted the late eighteenth century. Robert Burns declared that 'I never met with a book that bewitched me so much', and spoke for a whole age.

Louise's was a society that thrived on parlour-games, and it clung to these harmless amusements, which a younger generation often found embarrassing and insipid, long after the passing of the old regime. One did not have to be silly or lacking in seriousness to find them diverting, but it helped to be unintellectual. Apart from such pleasures, Louise prided herself on providing for her guests 'the best music to be heard at that time'.[42] Not everyone agreed that she actually did: the young Talleyrand, for instance, was unimpressed. According to his memoirs, before the Revolution he went more out of curiosity than because of a pronounced musical taste to salon concerts, but he found Louise's 'learned and boring'.[43] Louise thought them enchanting, was flattered that composers like Grétry, Sacchini and Martini allowed airs from their operas to be sung there before the official première, and clearly liked being told by Grétry that her untrained voice produced 'silvery sounds'.[44]

When not giving light and memorable suppers herself (of another occasion: 'We sat down to eat at ten o'clock, and my supper was as simple as could be ... a fowl, a fish, a dish of vegetables and a salad; and if I was tempted into inviting some visitors to stay, there really was no more than that to eat'),[45] Louise often ate in town, went to a ball 'where there was nothing like the crush one encounters today',[46] or joined in amateur performances of drama and comic opera, which she greatly preferred to dancing. Sometimes professionals helped out, but the evening's entertainment was not necessarily the better for it. The future acting star Talma, who played the romantic rôles, was gauche and embarrassed, and gave no sign of the great talents he would develop. 'I was enormously surprised,' she writes, to see our young 'lead' overtake Larive and replace Lekain. But the time it took for this metamorphosis to come about, like all others of the same kind, simply proves to me that dramatic talent is of all talents the one which develops latest. Note that not a single great actor was great in his youth.[47]

For the time being she preferred performers closer to home – her brother, a predictably accomplished declaimer, his wife Suzanne, and Auguste Rivière, a fine comic who would later mysteriously accompany Louise on her travels over Europe with Julie Le Brun. There is no mention of Jean-Baptiste-Pierre Le Brun in all this, much though he loved dressing up. Clearly his wife and he kept their social lives separate.

'My time was never my own until the evening,'[48] Louise writes, meaning that she was furiously busy painting all day. But she resented her husband's intrusion into her professional life when what she describes as his greed for money made him suggest that she should take on some pupils.[49] It is hard to imagine that Louise earned more from this activity than from her painting commissions; and the pleasure one might have expected her to derive from helping women develop their artistic skills seems to have been completely absent. It was simply one more grudge to bear against Le Brun, the rash speculator, outrageous philanderer and shameless sponge.

> I agreed to what he wanted, without stopping to think about it, and soon I had flocks of young ladies wanting me to show them how to do eyes, noses, ovals which I constantly had to retouch and which distracted me from my work and thoroughly annoyed me.

It is a striking illustration of Louise's single-mindedness, not to say self-preoccupation. Having had to struggle to win the success she knew was her due, she found it worse than irritating to be asked – even for a consideration – to help others achieve something comparable. For most of her pupils, of course, it would not be comparable at all, because they lacked her natural talent and probably her determination; but she did acknowledge an exception in Marie-Guilhelmine de Laville Leroulx.

Yet her attitude remains faintly disquieting. At what point does single-mindedness become egoism? It is a question we have to ask ourselves as we follow her career, observe her triumphant progress through the courts of Europe, attempt to untangle the complexities of her relationship with a daughter she smothered with possessive affection and then allowed to die in distress, and consider the nature of her achievement as a portraitist.

When she stayed at the surface of her sitters' characters – as she does in the case of more than one glamorous woman – was it because they lacked profound natures, or because she lacked the sympathy to penetrate them deeply? Is she a 'deeper' portraitist of men because they interested her more, or because she was always matching herself against them? Did she take an essentially reductive view of her own sex, such that, far from wanting to avenge its social and institutional downtroddenness, she merely connived at the Rousseauist view of its proper limitations?

She would not have been the first, and has not been the last, to win the laurels in a man's world and then make little or no effort to help other women do likewise. The marquise de Merteuil's 'I am my own creation'[50] is not far removed from Louise's 'I had no master as such'.[51] When she returned from her exile in 1802, she says, she was undismayed to find her old position of supremacy usurped by a new generation of portraitists. But they were all male portraitists, and their idiom was different from her own. Perhaps she would have been less forgiving of female competition; she never has a generous word to say about the contemporary painter whom some saw as her rival, Adélaïde Labille-Guiard. The self-portrait with girl pupils which Labille-Guiard exhibited at the 1785 Salon incidentally suggests that she took the training of women artists much more seriously than Louise, who gave up teaching students as quickly as possible.

It would be simplistic and inaccurate to suggest that Louise's portraits of men invariably plumb the depths of the male psyche, while her female ones fail – for whatever reason – to do the same for her own sex. Some of her women were, and look, substantial and complex – the Birmingham Countess Golovina, for example, or the Viennese Countess Bucquoi. Nor could it be assumed that male subjects would, like Calonne, be granted a weightiness they did not necessarily deserve. A case in point is the rather weak portrait Louise painted in 1784 of the comte de Vaudreuil. He may have been a lover of Louise's – rumour claimed as much, at least – and was one of the glossiest noblemen of *ancien régime* France. The Louvre ultimately benefited from his astute picture-buying, for he was a passionate collector. He lived life magnificently, as befitted an elegant epicurean, and, despite having a large income from family plantations in the Caribbean as well as various minor Crown appointments, repeatedly slipped into debt. Usually his royal contacts bailed him out, but occasionally he had to hold picture-sales (which Jean-Baptiste-Pierre Le Brun organised). Although Marie-Antoinette detested him, he felt none the safer for it at the outbreak of the Revolution, and left Paris in July 1789.

Louise painted him sympathetically, and certainly had grounds for feeling well disposed towards him. His acquaintance gave her an entrée to the best social circles, and Vaudreuil had flatteringly let it be known that he preferred an evening at her salon to any of the amusements Versailles could offer.[52] But the picture is a feeble one, ineptly constructed, awkwardly posed and hinting at Vandreuil's own superficiality. He is, admittedly, as pleasant-looking as Louise's pen-portrait of him in the *Souvenirs* suggests:

> he was tall, a fine figure of a man; his bearing was remarkably noble and elegant; his gaze was gentle and shrewd, his expression extremely mobile like his ideas, and his obliging smile predisposed you immediately in his favour.[53]

But there is a polished emptiness to him that reflects the court milieu in which he flourished, and which he affected to despise. Remembering that he was one of the most accomplished stage performers of the day, we may also recall what Diderot said about actors in the *Paradoxe sur le comédien*: '. . . the great actor is everything and nothing . . . And perhaps it is because he is nothing that he is *par excellence* everything, his particular form never opposing the foreign forms he must assume.'[54] Great actors are 'marvellous puppets', characterless creatures who can become any character because of the void inside them.

> The great actor . . . has no chord of his own, but strikes the chord and tone that go with his part, and he has the skill to adapt to any . . . The person who, in society, has the intention and possesses the unfortunate talent of pleasing everyone is nothing, has nothing proper to himself, nothing distinguishing him, which enthuses some people and tires others. He always speaks, and does it well; he is a professional sycophant, a great courtier, a great actor . . . A great courtier, accustomed from the cradle to the rôle of marvellous puppet, assumes all kinds of forms at the whim of the string in his master's hand.[55]

Perhaps to compensate for the Grand Falconer's lack of personal weight, Louise loads him down with finery and insignia, picking out the heavy embroidery of his coat and waistcoat, detailing the ribbons of the order of chivalry he wears on his chest, and highlighting the exquisite lace of his cuffs. He is intended, evidently, to appear relaxed; yet the marks of office and rank, about which it is too much to imagine him feeling embarrassed, seem to constrict him slightly.

The same year Louise painted a sitter who lacked all the elegance of Vaudreuil, but whom, because he was male, she did not have to glamorise.

The expensive lost portrait of Monsieur Beaujon shows an affable plump body, but in no way suggests the physical decrepitude that necessitated Louise's painting him in his own house. The irony of Madame de Bonneuil's attachment to him was not lost on the world, for this obese, blind, rheumatic, dropsical and gouty one-time reveller kept a seraglio of beauties – called his '*berceuses*', or lullabies – whose favours he could not enjoy. Louise found the unfortunate millionaire alone in a bath-chair, his hands and legs so swollen that he could use neither. An exquisite dinner had been laid out for his beautiful minders, but Beaujon himself had nothing except a dish of spinach to eat.

Touring his sumptuous dwelling – formerly the home of the marquise de Pompadour – Louise felt she was in the palace of a king:

> everything was of great richness and in exquisite taste. A first drawing-room contained 'show' pictures, none of them particularly remarkable – so easy is it to deceive amateurs, however much they can afford to pay for their acquisitions. The second was a music room: grand pianos and smaller ones, every kind of instrument, nothing was lacking; other rooms, along with the boudoirs and closets, were furnished with supreme elegance. The bathroom was especially charming; a bed, a bathtub were draped, like the walls, with sprigged muslin lined with pink fabric; I have never seen anything so pretty; one wanted to have a bath there and then. The apartments on the first floor were furnished with equal care. In the centre of one particular room, adorned with columns, there was an enormous gilt basket, surrounded by flowers, which contained a bed no one had ever slept in.[56]

This epitome of *ancien régime* splendour, a perfect house with perfect furniture and its own architect-designed park, ought to have been a focus of elegant social life. But Beaujon, a generous man who wanted to make reparation to society for the dubious speculations which had founded his colossal fortune, was unable to derive any real pleasure from it. Louise illustrates the sad truth with an anecdote:

> An Englishman, keen to see everything that was said to be a 'sight' in Paris, asked to be given permission by Monsieur de Beaujon to visit his fine *hôtel*. Arriving in the dining-room, he found the great table laid, as I had found it myself, and turning to the servant who was accompanying him he said: 'Your master must eat very well?' 'Alas, Monsieur,' replied his *cicerone*, 'my master never sits down to eat, he is simply served a dish of vegetables.' As the Englishman

passed into the first drawing-room, he continued: 'These, at least, must delight his eyes', pointing to the pictures. 'Alas, Monsieur, my master is nearly blind.' 'Ah!' said the Englishman, going into the second drawing-room, 'he finds consolation for that, I hope, listening to good music.' 'Alas, Monsieur, my master has never heard what is played here; he goes to bed too early, hoping to snatch a few seconds' sleep.' Then the Englishman, looking at the magnificent garden stretching out beneath the windows, said: 'But your master can at least enjoy the pleasure of walking.' 'Alas, Monsieur, he no longer walks.' At this point the people invited for dinner arrived, among them some very pretty women. The Englishman continued: 'Well, there is more than one beauty here to provide some very pleasant moments for him?' The servant, in reply, merely repeated two 'alases' instead of one, and said no more.[57]

According to the *Souvenirs*, Beaujon was exceedingly small as well as very fat, and so was the reverse of the elegant Calonne. A wit who saw their two portraits hanging side by side at the Salon called them the images of mind ('*esprit*') and matter respectively.[58] Louise was obliged to withdraw the Beaujon portrait because the subject was so indignant at the epigram, particularly as he had become the spirit of benevolence, and wanted the portrait to hang in the hospice for orphans he had founded in the faubourg de Roule.

The impotent Beaujon was probably not the client who commissioned from Louise the provocative picture of a bacchante which caused a sensation in the Salon the following year. She was not averse to doing such pictures for besotted lovers, as her later portraits of Emma Hart for Sir William Hamilton reveal. But who was the model in this case? The work may have been a concoction rather than a portrait, yet we must assume that Louise painted the wantonly posed creature from life. It is possible that she was her own model, but perhaps unlikely: she was by this time thirty years old, and her well-endowed nymph looks younger. Probably she hired a nameless woman to pose in her own studio and dressed her with the appropriate props.

In theory, the female model who sat to a woman painter should not have been subject to the same assumptions about her virtue as those who sat to men, but the sheer sensual exuberance of Louise's *Bacchante* makes one wonder. And not simply about the model; for tongues were already wagging about Louise's own morals, and the picture may have been a risky one for her to paint for that reason. Adélaïde Labille-Guiard, to whom sexual scandal also attached, had painted a comparable study of erotic abandonment a few years before – the *Heureuse Surprise* of 1779 – and probably both commissions had been impossible to refuse. Louise never painted even a semi-nude male, possibly because she had never studied one from life, but with women it was a different matter. The *Bacchante* showed what the pictures of Emma Hart would confirm, that she could handle the female form as erotically as any man.

Louise embodies the paradox of the conservative artist, wedded to and dependent on an established and unprogressive *monde*, who was also ambitious enough to want to move on. By her twenties, she was fully aware of her saleability, and she was adroit enough always to fit into her adoptive world. It was provoking, then, to know that the conservatism of the establishment could work against her and halt her progress as a female artist. The recognition which the court and the faubourg Saint-Germain willingly extended to her was gratifying, but wider recognition was dependent on access to the Académie royale, with its fixed hierarchies, Crown commissions and regular opportunities for exhibition. And here Louise's sex would inevitably count against her. It had not been intended thus at the time of the Académie's establishment by Louis XIV: the King had meant the institution to be open to all gifted artists irrespective of sex. But this liberal policy ended in 1706, by which date only seven female academicians had been elected. (The English Royal Academy had an even worse record: it elected no women at all between the founding members Angelica Kauffman and Mary Moser in 1768 and, in the early twentieth century, Dame Laura Knight.) Louise faced an additional obstacle to election, namely the fact that she was married to a picture-dealer. The Académie wanted to protect the status of painting as a liberal art, and hence would have no truck with trade. Any connection with it automatically entailed exclusion, at least in theory.

This particular difficulty was removed when Marie-Antoinette, who by the early 1780s had developed a close personal friendship with Louise, decided to suggest to the Académie that it forget about Jean-Baptiste-Pierre Le Brun's profession and admit his wife forthwith.[59] Louise's reference to this intervention is deliberately casual: 'I believe, indeed, that the King and Queen had been good enough to wish to see me enter the Académie; but that is all.'[60] It certainly did not suit her to have it assumed that she owed her election to outside influence, though it was convenient to foist the blame for circulating this story onto the apparently misogynistic First Painter to the King, Jean-Baptiste-Marie Pierre. 'Monsieur Pierre spread the rumour at that time that a court order had led to my admission.' Whether or not the rumour had been spread by Pierre, it was apparently true. The effect of Marie-Antoinette's move may have been to increase the devotion Louise showed her throughout her life, whether or not she was embarrassed by the 'court order'. Possibly the Queen was inspired to help her favourite portraitist for reasons other than friendship, however, for the director of the Académie, d'Angiviller, presented her with a document arguing that Louise, to his best belief, was herself quite uninvolved in picture-selling. Marie-Antoinette seems to have needed little persuading.

Concerned as ever with correct self-presentation, Louise is careful to emphasise that the original idea of standing for membership was not her own, but Joseph Vernet's. The success of one particular portrait was decisive. During the trip to Flanders with her husband, in Antwerp she had been so moved by Rubens's picture of his sister-in-law Susanna Lunden – the so-called 'Straw Hat' now in London's National Gallery, which actually shows the sitter wearing a felt hat adorned with feathers – that she decided to paint her own picture in homage. The resulting work, done in Brussels, greatly impressed her public at home, though it is in fact less captivating than some of Louise's other self-portraits, like the 'Cherry-Red Ribbons' of 1782. In the 'Straw Hat', Louise gives herself a slightly vacuous prettiness resembling the enamelled emptiness of some of her female subjects, but does compensate with a dazzling display of colour – puce dress with ruffled lace edging, gold gauze sash, black lace-trimmed mantilla and opalescent ear-drops. 'This portrait and several other works of mine,' she writes,

> decided Joseph Vernet to put me forward for membership of the Académie royale de peinture. Monsieur Pierre, at that time First Painter to the King, opposed it violently, saying he did not want any women admitted, and yet Madame Vallayer-Coster, who painted flowers so perfectly, had already been elected, and so, I believe, had Madame Vien.[61]

Louise was right. Anne Vallayer-Coster, significantly a practitioner of a 'minor' genre, and Vien's wife Marie-Thérèse Reboul (a miniaturist and still-life painter) were both academicians. It had been accepted since 1770 that the Académie might have four female members at any given time. D'Angiviller had supported this limit on the grounds that it was a sufficient number to recognise talent: women could never assist in the progress of art *en masse*, he thought, because the modesty of their sex meant they could not study from life. When Anna Therbusch, who had been admitted in 1767, died in 1782, there were only two female academicians left; the painter Roslin's wife Suzanne Giroust had died ten years previously and not been replaced. With two vacancies thus existing, it seemed timely for Louise and her slightly older contemporary Adélaïde Labille-Guiard to put forward their names.

Louise was not alone in believing Pierre to be opposed to her election. A couplet circulated at the time claimed that anyone wanting to deprive her of that honour must have a heart 'of stone [*pierre*], of stone, of stone'.[62] Was his own mediocrity at fault, making it impossible for him to accept that a 'mere' woman should earn the accolade of being elected Academician? However unlikely this seems, it is true that Pierre's talents were widely regarded as inferior. For Louise he was 'a very indifferent painter, for he saw in painting nothing more than the wielding of the brush; [but] he was witty, and besides was rich, which gave him the means to entertain artists lavishly – and artists then were less well-off than they are today.'[63] It may be a cruel dig, but Diderot's *Salons* contain some crueller ones. Diderot's opinion of the painter barely changed over the period of his activity as a Salon critic. In 1761 he is scathing.

> I don't know what is happening to the man. He's rich; he's had an education; he's made the pilgrimage to Rome; he's said to be witty; nothing's pressing him to finish a work off, so why the mediocrity of nearly all his compositions?[64]

He accuses Pierre of plagiarism as well as ineptness, but blames his lack of genius for the overall second- or third-rateness of his productions. Two years later Pierre is called 'the vainest and most tedious of our artists',[65] and in 1767 accused of professional jealousy:

> Do you think we've forgotten the dullness of that *Mercury* and that *Aglaura* you endlessly redid and which always needed re-doing, and that second-rate *Crucifixion*, always second-rate despite being copied from one of the most sublime compositions of Carracci? There are some men who are eaten up with a very insolent, very base jealousy. Monsieur le Chevalier, earn the right to be disdainful, don't be it; that's the best thing.[66]

It should probably be assumed that Pierre, jealous or not, *was* opposed to Louise's election, but if so it may have been on personal grounds rather than because he disagreed with the admission of women. In 1770, after all, he had been one of the signatories to the ruling which simply limited the admission of women to four at any given time, and which in fact also made provision for that number to be exceeded in exceptional circumstances. (It never was.)[67] After the Revolution, Labille-Guiard had a motion passed that the limit be abolished, but ironically the much more misogynistic Institut de France, which replaced the Académie royale in 1793, admitted no women at all.

Pierre could not stop the tide of support for Louise, the backing of what she calls a 'cabal' of art lovers, and she was elected with Labille-Guiard on 31 May 1783, at the age of twenty-eight. The art lovers were surely right, for these two were the most distinguished women painters then living in France. But Louise must have been disappointed not to be admitted to the top category in the Académie's hierarchy, that of history painter. She had no intention of breaking her lucrative links with portraiture, but she naturally wanted the highest accolade. She submitted a mythological painting (which counted as historical) as her reception-piece, a picture called *Peace Bringing Back Abundance* which she had painted in 1780. Provokingly, though, the Académie never stipulated the category into which she had been received. Perhaps it was misogynistic enough not to want a woman at the top of the hierarchy, but more probably it gave Louise no official rank because she had – exceptionally – been admitted by royal order, not by the submission of a '*morceau de réception*': the evidence suggests that Louise's picture was received *after* her admission.[68] Labille-Guiard, either more realistic or less ambitious, had presented a pastel of the sculptor Pajou as her reception-piece, and was admitted as a 'painter of portraits'.

Louise had been confidently handling oils since the 1770s, and knew that large historical canvases could not be executed in any other medium. Not that she spurned the medium of pastel: it was one in which Louis Vigée had shone, and his daughter greatly admired the pastel portraits of the Italian Rosalba Carriera. But she knew that oils were less 'female', which was one reason why her ambition propelled her towards them. There was not much else she could do to impress the Académie, and both her reception-piece and other works of the same type she did between 1780 and 1783 are competent enough performances. If the official response seemed slightly grudging, she could always blame it on vested interests. In any case, she now had the official sanction as an artist none of her worldly achievements had been able to provide, and could regard herself as a member of the establishment.

CHAPTER THREE

THE LAST OF THE OLD REGIME:
'The extreme goodness with which they treated me'

It was a sign of approval to tell a woman that she painted like a man, and both Louise and Adélaïde Labille-Guiard received the compliment more than once. The reference was less to subject-matter – for instance, a man rather than a woman being thought the 'proper' painter of the erotic female nude, though both the new *académiciennes* did so with striking effectiveness – than to technique. To be called 'virile' or told that one wielded a 'male brush' meant, broadly, that one painted with vigour and competence (all the more surprisingly in view of the institutional disadvantages one's sex suffered). But the 'male' virtue of correct draughtsmanship was more commonly associated by critics with Labille-Guiard than with Louise. Louise was praised for the 'female' seductiveness of her colouring.

This was merely an old opposition revived, and there was originally nothing specifically sexual about it: the great artistic quarrel in the seventeenth century between the Poussinists and the Rubenists had been about *disegno* versus *colore*. But when the two terms were used as a way of contrasting Labille-Guiard with Louise, they generally signified that the one epitomised sense and the other sensibility. Labille-Guiard painted in a more studied fashion than Louise, and less rapidly: she rarely completed more than a dozen works in any one year, while Louise frequently produced more than thirty. Possibly as a result, the older woman can appear more profound, less facile. But the opposition of draughtsmanship and colour has little to do with it.

If Adélaïde Labille-Guiard seems more dourly serious, it may be for the trivial reason that she does not evidently idealise her looks in her self-portraits, whereas Louise emphasises her own feminine charm. A different kind of seriousness, too, is implied in Labille-Guiard's attitude to the training of woman artists. There seems as well to have been a general view, which may or may not have been justified, that she deserved her election to the Académie more than Louise, because she owed it to no one but herself: this was the message of a couplet circulating in Paris at the time.

And it is possibly significant that she never had painting links with Marie-Antoinette, though she did become the official portraitist of Louis XVI's aunts, Madame Victoire and Madame Adélaïde.

Were the women genuinely rivals?[1] The fact that they were both portraitists and both made their Académie 'début' at the same time encouraged others to discuss them together, but the *Souvenirs* never mention Labille-Guiard by name. On the other hand, she is surely the subject of the following remark, which Louise drops apropos of *Mesdames Tantes*:

> I was not unaware that a woman artist, who for reasons I cannot fathom has always shown herself to be my enemy, had tried by every imaginable means to blacken my reputation in the eyes of these princesses; but the extreme goodness with which they treated me soon reassured me as to the slight effect these odious scandals had had.[2]

(Perhaps, as Germaine Greer suggests, the far-fetchedness of the accusation simply reflects Louise's own vanity and insecurity.[3]) Her reference to the envy she aroused by succeeding in selling her pictures expensively is possibly a dig at Labille-Guiard, who was known for the comparative modesty of the prices she charged.

> Though I was, I believe, the most inoffensive being who had ever lived, I had enemies; not only did some women bear me a grudge for not being as ugly as they were, but several could not forgive me for being fashionable, and selling my pictures for more than they did.[4]

Of course, Louise's neglecting to mention Labille-Guiard directly could itself indicate dislike, if not necessarily rivalry. Since Labille-Guiard did much to attempt improving the lot of women painters, it is hardly likely that she would have engaged in aggressive competition with another successful artist of her own sex, or even tried to blacken her reputation with *Mesdames Tantes*. It seems more plausible that the so-called rivalry was invented by critics than that it actually stemmed from what the nineteenth-century writer Charles Oulmont, in a book on woman painters, called the 'Eve mentality', or the natural competitiveness of career women.[5]

It is most probable, in fact, that Salon critics paired the two artists in order to avoid answering the question of their possible superiority to men: setting woman against woman neatly deflected attention from the troublesome issue of how female excellence might detract from male achievements. At the end of the *Souvenirs* Louise reports David's comment on a picture of his and her portrait of Paisiello, done during her stay in Italy: 'One would think my canvas had been painted by a woman, and the portrait of Paisiello by a man.'[6] This comparison is explicit, and Louise is quick to acknowledge that David never denied her the praise that was her due, however much they disliked each other personally. If Louise was never the equal of David, she needed to fear no comparison with contemporary male portraitists like Alexandre Roslin – who was thought to produce good likenesses – and Joseph-Siffred Duplessis, who was better known for his glossy technique than for the resemblance of his portraits ('Very like, except for the head' was one verdict on his 1777 picture of Louis XVI). Bachaumont, writing of the 1783 Salon, is unusual in frankly declaring Louise's superiority to all-comers:

> . . . despite the excellence of numerous masters who have entered the lists of the grand genre, who would believe it – the sceptre of Apollo seems to have become a distaff, and it is a woman who has won the palm. Let me explain myself: I do not mean that there is more genius in a picture with two or three three-quarter-length figures than in a vast composition with ten or twelve life-size ones . . . I simply mean that the works of the modest Minerva attract the spectator's attention first, constantly summon it back, seize it, take possession of it, and draw from him those cries of pleasure and admiration of which artists are so jealous.[7]

But in case his praise sounds over-generous, Bachaumont quickly qualifies it. The fact that Louise is so widely talked about, he continues, has much to do with her being young and pretty, moving in the right circles, giving artists, writers and people of quality elegant suppers, and having protectors in the highest places.[8]

Other critics are keen to insist that they are judging women artists by the same independent criteria as they apply to men, and do not apportion praise or blame according to the artist's prettiness and charm. The *Année littéraire* explicitly places Louise at the head of portraitists, not merely *women* portraitists.[9] But designating Labille-Guiard an honorary male in virtue of her drawing skills, and Louise – however frequently she might be called a *grand homme* – a quintessential female, both attractive in herself and a mistress of sensuous colour, was a convenient way of banding the two women and keeping them apart from the male mainstream. Louise's faults in draughtsmanship, often commented on in the 1783 and 1785 Salon criticism, were rightly seen to stem from her (woman's) lack of training, but the weakness was frequently noted without sympathy. One commentator remarked of the 1785 *Bacchante*:

> To paint a half-length of a woman without having studied from life . . . to have not the faintest idea of the style of drawing and expression suitable for a Bacchante, to ignore even the fact that the thyrsus is one of her principal attributes, and yet call oneself a history painter . . . is utterly astonishing.[10]

This was one solution to the problem: to deny, against the evidence of public acclamation and professional success, that a woman could paint at all. Another – which in fact amounted to the same thing – was to acknowledge the skill of a painting, but question whether the woman who put her name to it had actually executed it. In this spirit Louise was accused of having had her canvases painted by Ménageot, an accusation Bachaumont regarded as a slander, but which, he said, was compounded by the two artists' living under the same roof (for they were also said to be lovers). Jean-Baptiste-Pierre Le Brun's 'life' of Louise remarked apropos of this that

> it is an injustice common to men and even women to affect to believe that a woman is incapable of occupying herself with anything but frivolities, and not to forgive her for wanting to penetrate the sanctuary of the arts and sciences.[11]

Labille-Guiard, meanwhile, was accused of claiming pictures that were really by François Vincent, her future husband, as her own. Some commentators even asserted that women were attracted to painting from life because it allowed them to indulge their indecent urges to see naked men – in other words, that sexual irregularity and female bids for artistic status went together. This ignores the fact that women found it extremely difficult actually to get sight of a male model.

When Louise's studio was being rebuilt in 1787, David obligingly agreed to be temporary tutor to her students, teaching them in his Louvre apartment free of charge. For this act of kindness he received an official reprimand, since it was assumed by the authorities that the girls were improperly attending his life classes. David wrote a letter of complaint to d'Angiviller, pointing out that the girls were kept rigorously separated from his male pupils and the nude model.[12] Besides, he said, they were of irreproachable moral character, which was the only reason why he had agreed to take them in the first place.

The notion that women wanted to paint in order to see a beautiful male body, always supposing that they could, also ignores the fact that the posed model is rarely arousing. In a letter to the *Journal de Paris* in 1785, the artist Renou recalls the wisdom of the Athenian legislator who had young men and women fight naked to extinguish the fire of their passions, and adds that those who are not initiated into an art are ignorant of the lack of sensuous pleasure experienced in 'observing nature'. Indeed, he says, this so-called pleasure is usually a type of disgust inseparable from the profession, as doctors and surgeons would confirm.

> Why, then, try by vague insinuations to deny women the resource
> which a decent talent offers them, when they are already deprived
> of every means of subsistence?[13]

Talent, he concludes, has no sex. But the less progressively minded went on insisting that it did. Louise's answer was simple.

> Monsieur Ménageot allegedly painted my pictures and even my
> portraits, though the quantities of people to whom I gave sittings
> could naturally testify to the contrary; this absurd rumour con-
> tinued to be spread around until the time of my admission to the
> Académie royale de peinture. As I was then exhibiting in the same
> room as the painter of *Meleager* [i.e. Ménageot], people had to
> acknowledge the truth; for Ménageot, whose talent and even
> advice I greatly appreciated, had a manner of painting entirely
> opposite to my own.[14]

Elsewhere she remarks that since she kept open studio, the sceptical could easily settle their doubts by calling in and watching her at work.

The misgiving which such suspicions make explicit was of its time, despite the apparent genuineness of the enthusiasm contemporaries showed for improving the education and civil rights of women (an enthusiasm which Napoleon would subsequently dampen). In the 1760s Rousseau was observing in *Emile* that the efforts of a talented woman at any of the arts are invariably 'improved' by a man:

> Very talented women always impress only the stupid. People
> always know who is the artist or [male] friend who guides the pen
> or brush when they work. People know the identity of the discreet
> man of letters who secretly dictates their oracles to them. This
> whole charlatanry is unworthy of a decent woman. If she had
> genuine talents, her pretension would debase them. Her dignity is
> to be ignored: her glory is in the esteem of her husband; her
> pleasures are in the happiness of her family.[15]

This indictment effectively dismisses the real accomplishments of eighteenth-century women – the *salonnières*, the learned Emilie du Châtelets, the much re-edited Françoise de Graffignys and Marie-Jeanne Riccobonis – and grants no validity to the 'alternative' ménages such as Louise's own, where a husband's own status could be enhanced by the glory of his wife, and where the family unit was at best unconventional.

Women artists were used to denigration. After all, Margarita Havermann had been expelled from membership of the Académie royale de peinture in 1722 because the quality of her work was thought to be suspiciously high, which meant it must have been due to the assistance of her former master Van Huysum. As a result of this 'scandal' it was declared that no women would ever be admitted to membership of the Académie royale again, and for thirty years none was. Even if their talents were acknowledged to be genuine, it was agreed that women were more likely to succeed in the world if they were pretty. Here Louise unquestionably had the advantage over the long-nosed Adélaïde Labille-Guiard. But at least Labille-Guiard did win the regard of serious critics. In his 1767 *Salon*, Diderot describes his attempts to help the Prussian Anna Therbusch during her stay in Paris and her efforts to win the attention of the artistic establishment. She was a talented woman, he wrote, and he preferred her portrait of him to the delightful but effeminate one by Louis-Michel Vanloo, but she still experienced difficulties in making her way in Paris, partly because of her unbridled temperament and relentlessly unsubtle self-promotion, and partly because of her reckless extravagance. He did far too much for her, in fact, and was inevitably accused of having an affair with her. But Anna Therbusch was also unattractive, lacking the beauty that would have smoothed her path as a woman in the painterly world.

This did not mean Diderot was untroubled by physical arousal while she painted him in the nude: artist and sitter 'chatted with a simplicity and innocence worthy of primeval times', but still 'since the sin of Adam one cannot control all the parts of one's body as one can one's arm; there are some parts that show willingness when the son of Adam does not wish it and none when the son of Adam would greatly like it'.[16] He had an answer, Diogenes' response to the young wrestler, if it were needed: 'My son, do not be afraid, I am not so wicked as *that!*' He did, though, like the way she insisted on painting the male nude, asking in the spirit of Renou why vice should have the exclusive privilege of undressing a man. Anna Therbusch's talents, however much hampered by her want of feminine beauty, were anyway sufficient in the end to win her membership of the Académie royale de peinture.

Louise's own reception-piece, *Peace and Abundance*, seems to have borrowed from a more famous woman artist, Rosalba Carriera, as well as her beloved Rubens. (Contemporary critics named Reni, Santerre and Cortoni as her models, but for someone who had already been told she painted none of her own pictures this accusation of plagiarism cannot have been very disconcerting.) Yet she must have known that portraiture was her real strength, as – despite the allegory of *Peace and Justice* which Louise had imitated – it remained Rosalba's.

One of the portraits most praised in the Salon at which, in Bachaumont's words, Louise's work outshone that of all other exhibitors was her picture of Madame Grand, Talleyrand's future wife. Louise makes the unlikely claim that she painted this woman first in 1776, when she was living in India and was only fourteen years old. The 1783 picture – said by a contemporary to be a very good likeness – depicts Madame Grand as a latter-day St Cecilia, her eyes rolled heavenward in Greuzian fashion and her mouth half open. She clutches a sheet of music in one hand and contrives to appear both desirable and silly. When asked about her origins, she habitually responded, 'Je suis d'Inde', which could be understood as 'Je suis dinde' – I am a turkey/a silly goose. According to Louise, she once congratulated the antiquarian and traveller Vivant Denon on his meeting with Man Friday, having confused Denon's travels in Egypt with Robinson Crusoe's adventures.

Madame Grand was a notorious courtesan at the time Louise's portrait was painted, and lived close to the hôtel de Lubert. In her *décolleté* dress and suggestive vacancy, she has a provocative look combining invitation with detachment – the aspect of the professional flirt. In 1783 she was being kept by a wealthy banker. She had many other lovers up to and after the Revolution, emigrated, returned to France, was imprisoned under the Directory – the government which presided over the Republic from 1795 until 1799 – on suspicion of espionage, and was bailed out by Talleyrand (who called her beautiful and astonishingly lazy). She became his mistress and then his wife; but Talleyrand tired of her, and in 1814 left for the Congress of Vienna – where heads of state and politicians would attempt to establish the size and shape of Europe in the post-Napoleonic era – in the company of a favourite niece. Madame de Talleyrand flounced out of the French capital, but subsequently returned and became a religious fanatic. As she lay dying in the rue de Lille the Archbishop of Paris gave her the last rites.

The duchesse d'Abrantès gives a cool, detached evaluation of this famous beauty.[17] She had a fine figure, she writes, but was not *graceful*; she was not *disgraceful* either, but started running to fat early. Her retroussé nose would have given finesse to any other woman's face, but failed to confer it on hers; her eyes and mouth lacked expressiveness, and her thoughts were as lumbering as her movements. Her hair, however, could be praised without reservation: it was of a ravishing blonde colour, luxuriant and beautiful. People were surprised when Talleyrand decided to marry her, according to the duchess, because she was no longer young and had lost her looks.[18] Like Louise's later subject Emma Hamilton, she became little more than a mound of flesh, and took to wearing a wig; her eyes were red-rimmed, and her whole person appeared very far from desirable.

Given her appeal as a portraitist of the *monde*, it is hardly surprising that Louise should have painted a number of naughty women. She seems herself, despite the strictness of her upbringing, to have had a sneaking admiration for expensively kept courtesans, whom she must often have inspected as they promenaded in the Palais-Royal gardens. There is no evidence that she actually painted any of them, though a mediocre portrait of the celebrated Mademoiselle Duthé in the Musée de Grenoble was once misattributed to her. Louise describes watching this pretty and elegant woman walking with other *filles* in the gardens,

> for at that time no men ever appeared with these demoiselles; if they met up with them at the theatre, it was always in boxes with grilles. The English show less delicacy in this respect. This same demoiselle Duthé was often accompanied by an Englishman, so faithful that eighteen years later I saw them again together at a spectacle in London. The Englishman's brother was with them, and I have been told that the three of them had set up house together. You can have no idea, dear friend, of the magnificence of kept women at the time I am talking of. Mademoiselle Duthé, for example, ran through millions; now the condition of courtesan is one for lost creatures; no one ruins himself any longer for a trollop.[19]

This statement is in fact completely inaccurate. Expensive courtesans flourished in the Empire and the Restoration as companions to the *nouveaux riches* Louise despised (and whose wealth they effectively advertised), and young nobles still ran through their inheritances on a *fille's* account.

Another habituée of the Palais-Royal gardens was the famous Mademoiselle Roland, of whom Louise would paint a dashing portrait in Rome; posed informally against a deep blue sky, this light-hearted woman strongly recalls Rubens's wife in the picture *Hélène Fourment in a Fur Coat*, which Louise could have known only from a print or copy. The fact that Hyacinthe-Gabrielle Roland met her future husband in the gardens says little for the reputation of either: she was a girl of modest origins who was free with her favours to men, and the Earl of Mornington – later the Marquess of Wellesley – was said to have ruined himself by excessive expenditure on women. They married in 1794 (having already produced three illegitimate children), but the Marchioness's renown continued to tell against her in the eyes of polite society. Perhaps sensing rejection, she refused to learn more than a few words of English, and did not accompany her husband to India after he was appointed the British monarch's representative there: clearly she was not regarded as a suitable consort. This separation strained the marriage, and after the birth of two more children the couple lived permanently apart. An intriguing footnote concerns the Marchioness's relationship to Queen Elizabeth II, who would presumably blush to admit such a woman as her ancestor. Hyacinthe-Gabrielle's second daughter, Anne, scandalously divorced from her first husband in 1816, married *en deuxièmes noces* Lord William Cavendish Bentinck; Nina Cavendish Bentinck, the daughter of their eldest son Charles, married the Earl of Strathmore and gave birth to the child who later became Queen Elizabeth the Queen Mother.

Louise painted these ornaments of society with unflagging energy, knowing that her adoptive world could not have enough of them. The *Souvenirs* do not mention her ever refusing commissions except when, during the Revolution, a sense of personal danger drove her from one country to another, or when – as in Russia – a paralysing melancholy gripped her. She was compliant and diplomatic as well as an astute businesswoman, and felt she had to satisfy demand. Perhaps it is not surprising that she never returned to her old ambition of winning acceptance as a historical painter: she was a pragmatic woman, and pragmatism may have supplanted idealism. On the other hand, it was not merely idealistic to want the highest rank her profession could offer; it also made sound business sense, because history paintings commanded the highest prices, and could win artists lucrative (and prestigious) Crown commissions.

It was not unheard of for painters to have their original rank revised, though the attempt to gain revision might be humiliating. When Louise's prickly old acquaintance Greuze tried in 1769 to have himself officially elevated from genre painter to *peintre d'histoire*, the Académie insultingly refused him the honour, and Greuze in turn refused to exhibit his work at the Salon again. Possibly Louise was warned off by Greuze's experience. She may, in any case, have felt disinclined to remind people of the irregularities attending her original admission to membership of the Académie, and expose herself to gossip again. So she stuck to what she was acknowledged to be good at, and painted according to the style that had won her favour. If the result was a certain uniformity and lack of adventurousness, it was a price she was prepared to pay.

One of the society women she painted the year after her admission to the Académie was the comtesse de Cérès, who caused her so much trouble at the time of the Calonne portrait by indiscreetly borrowing her carriage. Louise depicts her as a ravishing beauty dressed in the height of fashion, her coquettishness in this portrait limited to the teasing way she is folding a letter she has just written. Another flirt, painted in 1785, was the comtesse de Chastenay. She would later bewitch Chateaubriand by receiving him in her bedroom, where for the first time he sat on the edge of the bed of a female who was neither his mother nor his sister. According to the *Mémoires d'outre-tombe*,

> She held out a half-naked arm and the most beautiful hand in the world, saying to me with a smile: We shall tame you. I did not even kiss that beautiful hand; I withdrew, all flustered . . . who was this Chastenay lady? I do not know. She passed through my life like a gracious shadow.[20]

At the time Chateaubriand met her, the countess was past the bloom of youth, though she could still inspire in young men the kind of devotion described in many early nineteenth-century novels – Balzac's *Le Lys dans la vallée*, Stendhal's *Le Rouge et le noir*, Custine's *Aloys* and others – dealing with a youth's calf-love for an older woman. Bachaumont knew how to interpret the come-hither look the countess wears in Louise's portrait – 'she *provokes*' – though another reviewer thought that she embodied 'innocence and naïvety itself'.[21] Perhaps he was taken in by her sage muslin fichu and unrevealing dress.

Where Louise depicted a female genuinely unconscious of the effect she could exert, genuinely naïve, it was most likely to be either because the sitter was considered plain – as with the vicomtesse de Vaudreuil, painted the same year – or because she was still young in the ways of the world. This had been the case with the duchesse de Chartres, first painted in the late 1770s. In the presumed portrait done in 1778 she looks unsure of herself, timid and tentative – the very image of the unworldly and well-brought up young woman who thought that *fille* could only designate an unmarried woman. By the time of the tender portrait which Louise painted in 1789 this has changed. The woman who is now the duchesse d'Orléans – and who according to the baronne d'Oberkirch always looked sad, sometimes smiled but never laughed[22] – has learnt a painful wisdom through experience. Dressed in white, she asserts an incorruptible purity against all the odds (marriage to a coarse philanderer and association with a corrupt, profligate court). Her face expresses a gentle reflectiveness, as though she were reconciled to the activities of her husband: now the darling of liberal writers, he supported the Republican cause, became a *député* and in 1793 voted for the death of Louis XVI. He consistently mis-used and neglected his wife, whose melancholy is emphasised in Louise's portrait by the Wedgwood medallion of Sterne's Poor Maria seated beneath a weeping willow pinned to her tasselled belt.

This elegiac tone was not perceived as a negative quality in the *larmoyant* climate of the late eighteenth century. Indeed, contemporaries found in it a confirmation of the duchess's essential virtue, contrasting so strongly with the supposed vice and rank profligacy of Marie-Antoinette. But in the duchess's resigned air there is surely a trace of the *taedium vitae* whose effects her husband's vigour could not neutralise, still less displace. The bitterness of her last years, tainted by disputes with her children over money, seems to be anticipated in Louise's portrait, but the stronger impression it gives is of a person wisely, regretfully detached from a world whose pleasures are empty.

Two portraits Louise exhibited at the 1789 Salon belonged to a world apart from the Versailles court. A pair of ambassadors had been sent by Tipu, the Sultan of Mysore, to seek political support from Louis XVI in his struggle against the English over trade and colonial possessions. Louise caught sight of them at the Opera and was struck by their superb bronzed heads and outlandish air:

> they seemed to me so extraordinarily picturesque that I wanted to do their portraits. Having communicated my desire to their inter-preter I was given to understand that they would never agree to be painted unless the request came from the King, and I obtained this favour from His Majesty. I went to the hotel where they were staying, because they wanted to be painted there, with some large canvases and my paints. When I arrived in their drawing-room, one of the men brought some rose-water and threw it over my hands; then the bigger, called Dervish Khan, sat for me. I did a full-length of him holding his dagger. The drapery, the hands, all were done from life, he was such an accommodating model. I let the picture dry in another room and began the portrait of the old ambassador, whom I painted sitting down with his son beside him. The father in particular had a magnificent head. Both were dressed in robes of white muslin scattered with golden flowers, and these robes, which were a kind of tunic with loose sleeves pleated from the shoulders, were secured with richly worked belts.[23]

Tipu Sultan spawned a number of legends, all woven around the romance of his person and the exotic mystery of the East. One legend follows the fortunes of the famous Yellow Diamond, or Moonstone, from its home in an eleventh-century Hindu temple to Seringapatam. Here Tipu has it set in the handle of a dagger, which is stolen at his death: the curse of the Moonstone, and along with it Wilkie Collins's novel, then begins.

Louise's pictures of the envoys reveal a taste for the exotic which may have been developed by her trips to Versailles. A full-length portrait by the English artist Tilly Kettle, showing Shuja-ud-danla and his son, had been presented to Louis XVI in 1778 and was displayed in the palace: the regal grace of the subjects in their surcoats, turbans and sashes, and particularly the skilful conveying of the different textures of silk, muslin and bro-cade,[24] in some ways anticipate Louise's treatment of Mohammed Dervish Khan and Mohammed Ufman Khan. Louise obviously relishes capturing a non-European idiom – scimitars, beards, tunics and oriental slippers – so striking in its particularity that there is no need of other accessory detail.

Eastern exoticism, or a toned-down westernised version of it, had been fashionable from the early eighteenth century. Louise must have known Aved's full-length portrait of Said Pasha, painted in 1742 and also at Versailles, which epitomises the enthusiasm for *turqueries*. Carle Vanloo did three pictures of Madame de Pompadour as a sultana, and even Empress Maria Theresa of Austria allowed herself to be depicted by Liotard in Turkish dress. Louise painted her mother and more than one society woman *en sultane*, and during her stay in London she would do the same with the soprano Josephina Grassini, showing her performing the part of Zaira in von Winter's opera of the same name.

If Louise liked the 'otherness' of the ambassadors from an artistic point of view, she found certain aspects of it unsettling. When she encountered foreign cultures, as would become clear during her exile, she liked them to be from the social point of view as French as possible. But the envoys were unaware of this, and thought they were complimenting her by inviting her and Madame de Bonneuil to a typically Indian dinner. The two women accepted out of pure curiosity, Louise writes, and lived to regret it.

> Going into the dining-room, we were a little surprised to find the dinner served on the floor, which obliged us to sit, like them, virtually horizontally around the table. They served us, with their hands, whatever they found in the dishes, one of which contained a fricassee of sheep's trotters in white sauce, very highly spiced, and the other some sort of stew. You may imagine that we had a

wretched meal: it disgusted us too much to see them use their tanned hands instead of spoons.[25]

The ambassadors were given an audience by Louis XVI on 10 August 1788, but he conceded nothing to their requests for military support. He was, however, more generous in the gifts he bestowed on them – Sèvres porcelain, Savonnerie carpets, and busts of himself and Marie-Antoinette (two of which were acquired in 1995 by the Victoria and Albert Museum). Marie-Antoinette in turn apparently toyed with the idea of installing wax images of the ambassadors at the Petit Trianon. In 1792 Jean-Baptiste-Pierre Le Brun offered the Keepers of the newly founded Muséum (the great national museum which would become the Louvre) the portrait of the older ambassador and his son in part-payment of a debt to the nation allegedly owed by an émigré whose collection he had sold. We do not know how the affair ended, but neither this picture nor the others he offered from his stock can be found anywhere in the French state collections. Louise simply remarks crossly that both ambassadorial portraits were sold after Le Brun's death, but that she is ignorant of their whereabouts. Her account omits to mention that when the envoys returned to Mysore empty-handed the enraged Tipu had them executed.

This commission probably served as something of a diversion from the society portraits Louise was painting with such regularity, but with the occasional sense that she was trapped by people's demands and expectations. (The official reason she gave for leaving for Italy in 1789 was that she had for a long time wanted to pursue her artistic education by visiting Rome and Florence, but been prevented by all the commissions she had accepted.) Painting children, on the other hand, always seems to have given her pleasure, and was not something she regarded as a routine business. The brilliant early portrait of Etienne Vigée had shown her ability – at the age of fourteen – to capture the essence of childhood, and she capitalised on it in her later work; the birth of her daughter in 1780, too, may have sharpened this sympathy. Among the many striking child-portraits of the mid-1780s is *La Petite Foucquet*, painted in 1786. The child was the great-niece of Calonne, and Goethe, who met her in the early 1790s, was smitten with her charms. The posture of Reinette, as she was called, echoes that of *Le Petit d'Espagnac*, whom Louise painted the same year. Both lean relaxedly on a wooden table, though Reinette looks the spectator straight in the eye, while young d'Espagnac glances mischievously over his right shoulder, amused like Etienne Vigée in the 1768 picture.

Contemporaries called the large portrait of Madame de Pezay and

Madame de Rougé with her sons (1787) a brilliant monument to motherly and filial affection, one of the great themes of the age of sensibility. The comte d'Espinchal, who in 1791 met the marquise de Rougé and her sons with the émigré court in Germany, observed that she looked more like a sister than a mother. In Louise's portrait the two women seem equally close, but they apparently fell out during the Emigration. As a result Madame de Rougé tried to cut Madame de Pezay's image out of the picture, but was prevented by the positioning of her right hand. Perhaps Louise is being diplomatic, therefore, in listing the portrait in the *Souvenirs* simply as of 'Madame de Rougé and her two sons'.

Louise often painted herself with her daughter, confident that she could make as beguiling a picture out of the two of them together as separately; and the great popularity of her 'maternités' suggests that she had gauged her public's responsiveness correctly. The mother-and-child studies were both traditional – often recalling the madonna paintings of the Renaissance – and modern, reflecting the special, post-Rousseau enthusiasm of her age for the child as a being in his or her own right. Like Louise's famous 1787 portrait of Marie-Antoinette with her children, and other *maternités* she did, the picture may also be in some sense a propaganda piece: she wanted to show that she was a loving mother, not an obsessive painter who neglected her daughter while she painted, or a social upstart who enjoyed scandalous liaisons with members of the court. So Julie may appear cradled in her mother's arms, more protectively – but in fact no more lovingly – than her mother cradles the palette in her 'straw hat' self-portrait. Louise also adored doing pictures of Julie alone, demonstrating a love all the more possessive, perhaps, for her having lost a second child in infancy, and she carried on doing so until after Julie's marriage in Russia. Then, possibly feeling that she had lost her headstrong daughter for good, she seems to have stopped.

Her enjoyment of her personal beauty may make her the narcissist Simone de Beauvoir's *Second Sex* dismisses her as, but there is no reason to conclude from this, as de Beauvoir does, that she lacked professional seriousness.

> Madame Vigée Le Brun never tires of capturing her smiling maternity on canvas. The woman writer [similarly] will still be speaking of herself even when she is speaking about general topics: one cannot read certain types of theatrical comment without being informed about the figure and corpulence of its author, the colour of her hair, and the peculiarities of her character . . . Woman's narcissism impoverishes her instead of enriching her . . .[27]

This is untrue of Louise. The *Souvenirs* tell us a little about the shape of her nose or forehead, but never the colour of her hair (which in her self-portraits she often rather unflatteringly winds in a scarf). In any case, it would have been quite perverse in her not to have noticed her own prettiness, given that appreciating and enhancing female beauty was her stock-in-trade as a portraitist. Bachaumont was simply being descriptively accurate in noting apropos of her success in the 1783 Salon that her graces contributed to the favour she enjoyed. Equally, the vanity which made her conceal the fact that she was ageing (in the 1789 self-portrait with Julie she looks younger than in the 1786 one) is no more than conventionally feminine. Some women artists have been more critical of their own looks than Louise was, but that does not necessarily make them more serious as painters.

She felt that she lived in a society which women governed, subtly but absolutely, and governed through both mental and physical seductiveness. This was part of the *douceur de vivre* whose loss after the fall of the *ancien régime* she regrets in the *Souvenirs*. The Napoleonic world, for her, was a brutalising and heavily masculine one in which the salon was the background to political debate, not society games and banter *à la* Marivaux, and material concerns outweighed more intangible delights.

So it mattered that women should continue to be portrayed as exquisite flowers, even if that entailed making them look brainless too. One such beauty was Yolande de Polignac, and Louise's portraits of her show a woman whose loveliness existed simply to be depicted. Madame de Genlis, it is true, wrote that no surviving portrait accurately conveyed her attractiveness, because she appeared at her best only when a change of fashion enabled her to conceal the prominent bulge of her forehead by brushing her hair over it, something which was not yet in vogue at the time of the Paris portraits.[28]

Yolande had probably been 'planted' at Versailles by Louis's adviser Maurepas to give Marie-Antoinette the companionship she was not getting from her husband, and to neutralise Marie-Antoinette's own political influence. The Queen was believed to have the interests of her native Austria more closely at heart than those of France, and popular dislike for her was compounded throughout the 1780s by her wild extravagance and rumoured misdemeanours. With her husband Jules de Polignac, Artois and Vaudreuil, Yolande formed the Queen's *société intime*, which was claimed to exercise a baleful influence. Marie-Antoinette was criticised for no longer holding court in her state apartments and retreating with the Polignacs to the privacy of the Petit Trianon. Louis, a quiet, shy man, also found it pleasant to relax in this company. Louise was at pains to present the duchess as an angel of innocence and guilelessness, which was the more necessary as she suffered as much slander for her association with

Marie-Antoinette and the ambitious Polignac clan as Louise did for her links with Calonne. 'There is no calumny,' she writes,

> no horror which envy and hatred have not invented against the duchesse de Polignac; so many libellous pamphlets have been written to destroy her reputation that, combined with the baying of revolutionaries, they must have left in the minds of some credulous people the idea that Marie-Antoinette's friend was a monster. I know this monster: she was the most beautiful, gentlest and sweetest woman one could hope to see . . .
>
> The duchesse de Polignac combined with her truly ravishing beauty the gentleness of an angel and a mind that was both as winning and as settled as could be. Everyone who knew her intimately can confirm how understandable it was that the Queen had chosen her as her friend, for she was truly the friend of the Queen; to this she owed her position as governess to the royal children; immediately the rage of all the women who wanted the post descended on her and robbed her of all peace; a thousand hideous slanders were unleashed at her. I often chanced to hear her enemies at court talk among themselves, and I confess that I was indignant at such persistent black wickedness.[29]

The accusation that Yolande was a 'monster' was presumably a reference to the rumours that she and the Queen had been lovers (anti-royalist pamphlets regularly accused Marie-Antoinette of lesbianism). Louise may not be very convincing in arguing that such a beautiful woman as the duchess must also have been an angel of innocence, but she does seem to have been correct in asserting that this essentially unambitious creature disliked being governess to Marie-Antoinette's children, a position which she occupied from 1780. She may have agreed to do the job to please the King and Queen, but

> her main ambition was for freedom, which meant that life at court suited her not at all; indolent, lazy, she would have rejoiced in complete repose, and the duties of her position seemed to her the heaviest of burdens. One day, when I was doing a profile of her at Versailles, our door opened at least every five minutes; people came to ask her for her orders, and the thousand things that were needed for the children. 'Well,' she said to me, looking overwhelmed, 'every morning there are the same requests, I have not a single moment to myself until dinner, and in the evening other fatigues await me.'[30]

Madame Campan, the First Lady of the Bedchamber to Marie-Antoinette, agreed with Louise in seeing Yolande as a blameless innocent, the victim of an elevation she had not sought;

> but if her own heart was incapable of forming ambitious plans, her family and friends saw their own fortune in hers, and tried to fix the Queen's favour permanently.[31]

Like Louise, according to Madame Campan, she was uninterested in finery – another disciple of the Rousseauist revolution, who preferred simplicity and ease to ornament:

> one almost always saw her *en négligée*, her appearance seeming choice only in the freshness and taste of her garments; nothing looked as though it had been put on self-consciously or even carefully. I do not believe I ever saw her in diamonds, even at the time of her greatest favour . . . I always thought that her sincere attachment to the Queen, as much as her taste for simplicity, made her avoid everything that could have suggested the luxury in which a favourite lives.[32]

The duchesse d'Abrantès thought Yolande too stupid to be capable of intrigue,[33] but the acerbic Madame de Boigne regarded her as more politically devious than she appeared, if less so than her sister-in-law Diane de Polignac.[34] Until Marie-Antoinette turned against her, with the ascendancy of Calonne, Yolande was reportedly in receipt of vast gratuities from the Queen; yet she was apparently unafraid of telling her home truths. In short, she provoked various responses. Many people were seduced by her startling looks; others called her calculating and meretricious, and were sure she played on them knowingly.

The duchesse d'Abrantès blamed Marie-Antoinette's friendship with the likes of Yolande de Polignac for the fall of the monarchy, because she saw it as symptomatic of a prevailing and fatal desire to descend from the necessary heights of regality. It was of a piece with the artificial cultivation of simplicity – pretending to be a dairymaid in the Versailles 'hameau', a collection of designer-cottages intended to epitomise rustic life, or wearing the kind of artless clothing that got the Queen into trouble when, in one portrait, Louise depicted her in a plain chemise dress. The most remarkable event during the reign of Louis XVI, the duchess wrote in her history of Paris salons,

> was the moment when the Queen, abandoning her royal supper

and the most generally observed etiquette, went to sup *without ceremony* at the house of the duchesse Jules de Polignac, and make music there to Gluck's accompaniment . . . in short, appearing as a person of the *monde*, and wanting to count in the circle of the duchesse de Polignac only as one person more among society.[35]

But in forgetting etiquette and luxuriating in all the familiarity of easy friendship, Marie-Antoinette was in fact simply forfeiting the respect due to her rank. Madame d'Abrantès concluded that the speeches of the Revolutionary Assembly, with their attacks on privilege and their baying for equality, had issued from the salons of Paris. Democracy was born of a muddle-headed longing for informality and deregulation, entirely characteristic of the age of sensibility.

Louise's clientele included many other courtly connections. The relic of an earlier royal liaison features twice in her list of sitters for 1787, though her portraits were not exhibited at the Salon. Madame du Barry had first sat to Louise in 1781, wearing a peignoir and a hat in the English style with upturned brim and feathers: it matches the description of a hat in a bill sent to Madame du Barry that year by Rose Bertin, the *marchande de modes*. The picture listed in 1787 – and its duplicate? – may be a replica of this one, for the *Souvenirs* are confused about the dates of the du Barry portraits. She was painted again in 1792, wearing a décolleté white silk gown, holding a wreath of flowers and leaning on a pedestal. A third portrait was begun in 1789 and completed in 1820, long after Madame du Barry's death. This is apparently the picture Louise was later annoyed to find retouched by its owner:

> the old general it belonged to must have daubed the head, for it is not the one I did; this one has rouge up to the eyeballs, and Madame du Barry never wore it. So I disown this head, which is not by me; all the rest of the picture is intact and well preserved.[36]

Louise's portraits show the former favourite as a luscious fruit, whose hot-house look is belied by her favouring of simple muslin or percale gowns in winter as well as summer, and her daily walks in the Louveciennes park irrespective of weather. In 1786, when she went to the château Louis XV had given his mistress there, Louise found her still beautiful:

> I was extremely curious to see this favourite, whom I had heard much about. Madame du Barry must then have been about forty-five years old. She was tall but not excessively so; she was plump;

a rather heavy bust, but a very fine one; her face was still charming, her features regular and gracious; her hair was ash-blonde and curly like a child's; only her complexion was beginning to spoil.[37]

The Goncourt brothers, who had seen a lock of the hair, described it in *La Femme au dix-huitième siècle* as Louise's portraits show it to have been, silky and unpowdered. However natural her taste in clothes and coiffure, though, Madame du Barry struck Louise as mannered:

> her look was that of a coquette, for her elongated eyes were never completely open, and her pronunciation had something infantile about it which was inappropriate to her age.[38]

Perhaps Madame du Barry was simply hanging on to youth as long as she could. By 1789, according to the diary of Gouverneur Morris, she was 'long past the day of beauty',[39] though the portrait Louise did that year must have discreetly concealed the fact. The comte d'Espinchal anyway disagreed with Morris's verdict. In her mid-forties she became a little plump, and there were some broken veins on her face,

> but she was still very desirable the last time I saw her, in 1789. There are still many attractions to her person which she owes to the most scrupulous cleanliness and the habit of taking a daily cold bath, which she does in all seasons and whatever the weather.[40]

Like Louise, he found her mind vacuous, but unlike her he called her conversation interesting. Since her withdrawal from court after the death of Louis XV, according to d'Espinchal, reading had been her favourite occupation after her toilette. All the pictures capture the special half-awake look, and also show the sitter with the same erotically inviting half-open lips as Louise gives herself in the 1786 self-portrait with Julie, and which Bachaumont, along with other critics, described as an affected *mignardise*.

The irregularity of her relationship with the former King meant that Madame du Barry had severed nearly all links with Versailles, but Tipu Sultan's envoys still felt the need to pay their respects to her. Louise was indirectly a beneficiary of this visit.

> Not only did they come to Louveciennes, but they brought Madame du Barry presents; among other things, lengths of muslin very richly embroidered in gold. She gave me one superb

piece with large raised flowers, whose colours are as perfectly nuanced as the gold.[41]

This length of muslin became a valued studio prop, and accompanied Louise on her travels all over Europe.

The former paramour had become the soul of discretion, never revealing unseemly details of her royal liaison and the court of Louis XV to Louise during their evening fireside chats, which is why Louise thought her conversation 'fairly empty'.[42] But she was also the soul of beneficence, and seems to have played the part of 'dame de charité' very sincerely. 'She did a great deal of good in Louveciennes,' Louise writes,

> where all the poor people were succoured by her. We often went together to visit some unfortunate person, and I still remember the holy rage I saw her in one day at the house of a poor newly-delivered mother who lacked everything. – What! said Madame du Barry, you have neither linen, nor wine, nor beef tea? – Alas! nothing, Madame. Immediately we returned to the château; Madame du Barry called her housekeeper and other servants who had not carried out her orders. I cannot tell you the fury she unleashed on them, while making them prepare a packet of linen which she had them carry at that very instant to the poor invalid, together with some beef tea and claret.

Louise lived at ease with her while the sittings continued. They had coffee together every day after dinner in Ledoux's neo-classical pavilion, where Louis XV had dined with his mistress. The drawing-room, Louise reports, was sumptuous:

> from it one enjoyed the most stupendous of views, and the fireplaces, the doors, were all as exquisitely moulded as could be; one admired the locks as masterpieces of the silversmith's art, and the furniture was of a richness and elegance that defied description.[43]

Below the apartment Louise herself inhabited, in a building situated behind the Marly machine which pumped water to the Versailles fountains, was a dilapidated gallery

> which housed a higgledy-piggledy collection of busts, vases, columns, the rarest marbles and quantities of other precious objects; you could have believed you were in the dwelling of the mistress of several sovereigns, who had all bestowed their gifts on her.[44]

The château itself had originally been a merely agreeable edifice, but by the time Madame du Barry had finished it was a veritable jewel-box lined with marble, gilded with bronze and carved boiseries, and filled with priceless furniture. If Madame du Barry's eye for art was less sure – she liked portraits and busts of herself more than anything, and rejected Fragonard's wonderful sequence *The Progress of Love* (now safely in the Frick Collection) in favour of dull neo-classical paintings by Vien – her overall taste was impeccable, and she spent a great deal on decoration. Yet for all the fabled simplicity of her dress, Rose Bertin made far more out of her than Vien or Greuze ever did. Over the years she paid 500,000 *livres* to dressmakers (a sum which excluded the actual cost of fabric), but invested less than 116,000 *livres* in paintings and porcelain.

The discretion Madame du Barry observed about her scandalous past extended to the present. At Louveciennes, Louise remarks,

> It was no longer Louis XV who lay down on the magnificent sofas, but the duc de Brissac, and we often left him there, for he liked to take his siesta. The duc de Brissac lived at Louveciennes as though it was his home, but nothing in his own manners and Madame du Barry's could have hinted at his being anything more than a friend of the mistress of the château. Yet it was easy to see that a tender attachment united these two people, and perhaps this attachment cost them their lives.[45]

For during the Terror Madame du Barry was captured on a reckless return from the safety of England, where she had gone to recover some stolen jewellery, to rejoin Brissac at Louveciennes. Shortly afterwards the duke was arrested and murdered, his body paraded through the town of Versailles, and his head finally thrown through a window of the Louveciennes château. The rest of the story is equally ghastly.

> It was not long before [Madame du Barry] too suffered the fate reserved for all those who possessed any fortune, like those who bore a great name; she was betrayed and denounced by a little negro called Zamore whom all the memoirs of the period mention, just because she and Louis XV had showered him with marks of goodwill. Arrested, thrown into jail, Madame du Barry was judged and condemned to death by the revolutionary tribunal at the end of 1793. She was the only woman, among all those who died during those frightful days, who could not face the sight of the scaffold with fortitude; she cried, begged the hideous crowd surrounding her for mercy, and this crowd was so moved that the

executioner hastened to end her torment. This has always persuaded me that if the victims of that dreadful time had not had the noble pride of wanting to die with courage, the Terror would have ceased much sooner.[46]

Louise, who was not in France to witness the Terror, still describes it in terms as extreme as Dickens' in *A Tale of Two Cities*. She was conservative enough to have felt all its murderous brutality, the indiscriminate and insatiable violence that raged from March 1793 to August 1794, as an assault on the *douceur* she cherished. It is not surprising that the memoirs of an old woman looking back on a lost era should also emphasise the carefree pleasures which those times had afforded, without thought for the misery that underpinned them. So the *Souvenirs* linger over the harmless apolitical pleasures of *ancien régime* life, her visits to the theatre, and the professional as well as amateur performers she painted; they are silent about the activities of republicans like Talma, who left the Comédie-Française for a more politically correct troupe and acted in plays that dealt sympathetically with revolutionary issues. The Talma she writes of is the young man who acted ineptly in private theatricals, not the star performer in Marie-Joseph Chénier's anti-monarchist *Charles IX*.

But her memories of the theatre may be sharpened by other reflections. Possibly a part of Louise's fascination with actors arose from an ambiguity in their social position that in some respects mirrored her own. Actors, like painters (especially women painters), had to fight for status and institutional recognition in the world, and were in one sense *déclassés* – being excommunicate – in another, privileged in the elevated circles which adopted them. They had fought throughout the eighteenth century for an academy, won it just before the Revolution, and then immediately lost it. They shared with Louise a delight in play and dressing up, and they understood the techniques of expression which she developed so successfully in her portraits. (The actress Mademoiselle Clairon, whom Louise once met, was the original model for the *tête d'expression* prize offered to Académie pupils by the comte de Caylus.) They also cultivated the arts of movement and masquerade which she explores in her work, where she poses her subjects as knowingly as a Talma arranging his body in imitation of ancient sculpture. Louise's 1789 picture of Prince Hendryk Lubomirski as a cupid, for example, borrows his attitude from a Hellenistic work, the *Crouching Venus*.[47] And she encouraged, even forced, the women she painted to dress up: her studio was as full of sartorial props as any actor's room backstage.

Like Reynolds, she often clothed her female sitters in costumes that were of no exactly definable period, but which allowed their grace full expression in the drifting transparency of lawns and muslins, the flowing lines of silk shawls and gauze mantillas, the dashing curve of feathers or hat-brims and the gentle wave of uncoiffured hair. Body-language was something she understood as well as any of the Comédie-Française's *sociét-aires*, and for all the naturalness she strove to convey in her work its effect can be to make her subjects appear self-conscious, intent on making an impression. Furthermore, actresses were past mistresses in an art Louise recurrently practised in her work, turning unpromising material into something seductive if not beautiful. Mademoiselle Doligny, whom Louise saw acting young female leads, had this self-transforming talent. 'She possessed at once such truth, such wit and such decency that her great gifts made one forget her ugliness altogether.'[48]

Sophie Arnould, one of Greuze's stunners, managed something similar; for she was far from pretty, 'her mouth disfigured her face, and only her eyes gave her an expressiveness which conveyed the remarkable wit that has made her famous'.[49] An example of her wit, reported by Louise but not attributed to Sophie, is provided by her reference to the performances of the two great dancers Gardel and the older Vestris with the extremely thin and small Mademoiselle Guimard as of two great dogs fighting over a bone.[50] A third performer whose effect on spectators was such as to make them forget her modest looks was Madame Saint-Huberti, whom Louise regarded as the queen of opera. She came to a hideous end after the Revolution, as Louise reports:

> The comte d'Antraigues, a very handsome man and with a very distinguished mind, fell so deeply in love with her that he married her. When the Revolution broke out he took refuge in London with her. It was there that one evening, as they were climbing into their carriage, they were both murdered, though no one has ever discovered either the identity of the murderers or the motives for such a hideous crime.[51]

In fact their servant had committed the deed, apparently for political reasons.

D'Antraigues was known as a staunch royalist, so it was hardly surprising that he should have escaped from France when revolution broke out. Long before that happened, though, Louise had become aware of the precarious position of the court society which provided her with her principal clients, and more particularly of the threat to the monarchy itself. The latter problem had much to do with the character and behaviour of Marie-Antoinette, though Louise would never admit the fact. Indeed, her increasingly hagiographical portraits of the Queen suggested that the French nation had at its helm a matriarch of austere virtue (an impression which her detailing of Marie-Antoinette's charitable acts in the *Souvenirs* is designed to reinforce) rather than the monster detested by the populace; or perhaps Louise, pragmatically, was simply making the best of a bad job, as she tells us she frequently did in her female portraits. It is scarcely possible, for example, to believe that over the period during which Louise was her official portraitist Marie-Antoinette's looks improved as radically as the pictures suggest. Louise was certainly not blind to the Queen's facial defects – the pendulous Habsburg lip, the bulbous forehead, the heavy bosom – though like other witnesses she was much struck by her dazzling complexion and superb carriage. 'If I were not Queen, people would say I have an insolent air,' she remarked to Louise. She simply found a number of increasingly elegant solutions to the difficulty presented by relatively unpromising raw material, as a courtier-artist was more or less bound to do. She was, without question, Marie-Antoinette's most flattering portraitist. Kucharski, who painted the Queen in 1780 and did a last portrait of her during her imprisonment in the Temple, presents a much less idealised image.

But Louise was not simply valued for her ability to beautify: she played her part in a serious attempt by the court to mend Marie-Antoinette's damaged reputation.[52] Perhaps she felt she had to make some reparation for the damage done by an earlier picture. The portrait of Marie-Antoinette she executed for the Austrian court in 1778 was greeted by Maria Theresa with the comment that it resembled an actress rather than a representative of the monarchy, so completely had glamour and gloss displaced the concept of majesty. In fact there is nothing actress-like about the portrait, which shows a plumply pretty woman with a luscious bosom and slightly pouting mouth, splendidly dressed in a panniered costume of white satin with gold trimmings and tassels and a court train of blue velvet with gold fleur-de-lys embroidery. The overall effect is simply magnificent, as befits the Queen of France.

Louise did her best to persuade the public that the Queen, who like Madame du Barry ran up enormous bills at Rose Bertin's, was really a woman of simple and frugal tastes when she did not have to dress up for court functions. Madame Campan actually blamed her familiarity with Rose Bertin for earning her a reputation for extravagance. The effect of inviting a clothes seller into her private apartments, 'in defiance of the custom which, without exception, excluded all persons of her class', was fatal. Until that time, according to Madame Campan, Marie-Antoinette had disliked ornament. It is true that she was apparently innocent of direct involvement in the notorious *affaire du collier* of 1785, in which the

Grand Aumônier de France, the cardinal de Rohan, was tricked by his mistress Madame de Lamotte into buying an enormously expensive diamond necklace in the belief that it was for Marie-Antoinette (whose favour he was desperate to win): the cardinal was arrested, tried and condemned, and the Queen's name was dragged through the mud during his trial. Thereafter, whether fairly or not, she was greeted with silence in the streets of Paris or hissed at the opera. But from the early 1780s Marie-Antoinette had begun to spend huge sums on personal adornment, and all the fashionable women of France wanted the same quantities of feathers and garlands as Mademoiselle Bertin introduced into the Queen's wardrobe, with a predictable general increase in expenditure.[53] It was even said that if the enthusiasm for plumes and high-rise coiffures had continued, it would have caused a revolution in architecture. Doors would have had to be made higher, along with the ceilings of theatre-boxes and the roofs of carriages.

Rose Bertin, incidentally, was another woman who reduced the young Chateaubriand to a state of confusion, though not, like Madame de Chastenay, because of her physical beauty. She was, in fact, rather coarse-looking, and grew very fat in middle age. In his memoirs Chateaubriand describes how he very shyly asked if he could share her carriage from Rennes to Paris, and how terrified he had been at the prospect of being shut up all night in such a vehicle with a woman, when he had never been able to look at a girl without blushing. Though he suffered dreadfully at being in close proximity to a large and very fashionable lady, she none the less kindly conducted him to his lodgings on arrival.[54] But the queen of *modistes*, whose origins had been even humbler than Louise's, was known to be a generous soul. She idolised the royal family and all the court, and was happy to give them credit, just as she later supported émigrés in England and elsewhere.

Louise's attempts to have the Queen pose in simple costume may have been part of a campaign to convince people that she was not bankrupting France – though of course simplicity does not necessarily come cheap – but it must also have answered to the Queen's fashionable taste for artlessness and the simple life. (Marie-Antoinette had issued orders that the stateliest court costume, the *grand habit*, should be worn only on the grandest occasions.) Yet when in 1783 Louise portrayed her *en gaulle* – a simple sheath of muslin fastened with a drawstring at the neck, which became known as a *chemise à la reine*[55] – she met with the disapproval of the establishment, who thought the costume inappropriate to royalty. After a few days Louise was forced to withdraw her picture from exhibition. But it still earned her great celebrity, featuring along with the artist in a contemporary vaudeville called *The Reunion of the Arts*. According to Louise,

Brongniart, the architect, and his wife, whom the author had taken into his confidence, rented a box for the first performance and came to fetch me that day to take me to the theatre. As I could not possibly have suspected the surprise that was being prepared for me, you can imagine my emotion when Painting arrived and I saw the actress playing her imitate me in an astonishing manner as I did the portrait of the Queen. At that same moment, everyone in the stalls and boxes turned towards me, clapping fit to raise the roof: I do not believe one could ever be as touched, as grateful as I was that evening.[56]

Louise became the delighted recipient of the Queen's special favour, drawing close to her in a way no royal painter since Titian had been to the monarch. There is a clear echo of Titian in the following story, told about the time Louise had missed a sitting because of illness during her second pregnancy and was thrown into confusion by Marie-Antoinette's unexpected goodness in offering her another one:

I remember that in my haste to respond to this favour, I seized my box of colours with such vivacity that it tipped over; my brushes fell onto the parquet; I bent down to repair my clumsiness. Leave them, leave them, the Queen said, You are too far advanced in your pregnancy to bend down; and despite all I could say, she picked everything up herself.[57]

One wonders whether the story is true. It bears a suspicious resemblance to the earlier one of Charles V's picking up Titian's brush when he had dropped it, which suggests Louise's desire to 'historicise' her position as a court artist more than anything else – and, of course, to underline her position as a female artist whose candidacy for membership of the Académie royale was supported by a queen. It is understandable in the circumstances that her feelings about Marie-Antoinette quickly developed into hero-worship, for even more than acceptance by the *monde*, proximity to the Queen underlined the distance she had travelled from her humble beginnings. So, like a happy child, she details every mark of Marie-Antoinette's graciousness, her excitement at being invited to sing duos by Grétry with her – 'though her voice was not very true'[58] – and all the gratification her conversation brought. Nor (despite the rumours) does she fail to mention the King's goodwill towards her: 'I don't know anything about painting, but you make me like it,'[59] he reportedly said of the group portrait of Marie-Antoinette with her children which she showed at the 1787 Salon.

75

Louise first had dealings with the future Queen in 1776–7 when she painted four copies of portraits of Marie-Antoinette by other artists. The pictures she did in the mid-1780s were all less grandiose than the 1778 portrait *en robe à paniers* for the Austrian court, though they emphasise the regal air on which contemporaries regularly commented. Some have an almost rococo charm: the picture of Marie-Antoinette *en gaulle*, for instance, makes her action of selecting a rose both playful and lightly provocative. The contrast between the muslin of her chemise and the heavy silk and brocades of the formal dress she wears in the Austrian picture is as striking as in the half-length picture based on the same pose in which the Queen lays aside a book she has been reading, and where her costume is in a subtly different idiom, from the muslin mob-cap to the point-lace collar and ruffled *engageantes*. Her hair, inevitably but regrettably from Louise's point of view, is lightly powdered, and the Queen looks benignly at ease. It was for work of this quality that Reynolds, according to his pupil James Northcote, paid Louise the compliment of setting her above Van Dyck, and calling her productions as fine as those of any painter, living or dead.[60]

Although Louise regarded herself, and was regarded by contemporaries at this time and later – in the Austria and Russia of the 1790s particularly – as an innovator in dress, one who reacted against the detailed heaviness of the formal style in favour of the lightweight 'naked' fashions associated with the classical revival, her work also epitomised the courtliness of the *ancien régime*. Balzac's Madame de Portenduère, in *Ursule Mirouët*, was one of those old women whose appearance recalled the spirit of the old order; her pansy-coloured straight-sleeved dresses, Balzac writes, were of a cut seen only in Vigée Le Brun portraits. Everything about her costumes, from the black lace mantillas to the old-fashioned hats, harmonised with her old-womanish walk, slow and solemn and as cautious as if she were balancing full panniers and a train, continuing to feel their phantom presence around her as a one-armed person still feels the presence of his non-existent hand.[61]

The flavour of the celebrated group portrait of Marie-Antoinette with her children, exhibited at the Salon of 1787, is in keeping with the mood of ceremoniousness. The picture perfectly illustrates the way portraiture was used as a political instrument in the eighteenth century,[62] intended as it was to drive home the message that the Queen was both a dutiful and loving parent and a worthy figurehead for the nation – concepts that needed demonstrating at the time. It was also meant to contrast with the exceedingly stiff portrait of Marie-Antoinette with her children which the Swedish artist Wertmüller had just painted. Critics generally admired the composition of Louise's portrait and the vigour of her colouring, said to rival that of Van Dyck; but there were dissenting voices, among them Bachaumont's. The Queen, he says,

> has been given a glow, a freshness, a purity which the skin of a thirty-year-old woman simply does not have. Her complexion eclipses that of Madame Royale [her eldest daughter], who admittedly is a little in the shade, of the Dauphin, who is meant to be at a distance, and even that of the duc de Normandie, who is meant to stand out with her, and should be a combination of lilies and roses.[63]

He also makes a more general criticism:

> the expressions do not correspond to the situation at all: the Queen, who is worried and distracted, seems to feel more affliction than the expansive joy of a mother who rejoices in the midst of her children.

Possibly, though, this is because she has just lost an infant daughter, whose absence from the cradle the young Dauphin signals. Retrospectively the sad expression must have seemed even more justified. When the Dauphin too died, the Queen was unable to bear looking at the picture, and ordered that it be removed from its prominent position in the Salon de Mars at Versailles.

If the picture had been intended to rehabilitate the Queen, it could not be regarded as a successful commission. Bachaumont, who had initially failed to locate it at the Salon, had been told by the organiser that it was unfinished; other painters had said it was *highly* finished – Louise's usual style – but could not be displayed

> for fear of enraging a maddened populace. What! I exclaimed, the Queen, this enchanting sovereign, formerly the idol of the French, who could not appear at the theatre, in the street, in her palace without that tumultuous applause which indicates general satisfaction? What! The Queen can have alienated people's affections to this extent! – To the extent, I was told, that her august husband has advised her not to come [from Versailles, the seat of the court] to Paris, where her own person might not be respected.[64]

Louise, who attached great importance to the picture, wrongly says in the *Souvenirs* that it was exhibited at the 1788 Salon (actually there was no exhibition that year), and remarks on the fact that the empty frame, which had been sent on ahead, had inspired malicious witticisms. ('*Voilà le déficit,*' someone said, in allusion to the fact that the profligate Marie-Antoinette was known as Madame Déficit.)[65] Louise's decision to paint her against the background of her vast jewel cabinet – made for her in 1787 by the *ébéniste* Schwerdfeger, with panels painted by Lagrenée and figures modelled by Boizot[66] – cannot be regarded as astute. It makes Marie-Antoinette appear, at the very least, unrepentant about the ostentatious prodigality which had so damaged her reputation, and which the *affaire du collier* had so painfully highlighted. What had actually been intended by the inclusion of the jewel cabinet was something much more edifying – an allusion to the Roman matron Cornelia's calling her children her jewels, and hence a celebration of adoring maternity. Marie-Antoinette presents her real jewels, not any old diamond necklace, to the French nation.[67] Louise, poorly educated as she was, rarely attempted to make classical references in her work, and perhaps this one would have been better omitted.

Because it had been removed from display, the painting escaped destruction during the Revolution itself. When Louise returned to France in 1802, she found it at Versailles in a private room, turned against the wall: Bonaparte liked it no more than many other opponents of the *ancien régime* had done. But the keeper at the palace informed Louise that several visitors still asked to see it; and after the Bourbon restoration it was again exhibited at the Salon.

In 1789 Louise appeared at the height of her powers, and the quality of her work is astonishing. But as the *Souvenirs* suggest, she was conscious of a growing threat both to the monarchy she supported so unconditionally and to the elevated classes from which she largely earned her living. The year before she had been filled with gloomy foreboding on her way to stay with the painter Hubert Robert at the maréchal de Ségur's property, Romainville. The deference of *hoi polloi* could no longer be counted on, and the sight of a wealthy woman's carriage no doubt seemed inflammatory to peasants who had been driven to the edge. In 1788 there had been a disastrous harvest, which resulted in bread prices being raised to unheard-of levels, and desperate attacks on aristocratic properties (partly arising from high taxes and the desire to destroy evidence of peasant debt) were spreading.

> . . . *en route* we noticed that the peasants no longer doffed their hats to us; on the contrary, they looked at us insolently, and some of them even threatened us with their sticks. Once we had arrived at Romainville, we witnessed the most terrible storm you can

imagine. The sky had acquired a yellowish background tinted with dark grey, and when these frightening clouds half-opened they released thousands of lightning flashes, accompanied by frightful thunder and hailstones so enormous that they laid waste an area of forty leagues around Paris. As long as the storm lasted, I remember that Madame de Ségur and I, pale and trembling as we were, looked at one another shudderingly; we felt we were seeing, in this sinister day, the harbinger of the misfortunes one could predict then without needing to be an astrologer.[68]

In both 1788 and 1789 Louise spent time at Malmaison, the future home of Empress Josephine, where the poet Delille was often to be found. One of Louise's oldest friends, Delille was virtually a professional ornament of society. He told stories with inimitable grace, was a superb conversationalist (though he celebrated the art of conversation very heavily in a poem), read his verse elegantly, and had an unrivalled facility at being wittily, frivolously agreeable: for this skill he was universally known as *chose légère*. His inadvertent marriage to a tyrannical woman was just one token of this airiness, though Louise describes it as fecklessness. At Malmaison she, like her hostess Madame de Moley (and later Madame de Staël), used to walk outside holding a sprig of greenery in her hand to signal that she wished to be left undisturbed, but on sight of Delille she apparently always threw it away.

Yet the signs of threat could not be ignored. During a dinner at Malmaison in June 1789, listening to the talk of the abbé Sieyès – author of *Qu'est-ce que le tiers état?* – and other friends of revolution, Louise was shocked by the anti-royalist tenor of their conversation, as well as by the fact that the comte de Moley loudly attacked the nobility:

> you would have thought it was a real club, and these conversations frightened me horribly. After dinner the abbé Sieyès said to someone or other: 'To tell the truth, I think we'll go too far.' 'They'll go so far they lose their way,' I said to Madame de Moley, who, like me, had listened to the abbé and who was also saddened by so many grim predictions.[69]

At about the same time there was a terrifying encounter at the Marly property of Madame Auguier, Madame Campan's sister, which also showed the way the political wind was blowing:

> we saw a drunken man enter the courtyard and fall on to the ground. Madame Auguier, with her usual goodness, called her

husband's valet and told him to give succour to this unfortunate, and take him to the kitchen and look after him properly. A few moments afterwards the valet came back. 'The truth is,' he said, 'Madame is too good; that man is a rogue! Look at the papers which have just fallen out of his pocket.' And he gave us several notebooks, one of which started like this: Down with the royal family! down with the nobility! down with the priests! Then followed the usual revolutionary litanies and a thousand hideous predictions, written in language that made your hair stand on end.[70]

When the authorities arrived to deal with the miscreant, and walked away from the estate with him, the disappointed valet saw them link arms and sing some revolutionary air together – or so Louise says.

Louise was predictably disappointed too, and felt the supposed forces of order betraying all that she and the class she revered – or most of it – held dear. But Marie-Antoinette's disbelieving reaction was still more unsettling. When shown the notebooks, she simply responded: 'Those things are impossible; I shall never believe they are plotting such atrocities.'[71] Probably this was a sign of that insensitivity to the mood of her people whose damaging effects Louise's grand portrait of 1787 had been designed to reverse.

The kinds of insubordination she had disapprovingly as well as fearfully noted in the course of her journey with Robert in 1788 seemed to grow more pronounced in 1789, her *annus horribilis*. She still went through the motions of civilised social living, organising concerts and *soirées* at her town house; but the vulgar disaffected world intruded, and its complaints grew more insistent. Her pity for 'les misérables' was always limited. Perhaps, having achieved an initially unlikely social success herself, she found little cause to extend her sympathy to others who seemed not to have made the same effort. Or perhaps she was not as compassionate a woman as the *Souvenirs* suggest. She liked the *petit peuple* as a picturesque background – in Naples, Vienna, Russia or France – rather than as a suffering reality. A distant kind of philanthropy, like the activities of the stocking-knitting aristocracy in Vienna, or a vague humanitarianism like Madame du Barry's ordering of *bouillon* for the pregnant mother, was one thing. Direct involvement with the proletariat was quite another. Similarly, the Louise who left alms for old ladies in her will was unwilling to support her daughter in her last, destitute years, let alone witness her death. Perhaps her beloved art of painting had encouraged her tendency to distance reality or transform it as the occasion demanded. In her work the artist effectively puts a screen – the canvas she paints on – between herself and the other; and the painter who has chosen a particular, ideal world to work in does not look sympathetically on forces that seem antagonistic towards it.

The fact that in 1789 there seemed to be a very real threat to her way of life would not in itself have explained the depths of depression into which she was sinking. Since she loved the old world in its own right, not just because its denizens paid her her living, she was fearful of the new one that promised to replace it. She began to slip into the melancholy that would regularly seize her when she felt disorientated – in Russia after her daughter Julie's marriage, for instance, or in France after her return from the years abroad.

The Louise who had suffered much from illness at her childhood convent, and often been taken away from it to spend time with her family, was physically robust in adulthood, at least after she had instituted the regular siesta to which she attributed her good health. But she was prone to neurotic disorders. Perhaps, indeed, they had been the real cause of her *malaises* in girlhood. Whatever the case, the political and social ferment of the late 1780s triggered a mental decline which worried solicitous friends like the Brongniarts. Louise claims that she gradually became unable to work, which the number of portraits listed in her memoirs for 1789 scarcely indicates; but it was clear that a fog had descended on her.

One stage of her life had passed. Most of her youthful ambition had been satisfied, and she probably felt that the future owed her something – that her struggles ought to be over, and a period of gentle development be allowed to succeed them. The passage of time had hitherto been something to smooth over in paint; now it represented the threat of a far more radical upheaval. Louise underwent an existential crisis that paralleled the political one, and was also its product. She describes it in exaggeratedly physical terms: when on the eve of her eventual departure from Paris she went to say goodbye to her mother, 'she only recognised me from the sound of my voice, though we had seen each other a mere three weeks before'.[72] But the suffering was psychological.

As her intrepid travels all over Europe suggest, at a time when travel by road was still an arduous and uncomfortable process, Louise was resilient. But like others of her time, particularly women, she was subject to bouts of debilitating *ennui*. *Ennui*, which announced itself as a new way of life from roughly mid-century onward (Madame du Deffand was one of its most celebrated victims), had a variety of causes, but all could be traced to a highly developed sensibility. An occasional means of escape used by Louise, and one which some doctors recommended, was retirement to the restorative calm of the countryside; this was her resort soon after she had returned to France from Russia. But travel was her more usual panacea. For her it was not so much a means of escape – for she sought out environments which matched as nearly as possible the social world she had left behind in France – as a way of anchoring existence, paradoxical as that sounds. It was to be a more productive disturbance to what the eighteenth century called the 'machine' – the organism – than the neurotic upsets she was suffering in the grip of political ferment. She would be shaken into some new perceptions, but also confirmed in many of her existing ones.

Until she reached the decision to leave France, though, she did her best to continue with normal life. Some excitement was provided by moving into the new house in the rue du Gros-Chenet (now the rue du Sentier), at least until Louise became convinced that *Sans-Culottes* were trying to sabotage the property: she saw them brandishing their fists at her when she stood at the window, and discovered that brimstone had been thrown into the cellar.[73] The garden of the hôtel de Lubert, which was huge, stretched diagonally across to the rue du Gros-Chenet, and the Le Bruns built their elegant dwelling of two apartments and a picture-gallery there.[74] The courtyard of the hôtel de Lubert became the site of a large saleroom. A biography of the architect Raymond describes him as having designed and built a house 'for the famous Madame Le Brun';[75] but Le Brun put matters slightly differently: 'I wanted my wife to have a comfortable studio there, and I personally wanted a gallery suitable for housing a collection of precious pictures and other *objets d'art* which I had been collecting for twenty years.'[76] He insisted that 'the strictest economy presided over its construction', but Louise always complained that he had spent her money recklessly on it, and had failed to clear some of the bills by the time he died.

Even the pleasure of inhabiting more spacious quarters, where *maréchaux de France* would no longer have to sit on the floor, could not counteract her general sense of distress.

> Society seemed to me in complete dissolution and decent people without support; for the National Guard was so strangely constituted that it presented a mixture as bizarre as it was frightening. And fear had gripped everyone; pregnant women whom I saw passing by wrung my heart; most had contracted jaundice out of terror. I have observed, besides, that the generation born during the Revolution is in general much less robust than the preceding one: how many children, at this sad time, must have been born weak and sickly![77]

She moved around from household to household, presumably (though she does not say as much) with her daughter in tow, seeking a security which the house on the rue du Gros-Chenet seemed unable to provide. The fact that Calonne was rumoured to have paid for the building cannot have increased her sense of safety, especially as she overheard some workers plotting revolution one day behind the Invalides:

'Do you want to earn ten francs?' one of them said. 'Come with us . . . All you have to do is shout: "Down with this one! down with that one!" and specially shout really loudly against Cayonne.' 'It would be fine to earn ten francs,' the other one replied, 'but won't we get clobbered?' 'Don't make me laugh,' the first one continued, 'It's me that will clobber them.'[78]

Louise was in this part of Paris because she had taken refuge with the Brongniarts, and Alexandre Brongniart, as a royal architect, had quarters in the Invalides which he pressed her to stay in for a few days. She was treated as solicitously as she describes Madame du Barry treating the newly delivered peasant woman, sustained with broth and claret. Another haven was provided by the Saxon chargé d'affaires, Monsieur Rivière, her sister-in-law's father, who enjoyed diplomatic immunity. But none of this support could really reassure her. ' "Why go on living? Why take care of oneself?" I often asked my good friends.'[79]

But why, one might equally ask, should Louise have felt more oppressed than most of her acquaintances? 'My friends', she tells us, 'were far less gloomy than I was.' Perhaps, in part, because of the closeness and explicitness of her links with Marie-Antoinette. But perhaps, too, because she suspected the ill-will of painters like David, who became prominent Revolutionary activists. David insulted Louise by calling her a 'servant of quality'[80] (that is, a lackey of the court), and proof of his antagonism was provided by his possession of a fat book written against Calonne which contained many slanderous attacks on Louise. She claims that the book was kept constantly in his studio, open at the page which relayed scandal about her. She later discovered his persecution of artists – notably Hubert Robert – during the Terror, and must retrospectively have felt that she had acted prudently in leaving France when she did. So perhaps she was not being altogether fanciful in calling the escape from Paris 'saving her skin', though there were clearly other motives behind her departure.

Although she writes that she could no longer paint because her stricken imagination had ceased to work productively, her eye could still be caught, as in the old days, by female beauty; but now primarily for the contrast it offered with the hideousness of the rabid mob. One day, she says, she saw a dazzling Amazon on horseback followed by two of the duc d'Orléans's grooms (serving, as their master now did, the Republican cause).

> I immediately recognised the beautiful Pamela whom Madame de Genlis had brought to my house. She was in full bloom and truly ravishing; and so we heard the entire crowd shout: 'Look, look at the woman we want for our queen!' Pamela came and went amidst this disgusting populace, which filled me with gloomy thoughts.[81]

Pamela was popularly believed to be Madame de Genlis's illegitimate daughter by Orléans, though Madame de La Tour du Pin was inclined to accept Madame de Genlis's claim that she did 'find' Pamela in England.[82] A celebrated beauty, Pamela is described in the *Souvenirs* as having been given a coquette's upbringing by Madame de Genlis, the governess of Orléans's legitimate children, and encouraged by her to develop the pseudo-art of 'attitudes' and expressions later made famous by Emma Hamilton.[83] Pamela took up acting in her 'mother's' mimodramas, her first rôle being that of Love in *Psyche Persecuted by Venus*. David, who was present at one of these performances, enthused over her talents.[84] It appears, however, that the beauty Louise noticed was not Pamela but the Revolutionary Théroigne de Méricourt, whose looks were less universally praised: d'Espinchal, for example, calls her 'barely pretty'.[85] Perhaps Philippe-Egalité was simply suing for her support.

The obvious threat of social dissolution, which Théroigne had declared it her intention to bring about, made Louise sick with worry for the King and Queen. On 6 October 1789 they were brought from Versailles to Paris by the people, who claimed they could be better protected against their courtiers in the capital – which, given that the same mob was also screaming for Marie-Antoinette's head to be cut off, her heart eaten and her liver stewed, cannot have been very reassuring. The day before, a crowd of women (perhaps led by male agitators) had assembled in Paris and marched to Versailles, shouting for bread and demanding that the King approve the Assemblée nationale's decrees abolishing various noble rights, as well as assent to the Declaration of the Rights of Man of 26 August (which proclaimed in the spirit of Rousseau that man had been born and should remain free). Louis was forced by a delegation of marchers to accept the August legislation, and promised in addition to rush food supplies to Paris. As he and his family were driven back to the capital the following day, the mob escorting them shouted that 'the baker, the baker's wife and the baker's boy' were on their way. The King and Queen and their children were finally deposited at the Tuileries, and the Assemblée nationale itself resolved to move to Paris.

Etienne Vigée was present to witness their arrival at the Hôtel de Ville. As this was the day Louise had set for her departure from the capital, he came to her house at ten that evening, and was able to reassure her as to Marie-Antoinette's poise:

> Never, he told me, had the Queen been more a queen than today, when she entered into the midst of this frenzied crowd so calmly and so nobly. Then he told me of this beautiful reply she gave to Monsieur Bailly [the Mayor of Paris]: 'I have seen everything and discovered everything, and forgotten everything.'[86]

Later that night Louise escaped along the deserted streets of Paris. She travelled down France by public coach, hungry, like all her fellow-travellers, for news of the royal family. Her anxiety was not allayed by the reports of horsemen who periodically approached the stagecoach to tell everyone that the King and Queen had both been massacred, and that Paris was ablaze. (The royalist couple who put her and Julie up in Lyon assured her that this was all untrue.) But she could not hide her fear for her own safety, even though she had taken the precaution of disguising herself heavily as a working woman. Her incognito, she says, was still cracked by a postilion at Mont Cenis who advised her not to try to cross the pass on foot:

> I replied to him that I was a working woman, well used to walking. 'Ah!' he continued, laughing, 'Madame is not a working woman, people know who she is.' 'Well, who am I then?' I asked. 'You are Madame Le Brun, who paints to perfection, and we are all very happy to know you have escaped the wicked ones.'[87]

Given that a 'crazed' Jacobin whom she had sat next to on the coach claimed to have seen the self-portrait with Julie exhibited at the recent Salon, Louise must have felt that some attempt at disguise was at least prudent. But apparently she did not deceive everyone. Nor can she necessarily have wanted to, if the reaction to discovering her identity was as positive as with the postilion. Yet both his recognition of her and the Jacobin's familiarity with her self-portrait sound like fabrications: Louise did not move in lowly circles, and many ordinary Parisians missed seeing the Salons altogether.

Louise liked celebrity. Her marriage had initially irked her for the simple reason that she was an independent woman who had earned fame under her maiden name; and keeping a clientele as a portrait-painter meant, more than with other types of painting, keeping in the public eye. But now circumstances were different. She was taking an enforced sabbatical from painting: as she says, 'I left several portraits barely begun'[88] at the time of leaving Paris, and turned down commissions as she would not do again until a similar debilitating melancholy gripped her in Russia. There was every advantage for the moment in remaining anonymous.

Even the resentment she had brought away with her from Paris dissolved as she contemplated a filthy and stinking individual who sat opposite her on the stagecoach. He was an avowed thief who had already stolen some watches and various other effects, but

> Happily he saw nothing on me to tempt him; for I had only a small amount of linen with me, and eighty *louis* for the journey. I had left in Paris my possessions and my jewels, and the fruits of my labours stayed in the safe keeping of my husband, who spent everything . . .[89]

The eighty *louis* was most of what she had been paid for a gorgeous portrait of the bailli de Crussol, whom she had painted in 1787 resplendent in the golden collar and sky-blue ribbon of the order of the Saint-Esprit. Providentially, she had been able to pocket it because of Jean-Baptiste-Pierre Le Brun's absence from Paris at the time. She cannot resist a last complaint -

> Far from Monsieur Le Brun ever giving me money, he sent me such pitiful letters about his distressed state that I once sent him a thousand *écus*, and at another time a hundred *louis* . . .

– but essentially she felt unencumbered and as relieved as her own parlous state allowed.

> For want of a homeland, I was going to live in places where the arts flourished and urbanity reigned; I was going to visit Rome, Naples, Berlin, Vienna and St Petersburg.[90]

And in all those places, she might have added, the prevailing urbanity would be translated into lucrative painting commissions.

CHAPTER FOUR

TO ROME: 'I thought I was dreaming'

> I cannot tell you what I felt as I passed onto the Pont Beauvoisin. Only then did I begin to breathe again; I was outside France, this France which was still my homeland and which I reproached myself for leaving with a light heart. The view of the mountains succeeded in distracting me from all my sad thoughts, I had never seen such high ones; those of Savoy seemed to me to touch the heavens, and to be mingled with them in dense fog. My first feeling was one of fear, but imperceptibly I grew used to this spectacle, and ended up admiring it.[1]

Louise was experiencing sublimity. This key aesthetic concept of the eighteenth century was not to be confused with the equally important one of the picturesque, which suggested something less dramatic, more quaint, but just as painterly. It was the '*pittoresque*' that had been lacking in the Chaillot property Le Sèvre rented after he stopped Louise's Palais-Royal promenades. But before her thirties she had never seen stupendous, wild nature. The Alps were so exciting as to cure her of her existential malaise instantly. Her adaptability was always selective: she was fixed in her political attitudes, but mutable – sometimes mercurially so – in other respects, a character-trait which was to become particularly marked in extreme old age. Here, her accommodating nature was expressed in the swiftness with which she embraced and was cleansed by a new environment. The elevation of the landscape answered to the new sensibility for the savage and awe-inspiring aspects of nature, and Louise was an enthusiastic convert.

She also revealed herself to be an unwitting Burkean. Burke's *Philosophical Enquiry into the Origin of Our Ideas on the Sublime and Beautiful* of 1757 had observed that 'terror is in all cases whatsoever, either more openly or latently, the ruling principle of the sublime'.[2] As she would later do in Austria, Louise got out of her carriage to be closer to nature, and duly experienced dread:

87

about half-way along the path, I was seized with great terror; for a part of the rocks was being mined by controlled explosion, which resulted in a sound like a thousand cannon shots, a noise which bounced from rock to rock and was truly infernal.[3]

But she craved emotional intensity, and a degree of pain seemed to be a necessary part of it. This was what distinguished the experience of sublimity from that of mere beauty.

The communicant's 'enthusiasm' – the 'divine madness' of the ancients – could only be generated by contact with elemental forces, antithetically opposed as they were to the rule-governed ways of polite society. When she felt more at leisure, on late travels through uncultivated countryside, Louise would allow her artist's enthusiasm practical expression, particularly when she visited Switzerland in her fifties. There, she filled sketchbook after sketchbook with mountain crags and raging torrents. Now, however relieved she felt at crossing the border into Savoy, there was a greater sense of urgency, and to pause to take the view would have seemed somehow improper.

She was still much more aware of her surroundings than some travellers. Those who chose to cross the mountains on the back of a mule were not obliged to pay any attention to them: the painter Northcote, for instance, followed his *vetturino*'s example and pulled a nightcap over his eyes, a kind of insensitivity which would have horrified Louise. She stuck to her path and often walked. Others thought it unreasonable to reject the comforts of modern transport when crossing Mont Cenis in the winter. Boswell, making the journey a quarter of a century earlier, had been lifted over on an 'Alps machine', a kind of throne carried in relays by six strong men.[4]

It was a difficult journey, especially at that time of year, though some travellers' accounts disguised the fact. The English, who might have been expected to be hardy and intrepid, could disappoint in this respect. The poet Gray remarked that he and Horace Walpole went as well armed as possible against the elements with muffs, hoods, beaver masks, fur boots and bearskins. Women were often braver and more resilient. Writing of the time of her own crossing, five years before Louise's, Samuel Johnson's friend Hester Piozzi (the former Mrs Thrale) observed that the Duke of Savoy was said to have had a road cut through the solid rock of the Alps, such that 'one of the great wonders now to be observed among the Alps is the ease with which even a delicate traveller may cross them'.[5] Rather earlier than Louise, Manon Roland also encountered the Alps for the first time, and concluded that any man held back from enjoying Alpine immensity by fear of fatigue or danger was a dreadful coward.[6] The

The artist's brother (Etienne Vigée;1773).
Saint Louis Art Museum, Saint Louis, Missouri

The Vicomte de Vaudreuil (1784).
Copyright © Virginia Museum of Fine Arts.
Gift of Mrs A. D. Williams

Bacchante (1785).
Sterling and Francine Clark Institute,
Williamstown, Massachusetts

Self-portrait (1782).
Reproduced by courtesy of the Trustees,
The National Gallery, London

Madame Grand (1783).
*The Metropolitan Museum of Art,
Bequest of Edward S. Harkness.*
All rights reserved

The Marquise de Pezay and the Marquise de Rouget with her two children (1787).
*Gift of the Bay Foundation in memory of Josephine Bay Paul and Ambassador Charles Ulrick
Bay. Copyright © Board of Trustees, National Gallery of Art, Washington*

Self-portrait with Julie Le Brun (1789).
Musée du Louvre, copyright © RMN

The Duchesse de Polignac (1783).
The National Trust, Waddesdon Manor

Madame du Barry (1782?).
The Corcoran Gallery of Art, Washington, William A. Clark Collection

Marie-Antoinette 'à la rose'
(1783).
*Musée National du Château de
Versailles, copyright © RMN*

Marie-Antoinette and her
three children (1787).
*Musée National
du Château de Versailles,
copyright © RMN*

descent might be a deflating experience, though; not everyone was accessible to the kinds of emotion Louise underwent. Arthur Young's *Travels in France and Italy during the Years 1787, 1788 and 1789* described the

> great delusion of the passage of Mont Cenis, about which so much
> has been written. To those who from reading are full of expecta-
> tion of something very sublime, it is almost as great a delusion as
> is to be met with in the regions of romance.[7]

Even after arrival in Italy, the sense of difficulty overcome was not always enough to induce real pleasure. Many of the *émigrés*, like Louise, were so relieved to have reached their destination that they saw everything with rapture, but others were less easily pleased. Chateaubriand took a deeply lugubrious view of what greeted him on the other side of the mountains:

> I was disagreeably struck at the beginning of the descent towards
> the Novalese: I was expecting, I do not know why, to discover the
> plains of Italy: all I saw was a deep black gulf, a chaos of torrents
> and precipices.[8]

From the heights one did not suddenly encounter the charms of Italy but a landscape very similar to the expanse one had just left.[9] Louise could never have regarded Savoy as sad, but in any case her reactions were conditioned by the mental set she had adopted. The journey to Italy, like the experience of art within it, was to be a tonic, the restorative draught her constitution needed. Admitting to any disappointment would be a defeat, because it would amount to denying the effectiveness of the remedy she had decided on. She seems to have been like her beloved Rousseau in finding movement itself stimulating, which explains why travel so regularly restored her. Rousseau had to walk in order to conceive thoughts. In the fourth book of the *Confessions* he notes that

> Walking has something about it that animates and enlivens my
> ideas: I can barely think when I am penned up somewhere; my
> body has to be in motion for my mind to get going.[10]

Louise's striding beside or ahead of her carriage is an expression not just of her nature-worship, but of her determination to reanimate herself after months of self-preoccupation and haunting fear. So she would not have countenanced the suggestion that Italy was initially unexciting. Since the journey mattered to her as much as the arrival, she would not chafe at the gradualness and unimpressiveness of the advance towards the cities of art; she was happy to take her country of refuge as she found it.

This is not to say that her arrival in her first proper staging-post, Turin, was particularly reassuring. She was already out of sorts from having been cooped up for days on end.

> I arrived . . . extremely fatigued in body and mind, since driving rain had prevented me from getting out of the coach to walk a little for the entire journey, and I know nothing more tedious than coachmen who eternally drive at a snail's pace.[11]

Her temper was not improved by being deposited at a very inferior inn. 'It was nine o'clock in the evening; we were dying of hunger; but as there was nothing to eat in the house, my daughter, her governess and I were obliged to go to bed without any supper.'

Bad lodgings were a hazard for the traveller, though they should have been easier to avoid than Louise found them. Turin was by now the seat of the *émigré* court, after all, and the standard of accommodation was generally high. Italy was still a 'friendly' country, its kingdoms and principalities ruled over by relatives and allies of the French Bourbons, and until Republican troops overran it it seemed as obvious a place of refuge as the Low Countries, Rhenish Germany and Switzerland. By the end of Louise's stay it would have become threatening, obliging her to move on to safer havens in Austria, Russia and Prussia. For the time being, as the temporary home of so many friends and former clients who had fled France, it ought to have seemed welcoming to Louise. But she could find nowhere decent to lodge – the prince de Condé and his retinue had taken up the whole of the grandest establishment, the Hôtel d'Angleterre – and ended up moving into a private house.

Whether she felt at ease in her new environment is difficult to say. Mrs Piozzi called it 'a lovely little place', although Arthur Young found the layout unappealingly rectilinear. Perhaps it was a suitable background in this respect for the French court-in-exile, anxious to impress supporters by its *gravitas* and orderliness. Louise offers no opinion on the adaptation of the French royals to a new way of living. Others were struck by their sober seriousness, contrasting as it did with their old pleasure-loving habits. According to Young,

> Nothing could be more regular and decent than the conduct of all the court; no licentious pleasures are here countenanced, and very little that looks like dissipation. How the Count d'Artois passes his time is not easy to conceive; for a prince who was dying with *ennui*

in the midst of Versailles, for want of pleasures that had not lost their lustre, one would suppose that of all the courts of Europe there was scarcely one to be found less adapted than this to his feelings, whatever it might be to his convenience.[13]

The revolution in the character of Artois, now living in the castle of Moncaglia, was indeed surprising. Once he had been a playboy, and his gambling, drinking and philandering had helped discredit both him and the monarchy. The frivolity of Marie-Antoinette's life until the mid-1780s was partly due to his influence – he seemed much more fun than the stolid Louis XVI – and his blazing extravagance as well as the enormous debts he incurred set the pace for a decadent aristocracy.[14] When Louise met him in London in the early 1800s she was impressed by the modesty of his establishment: he received a pension from the British government, which supported the French Crown, but the representative of Louis XVIII might have been expected to want to make more show. The influence of his mistress Louise de Polastron was thought to have had much to do with his character-transformation, but perhaps the threat to courtly values which the future Charles X could everywhere perceive had finally cured him. In any case, in Turin he already seemed a wiser man.

Another former social butterfly, the comte d'Espinchal, commented on the stiffness of Turin court life:

> But I am far from blaming the strictness of this etiquette, which I think more than ever necessary in all courts to preserve decency, respect, the consideration due to the majesty of the sovereign. We are, at the moment, too deadly an example of the adverse consequences which follow on the relaxing of the former habits of etiquette, and our Queen is paying a high price for the pleasure she took in a free and much too easy life.[15]

It all sounds very much like the criticism the duchesse d'Abrantès voices of the Queen, and her observation about the heights from which royalty should not descend. Despite the familiar, or according to Louis XVI over-familiar, nature of her relations with Marie-Antoinette, Louise would surely have echoed d'Espinchal's sentiments. She was too reliant on courtly patronage for it to be prudent to do otherwise.

One counter-revolutionary refugee from the court of France seemed not to have acquired the weight which observers found in the King's brothers and their acolytes. Calonne, who had joined the party after being hospitably treated by the Crown during his stay in London, worried d'Espinchal on this score, because of the political influence he still exerted.

Our Princes seem to place every confidence in him, and he is becoming the virtual head of their council. Will our affairs prosper any the more for that? Misfortune should have matured Monsieur de Calonne and given more solidity to the lightweight character with which he governed the nation during his ministry; but I doubt whether there is the slightest change in him.[16]

Louise is surprisingly silent about the members of the royal family in Turin at that time, though she does mention having seen the duc de Bourbon and the duc d'Enghien at the theatre. She never refers to Calonne, perhaps still smarting at the scandalmongering she had endured in France on his account. She can scarcely have felt that it would be out of place for her to attempt to mingle with the court, given the entrées she had enjoyed in Paris (and the fact that she had done a portrait of the future Louis XVIII, then the comte de Provence, as early as 1781). She was never shy of using contacts – it was not in her nature – and her aloofness in Turin is not easy to explain: perhaps she simply felt that she would defer rebuilding a clientele until she reached Rome. Turin was merely a stopping-place, and she probably regarded recovering her mental equilibrium as more important than socialising.

But she did eagerly seek out one artistic contact. The day after her arrival, 'very early in the morning',[17] she let the famous engraver Porporati know that she was in the city. She had seen much of him during an earlier stay of his in Paris, and he was now a teacher in Turin. Besides being a superb engraver, he appears to have been a very obliging man, and came immediately to Louise's rooms.

> Finding me so badly lodged there, he asked me most pressingly to go and stay in his house, which I did not immediately feel able to do; but he was so earnest and open in urging it on me that I forgot my hesitation, and after arranging for my packages to be carried to his home, I followed them straightaway with my child. I was received by his daughter, a girl of eighteen who lived with him, and who joined with her father in giving us every imaginable attention for the five or six days we spent with them.[18]

When, more than two years later, Louise was passing through Turin again, Porporati repeated his hospitality, and offered her party use of the farmhouse he owned outside the city. She thought she could do nothing better to thank him than paint his beautiful daughter. It is a lovely picture (at present in Turin's Pinacoteca), and shows how good Louise was at capturing the serene radiance of young faces: the much earlier drawings of girls now in the Louvre have the same kind of angelic purity. Porporati's re-action could not have been more gratifying. 'He was so enchanted with it that he engraved this portrait immediately, and gave me several charming proof copies.'[19]

The relationship between artist and engraver was a mutually satis-factory one. Each profited from the other: the easy availability of prints meant Louise's fame could spread, and Porporati found her subjects congenial. But his hospitality in Turin does not seem to have been due to anything but good nature. He had a low opinion of the artistic sensibilities of the natives, Louise discovered. Although there were wonderful riches in the royal museum (of which he was to become curator in 1797), and although musical life seemed to be flourishing, he denied that Turin possessed many connoisseurs: they 'have no idea' he told her. 'and look what has just happened to me: a very grand person, hearing I was an engraver, came to me recently to ask me to engrave his seal'.[20]

At her next stop, Parma, Louise spent a lot of time looking at Correggios. This is hardly surprising, but it does suggest that her later attempts to get her name removed from the list of *émigrés* on the grounds that she had 'emigrated' to further her artistic education may have been partly made in good faith. She probably felt that with the approach of winter she should be hastening on towards Rome, but in fact she did not give the appearance of being in a hurry. In Parma she allowed her-self to do what she did well, present her compliments to royalty. The comte de Flavigny, Louis XVI's minister there, took her to Maria Amalia, Marie-Antoinette's sister and the wife of the Duke of Parma. 'She was in deep mourning for her brother Emperor Joseph II [of Austria],' Louise writes; 'her apartments were all draped in black, and she seemed to me like a ghost, the more so as she was very thin and excessively pale.'[21] She was mannish too, which displeased this very feminine woman; and though she gave Louise a polite reception, she quite failed to charm her. The network of Habsburgs Maria Theresa had created all over Europe in her determination to ensure political stability by dynastic means was holding relatively firm, but weaknesses were appearing. Louise noted signs of strain in Maria Amalia, as she would later do in her much more politically ambitious older sister Maria Carolina of Naples, and sensed that a canker was spreading through the family and through Europe.

However much Louise was enjoying her new sense of liberation, how-ever glad to be away from the insistent remainders that all was not well in France, she still missed Frenchness. In Parma, where she otherwise knew no one, she was grateful to the Flavignys for looking after her, and she was glad when they put her in touch with another well-born compatriot, the vicomte de Lespignière, who offered to accompany her on the rest of her journey to Rome. Flavigny, who had been alarmed at the thought of this entirely female party travelling alone over the mountains, was also relieved.

It is easy to underestimate the intrepidness Louise showed in travelling the length and breadth of the continent unaccompanied, because she so rarely refers to it. It is true that at the start of her later trip to England she revealed an uncharacteristic terror (if one typical for its times) of highwaymen and footpads, and that when she did acquire a travelling companion – Suzanne Vigée's brother Auguste Rivière – she often found him of limited help in guaranteeing her security. After the journey down France she was never again obliged to use public transport, and must have derived some comfort from having her own coach. But for much of the time she was alone with her young daughter and Julie's governess, Madame Charrot. She braved strange and sometimes deplorable inns, used contacts when she had any, and accepted the occasional offer of company en route – the dour Monsieur Duvivier, whom she called her 'wet blanket',[22] on the journey to Naples, or, more happily, a Polish couple, Count and Countess Bystry, on the way to Vienna. But she had a fiercely independent streak, as the story of her marriage also reveals. And in travelling from country to country she was often thrown back on to her own resources.

She did not stay long in Parma, aware that the mountains around Bologna still had to be crossed in what was now becoming wintry weather. But despite the brevity of her stay, the city – like others in Italy – paid Louise the professional compliment of electing her to membership of its academy, the Accademia Clementina. If political turmoil in France seemed to threaten the future of the arts, with dwindling commissions from Crown and aristocracy alike, compensation could clearly be found elsewhere. D'Angiviller remarked on this in a letter of February 1790 to Ménageot, then the head of the French Academy in Rome, saying that Louise could not have chosen a more propitious time to make her Italian journey.[23]

In gratitude towards the Bolognese, her next hosts, Louise presented them with a portrait, the bust of Julie Le Brun at present in the Bologna Pinacoteca, which shows her wearing a wreath of flowers and looking demurely at the spectator over her left shoulder. Louise does not list this work by name in the *Souvenirs*, but mentions a 'small bust in oils for the Bologna Institute', which is presumably the same piece. She wanted to spend at least a week immersing herself in the masterpieces of the Bolognese School, but her hopes were nearly dashed on arrival:

> I was hurrying to unpack my bags, when the innkeeper said to me: 'Alas, Madame, you are wasting your time; as a Frenchwoman you may spend only one night here.' I was in despair, the more so as that very moment I saw a tall dark man enter, dressed exactly like Bartholo [in Beaumarchais's *Le Barbier de Séville*], which made me recognise him immediately as a nuncio of the papal government.[24]

But if she initially appeared to be a victim of this government's mistrust of French *émigrés*, all turned out happily. Although 'his clothes, his pale serious face gave him an appearance which struck me with dread',

> He held in his hand a piece of paper which I naturally took to be an order for me to leave the town within twenty-four hours. 'I know what you have come to tell me, Signore,' I said to him, looking rather deflated. 'You are bringing me an order to leave.' 'No, on the contrary, I am bringing you permission to stay here as long as you wish, Madame,' he replied.

Apparently the Turin authorities were giving the papal government the names of all the French travellers crossing the Roman states, and perhaps because the Italians, unlike the authorities at home, accepted Louise's *bona fides* as an artist travelling to extend her artistic knowledge, her stock was good enough to have won her this privileged treatment.

If she was seduced by the other attractions of Bologna, Louise gives little sign of it. One would scarcely have expected someone who disliked *gourmandise* to pay much attention to being in such a gastronomic paradise, even though her meals no longer had to be restricted or curtailed because of painting commissions. Nor does she seem to have been particularly struck by the character of a city whose essence Mrs Piozzi found ambiguous, superbly sited in countryside of exceptional beauty, but itself oddly sorrowful despite the handsomeness and regality of its architecture.[25] What really drew her, arousing an enthusiasm which seems as strong as she looks back over the years as it was at the time, was the miracle of Bolognese art. When she visited one palazzo,

> the attendant followed me, determined to tell me who had painted each picture. He made me very impatient and I told him gently that he was troubling himself needlessly, because I knew all these masters. So he contented himself with carrying on accompanying me; but as he heard me in ecstasies in front of the most beautiful works, and calling the artists by their names, he left me

and went to ask my servant: 'Who is this lady? I have shown real princesses round, but I have never met anyone who knew as much about art as she does'.[26]

Lespignière continued with the party to Florence, the next stage of their journey. Louise found the prospect of staying there irresistible, despite her impatience to reach Rome, and did not suffer the disappointment other travellers have occasionally felt: 'when I entered the famous city, I was instantly surprised and charmed by its beauty and by the views.'[27] The Italophile Germaine de Staël, later to become a friend of Louise's, was less ready to be won over, possibly because she had no real feeling for art. Words were the thing for her, and apart from Louise she did not know any artists well. Her best-selling novel *Corinne* (1807) does its best to persuade the reader that this indifference was more apparent than real: there are laboured pages on pictures and statues which are as uninteresting to read as they evidently were to write, and except in its rhapsodic 'Staëlian' moments the section on visual art rarely rises above the level of torpid guidebook prose. Germaine thought Florence a sad place, melancholy in the way Mrs Piozzi found Bologna: she was wearied by the quantities of churches, nearly all of them said to be essential viewing, and bored by all the museums and monuments.[28] Louise refused to notice any painting predating Raphael, but there is nothing else surprising in the *Souvenirs'* account of Florence's treasures, and nothing that gives the writing a quirky personal accent. Anecdotalism is much more Louise's *forte*, surprisingly enough, than the vivid evocation of art. She is better on infernal inns, intolerable food and universal din than she is on Reni, the Carracci, Palma Vecchio and the rest. Still, she was characteristically energetic, saw all the important monuments and works of art, and ensures that her reader knows it. She was, in fact, making up for lost time with far more determination than the average Grand Tourist, whose desire to acquire an artistic education was more often a dilettante's stray inclination or a concession to someone else's will than genuine keenness.

The Uffizi paid Louise the same compliment as the Accademia di San Luca in Rome would later do, asking for her self-portrait. She was proud to think that she would hang in the same gallery as Angelica Kauffman, 'one of the glories of our sex',[29] and agreed (though she did not paint the portrait until she reached Rome). It is an extremely attractive work of which she produced various replicas; the one for Lord Bristol, the Bishop of Derry – himself to be painted twice by Louise – draws great crowds at the family seat of Ickworth, despite its clear inferiority to the original. Louise shows herself painting, and on her easel, from which she has turned to face the onlooker, is the roughly-sketched image of Marie-

Antoinette. This indicates less any current painting commission than the fact that she wanted to be remembered by posterity as her preferred portraitist. (The Ickworth version has a different, unidentified head on the easel canvas.) If the Queen's face is insufficiently defined to reveal much about how she would have looked in the completed picture, Louise's version of herself is certainly a flattering one. This is not so much because she makes herself extremely pretty (in 1818, a quarter of a century later, Natalya Kurakina saw the portrait in the Uffizi and said that Louise still retained the beauty she had depicted)[30] as because she appears so young. In 1790 she was thirty-five years old, but in this picture she looks no more than twenty. Again she gives herself the half-open mouth Bachaumont disapproved of, and again she wears an unlikely painting costume – a velvet dress tied at the waist with a sash, with lace trimmings. But it is, all the same, a winning image. In later life, according to the painter Jean Gigoux, Louise was pleased to be told how the portrait continued to delight visitors to the Uffizi, and was constantly being copied by artists.[31] Ménageot, writing to d'Angiviller from Rome in March 1790, referred to the work as one of Louise's finest productions. 'In my opinion,' he states, 'she has scaled new heights since her departure from Paris. This picture has astounded everyone who has so far seen it; Rome is quite unfamiliar with this kind of talent.'[32] It is easy enough, he adds a few days later, to win praise when one is an 'amiable' woman painter,[33] but there is nothing ambiguous about the acclaim accorded to Louise on technical grounds. The director of the Uffizi, Petti, told her that her portrait had been enthused over by professionals and *cognoscenti* of every persuasion as well as by the French resident in Florence.[34]

People saw something classic in the glamorous image Louise had painted. Perhaps she had encouraged this response by showing herself in a Van Dyck costume; but at any rate there was only one verdict on the skill of her portrayal. From at least the time of her 1787 self-portrait with Julie, which is in some ways indebted to Raphael's *Madonna della sedia* (a painting she reports seeing in the Palazzo Pitti, but which she doubtless knew earlier from engraved reproductions), Louise had been measuring herself against earlier masters.[35] Her homage to Van Dyck in the Uffizi picture, and the different kind of homage she paid Raphael both in copying what she believed to be his self-portrait and in elevating his works above everything else she saw in Florence, assume a particular significance in the light of her own implicit claims to be considered a great painter. Louise both affirms Raphael's supremacy and asserts her own right to follow in his footsteps, imitating him as Gigoux later describes young and old painters imitating her Uffizi picture. Absence from France had left her feeling out of touch and needing fresh confirmation of her status as an artist. By appropriating the Old Masters, she was simultaneously matching herself against them. Reynolds, after all, had told Northcote that Louise's best portraits were the equal of any, and even superior to Van Dyck's.

Eventually Louise reached Rome. A letter she sent Hubert Robert on 1 December 1789 refers to her desire to go back to the 'beautiful city of Florence',[36] so enchanting had she found it; but first she had to give her undivided attention to another place. About the dreariness of the approach she says nothing. *Corinne*'s Oswald, the typically irresolute and melancholic male of early nineteenth-century French fiction, cannot be seduced by the environs of the eternal city:

> the deserts surrounding Rome, this terrain tired by glory and which seems to disdain to produce anything, are merely a wild, uncultivated stretch of land for the person who considers them only from the point of view of utility. Oswald, accustomed from childhood to the love of order and public prosperity, initially received a painful impression as he crossed the abandoned plains which announce the proximity of the city that was once Queen of the world ... Lord Neville [i.e. Oswald] judged Italy like an enlightened administrator ... [and did not feel] the effect which the Roman Campagna produces on the imagination when one is filled with memories and regrets, with the natural beauties and illustrious misfortunes, which cast an indefinable spell over this country.[37]

Chateaubriand can find little that is positive to say about the Campagna: he offers the tired, limp 'imagine something of the desolation of Tyre and Babylon', but does admit that the whole has an 'inconceivable grandeur'.[38] Mrs Piozzi is brisk: 'The melancholy appearance of the Campagna has been remarked and described by every traveller with displeasure, by all with truth'.[39] Pre-Romantic and Romantic melancholy had to have a touch of poetry about it to fire the imagination, otherwise it simply seemed a kind of barrenness; and the promise of Rome, surprisingly enough, was rarely sufficient to kindle the imagination.

If Louise had contemplated arriving in early winter with some trepidation, she need not have worried. There were advantages to travelling at this time of year. It is true that late eighteenth-century travellers did not suffer in the same way as modern ones do from the clog of summer or the fog of polluted air; but, sensitive as Louise was to light, she must have welcomed the clarity which the Roman atmosphere acquires only in cold winter sunshine. For an artist who needed to feel as unflurried as she did, the tranquillity of Rome in November was a boon. And for one who knew how to use patrician introductions as adroitly as she did, the intermittent closedness of the city was no disadvantage.

Like Louise herself, Rome was in some respects snobbish. Its masculine grandeur, which can seem overwhelming, might appear as obvious as that of nineteenth-century Vienna, but its true character lay in the intermingling of private and public space. Louise had access, at least after a while, to some of the most select drawing-rooms in the capital. Though she never abused her status, she enjoyed the entrée which her charm and professional standing gave her to these halls of privilege.

She looked at St Peter's and was faintly disappointed, not finding it as grand as she had expected, and moved on (as one then could, but no longer can) via the Bernini staircase to the Sistine Chapel. Energetic as she was, she seemed quite unspent when, not long after this, she faced the Vatican museum. To judge by the tones of the *Souvenirs*, she was undismayed by the thirteen and a half acres of the collections, the three sets of state apartments, the gallery of courtyards and all the encompassing vastness. Perhaps there is even something faintly unseemly in the dauntlessness of her progress across this huge expanse. The reader may be disconcerted, too, by the evident fact that Louise, guided over the terrain by the courteous Ménageot, was content simply to repeat the art historian Winckelmann's famous judgements on Greek sculpture and its approximation to ideal beauty. The routine nature of the enthusiasm she expressed for the precious relics suggests that she has learnt what to say about antiquity, rather than that she has any deep feeling for its remains; though, to be fair, the fact that she wrote the *Souvenirs* so long after the original encounter with Rome may adequately explain the dull derivativeness of the reflections.

There is, however, nothing ritualistically pious in the rapture she expresses at sight of the Vatican's Raphaels. She was moved to reflect regretfully on Raphael's early death. These thoughts were initially prompted by a visit from the *pensionnaires* of the French Academy in Rome, who presented her with the palette of Jean-Germain Drouais, who had recently died aged twenty-four:

> they asked me in exchange for some brushes I had used for painting. I cannot hide from you, my friend, how touched I was by this exceptional homage, this flattering request: I shall always retain a happy, grateful memory of it. How deeply I regret not finding here the young Drouais, whom death has just removed so cruelly from us! I had known him in Paris, he had even dined at my house with his comrades one day before they all left for Rome . . . Alas! death is no respecter of persons: did it not strike Raphael before he was

thirty-eight? Did it not deprive the world of this genius when he was in his prime, at the peak of his vigour?[40]

She then rehearses the 'slanderous' stories of Raphael's dissoluteness, which she hotly denies (rather naïvely, too: 'Raphael was no libertine; you only have to look at the heads of his Madonnas to be persuaded of the contrary').[41] Perhaps she was still smarting from her own persecution over the Calonne 'affair' and the other rumours that had attached to her.

However much the *pensionnaires'* homage touched her, in other respects she had doubts about them. Most of the young men were sympathetic towards the new political order in France, and attempted to spread Revolutionary doctrines among the population of Rome.[42] Eventually, she writes, they made the Academy into a den of Jacobins (the extreme Republican faction under the Revolution), and she had as little to do with them as possible. D'Espinchal's *Journal d'émigration* complains about the rank ingratitude of the *pensionnaires* as guests of the Crown.

> This kindness on the part of the sovereign does not prevent these young artists from being the apostles of a revolution which aims to dethrone the very one who feeds them ... The wretch David owes his existence and his talent only to the goodwill of the generous monarch of whom he clearly shows himself to be the ungrateful persecutor.[43]

David's conduct filled Louise with revulsion. She must also have sympathised with the problems facing her old friend Ménageot in his capacity as Director of the French Academy. He tried to maintain order, but complained about the independence of the boarders. On 25 August 1790 he wrote to d'Angiviller in despair:

> The spirit of liberty and equality which is spreading everywhere is making this institution very different from what it was before, when young men did not regard themselves as the equal of their director, and people respected differences in age, status etc.[44]

These difficulties may partly explain why Louise herself did not stay long as a guest of the Academy. In an earlier letter to d'Angiviller Ménageot had explained her position when she and her party arrived in the city:

> as it is almost impossible at the moment to find lodgings in Rome, I gave them one in the palace [the Palazzo Mancini, where the

Academy was then located] which formed part of the Director's apartments, and which I occupied during the winter; it is the wing which overlooks the little street; she will be fairly comfortable there and will be able to devote herself peacefully to her art, as she intends to do, and more conveniently than anywhere else.[45]

Probably Ménageot had never tried living in these rooms for any length of time. Louise disagreed, anyway, that their position was conducive to either work or rest. She was not sorry to leave, she writes, because of the constant noise of horses and coachmen in the street:

> besides, there was a Madonna at the corner, and Calabrians, whose patron saint she must have been, came to sing and play the accordion in front of her shrine until daybreak.[46]

In mid-century Winkelmann, who lived near the Piazza di Spagna in the Palazzo Zuccari, had complained that rest was impossible at night, when all hell was let loose in the city: people shouted, fired pistol shots and let off fireworks till daybreak with such relentless exuberance that the only way of ensuring sleep – however inadvisable in the heat of summer – was to get dead drunk.[47] More delicately, Louise simply decided to leave for different quarters. But she also, rather rashly, chose the Piazza di Spagna, where she found lodgings with the landscape painter Simon-Joseph Denis. This beautiful square and its environs, overlooked by the church of Trinità dei Monti, had long been popular with foreign artists. In the seventeenth century Claude and Poussin lived in neighbouring streets, and in the eighteenth the area was so much favoured by English painters that it was called the Ghetto degl'Inglesi. Nowadays smart antique shops and jewellers have driven the artists out. What caused Louise to move on, predictably enough, was the noise.

> all night long carriages went to and fro across the square, where the Spanish ambassador had his residence. Then a crowd of people of the working class flocked there when I was in bed to sing choruses of songs which the young men and women improvised charmingly, as I cannot but admit – for the Italian people seem to have been born to make beautiful music – but I could not endure this constant concert at night, however much it would have enchanted me by day.[48]

She continued to strike unlucky in her search for living quarters, usually for the same reason (though once the cold and damp were responsible).

One perfect-seeming small house was made uninhabitable by the din of washerwomen pumping water in the small hours,[49] and in another wood-worm chewed the beams and rafters throughout the night, apparently deafeningly.[50] Louise concluded, understandably enough, that tolerable lodgings were the most elusive of Rome's treasures. Sightseeing provided some respite from the shattering of her calm. She went to the Colosseum, and was reminded of an exploit of Hubert Robert's when he was a student at the French Academy:

> Robert was twenty years old at the most when he bet his comrades six grey paper sketchpads that he would climb unaided right to the top of the Colosseum. The madcap, despite repeatedly putting his life at risk, indeed managed to get to the summit; but when he wanted to return to earth, since he could no longer use the pro-truding stone which had helped him to climb up, he had to be thrown a rope through one of the windows; he grabbed it, fastened it round himself, pitched himself into the air, and was lucky enough to be pulled inside the monument. Just describing this *tour de force* makes one's hair stand on end. Robert is the only man who has ever tried it, and all that just for six pads of grey paper![51]

At the same time, she wrote to Robert to tell him that the cross he had planted on the summit was still there. Her love of sketching accompanied her everywhere she went. She could not walk around the city, she writes, without feeling the need to use her crayons, and never undertook a journey from which she did not return with a handful of drawings. Anything might be turned to account, and any surface might serve as a sketchbook. Once, on the terrace of Trinità dei Monti, she suddenly felt impelled to capture a sunset, and could find no other paper than a bill of exchange from the banker Laborde for the two pictures she had sold him before leaving France, her brilliant portrait of Hubert Robert in the grip of divine enthusiasm and a self-portrait with Julie. She was retrospectively annoyed with herself for not having cashed the bill.

> Three years later, as I was thinking of returning to France – though I then changed my mind – I cashed ten thousand francs, which I only in fact got eight thousand for, so bad had the exchange rate with Paris become. Subsequently, when I did return to France, since Monsieur Alexandre de Laborde either could not or would not settle the balance of eight thousand francs which remained to be paid, we cancelled the transaction, he gave me

back my two pictures and I returned to him the bill of exchange
with my sunset sketched on the back.[52]

The two portraits were eventually given by Louise's niece Eugénie Tripier
Le Franc, who had inherited them, to the Louvre.

Louise made some friends too. One would have expected her to enjoy
finally meeting Angelica Kauffman, and with a minor reservation she did.
They were, after all, two of the most successful women artists in the
history of painting before the end of the nineteenth century, and Angelica
was already celebrated throughout Europe – not just for painting (unlike
Louise she had actually trained in Italy), but for her etchings, engravings
and designs for decorative work. She cast her net more widely than Louise
ever did, her subjects varying from classical and medieval history and
mythology through the Renaissance to the contemporary literature of
England, France, Germany and Italy. Her life contained enough incident
to be worthy of a novel: Anne Thackeray, William Makepeace Thackeray's
daughter, actually made her the heroine of her *Miss Angel*, published in
1875, and other novels were written about her. It is surprising that Louise,
whose life contains as much incident, never received the same treatment:
she too rose from humble beginnings, had an unconventional marriage
(though not to a bigamist, like Angelica), was romantically or sexually
linked with some of the most influential men of the day, and moved in
the best circles. Louise, fourteen years her junior, probably felt some
trepidation at the prospect of getting to know this 'glory of our sex'. The
first encounter was entirely reassuring, however.

> I found her very interesting, quite apart from her fine talent, in her
> intellect and knowledge. She is a woman of perhaps fifty, very
> delicate, her health having been affected by the misfortune she had
> to marry an adventurer who ruined her. She has married again, an
> architect [sic] who takes care of the business side of things for her.
> She talked for a long time with me, very informedly, during the two
> evenings I spent at her house. Her way of conversing is gentle; she
> is formidably learned, but has no enthusiasm, which (given my own
> ignorance) did not electrify me.[53]

Goethe suggests in his *Italian Journey* that Angelica's second husband, the
decorative painter Antonio Zucchi, was responsible for a part of Angelica's
frailty, because of his liking for the money her incredible industry produced:

> She is not as happy as she deserves to be, given her huge talent and
> a fortune that grows daily. She is tired of painting to order, but her

husband finds it wonderful that she can earn such good money for often rather little effort. She now wants to work for herself, taking more care and trouble, and putting more study into it, and *could* do so . . . She has an unbelievable talent, a really massive one for a woman.[54]

It sounds a familiar story: the richly gifted woman painting successfully, and the husband enjoying the proceeds. Goethe's view of Zucchi's role in all this is rather different from Louise's, but in fact all the evidence suggests that Angelica, like Louise herself, had an excellent head for business. Another note of Goethe's, for February 1788, mentions that she had just bought two pictures, both expensively, but that she is so rich that she can well afford to give herself pleasure.[55]

Perhaps Goethe is right to suggest that the 'unbelievably modest' Angelica painted furiously to keep her husband happy; but perhaps there was more to it than that. As we know, Louise thought that she herself produced too much indifferent work simply because the security of earning more than she strictly needed was essential to her peace of mind. Possibly Angelica also felt the urge to show that women could be more than dilettante practitioners of the polite arts, though if that is the case it is paradoxical that she so often sacrificed quality to quantity.

In the course of her phenomenally successful career she built up a clientele as distinguished as Louise's own would be, and as cosmopolitan. During her fifteen years in Great Britain between 1766 and 1781, for instance, the royal family, dukes and duchesses sat to her; when she returned to Italy, Grand-Duke Paul of Russia, the future Tsar, was one of her first patrons, and Joseph II of Austria gave her a precious jewel-case in gratitude for the two pictures he had bought from her.[56] Some of her clients were the same as Louise's. She painted Hendryk Lubomirski,[57] the Bishop of Derry[58] (and his daughter Lady Elizabeth Foster, whose triangular relationship with the Duke and Duchess of Devonshire was infamous), Countess Skavronskaya and Ferdinand and Maria Carolina of Naples with their family. She rather reluctantly gave the royal children drawing-lessons, no doubt feeling like Louise that she had better things to do with her time.[59]

Catherine the Great preferred Angelica to Louise as an artist because she believed her to have a better understanding of ideal beauty. The fact that she often painted effete-looking men may be as much because she had fallen under the spell of Winckelmann in Rome as because she had, as a woman artist, been forbidden to draw the male nude from life: Winckelmann, the greatest living authority on classical art, the founder of modern art history and a well-known homosexual, praised the androgynous qualities of Greek sculptures like the *Apollo Belvedere* and other softly contoured male forms.

Both Angelica and Louise were attractive (Angelica's Uffizi self-portrait of 1788, painted when she was forty-six, makes her look ten years younger, which suggests that she shared Louise's female vanity), and both were regarded as ornaments of society. Correspondingly, they moved in the best Roman circles. The cardinal de Bernis invited both of them to one of his famous dinners in the Palazzo dei Caroli (now the Banco di Roma), along with members of the diplomatic corps and other foreigners.[60] He had refused to take the oath demanded by the new civil constitution of the clergy, which meant that he had effectively ceased to be French ambassador; but he still did *émigrés* the honours for which he felt himself responsible.[61] His chef was nearly as famous as Bernis himself. Lady Anne Miller's *Letters from Italy in the Years 1770 and 1771* remark of Bernis twenty years before Louise's arrival:

> The cardinal, being subject to the gout, starves at his own table, as he thinks living low the only means of keeping the fit off. He feeds on nothing but herbs boiled and all the juice pressed out; neither gravy, butter, salt, cream, eggs, oil, nor any kind of meat, fish or fowl does he ever taste, eats very little bread, and that extremely stale. Though he is himself thus suffering famine, his dishes are of the best kinds . . .[62]

Despite this Beaujon-like fasting he was, Lady Miller adds, 'rather inclined to corpulency'.

Unfortunately, Louise never painted his portrait. But he did lend her an important prop for a portrait said by contemporaries to be one of her masterpieces, the picture of Lord Camelford's daughter Miss Pitt, which Louise did soon after her arrival in Rome. (The portrait is now in an English private collection, but the Hermitage possesses a replica.) She chose to paint this extremely pretty sixteen-year-old as Hebe, bearing a cup from which an eagle is drinking. Miss Pitt's slightly vacant look suggests either a habitual state or the fact that she is quite unperturbed by the presence of this huge bird. For some reason the equipment of the Palazzo dei Caroli included a tame eagle; Louise, whose admiration for wild nature was sometimes qualified, was more frightened of being devoured by it than her serene sitter seems to have been. 'The accursed beast, which was used to being always in the open air, chained up in the courtyard, was so furious at being in my room that it tried to attack me.'[63] But the commission seems to have passed without further incident.

In 1790, according to d'Espinchal, Bernis was the only foreign plenipotentiary in Rome to serve his guests serious food.[64] A contemporary English witness reported that the usual Roman substitute for banquets were *conversazioni*, occasions on which one enjoyed no conversation but put up with being squeezed and jostled in the most select and best-dressed company.[65] It was said, indeed, that the aristocracy of Rome found *conversazioni* the most effective means of excluding foreigners, or making them feel unwelcome. But the version Bernis presided over was different. Fragonard's patron Bergeret reported in 1773 that his were characteristically well-fed affairs, with *valets de chambre* pressing refreshments of every kind on guests. Canny Italians, knowing how rare such luck was, would swallow fifteen ices in a single evening.[66]

If the Roman *monde* was in some respects inhospitable, in others it seemed to Louise remarkably generous. Nowadays many of the noble palaces she visited, which contain unbelievable artistic treasures, are owned by banks, but in Louise's day they were family properties (like some of Rome's great churches). The eager sightseer rarely needed a personal invitation to visit them. Louise allowed herself time off painting to view the homes of great Roman dynasties – the Palazzi Giustiniani, Farnese (the most magnificent Renaissance palace in Rome, and now the French embassy), Doria-Pamphilj (whose gallery is at present home to the city's greatest patrician art collection), the Barberini (part of which is now a national gallery, housing Raphael's *Fornarina*), and the huge Palazzo Colonna, itself a work of art. She preferred being alone while she inspected the riches of these places. As in Bologna, she resented being told what she was looking at by people who knew it less well than she did herself. However sumptuous the collections, though, she was critical of the appearance of the pictures, most of which needed cleaning.

When not looking at pictures, or listening to music (on Good Friday she heard Allegri's *Miserere* sung unaccompanied in the Sistine Chapel: 'It was truly the music of angels'),[67] Louise spent time, as a portraitist would, looking at faces and people. Mrs Piozzi had been struck by the sheer showiness of Roman women:

> This is the first town in Italy I have arrived at yet where the ladies fairly drive up and down a long street by way of showing their dress, equipage, &c., without even a pretence of taking fresh air.[68]

Louise remarks on the alternative form of self-advertisement employed by women of humble birth, who could not afford carriages:

> What surprised me greatly in Rome was to find on Sunday mornings at the Colosseum quantities of women of the lowest classes

extraordinarily decked out, covered with jewels, and wearing enormous paste diamond baubles in their ears. They presented the same appearance at church, where they went followed by a servant, who as often as not was only their husband or lover, and whose employment was usually that of a valet. These women do nothing in their own homes; their indolence is such that they live in wretched poverty and mostly become prostitutes. You see them at their windows, looking out onto the streets of Rome, with flowers and feathers in their hair, their faces covered with rouge and white lead; the top of their corsage, which you catch a glimpse of, promises a splendid toilette, so that a novice who wants to become acquainted with them is astonished when he goes into their bedrooms to find them dressed only in a dirty petticoat.[69]

(D'Espinchal notes that it was normal for Roman women to wear white lead, but not rouge.[70]) It is a shame, though hardly surprising, that Louise sketched none of these women during her stay in the city, and none of them could conceivably have afforded to be painted by her: during her career she depicted only high-class courtesans. It was well known that Italians were comparatively uninterested in sitting for their portraits,[71] which is why native painters like Pompeio Batoni had a predominantly foreign clientele. And although Louise notes that she did have (un-specified) artistic links with Romans,[72] most of the portraits she painted were of Polish, Russian and English aristocrats.

She also frankly admits that she sought out the company of her own compatriots for recreation, though she largely avoided the Polignac clan (who had also crossed the Alps to Italy) to escape gossip. In 1789 and 1790 the city was full of émigrés, most of them known to her. When not gathered in the palazzo dei Caroli, they would often assemble at the residence of the prince de Rohan, the other mainstay of the French in Rome. 'The arrival in Rome of so many people bringing news of France,' Louise writes,

> made me every day feel emotions, often very sad, but sometimes very sweet too: for example, people told me that shortly after my departure, as the King was being beseeched to sit for his portrait, he replied: 'No, I shall await the return of Madame Le Brun, so that she can do my portrait as a pendant to the Queen. I want her to paint me full-length, giving Monsieur de La Pérouse the order to set out on his round-the-world voyage.'[73]

But he had been dead for nearly ten years when Louise did finally return. Another potentially great commission she missed was painting the portrait of Pope Pius VI. The abbé Maury came to see her to present the request:

> I wanted to do it a great deal, but I would have had to be veiled to paint the Holy Father, and the fear of being prevented by this from doing a picture I would be satisfied with forced me to refuse this honour. I was very sorry about it, for Pius VI was still one of the handsomest men imaginable.[74]

She worked hard, but took time off occasionally to see the sights. Once she travelled the few miles to the Tivoli waterfall in the company of her daughter, Ménageot and Denis. The cascades of the river Aniene – the classical Anio – drew countless visitors in the eighteenth century, as they still do despite now being miracles of hydraulic pumping rather than (as in Louise's day) miracles of nature. She was much moved by the picturesqueness of the place, surrounded by olive-groves and overlooking the Campagna. Winckelmann, before her, had responded similarly, finding the beauty of the natural surroundings overwhelming after the 'desolation' of Rome's environs.[75] The obsessively acquisitive Earl of Bristol actually bought the Temple of Vesta there, planning to remove it to Ickworth or to his country seat in Ireland, but was frustrated in his project by the intervention of the Roman government.[76] Hubert Robert loved the spiralling, scattering surge of the Cascata Grande at Tivoli, and the incredible limpidity of the Aniene's waters.

Louise too was under Tivoli's spell. Neither Ménageot nor Denis could move her from the spot where she sat sketching the cascades and trying to capture the rainbow colours of the falling water. 'When we finally finished with the waterfalls,' she writes, 'Ménageot took us by a rough, steep path to the temple of the Sibyl [i.e. Vesta], where we ate with hearty appetites; then I lay down at the base of the columns to take a siesta.'[77] Louise, who was lulled by the splashing of the water, describes her peculiar impressionability to sound. For her it had an almost visual or tactile quality.

> To say nothing of the dreadful noise of thunder, there are unbearable ones for me, and I could trace their form according to the impression they made on me: I know round sounds, pointed ones, but there are some which have always been agreeable to me: the sound of waves at the seaside, for instance, is soft and inspires one to gentle reverie; I think I could write a treatise on *noises*, so great is the importance I have attached to them throughout my life.

The party stayed the night at an inn, and Louise returned the next morning to complete the sketch of the scene. Tivoli had all that her artist's soul desired – wild beauty, colour, form, and for all the energy of the cascades a soothingness she missed in the bustle of Rome.

View-painting was the enthusiasm of the age, as travel was the passion of the Enlightenment, and Louise incorporated what she saw into her Italian portraits. Her 1791 portrait of Countess Potocka – a different Countess Potocka from the one to whom Louise addresses the letters about Switzerland included in her memoirs – shows the sitter against a background evidently based on the celebrated gardens of Tivoli, with a series of waterfalls and a mass of ivy-covered rocks. It is the very scene Louise describes in the *Souvenirs*:

> We went to see the grotto of Neptune, at the top of a huge water-fall, which after cascading furiously over great black stones calmed down into a broad white limpid stretch of water. From there we went into what is called Neptune's cave, which is nothing other than a pile of rocks covered with moss, onto which pound the cascades; it makes this cavern very picturesque.[78]

The Potocka portrait, painted at about the same time as the one of Miss Pitt, shows its subject reclining elegantly on a rock and superbly dressed, the shimmering fluidity of the textures – shining grey satin gown, auburn hair, gold-fringed scarlet shawl – harmonising with the background of the cascades. The Countess looks calmly inviting in this most poetic of compositions, perhaps too knowingly so. She was married four times: her second husband Prince Saphieha (not, as Louise wrongly says, her first one, the deceased Prince Sanguszko) was a drunkard whom she nevertheless told Louise she preferred to Count Potocki, still married to her at the time the portrait was painted.

When she had finished this picture and the one of Mademoiselle Roland, Louise painted her self-portrait for the Roman Accademia di San Luca, which elected her to membership in early April 1790. In this picture she avoids flattery, making herself a great deal less glamorous than in the Uffizi portrait (and incidentally less glamorous than Reynolds makes Angelica Kauffman in the portrait which hangs next to her in the Accademia). Louise has a workaday appearance, and wears a plain painter's costume, untrimmed grey dress and roughly tied white neckerchief, with a white scarf wound round her head. It is not a polished work, and seems to have been done in haste, but possesses much charm as the practical image of a practical woman, now merely attractive rather than the stunner of the 'cherry-red ribbons' and 'straw hat' self-portraits.

At this time Louise also painted the replica of her Uffizi self-portrait for the Earl of Bristol, as well as a three-quarter length picture of the Earl himself (whom she would later paint again in Naples) and a portrait of a young Portuguese woman, Señora Silva. In short, she says, 'I worked prodigiously hard'.[79] But after seven or eight months it was time to move on.

She tells Hubert Robert and Brongniart in a letter of 16 March 1790[80] that she is writing to them jointly to save her eyes, worn out by all the painting she has done in Rome. She has obviously been happy there, but misses the gatherings in the rue de Gros-Chenet, wishing she was

> in the gallery on the great sofa, next to all of you, for I so loved to see you all gathered there, making music for all you were worth, or listening to it, which is not so common here . . . People in Rome at the moment have less pure taste than at home, with the exception of a few true connoisseurs who have retained it.

She has other reservations too. Roman hospitality remained stiff, she reported, even though her public success had been considerable and she had received many invitations.

Realising that all the foreign residents she knew – that is, her clientele – were leaving for Naples, she decided to go there too, planning to set off at the end of Holy Week on 7 April 1790. She probably scented new commissions: the letter to Robert and Brongniart mentions that she is 'expected' in the city, and Ménageot wrote to d'Angiviller that she intended to spend part of the summer as well as the spring there, since she had much work to do.[81]

Louise, who was not actually as self-deprecating as she makes herself sound, claimed that none of the flattery she had received had made her any vainer, and that her friends knew her too well to expect otherwise. 'It has astonished and encouraged me, that is all.' But her insistence in the letter to Robert and Brongniart on detailing the public appreciation of her Florentine self-portrait argues rather differently:

> My picture for Florence is enjoying the greatest possible success. I would seem conceited if I went into all the details of its favourable reception . . . never in my life have I been encouraged to this extent; it pleased me all the more in that the Romans concede almost no worth to our school . . . all the artists have come more than once, and so have princesses of every nation . . .

There is more than a hint of self-congratulation too in her airy reference to the poems of praise she has received: 'I shall send you the best'. People call her Madame Van Dyck and Madame Rubens, she continues, which is highly gratifying, but the masterpieces of Italian art are there to deflate whatever pretensions such praise may have encouraged. This is no doubt sincerely meant, but the coquettish tone of self-admiration can hardly be missed either. She was brimming with confidence as she prepared to leave for Naples.

CHAPTER FIVE

TO THE SOUTH AND BACK: 'Naples too wants my daubs'

Louise was doing more in Naples than pursue clients. Official, as opposed to private, commissions had eluded her in Rome. The reason she gives for having declined to paint Pope Pius is unconvincing – no (woman) artist could have been expected to paint the Pontiff when she was unable to see him properly – and the story of the commission is perhaps invented, just as the later one of Catherine the Great asking her to paint her portrait in St Petersburg seems to be. Naples could offer something better: a royal court with a Bourbon monarch (though of the Spanish dynasty) and his Habsburg consort (who was the sister of Marie-Antoinette). The Queen of France's favourite portraitist would surely find a welcome at the court of Maria Carolina.

Besides, Naples was also a fabulously cosmopolitan place, for two centuries a province of Spain and Austria, but from 1734 the capital of an independent kingdom. The cosmopolitanism had been enhanced by the Bourbons' importing of foreign artists to furnish and decorate their residences; the discovery of Herculaneum and Pompeii had added to the fame of the city; and its opera house, the vast San Carlo, drew thousands of visitors. At the time of Louise's stay it was the third largest city in Europe after London and Paris, with 400,000 inhabitants. Stendhal would later say that it made anywhere else appear provincial.

Louise was accompanied to her new destination by the Monsieur Duvivier whom Bernis had recommended to her, but the journey was apparently trying. She was offended by being made to sit close to Duvivier's enormous valet in the coach, and by her travelling-companion's resolutely anti-picturesque attitude to the country they traversed. Furthermore, despite Duvivier's promise that they would prepare their own food *en route*, the party was reduced to eating bad meals in inns. It was not enough to dampen Louise's enthusiasm; but she was heartily relieved to part from her 'wet blanket' when they reached Naples after two-and-a-half days of travelling.

The first sight was ravishing.

I cannot find words to describe the impression I felt on entering the city. The brilliant sun, the wide expanse of the sea, the islands glimpsed in the distance, Vesuvius with a great pillar of smoke coming out of its summit, even the population, so lively, so noisy, so different from Rome's that you would think a thousand leagues' distance separated them: everything transported me, but the pleasure of parting from my tedious companion perhaps counted for something in my satisfaction.[1]

Winckelmann, with his fixation on Rome above all other cities, had inevitably been critical, claiming to have been crushed by the Neapolitan throng and deafened by the unbelievable din of the place.[2] Saint-Non, the author of a famous *Voyage pittoresque de Naples*, is more tolerant of this pullulating life:

The Neapolitan populace is excessively noisy, but lighthearted and indolent in character; it is incapable . . . of pursuing revenge for long. You can win it over completely by escaping its first movement of rage. It takes little to calm it and little to satisfy it. More peaceful and good-natured than any other people, it has no interest in the affairs of government. Give a Neapolitan his basic needs, frugal but easily obtained, and he will never complain . . .[3]

Travellers reacted in different ways to the city itself. Dupaty thought that, contrary to the proverb, one should see Naples and live, Creuzé de Lesser that one should see Naples and immediately leave. Germaine de Staël, who went to Naples in 1805, is famous for saying that she would not open her window for a first view of the bay – that masterpiece of Romantic scenery – but would travel 500 leagues to converse with an intelligent man. Yet *Corinne* suggests that she was intoxicated by the natural world there.

Every step, as one trod flowers underfoot, made them exude delicious perfumes. Nightingales took their rest by preference on bushes covered with roses. Thus the purest songs mingled with the most divine scents; all the charms of nature attracted one another mutually; but what is most ravishing and inexpressible is the sweetness of the air one breathes.[4]

The *laissez-faire* attitude of the Neapolitans irritated her, because her approach was more bracing, and she disliked their inclination to let everything happen of its own course, as oranges and lemons fall from trees. Still she enjoyed the prevailing anti-intellectualism.[5] Naples might lack the solemn grandeur of Rome (which so often casts a pall over the more unreadable sections of *Corinne*), but it was correspondingly more liberating.

It was also wealthy, though here too it seemed a place of contrasts. Its palaces were supremely elegant, but it had the most squalid of slums; its nobles were cultivated, but capable of sudden acts of violence and revenge. Saint-Non found much of the magnificence a matter of show, not substance.

> You come across huge, spacious palaces, richly furnished, but three-quarters of them are uninhabited. Families possess the most superb plate, but never serve food on it; and apart from a few houses which do things in the French style, everything which seems to indicate a state of the greatest ease is simply a display put on for one or two days a year . . . Noblemen with vast incomes and the most brilliant households often lack basic necessities . . . From time to time the leading families have *ricevimenti*, of 300 or 400 people, where the most substantial food you are offered is a biscuit; nothing could be more dazzling than these *ricevimenti*, pages in embroidered costume, jackets richly trimmed with silver braid, *maîtres d'hôtel* one is tempted to take for masters of the house, buffets with an inexhaustible supply of ices, sweetmeats and *rinfreschi* of every kind; but it is all like a firework display, and the very next day all this great splendour has disappeared.[6]

These luxurious-seeming affairs, in other words, could actually be as unsustaining as Roman *conversazioni*.

Louise again found herself approached for portrait-painting commissions by foreign rather than native clients – perhaps because of the usual Italian indifference to portraiture, but perhaps also because of this tradition of financial uncertainty, not to say parsimony. It was probably his own experience of the Neapolitan way with hospitality that encouraged the Russian ambassador, Count Skavronsky, to send her a delicious dinner on the day of her arrival. Louise, who had taken rooms next door to the Russian embassy in the hôtel du Maroc, was touched by this neighbourly gesture and its sequel:

> That very evening I went to thank him, and there I met his charming wife; both pressed me to have no other table but their own, and although it was impossible for me to accept this offer unreservedly, I often availed myself of it during my stay in Naples, so agreeable did I find their society.[7]

The Skavronskys were an intriguing couple. He was a very wealthy Livonian aristocrat, one of the foreigners rich enough to commission a portrait from Louise, and an Italophile whom Catherine II had sent as ambassador to Naples in 1784. At the start of his posting his wife Catherine stayed in St Petersburg with her uncle Potemkin, who had made her and two of her sisters his mistresses. Through his influence she became a lady-in-waiting to the Tsarina, but eventually the ill-health of her husband obliged her to move to Naples. When he died in 1793, she returned to Russia.

The *Souvenirs* refer to Skavronsky's extreme pallor, but note that his sickliness did not prevent him from being perfectly mannered. Louise thought his wife a picture of loveliness, but hints too at her vacuousness.

> The Countess was gentle and as pretty as an angel; the famous Potemkin ... had showered her with riches of which she made no use. Her idea of happiness was to live lying on a sofa, wrapped up in a great black pelisse and wearing no corset. Her mother-in-law had her sent from Paris cases full of the most charming articles of apparel made at that time by Mademoiselle Bertin, Queen Marie-Antoinette's *marchande de modes*. I do not believe the Countess ever opened a single one, and when her mother-in-law expressed the desire to see her wear the delightful dresses and hair adornments these cases contained, she replied nonchalantly: What is the point? For whom? Why? She gave me the same answer when she showed me her jewel casket, one of the most sumptuous you can imagine: it contained some enormous diamonds which Potemkin had given her and which I have never seen her wear.[8]

The comte de Ségur wrote that she might have served any painter as the model for Love itself, which is not to say that her face had much character.[9] Indeed, Louise's first picture of the Countess – which according to a letter she sent Madame du Barry she was painting by early July 1790 – seems perfectly to illustrate the principle she announces in the *Souvenirs*, that when she found her female sitters lacking in physiognomy (or expression) she gave them a look of reverie which almost up for it. Her Naples portrait of this beauty, nerveless and masklike as she appears, borrows its pose from the much more moving 1789 portrait of the duchesse d'Orléans: both women sit relaxedly on a velvet sofa and lean on a cushion. (Countess Skavronskaya's crescent smile would later be 'recycled' in the pictures of Countesses Potocka and Schönfeld).[10] But Louise refuses to confer on Catherine Skavronskaya a depth she did not possess, and the *Souvenirs* confirm her shallowness.

I remember she told me that to make her fall asleep she kept a woman slave under her bed to tell her the same story every evening. By day she was perpetually idle; she had no learning, and her conversation was as empty as could be; despite all that, thanks to her ravishing face and angelic sweetness she possessed invincible charm. Count Skavronsky was very much in love with her . . .[11]

Ironically, a drawing Louise did after the 1790 portrait, sold in New York in 1993,[12] shows the artist paying far more attention to the sitter's costume than she did herself, with detailed annotations on the satins, muslins and gauzes she wears and the shade of the velvet covering the settee on which she reclines. 'Dress of deep mauve satin,' the description reads, 'sleeves of white muslin like the bonnet; gold gauze sash, green velvet settee . . . cushions. Greyish background . . . The small portrait black on its reverse side, and stamped with a gold letter . . . she looks at the portrait.' Although an empty picture, the portrait in oils is a *tour de force* precisely because it has to be empty: as far as we can tell, it is one of the most truthful images Louise ever painted. Angelica Kauffman also did two portraits of the Countess, but somehow Louise seems the right painter for her.

Perhaps Louise would have welcomed more leisure to enjoy the sheer beauty of her surroundings, the prodigality of colour in Naples – pastel houses, majolica-tiled cupolas and bell-towers, polychrome frescoes and inlaid marbles – the deliciousness of place which Boswell, quoting Horace, said smiled beyond all others.[13] She loved her quarters, with some reservations:

> I was enchanted to be living in the hôtel du Maroc, to say nothing of the charm of my surroundings. From my window I had the most magnificent view and the most delightful spectacle. The sea and the island of Capri in front of me; to the left Vesuvius, which seemed to promise an eruption by the quantities of smoke it was emitting; on the right the hillside of Posilippo, covered with charming houses and superb vegetation; then the Chiaia quay is always so lively that it presented me with a constant stream of varied and amusing pictures: sometimes *lazzaroni* [the Neapolitan beggar class] came to quench their thirst at the beautiful fountain beneath my windows, or young laundresses came to wash their linen there; on Sundays young peasant women in their finest attire danced the tarantella in front of my hotel, playing the Basque tambourine, and every evening I saw fishermen with torches whose bright light cast fiery reflections on the sea. After my bed-

room there was an open gallery which gave onto a garden filled with orange and lemon trees in blossom; but as everything on this earth has its drawbacks, I had to resign myself to one in my apartment. For several hours in the morning I was unable to open my windows onto the quay, because a temporary kitchen had been set up underneath where women cooked tripe in huge cauldrons, with rancid oil whose smell wafted up to me. So I was reduced to looking at the sea through my window-panes. How beautiful this Naples sea is! I often spent hours gazing at it at night, when the waves had calmed down and were silver-tinged by the reflection of a superb moon. Often, too, I took a boat to go for a trip and enjoy the magnificent panorama of the city in its entirety, rising up like an amphitheatre.[14]

But her clients were not prepared to leave her in peace. In February 1791 Ménageot wrote to d'Angiviller of her busyness and consequent tiredness:

> Madame Le Brun, who has been enjoying the most gratifying success in Naples, plans to come back to Rome very soon for a six-week rest from work and from the Naples air, both of which have affected her health.[15]

An earlier letter had reported that Louise's sight was giving her problems, and she herself writes that going to court for a midday session of painting Crown Prince Francesco was particularly painful for this reason. To get to the palace she had to follow the Chiaia road at the time of greatest heat:

> The houses built on the left, facing the sea, were painted *brilliant* white; the sun was reflected off them so strongly that I was blinded. To protect my eyes I had the idea of wearing a green veil, which I had never seen anyone do, and which must have seemed strange, for women wore only white or black ones; but a few days later I saw masses of Englishwomen copying me, and green veils became the fashion. I was also very glad of my green veil in St Petersburg, where the snow is so dazzling it would have made me lose my sight.[16]

Her subjects were not only royal or aristocratic. Barely had she begun the portrait of Catherine Skavronskaya than Sir William Hamilton, the British ambassador to Naples, presented himself to her and asked her to paint his superb mistress and future wife, Emma Hart, before she took on any other commissions. Louise could not immediately comply. Not only was she under an obligation to Count Skavronsky, but she was also engaged on her second portrait of Lord Hervey, the Bishop of Derry, a three-quarter-length showing him against the background of Mount Vesuvius. There could not have been a more appropriate background – though Byron thought Vesuvius hackneyed – since Lord Hervey climbed the volcano every day. In Louise's picture he appears affable and convivial, a state no doubt stimulated by this regular exercise. (The affability was disliked by Pompeio Batoni, who found the Earl-Bishop's chatter as he sat to him for another portrait condescending.) Mrs Piozzi was conscious of the perils he underwent in indulging his enthusiasm: '[the] Bishop of Derry did very near get his arm broke'[17] from venturing too close to the crater while red-hot stones were being flung up into the air.

Louise's portrait is refreshing in its approachability, reflecting the informality of her subject: it differs from a standard portrait by Batoni in its delicate sensitivity and its avoidance of grandeur. There is often in her work a stylistic tact or muteness that recalls Ramsay, and in the picture of Lord Hervey this understatement provides a compelling contrast with the threat of the adjacent volcano. The Bishop sits in contemplative stillness, exuding a sense of order and balance. According to some contemporaries, though, this kind of steadiness was precisely what he lacked. Lord Charlemont called him a man of no firm principle, a bad father and a worse husband – rapid, noisy, diverting but useless, like a shallow stream. Elisabeth, Lady Webster, described him as clever and bad.[18]

The Bishop had been a friend since schooldays of Sir William Hamilton, and it was while staying with him in Naples in 1765 that he had been struck by the red-hot stone on Mount Vesuvius. Sir William had a house, the Villa Angelica, which Dr Burney described as being at the very foot of the volcano, and which served as a base for his own frequent excursions up the mountain.[19] Both men were connoisseurs. Louise's Naples portrait of the Earl-Bishop is no longer part of a great picture-collection, for that was confiscated when he was arrested by the French in 1798 (he subsequently recovered it only for it to be seized again by Napoleon's troops); but the huge rotunda of Ickworth, where this picture and the replica of her Uffizi self-portrait hang, was originally meant to be the home of a superb gallery.

His friend was famous as a collector too. Talleyrand's son said that the arts protected Sir William more than he did them,[20] meaning that he was clever at speculating on the art market. But to call him a mere speculator is unfair. Sir William had the true collector's passion for *things*, and speculated less to make money than in order to buy more art. His collecting, in any case, was often disinterested: he made generous donations to the fledgling British Museum, for instance, which gained incalculably from his passion for ancient Greek vases and sculpture. Louise either was ignorant of this generosity or – rather inconsistently – chose to be supercilious about the commercial possibilities of trading in art. Predictably enough, she minded most where her own art was the object being traded. When she went to Warwick Castle during her stay in England, she notes, she was surprised to find Lord Warwick in possession of two charming *têtes d'expression* which she had sketched in charcoal as a pair of overmantels at the Villa Emma, Hamilton's summer residence in Posilippo. The collector had sawn them off and sold them to Lord Warwick, although, as Louise remarks, she had not sold them to Sir William in the first place.

Sir William was as well known as an antiquarian as he would later be as a cuckold, celebrated for the book on Greek antiquities he sponsored – d'Hancarville's *Antiquités étrusques, grecques et romaines* – and his own *Campi phlegraei*. This is the aspect of his character that is emphasised in Reynolds's portrait of 1777, now in London's National Portrait Gallery: the slightly bloodless, spare, scholarly man, supremely civilised, dignified and elegant, with his passions kept well in check.

There was, of course, a playful side to Sir William, which helps explain why he was such an agreeable companion on hunting and fishing trips to King Ferdinand IV of Naples. The King, who had been given a deliberately unacademic education, remained a boisterous boy at heart, and could take any amount of physical exertion; reading and writing, on the other hand, were obnoxious to him, and he found his wife far too bookish. Sir William's liking for blood sports had not appealed to his cultivated first wife Catherine, who once wrote to his nephew that the King and her husband had just killed 376 wild duck on a single shooting expedition: 'What slaughter!'[21] Perhaps his greatest passion, though, was the one he developed for his nephew Charles Greville's former mistress Emma Hart.

Ménageot said that Sir William regarded the picture Louise painted of her, *Lady Hamilton as a Recumbent Bacchante* (or *Lady Hamilton as Ariadne*), as one of the most beautiful he had ever seen.[22] It was also Nelson's favourite portrait of Emma, who became his mistress after Sir William had married her: he bought it from Sir William in 1801 for 300 guineas, and left it in his will to Emma herself. She later sold it to help pay off her enormous debts.

Louise's decision to paint her as Ariadne was a somewhat mischievous one, though the way she tells the story rather disguises the fact.

> I painted Madame Hart as a bacchante lying by the sea, and holding a goblet in her hand. Her beautiful face was highly animated, and contrasted completely with the Countess's [i.e. Catherine Skavronskaya's]; she had an enormous quantity of lovely chestnut

hair which she could entirely cover herself with, and as a bacchante, with her hair loose, she was admirable.[23]

Louise actually chose the moment after Ariadne had been dropped off at Naxos by Theseus against her will, when she ought to be indignant if not distraught (particularly as, according to one version of the story reported by Plutarch, Theseus has got her pregnant). But Louise's Ariadne looks anything but desperate. The daughter of Minos and Pasiphaë, lounging luxuriously, gazes at the spectator with a wide-eyed candour, forebearing to glance at the horizon where a tiny ship – presumably the one commanded by Theseus, whose life she has just saved – can be discerned.[24]

She is manifestly a courtesan, quite obviously out to please the onlooker, and the whole painting wears a directly suggestive smile. Theseus may have left his woman to die, but Ariadne is far from finished. Like Emma herself, she may safely trust that something or someone will come to rescue her. It is an impudent and frolicsome image because Louise has got the measure of her subject, but not *too* impudent: the mockery had to be tempered for the sake of Emma's infatuated lover, ravished as he was by her beauty. Louise must have calculated that Sir William, as well as his innocently vain mistress, would see in the picture only a testament to her all-powerful charms, and she apparently calculated correctly.

She painted Emma several times. The full-length *Lady Hamilton as Sibyl* was done in Rome for the duc de Brissac. After his murder in 1792 Louise kept it by her, eventually selling it to the duc de Berri in 1819. She seems to have copied this picture for herself or another client, and her husband also possessed a version. The head and bust were replicated for Sir William Hamilton, and sold in 1801 for £32 11s., while a picture of Lady Hamilton as a bacchante dancing against the background of Vesuvius and holding a tambourine remained in Louise's possession until she bequeathed it to her niece Eugénie. Apart from the arms and tambourine, it closely resembles Romney's *Lady Hamilton as Bacchante* of about 1784. Louise had painted a dancing woman with a tambourine before, the 'portrait d'une danseuse' of 1783–5 (formerly thought to be of La Camargo) at present in the Musée Cognacq-Jay in Paris. But the tone of the Emma Hamilton picture is quite different, sultry and erotic in comparison with the almost vernal freshness of the earlier portrait.

'The life of Lady Hamilton is a romance,'[25] Louise remarks in the *Souvenirs*. She came to an unromantic end, an obese alcoholic who lived beyond her means, was imprisoned for insolvency, and eventually died destitute in Calais (where in 1995 a monument to her was erected in a public park). Louise would meet her again in 1803 during her stay in

London, when Emma was well on the downward slope, and notice her prodigious capacity for drinking porter. But in Naples she seemed to reign supreme, and scandalous stories even circulated about her 'intimate' relationship with Maria Carolina.

Emma Hart was of obscure origin, born in Lancashire of a blacksmith and a servant but brought up by her grandmother in Wales. The adolescent Emma migrated to London, where, according to Louise, she 'calculated that she could find a more suitable situation' than the one of children's nanny she had held in a middle-class household. It is unclear whether or not this new situation became prostitution, but what is certain is that Emma's beauty won her many lovers. 'The Prince of Wales,' Louise writes, 'told me that he had seen her at this time wearing clogs at the door of a fruiterer's, and although she was very poorly dressed, her charming face drew attention to her.' She then, also according to Louise, began working as a chambermaid for a lady of good family and irreproachable morals. 'In this house she acquired a taste for novels, then a taste for theatre. She studied the gestures and voice-inflections of actors, and reproduced them with amazing facility. This talent, which was very far from pleasing or suiting her mistress, got her dismissed.' And she soon began to practise the 'attitudes' for which she would become famous, posing as the goddess Hygiene in the household of the quack Dr Graham.

At this point artists became interested in her, Romney in particular: she sat to him about forty times, as a bacchante, Circe, Calypso, Euphrosyne, St Cecilia and so on. She was also painted by Reynolds, Hoppner, Gavin Hamilton (who depicted her as a classically severe and austere sibyl) and Lawrence.[28] One of the Hamilton residences, the Palazzo Sessa, would eventually contain dozens of portraits and fancy pictures of Emma, for Sir William could not have enough of them. Perhaps reflecting her actress-like ability to assume different appearances, painters showed her in various guises. Louise's tambourine picture of Emma is based on the famous frieze of Herculaneum dancers: the tambourine was one of Emma's favourite props. In the Ariadne portrait she reclines on a tiger skin, like Elinor Glyn, and in her succulent voluptuousness there is a hint of the fleshiness that would later spoil her looks. By contrast, Romney's 1785 portrait *Lady Hamilton as Ariadne*, in the National Maritime Museum in London, is sober, demure, almost virginal, and quite without the frisky softness of Louise's *Ariane gaie*. Louise comments on Emma's actress-like skills:

> Nothing was more intriguing than the faculty Lady Hamilton had acquired of suddenly giving all her features the expression of grief or joy, and posing wonderfully to portray different characters.

> With fiery eye and flowing hair, she would give you a delicious
> bacchante, then suddenly her face conveyed grief, and you saw an
> admirable repentant Magdalen.[29]

Charles Greville, the son of the Earl of Warwick, discarded her for an
heiress (whom he then failed to secure) when he found himself chronic-
ally short of money. He took Emma with him to Naples for the express
purpose of raising cash from Sir William by having the latter recognise
him officially as his heir, and 'trading' Emma to him in return. (Louise's
account, which she had from Greville, gives a more flattering version of
his part of the affair, claiming that he had taken Emma along merely to
plead his cause.) Emma could hardly have been more different from his
first wife, but Sir William was susceptible to her charms, and they lived
together for some years before marrying. He was drawn by her beauty and
innate decency, and encouraged her to perform her attitudes.

Although Goethe reports seeing Emma in a Grecian tunic in 1787,
Louise seems to take some credit – as she would later do in the case of
society women in Moscow – for dressing her *à l'antique*. Emma's own
taste in clothes, she writes, was execrable: 'She had no style, and dressed
very badly when it was a question of wearing ordinary costume.'[30] But

> The day the chevalier Hamilton presented her to me, he wanted
> me to see her in action; I was thrilled; but she was dressed like
> everyone else, which shocked me. I had some dresses made for her
> like the one I was wearing to paint comfortably in, and which are
> called smock-dresses; she added some shawls to drape herself in,
> having an instinctive feel for such graces; and from that point on
> you could have copied her different poses and expressions and
> produced a whole gallery of pictures ...[31]

It was Emma, according to the novelist Madame de Krüdener, who first
revealed the artistic qualities of the shawl-dance, showing how teasing,
dramatic and utterly Pompeian it was.[32] Her dancing, as well as her
attitudinising and singing, was widely regarded as one of the most
voluptuous spectacles in Naples.[33]

Of course she remained vulgar, as Louise's Ariadne portrait suggests,
though contemporaries remarked on how many of the social graces she
had learnt from mingling with the great and taking various kinds of lesson. Gouverneur Morris met her in 1791 in Paris, and thought that she still
had the air of a kept woman.[34] The Duchess of Devonshire, who encountered her the same year in Bath, found her appearance coarse, and said
that Lord Hervey's judgement on her must stand: 'Take her as anything

but Mrs Hart, and she is a superb being – as herself she is always vulgar'.[35] Common-seeming or not, she had a power to transform herself which made her an acceptable companion not just to Sir William (whom she married that year), but also to the Queen of Naples. Louise refers only discreetly to the rumours about the two women's friendship, but says that the intimacy was politically based: 'Lady Hamilton, being very indiscreet, put her in possession of quantities of little diplomatic secrets, which Her Majesty took advantage of for the running of the Kingdom.'[36]

Maria Carolina was much brighter than her sister Marie-Antoinette – though Louise would never have admitted such a thing – and infinitely more intelligent than her husband Ferdinand. But Louise had no high opinion of Emma's mind.

> Lady Hamilton had no wit at all, though she was greatly given to mockery and denigration, to the extent that these two faults formed the only backbone of her conversation; but she was also canny, and used the canniness to get a husband.

It is typical of Louise to believe that the vulgar woman bagged the unsuspecting aristocrat, rather than that the besotted aristocrat should have wanted to make the vulgar woman his wife: she was, after all, '*attaquée de noblesse*'.[37]

For all her instinctive knowledge, Emma lacked the painter's eye. She could not, according to Louise, see how she was beautified by classical costume, or by the turban she wore for the sibyl portrait. The comtesse de Boigne confirmed that when she discarded 'antique' tunics and robes for more ordinary dress, Emma instantly lost all distinction. As Madame de Boigne also notes, she was someone whom it was easy to describe in terms of ridicule, but who in reality ravished the onlooker. The proof of her exceptional quality was that when others tried to do as she did, they completely failed. In her, a hair's breadth separated the sublime from the laughable.[38]

Other forms of sublimity awaited Louise's closer inspection, in particular the grandiose horror of Vesuvius. She set off with her Portuguese friend, Señora Silva, and a French abbé to become as closely acquainted with the mountain as the Earl-Bishop and Sir William. The threat of volcanic activity was probably an unstated 'draw' for this apparently fearless woman, and Vesuvius was notably active in the eighteenth century: there were spectacular eruptions in 1737, 1754, 1766, 1771, 1779 and 1790, and there would be another in 1794. Vesuvius's attraction for tourists at that time was understandable. Volcanoes represented the most elemental of natural phenomena, and so appealed to the nascent forces of Romanticism, the love of natural spectacle, and the Enlightenment interest in empirical investigation. Sir William Hamilton won praise for his cool, scholarly cataloguing in the *Campi phlegraei* (1776) of the different processes that attended its eruption, and those travellers who failed to see fire, lava and pillars of smoke issuing from the crater were apt to feel cheated.[39] Louise showed proper gratitude for the volcano's obligingness, as is clear from a letter she sent Brongniart:

> Now I am going to talk to you of my favourite spectacle, Vesuvius. For two pins I'd become a Vesuvian, I so adore this superb volcano; I think it likes me too, for it fêted me and welcomed me in the most grandiose fashion. How the finest firework displays, not excepting the great girandole of the Castel Sant' Angelo, pale into insignificance when one thinks of Vesuvius![40]

She remained determinedly thrilled despite the unpropitious weather conditions on the trip:

> The first time I did the climb, my companions and I were caught in a dreadful storm, and rain so heavy it was like the Flood. We were soaked, but we still took a path up to the heights so as to see one of the great lava-flows right at our feet. I thought I was at the gates of hell. An inferno, which asphyxiated me, was snaking away under my very eyes; it was three miles in circumference. Since the foul weather stopped us going any further that day, and the smoke as well as the rain of cinders that showered down on us made the summit of the mountain invisible, we got on our mules and went down towards the black lava. Two thunderstorms, in the sky and in the volcano, mingled continually; the noise was hellish, the more so as it was echoed in the cavities of the surrounding mountains. As we were just beneath cloud-level, I was trembling, and our whole cavalcade with me, fearing that our movement as we walked might draw a thunderbolt down on us . . . I arrived home in a pitiable state: my dress was nothing but soaking cinders; I was dead with fatigue; I dried myself off and went to bed very happily.

Although she was prone to domesticate the savage – even after this baptism by fire she insisted on calling the volcano 'my dear Vesuvius' – Louise respected its sublime wildness. She was diverted by the fact that on her second visit, in perfect serene weather, Vesuvius was in a more furious mood than ever, putting on a show she could not resist capturing:

> as, during the day, one cannot make out any flames, we saw com-
> ing out of the crater, along with the clouds of cinders and lava,
> only a huge mass of white-silver smoke, which the sun lit up in a
> wonderful way. I painted this effect, for it is divine.[41]

Some years later, Chateaubriand would be impressed by the way this great
natural spectacle dwarfed and humbled the efforts of man. He experienced the same terror and sense of powerlessness as Louise, but felt
diminished by it rather than enhanced as a human being.

> In effect, what do the famous revolutions of empires count for in
> the light of these accidents of nature, which change the face of the
> earth and the seas? Men would be happy, at least, if they did not
> devote the few days they have to spend together to tormenting
> each other! Vesuvius has never once opened up its depths to
> devour cities without its fury surprising people spilling blood or
> shedding tears. What were the first signs of civilisation, the first
> proofs of man's passage to be found in the dead cinders of the vol-
> cano? Instruments of torture, skeletons in chains.[42]

Louise was not inspired to such philosophical reflection. But, like
Chateaubriand, she found the human factor misplaced in this immense
environment, more troubled by hearing of a dead body in the resident
hermit's cell than she could imagine being in the presence of natural
peril.[43] Yet however puny Vesuvius made Louise feel, she kept being drawn
back to it, attracted by the elemental forces it contained and might at any
moment unleash.

The slothfulness of the humans she encountered in Naples could scarcely
have contrasted more with this potential destructive energy. The *dolce far
niente* of the Neapolitan beggar-class superficially resembled Countess
Skavronskaya's, but seemed more a conscious philosophy. The *lazzaroni*
aroused almost as much curiosity amongst eighteenth- and early
nineteenth-century travellers as the excavations and discoveries at
Herculaneum and Pompeii did: they became a byword for thievery,
corruption, indolence and sedition, but were an essential part of the
colourful open-air Neapolitan scene, a perpetual comic opera. At the
beginning of the eighteenth century Addison stigmatised the Neapolitans
in general for *lazzaronismo* – the leading of a lazy, pleasure-seeking life.[44]
Goethe realised that it was pointless to carp against this rabble class's

chosen *modus vivendi*, which was defensible in both philosophical and practical terms. Naples, in his opinion, actively encouraged one to indulge in blissful idleness, enjoying oneself as the natives did in their paradise city.

> When one simply considers what a quantity of food the fish-filled sea provides, food which those people must lawfully nourish themselves with several days every week; how there is a super-abundance of fruit and vegetables in all seasons; how the area around Naples has earned the name *Terra di lavoro* (not 'land of work' but 'land of agriculture') and the whole province has for centuries borne the honorary title of 'happy country' (*Campagna felice*); it may readily be understood how easy it is to live there.[45]

The *lazzaroni*, in any case, were not simply feckless prodigals. Since Masaniello's revolt in 1647 – a rebellion by the peasantry against aristocratic privilege – they had given rise to a fantastic legend, and were regarded as a political force. The attempt by their Spanish rulers to tax the populace's basic foodstuff, fruit, as a way of increasing revenue was answered by an uprising whose significance became archetypal. The whole point, as Goethe saw, was that fruit had to be freely available for the *lazzarone* ethos to continue. D'Espinchal remarks in his journal that Ferdinand IV was acute enough, whatever his general intellectual deficiencies, to see the importance of currying political favour with this class.

> The King protects the *lazzaroni* in order to be protected in turn, for they make the government tremble. One contains them by favouring their idleness and not letting them go without bread or macaroni, or ice in summer. With such a horde and such enforcement of law and order, one lives in perpetual fear of being robbed at home. It is not prudent to leave one's key in the lock, or even put anything on the window-sill in the lower storeys. One is stolen from here with amazing skill and with no hope of ever getting back what one has lost. Despite that, everyone uses the *lazzaroni*, and there is not a house that lacks its regulars.[46]

Louise, though, suggests that the *lazzaroni* were not thieving by nature (just as during Masaniello's rebellion there was no looting at all except for the stealing of a silver cup by a small boy). They desired only what they needed, not superfluous luxury. During her stay she only once heard of a theft by a *lazzarone*, and it had a quality of restraint that was equivalent to innocence.

One day when the baron de Salis was giving a grand dinner, and was quietly going down the stairs to the kitchen, he stopped short at the sight of a man who, thinking he was unobserved, went up to the pot-au-feu, took a piece of beef and made off with it. The baron was happy just to watch him go away, for all his silverware was spread out on a table; the *lazzarone* had certainly seen it, yet the poor man confined his theft to the piece of beef he took.[47]

Perhaps Louise took this lesson about moderation to heart, for immediately after telling the story she criticises herself as an artist for having so often lacked restraint.

> sometimes the need to make money, for I had not a penny left of the fortune I had earned in France, and sometimes the weakness of my character, made me take on too many commitments, and I killed myself painting portraits. The result is that after devoting my youth to work, with an assiduity and persistence that are rare enough in women, and despite loving my art as much as life itself, I can barely count four works (including portraits) which I am really satisfied with.[48]

For all the frugality of her tastes, Louise was in danger of becoming obsessive about money. But the amount of work – or overwork – she did in Rome and Naples, quite apart from the high prices she charged for her pictures, had unquestionably made her a wealthy woman. She seems to have been unreasonably upset by the profit which clients like Sir William Hamilton made selling her portraits, as though she herself had not earned enough from them, and was particularly offended by Sir William's haggling with her over the price of the *Ariadne* picture:

> The fact is that after bargaining with me for a long time over the portrait of his mistress, he got me to agree to do it for 100 *louis*, and then sold it in London for 300 guineas.[49]

She often returns in the *Souvenirs* to the subject of the money she earned and then lost over the years. But the *lazzarone* and his whole breed made her rethink her attitude to material wealth, and to regret the routineness of the work she did in order to amass more of it. Of her return to Rome she writes:

> There I once again undertook to paint a great number of portraits, which, to tell the truth, gave me little satisfaction. I had

regretted in Naples, and I regretted above all in Rome, not spending my time painting a few pictures on subjects that inspired me.
I had been elected to membership of all the academies in Italy,
which encouraged me actually to earn the distinction I had been
accorded, and yet I was going to leave nothing in this beautiful
land that would greatly add to my reputation.[50]

It is true, of course, that a courtier-artist like Louise was obliged to answer
her patrons' bidding, and given that she had had to acquire a new set of
clients after leaving France she could not afford to be over-selective, or to
ruffle feathers. She was unenthusiastic about painting the children of the
royal family in Naples, but could hardly turn down a royal request. So
while Maria Carolina was away in Vienna with her husband, arranging
dynastic marriages for their children, Louise set about promoting them as
best she could in paint.

It was not a particularly easy task. Maria Carolina herself wrote of the
two eldest daughters that they were neither beautiful nor agreeable, but
that she hoped they would make good wives.[51] In the case of Maria Luisa,
later Grand-Duchess of Tuscany, she feared that it was a battle lost before
it had been joined. The girl was astonishingly ugly, with a grimacing face;
but she succeeded in marrying the Grand-Duke, though she died shortly
afterwards. Whatever the truth about her unattractiveness, Louise's portrait is of an unobjectionable-looking girl with an alert, slightly *gamine*
charm. The eldest daughter, Maria Teresa, managed without the assistance
of Louise's winning portrait to secure betrothal to Franz II of Austria:
Maria Carolina announced the success of her mission on return from
Austria, and the composer Paisiello composed a celebratory *Te Deum*. The
youngest sister, Maria Cristina, is captured with delightful informality sitting in a garden picking roses.

If Louise suffered from the heat painting Crown Prince Francesco, cold
would take its revenge when she embarked on her next work, the Paisiello
portrait so admired by David. Though she lit a fire in her studio, she soon
discovered that the chimney was blocked: obviously the fireplace had
rarely been used. Mrs Piozzi remarked that Italians seemed to have no
feeling for the cold, flinging open windows with a joyous cry of '*che bel
freschetto!*' and moving yards away from a few flashing twigs in a grate for
fear of being scorched, while the wind whistled round their ears.[52] Both
Louise and Paisiello were choked and blinded by smoke, which makes it
all the more extraordinary that Louise's portrait is the masterpiece it is.
Ménageot describes it in a letter to d'Angiviller of 30 March 1791 as a 'very
fine thing',[53] vastly superior to her self-portrait of the previous year (presumably the one for the Accademia di San Luca).

At this time, Louise writes, Paisello was the toast of Naples.[54] In the late 1770s he had been fêted by Catherine the Great in St Petersburg, moved on to similar acclaim in Vienna, returned to Rome, where his latest opera was deemed a failure, and indignantly decided to settle in another city. When Louise met him he had just completed *Nina o la pazza d'amore*, whose première she attended at the San Carlo opera house. The score of this work is displayed on the clavichord at which he sits playing in Louise's portrait, along with that of the *Te Deum* commemorating the King and Queen's successful journey to Vienna. In later life Paisello fell into disgrace, having supported the new government when the Neapolitans revolted against the Bourbon monarchy, and so suffering Ferdinand's displeasure on his return from exile. He worked for Napoleon in Paris, but without great success, returned to Italy, flourished under Joseph Bonaparte, Napoleon's brother, and Joachim Murat (successively Kings of Naples from 1805 to 1815), and was again in disgrace on Ferdinand's restoration. A year later he died, a broken man.

None of the troubles of his later years is foretold in Louise's picture, which shows a genius in his prime. His eyes – which the freezing weather actually made stream – are rolled inspirationally heavenward; artistic licence enables Louise to show his fingers scurrying over the keyboard at which he sits, though in fact they were covered in chilblains and refused to move. David was not alone in admiring the picture extravagantly. Louise sent it rolled around Ménageot's *Meleager* to the 1791 Salon,[55] and the response of the critics was ecstatic. Even Jean-Baptiste-Pierre Le Brun took up his pen in praise, writing in *Le Salon de peinture* of the portrait's flawless draughtsmanship, subtlety of tone, noble composition and sublimity of expression. The ancients, he concluded, had nothing to teach Louise.[56]

The painting in some respects recalls the earlier 'enthusiastic' picture of Hubert Robert, where the artist is shown exuding the same artistic intensity and visionary inspiration. (Labille-Guiard's picture of Robert has him looking much sprucer, wearing a top hat tilted at a rakish angle and a smart frock coat, though with his hair as undressed as in Louise's version.) It is also close to the portrait of an enthusiastic Gluck by Duplessis, now in Vienna's Kunsthistorisches Museum, but which Louise had probably seen in the 1775 Salon.[57]

Stendhal said that Ferdinand, again astutely, had shown a crucial awareness of the importance music had for the Neapolitans. Of the San Carlo opera-house he wrote:

> There is nothing in Europe, I do not say approaching it, but which can even give a remote idea of this auditorium. It is . . . a veritable

coup d'état. It attaches the people to the King more than the best law could do; the whole of Naples is drunk with patriotism. The surest way to get yourself stoned would be to find some fault with it. As soon as you mention Ferdinand: 'He rebuilt the San Carlo' [after a fire], they say – so easy is it to make the people adore you . . . Personally, when I think of the meanness and the *prudish poverty* of the republics I have seen, I feel thoroughly royalist.[58]

Along with his cultivating the *lazzaroni* (which actually led to his being called *il Re lazzarone*), this reconstruction of the San Carlo was probably the cleverest political move Ferdinand ever made. Certainly, the city had other claims to attention than its superlative opera house; but the San Carlo epitomised music, and music compensated for the barbarity and ignorance of the people and their boorish ruler.

Rousseau describes the musical glory of Naples in his *Dictionnaire de musique*. The article 'génie', almost anticipating Louise's portrait of the rapt Paisiello, asks rhetorically: 'Do you wish to know if some spark of this consuming fire has touched him [the genius]? Run, fly to Naples to hear the masterpieces of Leo, Durante, Jommelli, Pergolesi.'

True, the mania for antiquity – which Louise does not much mention in the *Souvenirs*, though she touches briefly on the excavations at Pompeii and Herculaneum[59] – led many visitors to neglect the opera; and this was at a crucial moment for music, when the followers of Pergolesi (not just Paisiello, but his rivals Cimarosa and Piccini too) were developing a more natural style, lighter in content but more melodious and harmonically richer than was current in the north. Piccini, who moved to Paris in 1776, fought a pamphlet war promoting the virtues of Neapolitan music against the supporters of the German expatriate Gluck; and the question of the relative merits of French and Italian opera divided the cultivated élite of the two countries. The sympathy evident in Louise's portrait of Paisiello perhaps suggests where her own allegiance lay.

Busy as she was, Louise ended up spending far longer in Naples than she had originally intended – six months rather than the planned six weeks. Soon after returning to Rome she met Maria Carolina by chance, triumphant at having concluded her Viennese business so satisfactorily. The outcome was predictable.

As our paths happened to cross in the crowd, she caught sight of me, came up and asked me with all imaginable grace to return to Naples to do her portrait. It was impossible for me to refuse, and I lost no time in setting off again.[60]

The commission cannot have been an easy one, but Louise rose to the challenge. Her portrait gives the Queen a dignified, almost restful majesty, not unlike the stillness she captures in the portrait of the duchesse d'Orléans. Maria Carolina has some of the familiar characteristics of Habsburg women – the heavy bust, the emphatic chin, the regal posture – but her physical deficiencies are only tactfully suggested. (The portrait of her attributed to Angelica Kauffman, now in the Museo Civico Gaetano Filangieri in Naples, is of someone much less attractive.) Louise defends both her looks and her moral character.

> The Queen of Naples, without being as pretty as her youngest sister the Queen of France, reminded me greatly of her; her face was tired, but you could still see that she had been beautiful; and her hands and arms were perfection, both in shape and in colour. This princess, of whom so much ill has been spoken and written, was affectionate by nature and very simple in her private life; her generosity was truly royal . . . she liked to relieve the misery of the poor, she never hesitated to climb to the fifth floor to help the wretched, and I know for a fact that her intervention saved from prison, and perhaps from death, a mother and four children whose father had just been declared bankrupt. And this is the so-called shrew who was calumniated under Napoleon in Paris with the most infamous and obscene engravings.[61]

A later generation has learnt to be more cynical about royal charity, and sceptical about alleged royal simplicity. But even in her own day, as Louise herself suggests, Maria Carolina had a mixed press. Henry Swinburne wrote that there was something very disagreeable about the way she spoke, and the way she moved her whole face *as* she spoke; her voice was hoarse, he added, and her eyes goggled, but he conceded that she had beautiful hands.[62] Others called her a Messalina, possessed of the same lubricious desires and vices as Marie-Antoinette, and even more impure than Catherine de' Medici.[63] Napoleon loathed her, and she him.

She was convinced that she had been born to rule, unsurprisingly in view of her upbringing at the Austrian court; and this fact must have made her marriage to Ferdinand less completely dismaying to her than it had originally appeared. Her influence over her husband was considerable – according to Louise, 'she alone carried the burden of government'.[64] She tolerated his deficiencies, and he apparently grew to love her.

Given her charity towards the poor, she did not like being reminded of Marie-Antoinette's contribution to the French treasury's deficit. Political and personal pressures on her accumulated over the years, and the baronne du Montet was shocked by her appearance in 1814, just before Ferdinand's restoration:

> I cannot find words to describe the impression which seeing the Queen of Naples made on me . . . How slumped and aged she is! All the vicissitudes of fate seem to have weighed down on her: her head is bent and grown white under this heavy crown.[65]

Louise still treasured their friendship, and kept Maria Carolina's present of a lacquer box (a supplement to the 'magnificent' fee she had been paid)[66] until she died.

However generally dissatisfied she was with the artistic quality of the work Louise did in Italy, some of the sitters she acquired succeeded in consoling her. It must have been particularly gratifying to be sought out when she returned to Rome by *Mesdames Tantes* (who had a mania for being painted), because their titular portraitist before their emigration from France – after Louis XVI approved the civil constitution of the clergy – had been Labille-Guiard.

One wonders why they should have turned to Louise with such apparent eagerness. The straightforward answer is that they had left Labille-Guiard back in France: she sympathised with the revolutionary ideals, and was never inclined to follow Louise into exile despite the hardness of the times and, at least initially, the virtual drying-up of commissions. Gradually, Louise's 'rival' acquired a new clientele, painting various portraits of députés of the Assemblée constituante who, like her, favoured a constitutional monarchy. Her apparent radicalism was not necessarily offensive to the King's aunts, since they disapproved of Marie-Antoinette's extravagance and Louis XVI's weakness. By the same token, of course, they might have looked askance at a painter who, like Louise, had so manifestly tried to glorify the Queen and who was so indelibly associated with her name. And they may have been aware of the common critical reaction to the exhibiting at the 1787 Salon of Labille-Guiard's portrait of Madame Adélaïde together with Louise's monumental picture of Marie-Antoinette with her children. The former was generally seen as a polemic on the virtues of antiquity, allegedly embodied by the court of Louis XV, and was said by commentators like Bachaumont to please real connoisseurs more; the latter looked forward, not back, and in some respects enshrined the new frivolity which Louise was occasionally accused of exalting. So to stern traditionalists it was clear where the moral and artistic preference should lie.[67]

But Louise had a glittering reputation, and still represented *ancien régime* values which the aunts held dear. Besides, she was once again a presence at the splendid Bernis salon, and *Mesdames Tantes* were Bernis's guests until they left Rome in 1796. It would have been hard for Louise to make these stolid, elderly women glitter themselves, and wisely she did not try. Rather, she presented moving and dignified images that mingled firm resolution and hope with a degree of resignation. They are, on the whole, emphatic portraits, and perhaps underplay the political naïvety of the aunts. Louise states that the sittings with Madame Victoire coincided with the royal family's flight from Paris in June 1791[68] – the episode in which Louis left the Tuileries at dead of night with his family and travelled incognito across his kingdom in a heavily curtained coach, only to be recognised at Varennes-en-Argonnes and returned to the capital – but they must actually have occurred later. Whatever the case, the aunt's response to the news was touchingly optimistic:

> This princess, at our last sitting, said to me: 'I have received some news which fills me with joy; for I have learnt that the King has succeeded in leaving France, and I have just written to him with the simple address: To His Majesty the King of France. They will know how to find him,' she added with a smile.

But such rejoicings were premature, Louise continues:

> that evening we heard my manservant, a very morose man who never sang, singing; since we knew him to be a revolutionary, we instantly said to ourselves, 'Some misfortune has befallen the King!' This was only too cruelly confirmed the next day, when we heard of his arrest at Varennes and return to Paris. Most of our servants were paid by the Jacobins to spy on us, which explains why they were better informed than we were about everything that was happening in France ...

Louise left Rome on 14 April 1792, intending to make her way back to France. She had begun the portrait of Emma Hamilton as sibyl, a work she rated so highly partly because she believed it showed her skills as a history painter rather than a mere portraitist, and which she would display to admiring onlookers in Vienna, Russia, Germany and England. This exceptional picture is probably chiefly modelled on a sibyl by Reni which is now in a private collection in London (but in the 1790s was located in Florence) rather than on one of the Cumaean sibyls of Domenichino, as has usually been suggested. It also shows what was of Louise's own time in the manner of the painting – though when she let some young painters in Parma see it, on her return trip to that city, they complimented her by suggesting otherwise.

All of them expressed a surprise which was far more flattering to me than the most gracious words would have been; several exclaimed that they had believed the picture to be the work of one of the masters of their school [i.e. the Bolognese], and one of them threw himself at my feet with tears in his eyes. I was all the more touched, all the more delighted by his testimony as my sibyl has always been one of my favourite works. If my readers, hearing this story, accuse me of vanity, I beg them to reflect that an artist works all his or her life to have two or three moments equalling the one I have described.[69]

But the lush sensibility of the portrayal, the slightly simpering look, the faintly bogus expression of rapture, are eighteenth-century, though they may simply reflect the sitter's vapid personality. (It was apropos of this sitting that Louise remarked on Emma Hamilton's lack of wit and *tournure*, style.) The portrait of Paisiello translates an almost exactly similar look of enthusiasm, head turned to the left and eyes upwardly rolled, but the effect is quite different. As a fount of divine inspiration, Lady Hamilton altogether fails to carry conviction: in some respects her closest resemblance is to the subject of one of Greuze's insipid *têtes d'expression*.

The claim by Roman journals that Louise had left Rome – whether before or after her second Naples trip – to join Calonne in London is, on the face of it, incomprehensible. She was seemingly intent, in April 1792, on returning to France, whether or not she was (or had ever been) sexually involved with Calonne; and her memoirs admit to no English trip before 1803. But the allegation perhaps suggests a significant shift in the way she was publicly regarded by the Italians. Louise herself gives no hint that she might have begun to feel uneasy in the city:

> As I climbed into the carriage, I was weeping bitterly. I envied the fate of all those who were staying behind, and once on the road I could not see a traveller go by without exclaiming: 'They are so lucky – they are going to Rome!'[70]

By the time of her final return from Naples, though, the political climate had changed from what it had been at the end of 1789; and *émigrés* – particularly artists who professed revolutionary views, like the members of the *jacobinière* from which Louise distanced herself – were much less welcome.[71] Besides, whatever their political persuasion, most refugees came to be seen as a drain on Rome's resources. Having arrived in Italy with next to nothing, they needed food, work, clothes and lodgings, and the Romans found that they even had to contribute towards the visitors' medical expenses. Louise, of course, paid her way, but she could not avoid being tarred with the same brush as her fellow-countrymen. Certainly attitudes had altered since d'Espinchal reported on the warmth of her initial reception:

> Madame Le Brun's reputation as an artist in Rome is greater than one had believed possible before she arrived. Her amiableness, her agreeable talents, her charming bearing, her pure and pronounced sentiments, the horror she expresses at the ingratitude of her colleagues [at the French Academy], everything conspires to make her sought-after in the best circles and treated with consideration.[73]

Whether or not Louise was beginning to feel hunted, she was still determined to enjoy Italy. She resumed her own Grand Tour through Florence, Siena, Parma and Mantua, but with her sights firmly set on Venice. However, when she eventually got there the city surprised her as much as it charmed her.

The modern reader may be surprised by the lack of enthusiasm so many eighteenth-century travellers express for the city. Winckelmann's experience was disappointing. 'Venice is a place which at first sight transports you but where you lose your initial admiration . . . at least, that is what I found.'[74] And again: 'Venice is a place which failed to please me.'[75] One wonders what had gone wrong. Perhaps his dislike stemmed from the city's atmosphere of poetry rather than (Roman) grandeur, or perhaps its delicate melancholy struck him as sickly and decadent. Rousseau, who was there in 1743, a dozen years before Winckelmann, devotes some indifferent pages to it in the *Confessions*. Writing nearly half a century later, Arthur Young – still seemingly obsessed with geometric regularity – is no more fulsome:

> The city, in general, has some beautiful features, but does not equal the idea I had formed of it from the pictures of Canaletti [*sic*] . . . There is not that species of magnificence which results from uniformity, nor from the uninterrupted succession of considerable edifices.[76]

Mrs Piozzi found it the reverse of melancholy:

> these dear Venetians have no notion of sleep being necessary to their existence, I believe, as some or other of them seem constantly in motion; and there is really no hour of the four and twenty in which the town seems perfectly still and quiet . . .[77]

Chateaubriand, though, simply called it against nature.[78] Germaine de Staël thought it more surprising than attractive, like Louise, and felt that it mostly inspired sadness.[79]

In other words, Venice had not yet become the unique paradise immortalised by Byron, Musset and George Sand. Louise seems to have been more impressed by its *originality* than anything else. Her spirits were lifted by meeting Vivant Denon, whom she had known in Paris and who called on her as soon as he heard of her arrival. At this time Denon was the reigning 'Diplomat of the Arts' in the city (under Napoleon he would become Director of the Imperial Museums and a baron of the Empire), but he had already enjoyed a thoroughly cosmopolitan career.[80] He had served at the French embassy in St Petersburg before being expelled from Russia by Catherine II for a minor social misdemeanour, then moved in 1776 to a diplomatic post in Naples, where he also engaged in archaeological work. He collaborated with Saint-Non on the *Voyage pittoresque de Naples*, but fell out with him. After being relieved of his diplomatic duties in 1785 he moved to Rome, went back to Paris – where he resigned from the diplomatic service – and in 1788 returned to Italy. He lived happily in Venice until the city expelled all foreign nationals; thereupon he proceeded to Florence, Bologna and Switzerland, before repairing to Paris in December 1793.

He proved to be just what Louise needed.

> His wit and his extensive knowledge of the arts made him the most agreeable *cicerone*, and I was delighted at this happy encounter . . . for it gave me as a guide one of our most pleasant Frenchmen – not, though, in terms of looks, for even as a young man Monsieur Denon was always fairly ugly, which did not apparently stop him attracting a great number of pretty women.[81]

Actually, he functioned as her *cicisbeo* as well as 'sightsman' (Evelyn's term): his mistress Isabella Marini assured Louise that such a companion was essential in Venice. However independent-minded she was, Louise was surprised to be taken to a café by Signora Marini,

> but I was even more taken aback when she said to me: 'Have you no male friend to accompany you?' I replied that I had come alone with my daughter and her governess. 'Well,' she continued, 'You must at least give the appearance of having someone; I shall lend you Monsieur Denon, who will take your arm, and I shall take someone else's arm; people will think we have fallen out, and it

136

will last for as long as you stay here; for you cannot go around without a man friend.'[82]

D'Espinchal confirms the importance of the *cavaliere servente* to a woman.

It is absolutely necessary in Venice. Two women would not dare to go out alone together, and one never meets any who have not at least the arm of a man . . . This continual assiduousness has put an end to every kind of gallantry, and one cannot give the name of 'favour' to what a woman gives or allows to be taken with facility, out of idleness or because of some obsession. A lady of the nobility cannot have a *cavaliere* except from her own class . . .[83]

Isabella Marini could afford to be generous with the mildly flirtatious Denon, who adored her. Louise calls her 'amiable and witty', 'pretty' and possessed of 'infinite expressiveness'.[84] A celebrated society hostess, she had enormous seductiveness, a highly cultivated intelligence and a supple oriental grace. She later married *en deuxièmes noces* the State Inquisitor, Count Albrizzi, and her salon was frequented by Canova, Madame de Staël, Chateaubriand and Stendhal. Byron called her 'la Staël italiana', but she was far more lovely; she was also learned, and wrote a book on Canova.

Vivant Denon wanted a portrait of her, and Louise obliged. The picture deservedly caused a sensation: it is a warm, intimate work, showing a woman whose voluptuousness is no less marked for being, unlike Emma Hamilton's, *pétillante* and alert. But it is also a study for a lover, and unabashedly depicts the woman's generous lips and part-exposed breast. Denon was so captivated that the same year he published *L'Originale e il ritratto*, a collection of poems dedicated to Isabella Marini prefaced by a short biography of the artist which Denon himself had written, and containing his etchings of both the sitter and her portrait. The biographical sketch comments on the 'Grecian delicacy', 'Italian passion' and 'French amiableness' which Louise found in Isabella Marini's face and translated onto her canvas, and adds that the artist has succeeded in conveying an essence which words alone could never have captured.[85]

Louise lost a large sum of money in Venice. She deposited her Roman and Neapolitan earnings there, and then failed to withdraw them at a politically opportune moment. This mishap gave rise to predictable complaints about her poverty, but it did not blight her subsequent recollections of the city. 'Venice is still well worth seeing,' she rather mechanically wrote, 'and I am charmed to have seen it.'[86] As much as anything, though, she had enjoyed *listening* in the city: hearing music was the essential pleasure it had always been from the days of her Paris salon. A reference to the wonderful singing of some girls makes one wonder whether she had read, and was unconsciously echoing, Rousseau's *Confessions*. This is Louise's description:

> no music equals that which I heard in Venice in a church. It was performed by young girls, and what they sang – so simple and harmonious, and sung by such beautiful, fresh voices – seemed truly celestial; these girls were standing on raised platforms, behind grilles; one could not see them at all, so that the music seemed to come from heaven, and to be sung by angels.[87]

Rousseau's story, in book VII of the *Confessions*, is more pointed. One of his greatest pleasures in Venice, he writes, was to listen to choirs of girls singing motets in the churches of the great *scuole*, also on platforms and behind grilles:

> I can imagine nothing more voluptuous, more touching than this music: the richness of the art, the exquisite taste of the singing, the beauty of the voices, the precision of the performance, everything in these delicious concerts contributes to produce an impression which is certainly not in accordance with the dignity of the place, but which no man's heart could resist.[88]

But at the church of the Mendicanti he was particularly provoked: 'What frustrated me was these accursed grilles, which let only the sounds through, and hid from me the angels of beauty of whom they were worthy.' So he arranged to be introduced to the girls privately.

> Going into the salon where these coveted beauties were to be found, I felt a shudder of love I have never experienced before. Monsieur Le Blond [the French Consul] presented these famous singers to me, one after another: all I knew were their names and voices. 'Come here, Sophie' . . . she was hideous. 'Come, Cattina' . . . she was one-eyed, 'Come, Bettina' . . . smallpox had disfigured her. There was barely one without some striking fault. The torturer laughed at my cruel surprise. Two or three, however, seemed passable, but they only sang in the choruses. I was desolate. During tea they were teased and cheered up. Ugliness does not exclude grace, and I could see they possessed it. I said to myself: 'no one sings like that without possessing a soul: they have

one.' In short, my way of seeing them changed so completely that I left almost in love with these ugly ducklings. I hardly dared return to their vespers. But I found consolation awaited me there. I continued to find their singing delicious, and their voices so embellished their faces that, for as long as they sang, I remained stubbornly determined to find them beautiful despite the evidence of my eyes.

Rousseau is the better writer, and makes an appealingly self-mocking anecdote out of his experience. But all he is really doing is applying the same vivid imagination as Louise does in a great many of her female portraits, from Marie-Antoinette downwards. The artist transforms a possibly ungrateful reality so that, like the ordinary-looking branch left in Stendhal's salt-mine,[89] it is crystallised into beauty. For both Louise and Rousseau, this crystallisation starts in the mind; then artistic impulse takes over, and a heavy Habsburg face is lightened, or the ugly Sophie or Cattina becomes surpassingly beautiful.

Reaching Turin via Vicenza, Padua and Verona, Louise initially felt happy. But events were about to take a sickening turn, and she was much farther from returning to France than she had imagined. The *Souvenirs* introduce another of the turning-points with which Louise varies the pace and increases the drama of her narrative. She was blissful, she writes, enjoying a bucolic idyll in the isolation of Porporati's farmhouse:

> Alas! it was in this peaceful situation, in this happy frame of mind, that the most cruel of blows struck me. The cart which brought letters had arrived one evening, and the carter gave me one from my friend Monsieur Rivière, my sister-in-law's brother, which informed me of the dreadful events of 10 August, and gave me appalling details of them. [On 10 August 1792 an armed mob invaded the Tuileries, which had been deserted by most of the Garde nationale. Nine hundred Swiss guards, who had been inactive during the Revolution, attempted to defend the palace with a few hundred courtiers, and sixty of their number were massacred.] I was shattered; this beautiful sky, this beautiful countryside became covered in my eyes with a pall of darkness. I reproached myself for the extreme peacefulness, the sweet pleasures I had just been enjoying; besides, in the anguish I was feeling solitude became unbearable to me, and I resolved to return immediately to Turin.[90]

But this did nothing to comfort her, for Turin was overflowing with French *émigrés*, most of them destitute. Nor was her personal situation as secure as she had supposed, for unknown to her her own name had been added to the list of *émigrés*. (It would be removed in 1800, but Louise chose not to return to France until 1802.) Her house in the rue du Gros-Chenet was scheduled to be confiscated, too, a crowning irony being that Etienne Vigée was, from 1775 to 1799, a member of the body responsible for selling off *émigré* property. But Jean-Baptiste-Pierre Le Brun had been prudent enough to register the house in his name, and to secure his divorce from Louise, so it was actually safe.

The shock Louise sustained had been sharpened, of course, by her determination to block out the world of Revolutionary politics from her life – moving out of the *jacobinière* of the French Academy, cultivating and being cultivated by bastions and supporters of the *ancien régime*, never reading the press. At times of strain her instinct was often to cocoon herself inside an impenetrable blanket of immobility. Her melancholia was itself a kind of insulation, because it directed her towards solitude as Madame du Deffand's had done. But she always, at moments of great bleakness, had one or the other of two crucial resorts, friends and travel. Up to now, travel had effectively distanced her from the place and occasion of threat, but she was temporarily at a loss to see how it could continue to do so. There seemed to be no alternative for the present to staying near Turin, which is what she did.

The second resort is more difficult to evaluate. Auguste Rivière's place in Louise's life is shadowy, but he clearly became an essential prop to her. What had brought him on the tail of his letter to Turin? We do not know; perhaps it was simply an obvious refuge from the horrors of bloody revolution. He must have been a very close friend to live with Louise and her household in the solitude of the small house she rented on the banks of the Po, as he would later share her isolation in the prince de Ligne's mountain eyrie above Vienna. But she never speaks of him in terms suggesting anything more than affection, and we should probably assume that her air of detachment conceals nothing. Certainly, they were partners – in travel (he would travel over Europe with her for the next nine years, more as an intendedly reassuring male presence than as another *cavaliere servente*) and in art, for Rivière was an accomplished painter who did oil miniatures of her portraits and helped her with landscape backgrounds to many of her works. But he eventually married the illegitimate daughter of Count Golovin, whose estranged wife Louise would paint in Moscow, and his relationship with Louise seems to have been platonic. He appears not yet to have begun his diplomatic career, but later on he became the Hessian ambassador to Paris and St Petersburg.

Having eventually moved on to Milan, Louise was persuaded by the Austrian ambassador, Count Wilczek, that Vienna should be her next port of call. The idea had much to recommend it. Vienna was an exceptionally sophisticated and cosmopolitan place, and as the home city of Marie-Antoinette it must have a sentimental attraction for Louise. She happened to meet a Polish couple, the Bystrys, who also intended to go there, and who obligingly advanced their travel plans in order to accompany Louise. She was delighted, and impressed by the Bystrys' moral character.

> It would have been impossible for me to find pleasanter travelling-companions. They showered me with attentions, and one can truthfully say that husband and wife were of a rare goodness: for instance, they took with them a poor old *émigré* priest and another young priest they had found *en route*, both of whom had just escaped the massacre at the Pont Beauvoisin . . . They cared for these two unfortunates, to whom they acted as guardian angels, like the closest friends or relatives. I was so edified by their behaviour towards these two wretched men that it attached me inexpressibly to this excellent couple, whom I saw constantly in Vienna.[91]

The scenery kept her eyes as agreeably occupied as the Bystrys' excellence did her thoughts, so she reached the Austrian capital in fine spirits.

CHAPTER SIX

THE HABSBURG COURT: 'The good city of Vienna'

On the face of it, Louise was made for Viennese society. The hand of the Habsburgs might be heavier than that of the Bourbons, and the natives less the *crème fouettée* of Europe – as the French were popularly called – than the clotted cream; but their weightiness was leavened in various ways. Germanic seriousness, for example, was tempered by the dash (some said the flightiness) of the Polish residents, many of whom inhabited splendid palaces in the *Innenstadt*. For Louise, they seemed to provide a breath of French air. Then there was the conviviality of the Viennese, their love of music and civilised pleasures, and their cultivation of salon life. And however grand the aristocracy – grand enough, certainly, to seem to offer rich pickings to a society portraitist – it was open and approachable too, less proud and less exclusive than the French. So it seemed more than likely that Louise would gain an entrée to the kind of world she understood and needed.

Admittedly, Vienna was a less splendid place than Versailles, and its palaces (with the exception of Schönbrunn) were rather second-rate. The accompaniments to elegant living which Louise had come to associate with court life were less select than she had known – the plate less splendid, the furniture less good, the china less fine. There was a more workaday seriousness to the place, particularly marked since the reign of Emperor Joseph II (who died in 1790): his concerns had been with practical achievements like weakening the power of the nobility over peasants and improving education and poor relief, rather than with empty ceremony.

It was probably as well that Louise was so determinedly apolitical; otherwise she might have wondered whether her welcome would be quite as fulsome as Wilczek had suggested. If her past position as portraitist to Marie-Antoinette, the late Emperors Joseph and Leopold's younger sister, was in her favour, the same was not true of her present position as *émigrée*. The new Emperor, Francis II (who had succeeded Leopold on the latter's untimely death in 1792), was known to mistrust the French. The

142

Austrian court might theoretically have been well disposed towards a nation of which *l'Autrichienne* was still queen (however precariously), but France and Austria had been at war with each other since 20 April 1792: the new political leaders in France had been troubled by the Austro-Prussian alliance concluded earlier that year, and elected to try to unite the nation by striking down the enemy abroad. It might have been thought that the heads of state in a war-torn Europe would rally to the cause of defending a besieged monarch in France, but Austria, like Prussia, was reluctant to attempt saving Louis XVI without more allied support. So Louise was prudent in continuing to stress the artistic, not political, origin of her self-imposed exile.

However widely French was spoken in Vienna, various antagonisms towards the French nation persisted, mostly connected with old territorial disputes and the infuriating French assumption of social superiority to everyone. This is possibly why Louise, who painted many members of the aristocracy, was never asked to do portraits of the ruling dynasty or the statesmen most closely associated with it. The imperial family reserved their favours for artists like Lampi, and the old potentate Prince Kaunitz – avowedly a great Francophile – invited her to his grand dinners, fêted her, but never sat to her. Perhaps, too, the memory of Maria Theresa's disapproval of the 'actressy' court portrait of Marie-Antoinette lingered.

It was certainly true that to be French was no longer a passport that opened all doors. According to the baronne du Montet, the support which many *émigrés* had hoped for simply failed to materialise, and they encountered the shock of indifference or rejection:

> by an oddity very common then among the great Austrian nobility, these great lords, so truly lords, and very lofty, were almost all friends of the French Revolution and hated the *émigrés* and the French nobility. I think that it can only be explained as a consequence of long-standing national rancour.[1]

Emperor Leopold had disliked the *émigrés*, regarded the doings of the French princes after their flight from France as insignificant, and had no time for Calonne. If his sister was in France, France itself was not his sister. Yet the comte de Vaudreuil, writing from the Austrian capital to Louis XVI's brother Artois in April 1792, had been keenly aware of Vienna's influence on his nation's fate: 'I keep returning to the same truth, possibly distasteful but incontestable . . . that despite the concern of other courts, even Russia, the Viennese is the centre on which everything focuses, and it is from here that our salvation or destruction will issue.'[2]

Leopold's *words* had been reassuring enough, but he had constantly deceived the French princes and never had any intention of doing anything for them. When Monsieur de Gallo, the Neapolitan ambassador to Vienna, let the Emperor know of his astonishment at the ways in which he was committing himself, the Emperor replied: 'So you believe all that?'

The perceived need to preserve the established order throughout Europe, in other words, which had led to the declaration of solidarity against the onslaught of French republicanism, was always likely to yield to the imperatives of enlightened self-interest. So, after Leopold, Francis II happily passed laws restricting the entry of *émigrés* into imperial territory, despite mistrusting the forces that had brought about the Revolution.[3] The general climate of constraint which developed under Francis lasted half a century, and created a systematic repression symbolised by the name of Metternich, the future foreign minister, whom Louise describes meeting in Vienna as a very young and very handsome man.[4]

The antagonism regularly aroused in the serious-minded by the fecklessness of the *émigrés* could not possibly be provoked by a working artist like Louise, who never subscribed to the ethos of the *joyeuse émigration*. At any rate, she detected no lack of enthusiasm in her own welcome, or admits none to her reader. *La bonne ville de Vienne*[5] showed itself to be as reliably enthusiastic as Rome had been early on, as Naples remained, or as St Petersburg was to prove on the next stage of her travels, and gave no hint that she was anything other than a favoured daughter. Little seems to have upset Louise's sense that she was being valued in her independent right. She continued to ignore what was happening in France – the gathering force of republicanism, bolstered by the royal flight to Varennes and the popular feeling that Louis had forfeited the right to his subjects' loyalty in attempting to escape the country, and the royal family's imprisonment in a mediaeval tower in the garden of Artois's town house, the Temple, where they would remain until the King's execution in January 1793 and the Queen's nine months later. Again she decided to spare herself the shock of reading the press after opening a gazette and discovering that nine of her acquaintances had been guillotined. For all its famed cosmopolitanism, the Austrian world could still seem as hermetically sealed in the 1790s as it has occasionally appeared since, when the desire for insulation remained.

In a sense, then, Louise wanted to hide. In another, she needed to circulate. The Viennese *monde* was known for the generosity with which it welcomed artists from other societies and ranks, and Louise used the letters of introduction Wilczek had given her to gain an entrée to the world from which she could expect commissions. If some members of the nobility supported the ideals of the French Revolution, there was seemingly no real desire for the social levelling which the republicans wanted: Francis II's evident aim throughout his long reign was to preserve the status quo in every last detail, and he completely lacked Joseph's reforming zeal. But the benign paternalism which flowed from the monarch via the ruling classes did duty, in a way, for genuine equality. Louise was struck by the standard of living the lower orders seemed to enjoy, and the charity which their social superiors showed them.

> As for the common people, I have nowhere seen it with an air of such happiness and well-being, which was a constant joy to my eyes during my stay in this great city. Whether in Vienna or in the surrounding countryside, I never met a beggar; labourers, peasants, carters, all were well dressed. One sees immediately that they live under a paternal government, and that is how it truly appears; moreover, the rich Viennese families, some of whom possess colossal fortunes, spend their income in the most honourable way, and most usefully for the poor. They offer all manner of paid work, and beneficence is a virtue common to all the well-to-do classes. One of the things that most surprised me was to see, the first time I went to the theatre, several women – including the beautiful Countess Kinsky – knitting thick stockings in their boxes: I found that very strange; but once I had been told the stockings were for the poor I took pleasure ever afterwards in watching the youngest and prettiest women working in this way, particularly as they knitted at the same time as attending to other things, without even looking at their work, and at a prodigious speed.[6]

Similar philanthropic urges led Princess Lobkowitz to found the Vienna Ladies' Society, an association devoted exclusively to charitable works, and which during the Princess's lifetime led to the splendid garden court of her palace on the Ungerstrasse being regularly filled with the helpless and destitute.[7] The original example for such benevolence had been given by Maria Theresa and her son Joseph, but the wealthy families readily followed their lead.[8]

Perhaps this paternalism resembled condescension more than anything else. The great nobles, after all, made no effort to disguise the extraordinary sumptuousness of their palaces, their splendid furniture and their glorious picture collections; but they seemed to enjoy wearing old clothes and affecting a generally unassuming appearance. Some said, rather dismissively, that this was just because the very rich liked being able to move around their city incognito and live more at their ease. But it probably also reflected the example set by their rulers.

In keeping with the mood of comparative sobriety they wanted to instil in the people, Joseph II and his successors imposed restrictions on the importing of French luxury goods. This was, of course, in part a nationalistic move. Just as Napoleon would ban the import of English fabrics in order to promote French ones, so the Habsburgs were actually intent on supporting such 'native' enterprises as the Belgian cotton industry and Vienna's own silk and velvet manufactories.[9] But it is fully in accordance with Joseph's own taste for plainness – he was a man of simple and austere habits – that he should have legislated in the 1780s against the tight stays and panniers worn by Viennese women.[10] His move, a blend of the Spartan and the Rousseauist, apparently failed, but the effort would certainly have been applauded by Louise, who at about the same time was championing natural outlines and freedom from sartorial constraint. The ideological origins of Maria Theresa's objections to Louise's portrait of Marie-Antoinette in superb French court costume become clearer.

So when Louise arrived in Vienna there was all the finery one would expect of a rich and powerful empire, but an accompanying sense of moderation. The dangerous extravagance of the French court would have alarmed the Viennese, and the feeling of superiority or disapproval they betrayed to some *émigrés* stemmed partly from their conviction that they were above French frippery. If the excesses of Versailles had rubbed salt into the wounds of starving, over-taxed peasants, the show of the Habsburgs may have struck their more contented subjects as no more than the grandeur necessary in any court culture. When the imperial family appeared on ceremonial occasions weighed down with diamonds, gold, silver, embroidery and lace, it was made clear that this was an exceptional display.[11] Otherwise, it was more likely to be the non-Germanic residents who dazzled the eye. Louise reports seeing one brilliant New Year's Day parade:

> One sees a great number of Hungarians then, all dressed in an elegant costume which becomes them marvellously, given that they are generally tall and have fine figures. One of the most remarkable was Prince Esterházy; I saw him pass, riding on a richly caparisoned horse covered in a blanket scattered with diamonds. The prince's costume was of an exceptional richness, and as the sun was blazing down one's eyes were quite dazzled by such magnificence.[12]

Apart from the Hungarians, it was the Poles who impressed most, seeming to enjoy life in the Habsburg capital as they did that of St Petersburg, and evidently feeling more at home in either place than they did in Warsaw. There was nothing in their outward appearance to suggest that the repeated carving up of their country by Russia, Prussia and Austria itself concerned them unduly. Louise was particularly attracted by the women, who possessed great style. She had a large clientele (starting with Countess Bystra), and painted them with brio:[13] their beauty was striking, and so were their vigour and sense of adventure. Louise captures all three qualities in portraits like the ones of Princess Sapieha – wrongly listed in the *Souvenirs* as being of Countess Zamoyska – and Countess Kinsky. Polish women were glamorous, sociable, and above all French-seeming: as Louise remarks, they used the language as though they were native speakers.

Stability and steadfastness were Austrian traits, but some observers thought that they made young Austrian women prematurely middle-aged. Louise's Viennese portraits do not necessarily suggest as much. She did an engaging rococo study of Princess Liechtenstein shoeless, for instance, scandalising the subject's family and obliging the Prince to place the 'forgotten' slippers at the foot of the full-length portrait.[14] But perhaps she felt less free to be as dashing with them as in the Paris pictures of women like the comtesse de Cérès, or as bold with erotic suggestiveness as in the portrait of Madame Grand. Although her Austrian women possess glamour, and hence a knowing desirability, on the whole they appear content within the bounds of prescribed form.

Despite everything, they could also seem snobbish. Louise tells a revealing story about Countess von Schönfeld, whom she painted in a *maternité* reminiscent of one of her own self-portraits with Julie. This very pretty young woman, 'as fashionable as it is possible to be', was provoked when her mother gave a part in an amateur theatrical performance to an undistinguished-looking cousin: 'as I was sitting next to Madame von Schönfeld, I asked her who this man was. She replied: "He is my mother's nephew", unable to bring herself to say: "He is my cousin".[15]

If seldom this hidebound by form, Viennese women were generally agreed to be on the dull side of obedient. They also often aged badly; like many contented and unchallenged beings, they ran to fat, though rarely as mountainously as the philoprogenitive Maria Theresa;[16] and their complexions, frequently 'improved' with cosmetics from an early age, spoiled quickly.[17] Louise did not care to trace this deterioration in paint, but she suggested its underlying causes in a number of society portraits of tamely self-satisfied women. One could, it is true, take a positive view of this semi-complacent conformism, as one French observer did. For Roger de Damas,

Germanic seriousness acts as a brake on the agitation, the whirl-wind impulses which become intolerable after the age of twenty; Vienna retains only enough of them to engage the attention or distract it, and not so much as to unsettle the most agreeable of societies; the youngest women, who in Paris might have been dissipated, are restrained by habit into observing the conduct appropriate to forty-year-olds, and the gap which in Paris might exist between middle age and the age of noisy pleasures is here filled, even among foreigners, by the prescriptions of the national character, namely a gentle gaiety and a social ease in gatherings, large or small, where one can always meet with distinguished people.[18]

True-blooded Viennese women perhaps toed the line too determinedly; certainly they seem to have found adherence to the social norm no hardship.

How did Louise establish a clientele? Partly, it seems, simply by exhibiting her *Sibyl* to hordes of admirers in her studio, but also through discreet introductions. It is unclear whether her entrée to one particular salon came via Wilczek or not, but according to Louise it was crucial:

> I first of all visited Countess Thun. She immediately invited me to her soirées, where the grandest ladies of Vienna assembled, and this house would have been enough to introduce me to all the high society of the town. I found many *émigrés* from our poor France there: the duc de Richelieu, the comte de Langeron, the comtesse de Sabran and her son, the Polignac family, and later on the good, amiable comte de Vaudreuil, whom I was delighted to see again.[19]

Louise's pastel portrait of the countess has been lost, but memoirs of the period tell us much about her character and influence. Born a von Uhlfeldt, she was the mother of the future Elizabeth Razumovskaya and Princess Lichnowska, two of Louise's triumvirate of supremely beautiful Viennese women (the other being Countess Kinsky). Mozart's letters tell us how vigorously she supported music, and along with Prince Lichnowsky involved herself in his life and works.[20] The English traveller Wraxhall makes her an exception to his general rule that Viennese women are unintellectual, saying that no European capital produced a person more distinguished in natural and acquired talents, or of a more liberal mind.[21] Her house was a rendezvous for all who pretended to refinement.

Louise was particularly fascinated by the life story of the ravishing

Countess Kinsky, regularly 'la belle Kinsky' in the records of the time. It seemed as much a romance as Emma Hamilton's. She writes in her *Souvenirs*:

> Count Kinsky's parents and her own had made an arrangement to marry their children, who were quite unacquainted with each other. The Count lived in some German town, and only arrived for the celebration of the marriage. Immediately after the service he said to his young and charming wife: 'Madame, we have obeyed our parents; I leave you with regret; but I cannot disguise from you the fact that for a long time I have been attached to a woman I cannot live without, and I am going back to her.' The post-chaise was at the church door; having said his farewell, the count climbed into the coach and went back to his Dulcinea.
>
> So Countess Kinska was neither girl, nor wife, nor widow, and this oddity must have surprised anyone who looked at her; for I have never seen anyone so ravishing.[22]

The Catholic faith of husband and wife prevented their legal separation until the papal nuncio decreed that the Countess had been virtually unconscious during the wedding ceremony (because of a terrible storm), and so could not be said to have consented to the marriage.[23] It was therefore dissolved, and she was free subsequently to marry Count Meerveldt, later Austrian ambassador to London. In his *Journal d'émigration* the comte d'Espinchal reports his own young son's hopeless love for this exquisite creature, a distant and respectful passion befitting his years.[24] This was regularly the effect of the Kinsky beauty on beholders, according to the baronne de Montet: every passion she inspired was profound yet seemly, a form of religious worship.[25] The Countess possessed all virtues and womanly graces, had poise, charm, expressiveness and an indefinably imposing air. Louise's portrait of her captures this complexity, but perhaps not (any more than Angelica Kauffman's) her sheerly ravishing looks.

Her virtue emerged in various ways. Quite apart from practising the usual beneficence of Viennese women – knitting stockings at the theatre and the like – she took it upon herself to reward a selfless action on the part of Madame Charrot, Julie Le Brun's governess, who had accompanied mother and daughter into exile. When Madame Charrot expressed satisfaction at having been put on the list of *émigrés* despite the loss of a pension which it entailed, because it meant that she had joined the ranks of *honnêtes gens*, the Countess contrived to pay her such a large sum for a smock-dress she made her (identical to the admired 'blouses' Louise wore for painting) that she recovered more than a quarter of the money.[26]

Paying her respects to resident painters was the first thing Louise did on arriving in a town: establishing a clientele by way of circulating in society had to wait until she had settled her artistic dues. So early on she went to see the sixty-year-old Francesco Casanova, who had settled in Vienna after several years in Paris. She remarks that he wore two or three pairs of spectacles one on top of the other, which recalls something she proudly said at about the same time concerning her own sight. At salon gatherings where women sat embroidering, she writes,

> I was sometimes called over to give advice about contrasts and nuances; but as the thing that most hurts my eyes is to look at bright colours by lamplight or candlelight, I confess that I often offered my opinion without looking. In general, I have always cared for my sight scrupulously, and it has served me extremely well, since even now I can paint without being obliged to wear glasses.[27]

Casanova was apparently less prudent than Louise about other things too. According to her, he had earned vast sums of money, but was so improvident that there was none left.[28] She, on the other hand, was said by Vaudreuil to have earned 75,000 *livres* during her stay in Vienna, which should have established her fortune comfortably, but she lost much of it subsequently. (Vaudreuil himself received over an eight-year period 2,885,000 *livres* of annual *gratifications* for doing absolutely nothing, quite apart from the money that came to him from his largely ceremonial post of Grand Falconer.)[29]

Casanova painted the celebrated Kaunitz, to whom Louise took her letter of recommendation from Wilczek, and so enjoyed a privilege denied to Louise herself. Perhaps Casanova's reputation as a painter of battle-scenes recommended him to the old statesman, whom the prince de Ligne reports as calling himself the best rider on horseback in the world. Louise said this harmless vanity was his only fault[30] (and in any case it was presumably redeemed by the fact that he rode in the French style), though others were revolted by the prolonged teeth-cleaning operation he obliged his guests to witness at the end of each of his dinners.[31] It may also be that Kaunitz was deterred by the high prices Louise charged, but he does not seem to have been made much happier by Casanova's: he lost an argument with him about the sum proposed for four pictures he had commissioned, defeated by Casanova's observation that, balancing the money asked against a painting's merit, he never considered that enough was enough.[32]

Louise, who seems to have been unaware that Kaunitz actually detested the French at the same time as admiring their style, was eager to make his acquaintance.

> This great minister was then at least eighty-three years old; he was tall, extremely thin, and held himself very upright. He received me with perfect kindness, and engaged me to dine the next day. As one only sat down at his table at seven o'clock, and I was used to dining alone at my own house at half past two, this invitation and the others that followed it, while flattering me greatly, vexed me a little; I did not like either dining so late or dining with so many other people; for his dinners, largely made up of foreigners, were always for thirty people and often more. From that day I resolved to dine at home, which I did before even going to Prince Kaunitz's house, and which I tried to conceal as far as was possible by taking half an hour over eating a boiled egg; but this little trick, which he noticed, annoyed him; and that, together with the pains I subsequently took to evade some of his invitations, was the cause of some minor tiffs he had with me; but he soon became a firm friend, which I was most grateful to him for.[33]

In any case, much could be forgiven in a man who adopted the cause of advertising Louise's *Sibyl* as enthusiastically as Kaunitz did, insisting on displaying it in his drawing-room for over a fortnight and so promoting her in the most effective way possible. Prince von Paar did something similar, and also earned Louise's great gratitude.

> I remember, for instance, that Prince Paar, who had taken delivery of the large portrait I had just done of his sister, the charming and good Countess Bucquoi, invited me to come and see it in his house. I found the picture displayed in his drawing-room, and as the panelling was painted white, which generally kills paintings, he had arranged a broad green drapery to surround the frame completely and hang down below it. Besides that, for the evening he had had a candelabra made with several candles and a reflector positioned in such a way that all the light was focused on my portrait. I need not say how touched a painter is by this kind of gallantry.[34]

Louise must have felt confident enough in both her artistic and social persona to risk ruffling feathers in the *monde*. She knew she needed peace and daylight to be able to paint, and that, as always, meant leading a relatively restricted worldly life. Yet Vienna offered as many pleasures as pre-Revolutionary Paris – plays, concerts, balls, and civilised salon conversation in French, the lingua franca.

Not surprisingly, Louise was impressed by the musical life, and particularly remembered hearing a Haydn symphony. Haydn had returned to Vienna from London in 1792, and taken Beethoven on – rather unsuccessfully – as a pupil, before going back to London for a further year in 1794. By the time he finally settled back in the Habsburg capital in 1795, he had an international reputation. Beethoven himself lived in Vienna from 1792 until his death in 1827, though Louise never mentions him, and in the 1790s he was much in demand as a virtuoso pianist in the private houses of the nobility. Mozart had died in Vienna in December 1791, but the *Souvenirs* say nothing about him either.

The aristocrats of Vienna often held private concerts (the standard of public recitals was generally lower),[35] and Louise attended many of them. Those of Princes Lobkowitz and Galitzin and Count Andrei Razumovsky were regarded as exceptional. Razumovsky's own talents as a violinist, and his wife's discreet charms, made their gatherings exceptional, and the setting in the Razumovsky palace on the Landstrasse was sumptuous. The couple also owned a palace resembling a small town in the suburbs – Andrei, the proud and arrogant Russian ambassador, could not endure resting his eyes on any property that did not belong to him – but it was in the town house that high society assembled.[36] It did so in considerable style,[37] and the Razumovsky salon became the foremost one in Vienna after Countess Thun's death. Surrounded by fine paintings and all the trappings of luxury, the guests conversed and listened to music in an atmosphere of Asiatic magnificence tempered by European taste. Here was no place for the unkempt look Viennese nobles sometimes favoured. Dress was always formal, and hair had to be powdered (otherwise the case only at court). Louise was now beginning to like powdered hair, though she had formerly found it repugnant, because it seemed to reflect a devotion to *ancien régime* values.

Some thought that all the Viennese, irrespective of class, were inclined to dissipate themselves in idle pleasure.[38] If true, the observation hardly fits the image of Austrian seriousness promoted by Maria Theresa and many, though not all, of her children. But Habsburg solidity did not preclude fun. The *monde*'s harmless diversions were principally dancing and play-acting, and Louise enjoyed both. She describes the Razumovsky balls as 'charming fêtes', a rather docile description given the frenetic activity they apparently involved:

> People waltzed with such fury that I could not conceive how all
> these people, spinning round as they did, did not become so giddy

as to drop; but men and women alike are so used to this violent exercise that they take not a second's rest for as long as the ball lasts. People also often danced the *Polonaise*, which was much less tiring; for this dance is nothing but an amble where you walk tranquilly two by two. It suits pretty women marvellously well, because one has all the time in the world to admire their figures and faces.[39]

But waltzes were lethal. As Louise remarks, a local proverb had it that there were three causes of death in Vienna, wind, dust and waltzing.[40] (It was the other two that decided her after the Bystrys' departure for Poland to move into the *Innenstadt*.) Another witness said that this craze proved an innately violent disposition in the natives more than it did their musical ear.[41]

Louise seems to have liked painting women dancing. The portrait of Princess Sapieha performing a shawl-dance like Emma Hamilton's was said to depict an innovation. D'Allonville declares disapprovingly that the Revolution introduced this dance along with the waltz and that the public sense of decency would never have tolerated it under the *ancien régime*.[42] But it would probably be mistaken to assume that the *monde* was regularly dancing its cares away in the 1790s: there is an element of artistic convention in images such as the one Louise presents. Her liking for a temperate neo-classicism – hints of Pompeii and Roman dancing girls – and a rococo charm, in which she resembled Angelica Kauffman, made these images doubly appealing in the lightly hedonistic ambience of Vienna.

She enjoyed amateur theatricals as much as she had done in Paris, and often found her expatriate friends to be their leading lights. The frivolous comte de Langeron, who later earned Louise's contempt by supporting Bonaparte, was usually the male lead at Baroness Stroganova's private theatre, where Louise describes the performances as exceptionally fine. Auguste Rivière had obviously travelled to Vienna with Louise, though she fails to mention the fact, and he acted comic rôles with great success there. According to Louise,

> this amiable man possessed every talent, which made the painter Doyen say he was an indispensable adjunct in society. The fact is that he painted very well, and did large miniatures in oils of all my portraits; he sang very agreeably; he played the violin and double bass, and accompanied himself on the piano. He had wit, perfect tact, and such an excellent heart that despite his distractions, which were frequent and numerous, he was as zealous in obliging

his friends as he was successful at it. Monsieur Rivière was small, thin, and always so young-looking that when he was sixty his figure and bearing would have made you think him thirty.[43]

Countess von Fries, of a famous banking family, also owned an impressive private theatre, and acted character parts there. She continued acting after she left Austria for Switzerland – having fallen out with her children – and met up with Germaine de Staël, herself a famously bad actor in serious rôles. Madame de Staël's lover Benjamin Constant called the countess 'a true Andromache preserved in spirits', and Staël herself said that she possessed talent: 'but how time passes!'[44]

If the apparent French superiority at acting seemed a further pointer to their regrettable lack of Austrian *gravitas*, Louise's comments about some of her fellow-exiles in the *Souvenirs* appear to confirm it. Among the many compatriots she describes finding in Vienna, those she singles out for particular mention seem to epitomise the values she associated with her lost French world – charm, wit and *savoir-vivre*, according to one interpretation, or alternatively giddiness and empty-headedness. Langeron, a man described by himself as more superficial and lightweight than profound and serious, was one of these social ornaments. Another was the chevalier de Boufflers, whom she calls a model of gracious wit. The playwright Brifaut writes of him in his memoirs that he was a charming companion in the *monde*, a delicious poet, agreeable painter, delightful musician and celebrated adorer of women. A third was the vicomte de Ségur, a man who had a mixed press, but whom the marquise de Sabran called a brainless philosopher and a ludicrous would-be roué. The fourth, the comte de Narbonne, was – at least according to d'Espinchal – a more successful Lovelace or Valmont, but also a pleasure-seeker of such insubstantiality that he was given the name 'Linotte' (scatterbrain or birdbrain). According to others, though, he was an impressive figure, an able and charming nobleman who – with his lover Germaine de Staël's help – became minister of war at the end of 1791, and genuinely wanted to make the constitutional monarchy work. Perhaps they were not a particularly select band, however diverting they may have appeared, but Louise's nostalgia for the elegancies of her Parisian world blinded her to their character deficiencies.

If the emigrant colony could give the impression of dancing life's cares away, Louise at least was brought rudely back to earth by shattering news from Paris. Her brother, knowing how she would be affected, was as brief as possible in his letter:

He told me simply that Louis XVI and Marie-Antoinette had died on the scaffold! Ever since then, out of pity for myself I have always avoided asking the merest question about what may have accompanied or preceded this horrible murder.[48]

Obviously Etienne Vigée had tried to spare Louise's feelings as long as he could, since the King had been guillotined several months before the Queen. But one wonders how Louise could possibly have remained unaware during the intervening period of what had happened: was her enclosed adoptive world to blame, or did she simply refuse to listen to all political news, even the most world-shaking, as it was being relayed to her? She can scarcely have been an intimate at the Austrian court to have missed the reporting of such an event, and the salons she frequented must have been exceptionally insular for the guillotining of the King and Queen of France to have passed unmentioned in them (particularly when the Queen was the ruling Emperor's aunt). Louise's obliviousness remains a troubling mystery. Nothing could have induced her to find out more about Louis XVI's and Marie-Antoinette's deaths but the decision – reached in Russia – to attempt a picture showing the King and Queen 'at one of the most touching and solemn moments which must have preceded their death', a painting she in the end found it too painful to undertake.

The blow of learning at the house of Madame de Rumbeke, a society hostess, that she had lost several acquaintances to the Terror had been dreadful enough;[50] but nothing could match the horror she now felt. The fact that Louise's very next words after describing her reaction to the double regicide refer to the coming of spring means simply that she had to overlay horror with its opposite, not that she was uncaring. It might have been an occasion to trigger the paralysing melancholia that gripped her at other times of great shock or stress, but seems not to have been. This time, Louise was resilient.

The same was not true of her friend and patron Yolande de Polignac. She was physically as well as mentally devastated. The duchess had moved to the suburb of Hietzing, Louise writes,

and it was there that she learned of Louis XVI's death, which so affected her that her health suffered greatly; but when she received the dreadful news of the Queen's, she was destroyed by it. Grief transformed her, and her charming face became unrecognisable: you could foresee her imminent end. She did indeed die shortly afterwards, leaving her family and several friends who had not left her side inconsolable.[51]

Another mystery: how can Louise, a friend of the Duchess's, have been unaware of Louis XVI's execution when Yolande had clearly known about it before the guillotining of Marie-Antoinette, unless Louise had expressly censored all such reports? And how can she have remained unaware of something so obvious as a friend's profound grief when she made a living from observing and then depicting the human countenance? A possible answer is that she in fact saw very little of the Polignacs in Vienna; another, that she sealed herself off from the world with an effectiveness that almost defies belief. It all suggests an overpowering self-preoccupation, the conviction that her art and life must at all costs be spared upset. This self-obsession was to become more marked later on, but even now the evidence is that only her own artificially constructed universe counted for her. The rest of her exile would see a continued effort to transport that universe intact from one friendly country to another.

The friend left most devastated at Yolande de Polignac's death, at least to judge by appearances, was her long-time lover Vaudreuil. Though he seems fairly quickly to have found consolation in marriage to a relative of his, his correspondence tells a different story. On 6 December 1793, for instance, he writes to the marquis de Vaudreuil of his reaction to Yolande's death:

> This morning, as I woke up (for I slept out of sheer fatigue, my eyes closed with the weight of my tears), how powerfully I felt that everything was finished for me! I have nothing more to say or do or think; for the person to whom my words, actions and thoughts were addressed is no more . . . this divine soul has been reunited with her Creator, who did not want to leave her any longer on an earth that was unworthy of her, and soiled with so many crimes. You might say that the King and Queen have won from God, as a consolation for their martyrdom, the reward of being reunited with a faithful friend, who never had a bad piece of advice or a harmful action to reproach herself . . . She made up to me for everything, consoled me for everything. The loss of my fortune, of my very existence, had never troubled me at heart because I found everything in her . . . I am no longer the person who matters above all else to anybody.[52]

Crocodile tears? It is perhaps too harsh a verdict, though Vaudreuil's acting skills were celebrated. At all events, he seems to have been reduced to a state of immobility by the disaster. Louise, more practically and therapeutically, set about painting a portrait of Yolande from memory, and the comte d'Artois succeeded in galvanising Vaudreuil into sufficient activity to ensure she was paid for it.[53] It records a beauty that is still startling, if a trifle bland, and must therefore be an imaginative reconstruction of the duchess as she had appeared before the death of either King or Queen.

Louise too decided to take a house in Hietzing,[54] feeling her old urge for country air and the charms of the natural world. Not that Vienna itself lacked open spaces, even though they could not satisfy her yearning for the wild. She enthusiastically describes the Prater, a public park whose bushes were regularly patrolled by the Commission for Chastity in Maria Theresa's time in case they sheltered courting couples. Nowadays it is filled with big wheels and popular pleasures, but then it was grand enough for Francis II to visit with his wife and children (though actually they liked walking around without ceremony).[55]

> It has been said with truth that the Prater was one of the finest promenades in existence. It consists in a long and magnificent avenue where a great number of elegant coaches go to and fro, and crowds of people sit on either side, as one sees in the main avenue at the Tuileries.[56]

But though many commented on the 'savage' aspect of the place,[57] the woods to which the central avenue led were inhabited by a half-tamed herd of deer – the perfect and typical eighteenth-century compromise between domestication and the elemental. Louise was more moved by the wild expansiveness of some of the outlying parkland, however carefully its owners had actually landscaped it.

> The countryside around Vienna is in general grandiose. One particularly notices the parks of Marshal Lansdon, Marshal Lassi and Count Cobentzl. All three are superb, and in a style quite different from English parks. The latter are more uniform, flatter and consequently less picturesque. Those surrounding Vienna have natural mountains, wooded at their summits; there are deep ravines which one crosses on elegantly shaped bridges, natural rivers and glittering waterfalls which crash down from the heights.[58]

One such waterfall, set in a sublime park, is depicted with disarming unnaturalness in Louise's portrait of Countess Bucquoi. The natural world, in this picture, is a *fond*, not an organic part of the whole (as with British artists contemporary to her),[59] and its picturesqueness offsets the sitter's almost regal repose. At the same time, it is tailor-made for the purpose it is called on to serve. The outcrop of rock the Countess props her forearm on is exactly suited to accommodate the female form, and the grassy ledge on which she sits is simply nature's version of the couch. But Madame Bucquoi herself is a triumphantly unnatural presence in this bucolic world, her shimmering bronze dress and stylish red shawl as incongruous as Louise's elaborate painting costume in the 'straw hat' self-portrait. The accessories all enhance an idea of character, and on those terms the wholly unreal look of the waterfall counts for nothing.

If real country was what Louise wanted for the purpose of living, not painting, she had to leave the *Innenstadt*. Nowadays Hietzing is an imposing suburb, where eighteenth-century and earlier buildings rub shoulders with Biedermeier solidity and Adolf Loos modernism, a mixture of broad approach roads and narrow inner streets, and what must be the most imposing post office in suburban Austria. There are still links with the France Louise regretted: Cléry, Louis XVI's valet, is buried in the church-yard along with Grillparzer, Otto Wagner and Klimt. But apart from the intermittent presence of the ruling family promenading during the summer months, the real attraction of the place for Louise was its proximity to sublime and picturesque nature. On one of her walks she was much moved by the sight of the huge mountain called the Kahlenberg, but which she calls the Caltemberg. The prince de Ligne tempted her into wanting to know it better by telling her it was the biggest mountain outside Vienna, and offering her lodgings on the summit. 'I did not hesitate to yield to my desire to spend some time there,' Louise reports.[60]

Ligne's motives for offering Louise this hospitality were not entirely disinterested. Andrei Razumovsky and several of his compatriots had been urging her to pursue her post-Parisian career by moving on to St Petersburg, 'where, they assured me, the Empress would greet my arrival with extreme pleasure'. Ligne was dismayed at the thought of losing her, and tried to detain her first with warnings about the winter snows *en route*, and then with the agreeable prospect of solitude on the Kahlenberg. He was not alone in feeling saddened by Louise's plans to leave: in early January 1795 Vaudreuil wrote to the marquis de Vaudreuil of his desolation at the prospect.[61] But Ligne, in a sense, had only himself to blame. He had told Louise about his travels to the Crimea with Catherine, and made her keen to see the Empress and empire for herself, despite the length of the journey she would have to undertake. Louise also had another motive. It is true that she was loving her stay in Austria.

> I was as happy in Vienna as it is possible to be away from family and homeland. In the winter, the city offered me one of the most pleasant and brilliant societies in Europe, and when the fine weather returned I had the delightful prospect of rediscovering the charms of my little country retreat. So I had no thought of

leaving Austria before it was possible to go back to France without danger . . .[62]

But, as was her nature, she also reflected that moving to a new court environment and circulating among fabulously rich nobles would enable her to round off the fortune she had promised herself to make before returning to Paris. This was despite the fact that, as she notes in the *Souvenirs*, 'I did a great deal of work in Vienna',[63] something confirmed by Vaudreuil's comment on the amount she had earned there. She still felt a pang, too, about money that had been lost or never paid to her, and perhaps one should not blame her. By the end of 1793, for instance, she had still not received what she was owed for the picture of Marie-Antoinette with her children, allegedly because *émigrés* were ineligible for such payments (and presumably because the Republic saw no reason to pay for 'royalist' works).

So the comte d'Artois, from his German exile at Hamm, set about providing Louise with the documents she needed for her journey. On 13 February 1794, over a year before Louise's eventual departure, he sent Vaudreuil a passport for her, along with a letter of introduction for Count Esterházy.[64] He was sure, he wrote, that Louise's reception would be both kind and lucrative, and that she was awaited with impatience in the imperial capital.[65] So Ligne, it seemed, could do little but attempt to delay her departure.

Though she never painted Ligne's portrait, presumably because he could not afford to have it done, their pleasure in each other's company was enduring. She calls him 'amiable',[66] but some verses of Langeron's which she quotes make him sound highly attractive to women, as well as a steadfast friend and brave soldier.[67] This Belgian was called the 'last of the French knights',[68] and was a devoted Francophile. Madame de Staël said of him that 'He is perhaps the only foreigner who has become a model of the French manner, instead of an imitation.' And elsewhere: 'Men, things, events have passed in front of the prince de Ligne; he has judged them without wanting to impose on them the despotism of a system, knowing how to be natural about everything.'[69] Louise called this naturalness one of the principal charms of Ligne's mind.

> His brilliant imagination, his subtle and penetrating observations about everything, the *bons mots* he constantly came up with, and which immediately ran the length and breadth of Europe, nothing had given the prince de Ligne the least desire to make himself heard; his manners and talk remained so simple that a fool could have believed him an ordinary man . . .

His generosity and insouciance about money, she writes – without reflecting on what Ligne might have thought about her own materialistic urges – made him a noble figure:

> not only did his extreme liberality constantly draw him into enormous expenditure without his ever deigning to count the cost, but when I met him again in Vienna, he arrived at Madame de Rumbeke's house one evening to tell us that the French had just seized all the property he possessed in Flanders, and seemed very little affected by the news: 'I have only two *louis* left,' he said: 'who will pay my debts?'[70]

He was more than welcoming to the French *émigrés*, who flocked to his house (called the Parrot-House, perhaps because of its pink colour) on the Mölkenbastei; every visitor noted the perfection of the French spoken there.[71] In Ligne's view only his *émigré* guests understood how to converse, an art of which Austrians were wholly ignorant.

However dispossessed in Belgium, Ligne was in 1791 the owner of two isolated monk's cells on the Kahlenberg, and rented two more. Ten years previously Joseph II had decided to dissolve the order of Camaldoli monks, which had an outpost on top of the mountain, because it did nothing useful – ran no schools, never tended the sick, but simply pursued the contemplative life.[72] (Joseph closed hundreds of monasteries and used their funds for good causes.) Louise thought that the religious generally were wise to lodge themselves at immense heights: 'deprived of worldly pleasures, they may at least taste the charm one experiences breathing pure air and contemplating grandiose nature'.[73] So when the monastery was closed in 1782 it seemed natural that those who had similar tastes should take the cells over. Actually Ligne was too convivial a soul to want total isolation for himself, as Louise reports.

> The great halls of the monastery had remained structurally intact; since then the prince had had them repaired and furnished so he could hold splendid receptions there. The balls lasted part of the night, the women guests remained fully dressed and went to bed on the couches which ran round the walls of these vast drawing-rooms. Personally, the Caltemberg appealed to me far more as it was when I lived there than at the time all these festivities occurred.

The faithful Rivière, who went up the mountain with Louise, Julie and Madame Charrot, was more of a city-lover, and during their three-week stay often had to leave the mountain for urban relief. But Louise loved it:

I was enchanted at being there; I preferred the cell I was about to inhabit to all the salons in the world, and I blessed the good prince de Ligne, heartily regretting the fact that he was not there to witness my happiness.

To get there, the party climbed the 'horrible rocky path' which led to the monastery (and which Ligne subsequently improved). The modern-day visitor to the Kahlenberg will incidentally find in this feat confirmation, if that were needed, of Louise's exceptional robustness, for however improved, the route remains tortuous, precipitous and very long.

Whatever the sufferings imposed by the journey, and the deprivations of life in a monkish cell, Louise loved this last Viennese adventure. If today the air is less pure, and the skyline spoilt by modern high-rise architecture, at that time one looked down from the heights onto what Louise describes as grandiose nature. While their rooms were being prepared,

I went and rested on a bench, from which one had a magnificent view. I hovered above the Danube, its course interrupted by islands embellished with the most beautiful vegetation, and gazed down on rolling countryside as far as the eye could see; in short, it was immensity . . . I quickly recovered from my fatigue, and soon hurried over to the other side of the mountain, where, from the edge of a wood, I saw in the background a very populous village, crossed by a calm, limpid little river . . .

Sublime wildness on the one hand, and bucolic domesticity on the other: both seemed the perfect antidote to the gloss of civilisation.

Ligne's verses on her weeks in his eyrie are characteristically bad, but at least have the merit of marking society's dismay at Louise's disappearance and his own pride in having prolonged her stay on Austrian soil:

> *Pour avoir fait à l'empyrée*
> *Le même vol que Prométhée,*
> *Vous méritez punition . . .*
> *Oubliez votre nation,*
> *Par votre génie honorée,*
> *Mais à présent, pays de désolation!*
> *Que ma montagne fortunée*
> *Par la fière possession*
> *Des talents dont la terre est ravie, étonnée,*
> *Soit par nos chants à jamais célébrée!*[74]

But this hermitic absence seems simply to have fuelled her ever-present sense of adventure. People might want her to stay, but it was not her habit to put the claims of friendship above those of professional self-advancement and the prospect of new lands to conquer. Louise was in many ways a likeable woman and trusted friend, but she was also a driven artist and a businesswoman. So on 19 April 1795, after a two-and-a-half-year stay in Vienna, she set off with her daughter, Madame Charrot and Auguste Rivière to renew herself and her clientele in a fresh environment.

CHAPTER SEVEN

CATHERINE THE GREAT AND ST PETERSBURG:
'I am charmed, Madame'

Increasing her fortune was not such an urgent preoccupation that Louise felt she had to hurry to St Petersburg. She spent three months on the journey, stopping in Prague, Dresden and Berlin: it was partly the desire to look at artistic treasures that slowed her down, but partly too her anxiety to preserve her royal connections.

In Berlin she felt the ghost of Frederick the Great, and knew that she had to stop at his younger brother Henry's palace, Rheinsberg, twenty leagues away. Having retired from the army, this warrior-prince spent thirty years at Rheinsberg cultivating the arts, and Louise found him a highly agreeable man. On first meeting him at the marquise de Sabran's house in Paris she had been repelled by his appearance, though.

> I cannot describe how ugly I found him. He must have been about fifty-five at that time, the King of Prussia being much older than he was. He was small and thin, and his figure, despite the uprightness of his posture, had no nobility about it. He had retained a very heavy German accent, and had an excessively guttural pronunciation. As for the ugliness of his face, at first glance it was utterly revolting. But despite his two big eyes, one of them pointing to the right and the other to the left, his gaze still had something gentle about it, which one also noticed in the sound of his voice; and since when one listened to him his words were always extremely obliging, one grew used to looking at him.[1]

Louise's portrait, predictably enough, tactfully improved the prince's looks. Henry was an ardent Francophile, and at Rheinsberg he had a troupe of French actors who performed some comedies during Louise's stay. But she must have been less charmed by the fact that he seemed to find even the recent political events in France praiseworthy, bent as he was on approving everything about her native country.

It was perhaps as well that Henry sent her on her way with enough food to feed a Prussian regiment, for the rest of the journey was appalling. The route was picturesque enough:

> The small towns we passed through are very well built; most of the countryside is fertile; but the sandy road was tedious beyond expression. We could only travel one post in seven hours, which often forced me to walk during the night.[2]

Far from getting better, the road became more dreadful. Day and night she and her party walked in horrible sands, the road running so close to the river Halle that half their carriage was tilting into it. Finally they arrived in Riga, and rested there for several days while waiting for their passports to St Petersburg. The approach to the capital was pretty, delightful rather than magnificent, and the air of domesticity seems to have been reassuring.

> I entered St Petersburg on 25 July 1795 by the Peterhof road, which gave me a favourable impression of the city; for this road is lined on both sides with charming country houses surrounded by the most tasteful gardens, in the English style. The inhabitants have taken advantage of the terrain, which is very marshy, to adorn these gardens, where there are kiosks and pretty rising ground, with canals and little rivers which criss-cross them.[3]

The magnificence of the imperial city contrasted completely with this village-like landscape. Much broader canals traversed the interior of St Petersburg, great granite constructions built by Catherine II to match the granite of the River Neva's quays. Louise was soothed as well as captivated by the sight of ships and barges, as she would be when she stayed in Bordeaux many years later. The grandeur of the architecture, massively immobile against this shifting scene, made her feel as though she had been transported to the time of Agamemnon. (Her knowledge of classical antiquity was never exact.) People told her that there was nothing more beautiful than the sight of these temple-like edifices by moonlight, but that was something she could not immediately judge for herself. She had arrived in the city during the 'white nights' of St Petersburg, when

> the sun sets at about half past ten at night; the mist lasts until dawn, which begins at about half past midnight, so that you can always see light, and I have often supped at eleven with the daybreak.[4]

Louise was forty years old when she arrived in Russia, apparently still eager for new experiences. What the country would offer her was strangeness tempered with familiarity, and she found the mixture satisfying enough to want to stay there for six years. As an artist, she needed – within very strict limitations – to have her world 'defamiliarised' in order to receive fresh stimulus. Russia would be glamorous and exciting in a way Vienna had not always been, and as Paris would no longer be on her eventual return. To see with fresh eyes, she had to undergo a degree of culture-shock. It must not be too extreme, but it must be sharp enough to renew her. Louise was never entirely happy being wedded to routine, either in painting or in life, however much she disliked certain kinds of change. Or, rather, she wanted change when it was relative and governable, wholly subject to her individual whim, not when its momentum made her lose her bearings. The portraits she did quickly and to order rarely satisfied her; as an artist she longed to stretch her wings, just as in life she relished new challenges. Perhaps it had been this essential adventurousness as much as her desire to increase her fortune that had led her to leave Austria.

A mixture of the known and the unknown was exactly what St Petersburg and its society represented. Comte Philippe de Ségur, who left his post as French ambassador to Russia soon after the fall of the Bastille, said that the city united barbarity and civilisation, the tenth and the eighteenth centuries, Scythian uncouthness and Parisian *politesse*.

> On the one hand elegant fashions, magnificent dress, sumptuous meals, splendid festivities, theatres like those which adorn and animate the select societies of Paris and London; on the other merchants in Asiatic costume, coachmen, servants, peasants dressed in sheepskin, and with flowing beards, fur hats, long hide mittens and axes hanging from broad leather belts.[5]

Louise's first impressions confirmed this view. St Petersburg seemed to her both ancient and modern. The city which Peter the Great had built and populated by force, a mirage rising from the marshes, held little attraction for Russians whose instincts were traditionalist; for them, Moscow remained the rightful centre of the empire.[6] But Peter's edicts, which had compelled noble families as well as traders and merchants to migrate to the new capital, ensured that Western influences continued to predominate. During the last years of Catherine's reign, and when her son Paul succeeded her, St Petersburg was famed as one of the most beautiful capitals in Europe, an extraordinary baroque complex of waterways, bridges, cathedrals and palaces, outwardly splendid and inwardly luxurious. When

Paul's dictatorial regulations came into force, it deteriorated into the type of a German provincial town (though still one of stunning visual grace), which is probably what Paul intended. But at its cosmopolitan height it was a cultural capital that seemed to outstrip even Vienna and – according to the prince de Ligne – Paris itself.[7]

Francophilia raged in St Petersburg during Catherine the Great's reign, though Catherine herself, a German by birth, was mistrustful of the French. (She still routinely corresponded in their language with her compatriot Grimm, the *philosophe* and diplomat.) After the outbreak of the French Revolution, and again later, she summoned all Russians living in France home, because they would find only bad examples to imitate there. This simply meant that worldly Russians attempted with ever great determination to recreate a Gallic spirit in St Petersburg. The salon of the socialite Elizabeth Divova was called 'little Coblenz', after the town in the Rhineland-Palatinate where supporters of the Counter-Revolution had assembled. French style was so widely admired that, according to Louise's patron and friend Princess Dolgorukova, good taste seemed to have leapt in a single bound from Paris to St Petersburg.[8]

When Catherine's son Paul and his wife Maria Fedorovna, calling themselves the comte and comtesse du Nord, toured Europe in 1782, they returned to Russia with quantities of French furniture, bronzes, porcelain and other *objets d'art*, some purchased by them, and some presented to them by Louis XVI and Marie-Antoinette.[9] If Paul was later to turn against 'tainted' foreign wares, especially those originating in a country that remained for him the seedbed of revolutionary republicanism, others retained their taste for Gallic artefacts, and devoted part of their colossal fortunes to decorating their palaces *à la française*. In 1793 Ligne was writing that Madame Vigée Le Brun would find herself as completely at home in St Petersburg as in Paris (where, in fact, she had stopped feeling at home).[10] Louise was indeed moved by the warmth of her reception – her fame, after all, had preceded her – though the Gallophobe statesman Count Rostopchin claimed that some of the best houses remained closed to her.[11]

> Every evening I circulated in the *monde*. Not only were balls, concerts, plays frequent, but I enjoyed the daily gatherings where I found all the urbanity and grace of a French *soirée* . . . Open houses were not lacking, and in all of them one was received in the most agreeable fashion.[12]

So her letters of recommendation from Razumovsky and others went largely unused. Clearly, her activity as a society portraitist could only benefit from this attentive enthusiasm. But, as usual, she had to keep a check on social pleasures, at the risk of offending the hospitable natives. 'I remember,' she writes,

> that towards the end of my stay in St Petersburg Prince Narishkin, a grand equerry, constantly kept 'open table' with twenty-five or thirty place-settings for the foreigners who were recommended to him. I experienced every imaginable difficulty in avoiding dining in town often; my sittings and my need to sleep after getting up from table were the only excuses that could win me forgiveness, so delighted are the Russians to have one dine with them.[13]

Meeting Catherine the Great was less of an ordeal than Louise had been fearing, though she apparently committed a gaffe by wearing a simple muslin chemise rather than court dress (which she had not had time to have made) and forgetting to kiss the Empress's hand.[14] A courtier attempted to reassure her by telling her that Catherine was a *bonne femme*[15] – a description that seemed to her surprisingly prosaic – and the Empress herself appeared unshocked.

Ligne had told Louise that Catherine, then in her mid-sixties, was a woman of unaffected charm and simple tastes. She sent for Louise within forty-eight hours of her arrival in St Petersburg, and Louise went, 'slightly trembling',[16] to her summer residence of Tsarskoe Selo, a few miles away. The palace of Tsarskoe Selo scarcely confirmed the simplicity of the Empress's tastes, though its manageable size and parkland setting make it feel more restful that Rastrelli's vast and imposing Winter Palace. Its profusion of gilt, amber and agate contrast with the informality of the grounds, where Catherine often walked her dogs in the morning.[17] (A picture by Borovikovsky in the Russian Museum of St Petersburg shows her doing this.) But even the informality was relative. Louise, who described the park as 'one of the most beautiful things you could see', notes:

> It is full of monuments which the Empress called her caprices. There is a superb marble bridge in the style of Palladio; Turkish baths, which are trophies of Romanzov's and Orlov's victories; a temple with thirty-two columns, and the colonnade and grand staircase of Hercules. This park has superb avenues of trees. Opposite the palace is a long, broad lawn, at the end of which is a cherry orchard where I remember eating excellent cherries.[18]

The grounds had originally been laid out by a pupil of Le Nôtre (the architect of the Versailles garden), but they had been restyled by Louise's time according to a more 'English' taste – that is, informally and picturesquely.[19] Some visitors, it is true, saw in their groves, Chinese pavilions, temples to friendship and supposedly Swiss chalets simply a move from Versailles to the Trianon.[20] But in general Catherine greatly preferred Capability Brown's kind of park to regular French ones, and his theories on landscape gardening much appealed to her. She called Peterhof, which had been built between 1781 and 1789, her 'English' palace, because its garden was designed according to Brown's principles. Many of the great Russian palaces had parks laid out by another Englishman (though possibly one of German extraction), the appropriately named Bush from Hackney.[21]

The autocrat of all the Russias put Louise at her ease. As a result of their first meeting, she invited Louise to spend the summer painting at Tsarskoe Selo, which flattered her but also filled her with trepidation:

> apart from the honour of being lodged by the sovereign, and the pleasure of living in such a beautiful place, everything about being settled at Tsarskoe Selo would have been a strain and an annoyance, for I have always had the greatest need to enjoy my own freedom, and have always infinitely preferred being in my own home so that I can live as I want to.[22]

In any case, a court intrigue seems to have prevented the plan from being carried out. It was claimed that there was no available apartment for Louise: according to the *Souvenirs*, courtiers suspected her of having come to St Petersburg to get Esterházy replaced as Artois's agent, and wanted her out of the way. Louise pooh-poohs the very idea:

> one has to be very ill-acquainted with my character not to know that I was too preoccupied with my art to be able to spend time on political matters, even if I had not felt the aversion I have always had for anything resembling intrigue.

It is indeed an unbelievable notion. Louise was no Madame Bonneuil, turning her beauty and adroitness to political ends. She satisfied her desire for adventure in other ways.

In person the Empress was delightful to her, quite charming enough to make up for this 'little court annoyance'. When Louise had been shown into her presence,

> she immediately said to me in an extremely gentle, if slightly guttural, tone of voice: 'I am delighted, Madame, to welcome you

here; your reputation has preceded you. I am very fond of the arts, especially painting. I am not a connoisseur of them, but a lover.' Everything which she added during this conversation, which was quite long, about her desire for me to enjoy Russia enough to want to stay there a long time had such a quality of warmth that my timidity disappeared, and when I took leave of Her Majesty I was entirely reassured.[23]

Louise observed her, more than anything. Having expected to find her as immense as her reputation, she was surprised at the Tsarina's smallness. She was, however, 'very fat'. The prince de Ligne confirms this: Catherine 'must once have had a blooming complexion and a lovely bust, but this was at the expense of her figure – she had been as thin as a stick, but one puts on a great deal of weight in Russia.'[24] According to Ligne, one did not particularly notice her smallness. But she grew so corpulent that at the time of her fatal stroke six men were needed to drag her from her closet to her bedroom.[25] Not everyone was complimentary. Some remarked that in old age she was toothless and had a rough, broken voice.[26] A wrinkle at the base of her nose – her 'utterly Greek nose', as Louise called it[27] – gave her face a rather sinister character: Lampi's state portrait failed to conceal it, and so was retouched on Catherine's orders.

Her moral qualities were ambiguous, though practised courtiers like Ligne and élitists like Louise would have been reluctant to admit as much. Ligne called her a 'mixture of soul and good sense, of elevation and energy'. He thought that her lofty brow, which for Louise spelled genius alone, said far more:

> Without being a Lavater, one could read on it genius, justice, exactness, courage, depth, fairness, gentleness, calm and firmness . . . frankness and gaiety were on her lips.[28]

For Ligne she was 'Catherine *le Grand*': he was more struck by her masculine traits of strength and purpose than, like Louise, her feminine warmth and tenderness. But the *bonne femme* who loved children and fed the birds when she rose at five in the morning, made her own fire and brewed coffee so strong that it gave everyone else palpitations – one pound of beans to every five cups –[29] was inevitably less known than the autocrat of all the Russias.

She did not forswear splendour, and could hardly have been expected to. Ligne said that she had all the goodness, that is all the greatness of Louis XIV. Her magnificence, her festivities, her pensions, her purchases, her show were like his. She ran her court better, because there was nothing theatrical or exaggerated about her.[30]

Besides, she had a moral justification for the magnificence, Ligne explains, namely the fact that it made money available. None the less, there was conspicuous extravagance under her long-time minister and one-time lover, Potemkin (who had been dead for several years when Louise arrived in St Petersburg) – the film-set villages and palaces, mere façades, which he had built for Catherine's journey to the Crimea so that she should be deluded into believing the region prosperous, the spoonfuls of pearls he had served at a banquet, and so on. To her credit, Catherine could firmly put a stop to such excesses when alerted to their inappropriateness.[31]

Nor was all of her St Petersburg life lived on the grandest scale. The so-called Small Hermitage – still an imposing edifice – was the scene of regular simple domestic gatherings,[32] where people danced, acted proverbs or played with Catherine's grandchildren, and everything ended at ten o'clock when Catherine retired to bed.

Despite this show of decorousness, Louise writes,

> there appeared in St Petersburg a lampoon in which Catherine was accused of presiding every evening over the most disgusting orgies. The author of this dreadful piece was discovered and exiled from Russia; but it must sadly be admitted, to the shame of humanity, that this libellist, who was a French *émigré* distinguished for his mind, had initially won the Empress's sympathy for his misfortunes, and she had even given him decent lodgings and a pension of twelve thousand roubles![33]

Rumours about Catherine's sexual appetite spread for other reasons. Some said that at the time of her stroke she had been trying to copulate with a horse, and many called her a nymphomaniac. Ligne was pragmatic on the question of her many lovers:

> Being the lover of the Empress of Russia is a court function. I have known nearly all the incumbents. The first was a Saltykov, the second the King of Poland, the third Orlov, the fourth Vassilchikov, the fifth Potemkin, the sixth Zavadovsky, the seventh Zovich, the eighth Rimsky-Korsakov, the ninth Lanskoy, the tenth Yermolov, the eleventh Mamonov and the twelfth Zubov.[34]

To those who remarked that she had a definite preference for younger men, Catherine replied that it was deliberate: if they were older, people would claim that the favourites ruled *her*. Platon Zubov, a pampered young sultan forty years younger than the Empress, was as richly rewarded as her other lovers for his services, and even allowed by Catherine's son Paul to keep all the riches he had amassed.[35] He rewarded the new Tsar by helping to assassinate him five years later.

Catherine denied to Potemkin that fifteen other lovers had preceded him, admitting to only five; but she did freely confess that her heart would not willingly remain a single hour without love.[36] Louise, who so indignantly repudiated the slander about Catherine's 'orgies' at the Small Hermitage, is too delicate to say much about the Empress's appetite for sex: 'one can only speak of her weaknesses as one speaks of those of François I or Louis XIV, weaknesses which in no way affected the happiness of their subjects.'[37] But Catherine herself barely attempted to conceal them, despite an otherwise rigid sense of propriety. The favourites simply provided her with much-needed recreation in the intervals of running a vast empire. As Louise remarks, she never granted anyone else any real authority.

Although she declares that Catherine '*le Grand*' had made herself into a man, Louise also states that the female sex should be proud to call her one of its own. She was unquestionably naïve in her attitude to the Empress, who, she says, was adored by her subjects.[38] Catherine undoubtedly forgot their interests when it suited her. She had nursed immense ambitions ever since arriving in Russia as a German princess and marrying the mentally subnormal Tsarevich Peter when she was sixteen: she may or may not have instigated his murder after he had succeeded to the throne as Peter III, but over the years she had learnt to play a waiting game. Whether or not she truly cared for her people, she did not extend her beneficence to her son Paul, and made every effort to keep him at a distance from power.

Her humanitarianism was certainly limited. In the course of her reign she gave new powers to the nobility over the serfs, and allowed atrocities to be committed during the suppression of the peasant revolts which ensued. After the great rebellion under the Cossack soldier Pugachev in the 1770s, she abandoned all thought of a general peasant reform and exiled the writer Radishchev to Siberia for his exposé of peasant suffering in the *Journey from St Petersburg to Moscow* (1790). The duchesse d'Abrantès thought this recourse to repression entirely natural in a despotic ruler.[39] Catherine now regarded Voltaire, whom she had once revered, whose statue by Houdon the diplomat and *philosophe* Grimm had bought for her collection, and whose death she had mourned in 1778, as a symbol of the unsettling new forces of free thought. She therefore removed his seated marble figure from the Small Hermitage, which contained the nucleus of what became the Hermitage's great collection. When Louis XVI was guillotined she was reportedly plunged into horrified grief, and ordered six weeks' mourning.[40]

Yet she was playing a double game, preaching a crusade without having any intention of joining the crusaders.[41] Madame de Chastenay has a crisp comment on this period in French and European history:

> The fatal conception of emigration began to be realised; the Empress Catherine sought to exalt it. She sent an ambassador to Coblenz and never a general; she gave a ceremonial sword to the comte d'Artois, and did not give him an army.[42]

She promised the *émigrés* financial support, but showed only limited commitment to the idea of a Counter-Revolution; and she admitted that she made such strenuous efforts to involve the courts of Vienna and Berlin in the affairs of France, urging them to support an imperilled monarchy, only in order to ensure that her own hands remained free. Besides, the luxury in which many of the *émigrés* insisted on living irritated her, particularly when it was at the expense of the public purse. Nor was Catherine prepared to be well disposed toward any member of the French colony in St Petersburg with a dubious background. If Louise's royalist credentials were impeccable, others who seemed less likely to comply with the tone of the imperial court were snubbed.

Catherine's 'enlightenment' may have been partly expressed in her patronage of the arts, but she does not seem to have liked Louise's painting very much. The first imperial commission was a débâcle, though Louise is less than straightforward in admitting it. After Catherine's return from Tsarskoe Selo in August or September 1795, Count Stroganov, the director of the Academy of Fine Arts in St Petersburg, came to commission a portrait of her granddaughters, the Grand-Duchesses Alexandra and Helen. Despite the ugliness of their father Paul (whose resemblance to Peter III was thought to be the only reason for assuming Catherine had not conceived a bastard child), they were apparently pretty. 'These princesses were probably thirteen or fourteen years old,' Louise writes,

> and their faces were celestial, though with quite different expressions. Their complexion in particular was so fine and delicate that you might have thought they lived on ambrosia. The elder granddaughter, Alexandra, had a Grecian beauty; she was very like Alexander [her brother]. But the face of the younger, Helen, had

infinitely more refinement. I had them posed together, holding and looking at a portrait of the Empress; their costume was slightly Greek, but very simple and modest.[43]

It was partly the costumes that caused the trouble. According to Zubov – who Louise later decided had invented the whole story – Catherine was scandalised by them. So, Louise writes, she quickly replaced the tunics with dresses, and regretfully painted sleeves over the originally bare arms. (X-rays show no significant repainting, which suggests that Louise did the entire picture again.) Paul told her later that she had been the victim of mischief-making, and she remembered that Zubov had tried to blacken her in Catherine's eyes in other ways – by claiming, for instance, that she was setting up a rival court to the Empress's when she moved opposite the Winter Palace. Esterházy, too, said that Louise gave herself 'impossible airs' in St Petersburg,[44] and Rostopchin remarked that she had provoked society women.[45] Was the *bonne femme* Catherine, who liked dressing in plain Russian costume, and who ate messily with a napkin tucked under her chin, slightly mistrustful of this elegant French newcomer?

What is clear from Catherine's correspondence with Grimm is that she was unimpressed with Louise's talent in comparison with Angelica Kauffman's.

> From the time of Louis XIV, the school of painting in France gave promise of painting nobly, and flattered itself that it could unite wit with nobility and attractiveness. Madame Le Brun comes in August: she has pretensions to be the equal of Angelica Kauffman. *She* certainly does unite elegance with nobility in all her figures; she does more: all her figures have an ideal beauty. The equal of Angelica, as her first effort, starts painting the grand-duchesses Alexandra and Helen; the first has a noble and interesting figure, the air of a queen; the second is a perfect beauty with a butter-wouldn't-melt-in-her-mouth look. Madame Le Brun has these two squatting on a settee, twists the younger one's neck, gives them the air of two pugs sunbathing, or, if you prefer, two ugly little Savoyard girls with hairdos like a bacchante's, with bunches of grapes, and dresses them in coarse red and purple tunics; in a word, not only is all resemblance missing, but the two sisters are so disfigured that some people are asking which is the elder and which the younger.[46]

It took exceptional stupidity to botch a portrait so completely, she went on. Another letter accuses Louise of making the girls look like monkeys pulling faces, or – worse – like a couple of prostitutes.[47]

People still flocked to Louise's studio to see the picture, presumably quite unaware of Catherine's opinion. Since there is nothing in the present portrait to explain the Tsarina's disgust, Louise presumably altered it radically in repainting it: it shows the granddaughters as perfectly attractive, if slightly simpering. Nor can her reaction simply be explained away as a predictably negative response to a French artist, caused by Catherine's basic dislike of the French nation, for she cultivated other compatriots of Louise's. Before the Revolution, indeed, so many artists were leaving France for Russia to help Catherine's efforts to raise artistic standards there that the Académie royale grew seriously alarmed. And although the tone of the Empress's letters to Grimm seems unequivocal, the fact that she instantly followed this commission with one for a portrait of her grandson Alexander's wife Elizabeth suggests that Louise was not without all merit as an artist in her eyes.

Louise had met Elizabeth on her first visit to Tsarskoe Selo, and been instantly struck. 'She was,' she writes,

> at most seventeen years old; her features were delicate and regular, and the oval of her face was perfect; her lovely complexion lacked bloom, but its very pallor was entirely in harmony with the expression on her face, whose sweetness was angelic . . . She was dressed in a white tunic with a girdle knotted carelessly around a waist as slim and supple as a nymph's.[48]

With her blonde hair floating in the breeze, she epitomised the *aimable antiquité* Louise loved. She thought Elizabeth so pretty that she was unwilling to paint her in an ordinary costume: her old ambition was rekindled, and she conceived the idea of painting a *tableau d'histoire* of Elizabeth and Alexander. But the recent fuss over the Greek tunics worn by Alexandra and Helen deterred her, and she eventually painted something much more straightforward: a portrait of the Grand-Duchess dressed in court costume, arranging flowers.

Yet if Countess Golovina's memoirs are to be believed,[49] Elizabeth still managed to offend Catherine with a sartorial faux-pas, and again Louise's 'classical' tastes were to blame. Countess Shuvalova, a member of the court, persuaded her to be dressed by Louise *à l'antique* for a masked ball during the official visit of the princesses of Coburg, one of whom was betrothed to the Tsarina's grandson Constantine. When Elizabeth approached the Tsarina to kiss her hand, Catherine refused to extend it, and stared at her with displeasure. The next day the Empress informed a courtier of her indignation at Elizabeth's appearance, and continued to treat her coldly for several days. Apparently she believed Elizabeth to be guilty of either exaggeration or pretentiousness, faults for which she had a strong aversion; but whether she learned of Louise's contribution to the affair, and hence disapproved of her even more strongly, is unknown.

Courtly patronage continued, though, and Louise went on to paint Constantine's bride. To judge by her earnings, she was busy from the start: she says she made 15,000 roubles during her first month in St Petersburg.[50] Since she apparently charged seven hundred roubles for a bust, three thousand for a half-length and more for a full-length, her income suggests that she painted at least five portraits in four weeks. Such productiveness was impossible even for her, so she must either have exaggerated the sum or sold her work still more expensively than was claimed. (Rostopchin remarked that she put a price of between one and two thousand roubles on a portrait which in London would have fetched a mere two guineas.[51]) The *Souvenirs* state, in any case, that she got little benefit from these massive earnings. First her Vienna money disappeared, stolen while she was at a private theatrical performance:

> When I arrived home at about one in the morning, I found my daughter's governess Madame Charrot on the staircase, all frightened and pale: 'Ah, Madame!', she cried out, 'You have just been robbed of all your money!' I was knocked all of a heap, as you may imagine. Then she told me that my little German servant had done this dreadful deed; that packets of my gold had been found under his bed and on his person; that he had even thrown some of it down the stairs, to make people think that the little Russian was the thief; and that he had just been taken away by the police.[52]

She recovered only half the sum. Then her fifteen thousand roubles went:

> I was advised to deposit them immediately with a banker who seemed to me a very honest man. This honest man has just gone bankrupt, and I shall never see my 15,000 roubles again. You must see fate's familiar hand in all of this. Up to now it has proved impossible for me to keep the least part of what I earn: I resignedly await a more propitious time.[53]

The Russian *monde* seems to have liked her work. Even Rostopchin conceded that she had rare talent – for a woman – but said that her mind was commonplace and that she knew little about art. He principally attributed her success to her physical charms (which, to judge by the self-portrait she painted in Russia, were less than they had been), her fashion sense and the support of the Polignac faction, which won her friends in high places. But her skill remained intact, and there was no need to resort to slander to explain the favour she enjoyed. Whether or not Louise had earned contempt for the airs she gave herself, she still deserved respect as an artist.

Most of her sitters were women. She painted one of her most memorable St Petersburg portraits of Catherine Dolgorukova, though she fails to list it in her memoirs. Having seen and enthused over the Sibyl picture, which Louise had transported to Russia, Princess Dolgorukova insisted that she be painted in the same pose. As payment Louise received a carriage and a bracelet woven of hair (presumably the princess's own), studded with diamonds which spelled the message 'Adorn her who adorns her century'.[54] In Louise's portrait Catherine Dolgorukova wears a turban similar to Emma Hamilton's, but of richer material, and leans on her right elbow while holding a book in her left hand. The score of the comic opera *Nina* (which another Princess Dolgorukova, the wife of the poet Prince Ivan Mikhailovich, had performed in so memorably that she became known in society as Nina) is by her. Her eyes are uplifted like Emma Hamilton's, but she looks more pensive and less rapturous than her model.

The ravishing Catherine Fedorovna, though married to a husband by whom she had five children, broke many male hearts. Count Cobentzl, the Austrian ambassador to St Petersburg whom Louise describes as very fat and unusually ugly,[55] was passionately and unrequitedly in love with her, and never sufficiently rebuffed by her coldness to keep his distance. According to Louise, he would rush through his despatches, which he wrote with great facility, in order to return as quickly as possible to her side; and his enormous girth never prevented him from engaging in any activity that might persuade her to look more favourably on him.

In St Petersburg, Louise painted another portrait of the beautiful Countess Skavronskaya. This picture, completed in 1796, shows the Countess to be as comely and self-admiring as the Neapolitan one, but a little less vacuous: she is plumply youthful, and has a sweet, slightly enamelled look. She leans on a cushion and contemplates the observer with an indolent, faintly mournful trustfulness. There is no hint, either in this picture or in the earlier portrait, that her uncle's forced attentions had impaired that trustfulness: she probably accepted them as a matter of course. Two years after the St Petersburg sitting she married Count Giulio Litta, whom Louise sketched during her Russian stay: though the ambassador of the Knights of Malta, an order which he defended to Paul I as a rampart against unbelief and Jacobinism, he persuaded the Pope to release him from his vows of chastity when he fell in love with Catherine Skavronskaya.[56]

Another beauty Louise painted was Catherine Skavronskaya's sister Tatiana Vassilievna Yusupova, whose estranged husband kept a seraglio on his huge country estate of Arkhangelskoye and embarked on an affair with an eighteen-year-old girl when he was eighty. But her gallery also includes *jolies-laides* and women who were not conventionally pretty, even if they had dash or charm. It may be, in fact, that Louise's style was developing into one which put a greater premium on character than regularity. This would help explain why her self-portrait in the Hermitage gives her a more workaday and less idealised look than some earlier ones. She certainly seems to have been conscious that she was living in a culture of strong-willed, forceful women, and there are fewer anodyne or simpering portraits than before.

One highly original picture is the portrait of Countess Golovina, now in the Barber Institute of Fine Arts in Birmingham. It may have been painted in Moscow, where Louise went towards the end of 1800; for the sitter, thought to have had an improper relationship with the young Grand-Duchess Elizabeth – twelve years her junior, and already unhappy in her marriage to Alexander – was forced to leave St Petersburg when Paul became Emperor: he presumably disapproved of her 'unhealthy' closeness to his daughter-in-law. (A note of Louise's earnings in Russia refers to her having been paid a thousand roubles in Moscow by 'Golovin'.[57]) The Countess was a niece of Ivan Shuvalov, the last favourite of Peter the Great's daughter Elizabeth I, and who himself sat to Louise during his stay in Russia. Against the wishes of her parents, she had married the wealthy and rakish Count Golovin, whose illegitimate daughter later married Auguste Rivière. Louise liked his wife a great deal. 'Countess Golovina was a charming woman, full of wit and talent, which was often enough to keep us company; for she entertained very little.'[58] This was possibly, though Louise does not say so, because some elements of society ostracised her. But there was a strong rapport between painter and sitter, which emerges from Louise's brilliant portrait.

She shows the Countess swathed in the same red cloak with gold embroidered palmettes and lyres – known as a 'Turkish' shawl – as is worn by Countess Bucquoi, Tatiana Vassilievna Yusupova and Princess Dolgorukova: clearly it was a studio prop. It is a discreetly erotic portrait of a dashing rather than beautiful woman, who holds her cape coquettishly against her cheek, and whose gaze has an almost masculine directness. The Countess quizzes painter and beholder with amused green-brown eyes in which the light dances: her slightly parted lips seem about to jest or challenge, and the arching of her left eyebrow adds to the note of interrogation. Louise disdains to idealise her subject, whose strength and humour are manifestly enough to answer any criticism: she preserves the imperfect nose and the cleft chin, and so succeeds in capturing a character.

A sterner beauty Louise painted in St Petersburg was Countess Catherine Apraxina, whose countenance earned her the nickname of 'enraged Venus'.[59] Pushkin used her as the prototype for his Queen of Spades, known as the 'Muscovite Venus' in her youth. (The model for the old Queen of Spades was the Countess's genuinely terrifying mother.) Louise portrays her daughter sympathetically: she is poised and collected, and evaluates the onlooker coolly. This Countess Apraxina was a small, svelte, elegant woman with large brown eyes; she wore more make-up than Louise would probably have approved, and continued to do so long after it had ceased to be fashionable.

With some exceptions – notably the sibyl-like Princess Dolgorukova – the Russian women Louise painted were dressed as fashionable Frenchwomen of the day would have been. There is nothing surprising in this, for French fashions had prevailed in St Petersburg from much earlier in the century. Rose Bertin had many Russian clients, and Catherine Skavronskaya was not the only court lady to receive shipments of clothes from her. Catherine II is unlikely to have approved of this, or of pointless and unpatriotic extravagances like Potemkin's sending to Paris for a pair of ball-slippers, as he once did post-haste for Princess Dolgorukova (whom he was besotted with). After all, in 1783 she had decided to check all French-inspired toilettes by imposing a uniform on all women attending her receptions, and the belles of St Petersburg were no longer permitted to wear Mademoiselle Bertin's creations. They were even obliged to forego coiffures *à la Reine* or *à la Belle-Poule*, because a new regulation prohibited hairstyles that rose above a certain height.[60] Some women did like the Tsarina, and asserted their national identity by wearing typical Russian costume – loose garments fastened with girdles and buttons, and with wide sleeves.[61] But far more of them dressed *à la française*, and so contributed to Louise's sense of having moved to a home from home. The new neo-classical style was abhorrent to Catharine, according to one writer:

> Madame Le Brun had just arrived [in St Petersburg], drawn by the hope of earning a lot of money; she had inspired a taste for Greek costume which everyone put together in their own fashion and often very clumsily. The enthusiasm she had aroused was distasteful to the Empress, a declared enemy of Greek costume because in her eyes it was linked with the Revolution.[62]

Given that the fabrics used for 'antique' drapery seemed to have been woven out of air, and the chemises and tunics appeared almost transparent, it is unsurprising that such dress was also called the naked style.[63] (Jane Austen writes, in a letter of 8 January 1801 to her sister Cassandra, of a woman 'expensively and nakedly dressed' in lace and muslin,[64] and John Carr refers in 1803 to the airiness of dress resembling a mist of incense.[65] An epidemic of flu in Paris that year was called 'muslin disease'.)

Women were as often indisposed in St Petersburg or Moscow as in Paris, receiving their visitors décolletée or bare-armed as they reclined against piles of cushions on a sofa or bed, while all around them people whispered of *vapory, migreny* and *spazmy*. Husbands shook their hands and blamed the *émigrés*, but the more obvious cause was the general prevalence of European fashions. Perhaps the addition of a specifically Russian ingredient – the sable and black fox of the East – might have palliated the mischief; but then the floating drapery effect which was so keenly sought-after would have been lost. In any case, as Louise remarks, Russian palaces were wildly overheated by European standards, so that except when venturing outside – which they were much more prudent about than Louise herself – the rich barely noticed that it was winter.

> The Russians have perfected the means of keeping apartments warm. Once you have passed through the *porte-cochère*, everything is heated by such excellent stoves that the fires kept burning in fireplaces are superfluous luxuries. The staircases, the corridors are kept at the same temperature as the rooms, whose communicating doors stay open without any inconvenience. Consequently, when Emperor Paul, who was then only Grand-Duke, came to France as the comte du Nord, he said to the Parisians: 'In St Petersburg we see the cold; but here we feel it.' Equally, after I had spent seven and a half years [actually six] in Russia and returned to Paris, where Princess Dolgorukova was living too, I remember going to see her one day when we were both so cold standing by the fireplace that we said to each other: 'We must go and spend the winter in Russia to get warm.'[66]

Everyone wore great padded boots of velvet when they went out in their carriages, and fur-lined cloaks. At seventeen degrees below freezing the theatres were closed, and people stayed at home. Louise had not realised the need to protect oneself against extreme cold when she decided to visit Countess Golovina at minus eighteen:

She lived quite a long way from me, in the great street called the Nevsky Prospekt, and from my house to hers I met not a single coach, which greatly surprised me; but I pressed on regardless. The cold was so intense that as soon as the Countess saw me come into her drawing-room she exclaimed: 'Good heavens! how can you have come out this evening? Don't you know that it's nearly twenty degrees below freezing?' At these words I thought of my poor coachman, and without taking off my pelisse ran back to my coach, and hastily returned home. But my head had been so affected by the cold that I was dizzy. My servants rubbed it with eau de cologne to warm it up, otherwise I should have gone mad.[67]

She was much struck by the common people's resilience and resistance to the cold, without thinking to ask herself whether they had not had to develop hardiness of necessity. Not that she was so preoccupied with upper-class clients as to be oblivious to ordinary existences, but she can appear thoughtless or condescending:

> it is a curious thing to see these little fellows [postilions of eight or ten], quite scantily dressed, sometimes even with their shirt wide open at the chest, and gaily exposing themselves to a cold which would certainly make a French or Prussian grenadier perish in a few hours.[68]

She was herself quite a considerate employer, as her cancelling of the evening engagement at Countess Golovina's suggests. None the less, she cheerfully observed, the number of centenarians in Russia might be attributable to the rigours of the climate. And every employer made some concession to arctic cold, if only to keep his servants alive and serviceable: coachmen were issued with fur-lined coats and gloves, and in exceptionally harsh conditions given wood to burn and strong liquor to drink while they waited outside for their masters. They can hardly have been overjoyed at freezing to death while the *monde* danced and gambled; but they were, Louise airily remarks, an obedient race. And despite the hardships they endured, she casually adds, drunkenness was unknown.

Was she untypically naïve or thoughtless, shockingly unobservant for one who earned her living from close scrutiny, blind to the evidence of despotism, or shielded from its more extreme manifestations? The comte de Ségur seemed to take a similarly rosy view of the *peuple*'s lot. 'During a stay of five years in Russia,' he writes,

I did not hear of a single act of tyranny or cruelty. True, the peasants live as slaves, but they are gently treated. One does not meet with a single beggar in the kingdom; if one found any, they would be sent back to their masters, who are obliged to feed them.[69]

But he does qualify this picture: 'these people still deserve to be pitied, since their fate depends on the capricious whims of fate, which assigns them to a good or bad master at random.'[70]

There was plenty to shock outside observers in prevailing mores. The habit of computing a man's wealth by the number of slaves he owned, for example, meant that the serf was simply seen as an object, property like a dog or a horse, and treated with no more consideration.[71] We should scarcely expect Louise to argue the need for social revolution, and it is no surprise that the *Souvenirs* say nothing about the miseries of the serfs or the hardships endured by the pauper-victims of the fabulously rich tyrants who employed her. When she remarks that the Russian people is 'simple and proud-seeming', 'the best souls in the world',[72] she speaks with an almost patrician insouciance.

This kind of condescension was apparent in cultural as well as social commentary, and Russian as well as foreign observers showed it. Often it was provoked by relatively unimportant factors, but sometimes the cause was serious. The Russian tendency to imitate more sophisticated nations was regarded dismissively, patronisingly, regretfully or admiringly, depending on the mood of the observer. Gogol's *Dead Souls*, for instance, mercilessly satirises the parrotting of French style prevalent in the upper and middle classes in Russia and their addiction to parlour games – charades, portraits, tableaux vivants[73] and other foolish things – seeing it as a forfeiting of national character and culture as well as a mindless waste of time. Where 'serious' art was at issue, this kind of observation could strike a warning note, though not everyone drew the conclusion that the Russian adoption of foreign ways was a bad thing. The prince de Ligne uncritically noted the effortlessness with which Russians mastered the various arts, how they became actors or painters as easily as they became surgeons, sailors or priests.[74] Much earlier in the century Lekain had remarked in a letter to David Garrick that Russians learned and retained the principles of acting so readily that they would soon outshine the stars of the Comédie-Française;[75] and the same theoretically applied to the principles of painting. In the second half of the eighteenth century most native Russian artists belonged to the lower orders of society, and might even be serfs who painted in between performing menial tasks for their masters. Ségur was dismissive of this facility, precisely because he thought it a proof of ingrained servility (which the burgeoning Romantic conception of creative genius found artistically reprehensible). But there is sympathy in his observation that the lack of personal liberty fosters the spirit of imitation – a remark which he then qualifies by noting that the Russian nobility displays the same tendency.[76]

Whatever its cause, it was often blamed for sapping the national character of energy. Perhaps the dislike Catherine II and Paul shared for the habit of copying everything French stemmed from this belief. If so, Catherine at least was inconsistent, for she did nothing to discourage imitativeness in the performing arts. As early as 1763 she had charged the French actor Clairval to recruit a troupe of actors in his own country and bring them to St Petersburg, and when their contract expired Diderot helped find more. He was rewarded by momentarily enjoying a far greater vogue on the Russian stage than he had ever had on the French: his *drame*, *Le Père de famille*, was translated twice, and the sole translation of its feeble predecessor *Le Fils naturel* went through three editions. Nearly all the great French plays were translated into Russian – the tragedies of Racine and Voltaire, and the comedies of Molière, Regnard and Marivaux.[77] Beaumarchais was especially popular. His *Mariage de Figaro* – the risky proto-Republican play which had been performed at the Petit Trianon in 1783, with Marie-Antoinette as the maid Suzanne, Artois as the ebullient servant Figaro and Vaudreuil as the decadent nobleman Almaviva – was put on at Tsarskoe Selo after much official resistance. Catherine, probably inevitably, was displeased, for more or less the same reasons as Louis XVI had been. Liberalism was dangerous, and social insubordination not to be encouraged.

But there were many amateur productions in the private playhouses of the aristocracy. Yusopov's palace on the Moyka embankment – now, disappointingly for its fabulous grandeur, an institute belonging to the Union of Educational Workers – had a splendid theatre, where Glinka's opera *Ivan Susanin* was premièred in 1836. (The palace itself is probably most famous as the scene of Rasputin's murder.) Opera flourished in the imperial city too. The Italian tenor Mandini was tempted there after a successful career in Italy and at the Parisian Théâtre de Monsieur, where he was engaged by the violinist Viotti to sing between 1788 and 1791. Louise raved over his talents and person: 'He was handsome; he was a great actor and he had just arrived from Paris, where several people can still remember having heard him.'[78] But he was as obstinately monoglot as Louise, and she had to listen to him singing in Italian. Among the cultural pleasures St Petersburg offered, music remained important to her. She describes listening to it at one court gala:

Beautiful, well-played wind music was to be heard throughout the meal; the musicians were stationed at one end of the room on the broad stage. I confess that it is a charming thing for me to hear music while I am at table. It is the only thing that has ever made me want to be a very grand lady or very rich: for I prefer music to all the conversation of fellow-diners, although abbé Delille has often said 'that things that have been gossiped over are easier to digest'.[79]

Catherine's reign was marked by a blossoming of musical life.[80] The Tsarina attached to her court the greatest Italian composers – not just Paisiello, but Cimarosa too – and in 1764 summoned the troupe of the French Opéra-Comique to St Petersburg. In time, admittedly, their work came to appear too liberal and democratic to her, for Catherine seems to have regarded opera as one of the causes of the French Revolution. But she proved to be as much a catholic and cosmopolitan in the way she encouraged Russia's musical development as in her promotion of native painting. She was, after all, herself the product of a cultivated German court, and had been horrified by the artistic barrenness of Russia when she had first come to the country.

Yet the Tsarina was tone deaf,[81] as she confessed in a letter to Grimm:

> I am no further advanced in music than before. The only tone I recognise is the barking of nine dogs which, turn by turn, have the honour of being in my bedroom, and which I can identify individually even from a distance by their voice or their organ; as for Paisiello's music, I listen to it and am astonished by the tones he combines, but I barely recognise it.[82]

In an earlier letter, Catherine had plaintively observed that she longed to listen to music and appreciate it, but could make out only noises. 'I feel like sending your new Medical Society a prize for whoever invents an effective remedy for insensitivity to inharmonious sounds.'[83]

In contrast to the pleasures of high society, there were also simple bucolic ones. Louise enjoyed the same blend of sophisticated worldliness and Arcadian simplicity as she had done in Austria. On very hot summer days the heat in St Petersburg became intolerable, and she took refuge in the country. On one boat trip she and her daughter came upon a delicious scene, like something out of Bernardin de Saint-Pierre's pastoral novel *Paul et Virginie*:

> We met a crowd of men and women all bathing together. In the distance we even glimpsed completely naked young men on

horseback, who were going to bathe with their horses in this state. In any other country such indecencies would create a great scandal; but it is different where innocence of thought prevails. Nobody had the idea of doing anything wrong, for the Russian people truly has the naïvety of primitive nature.[84]

It was easy to yield to a sense of idyll – to walk in a neglected 'English' garden on another island, to rent a *dacha* on the banks of the Neva and watch the boats go by, to enjoy the luxurious hospitality of a general who had served in Turkey and lived nearby, eat superb fruits in his Turkish tent, or spend evenings talking with Countess Golovina and her friends.[85] But was it real? Louise admitted to a sense of guilt: 'The peace and happiness I was experiencing did not . . . prevent my often thinking of France and its misfortunes. In particular I was beset by the memory of Louis XVI and Marie-Antoinette . . .'[86] In other words, she felt a prick of disloyalty. Was it right not to be suffering when those she idolised had suffered so horribly for not escaping their country as she had done? She loved all the luxury of St Petersburg, the apartments scented with warm, mint-infused vinegar, the sumptuous long divans, the sofas on which she posed many of her subjects (so divinely comfortable that she became incapable of sitting in an armchair), the refined gatherings at which one drank excellent Georgian tea or a kind of mead called hydromel. Above all, she loved the fact that everyone spoke French; but it made her feel where her loyalties should lie. Louise was not the only traveller who disdained ever to attempt mastering the language of the countries she visited: almost none of the exiles learned how to converse in Russian, and after nearly thirty years in the country the comte de Langeron knew only how to address his dogs in it. Many Russians, too, were said to speak French better than their own tongue. But since the fact of her nationality was ever-present in Louise's mind even at a remove from France, she could not remain completely unaware of what had been happening there, nor forget the cause of her departure.

Hers had not been a thoughtless *joyeuse émigration*; she was a serious working artist who had 'emigrated' for more or less good reasons, and would never have countenanced the claim that she had left in order to enjoy greater comforts than were available in France. But no more than Austria could Russia be argued to offer her an artistic education, her pretext as she had set off for Italy. She knew, too, that Madame Labille-Guiard had stayed behind, though she could console herself with arguing that this was simply because she was pro-Republican. Despite such reasoning, Louise's determined effort to blot out what had gone on in France was beginning, even to her, to look like complacent self-protection.

Self-portrait (1781).
Kimbell Art Museum, Fort Worth, Texas

Charles-Alexandre de Calonne (1785).
The Royal Collection, Windsor Castle. Copyright © Her Majesty Queen Elizabeth II

Hyacinthe-Gabrielle Roland, later Marchioness of Wellesley (1791).
Fine Arts Museums of San Francisco, Mildred Anna Williams Collection

Countess Golovina (1797-1800).
The Trustees of the Barber Institute of Fine Arts,
University of Birmingham

Louise, Queen of Prussia (1801).
Schloss Charlottenburg; Preussischer Kulturbesitz, Berlin

Giuseppina Grassini in the role of Zaïre (1804).

Musée des Beaux Arts, Rouen

Mont Blanc (1807).
Musée Savoisien, Chambéry

Madame de Staël as Corinne at Cape Miseno (1808).

Copyright © Musée d'art et d'histoire, Ville de Genève

There was nothing for it but to inform herself about horrors she had wanted to ignore. She wrote off to Cléry, who she knew had taken refuge in Vienna after Louis XVI's execution, to discover the 'sad details' she now needed to know in order to do a penitential picture of one of the scenes preceding Louis's and Marie-Antoinette's deaths. The former valet's notes relating to the events up to the guillotining of the King would later be published as the *Journal des événements à la Tour du Temple pendant la captivité de Louis XVI*, a bestseller at the end of the eighteenth century. For the time being he sent Louise a detailed letter describing six 'grievous scenes' which might be used in a picture.

In fact, they were too heartrending. Whatever her intentions, however strongly she now felt that she should make amends for not having suffered enough, Louise could not endure the thought of the pain she would be inflicting on herself. 'This letter made such a cruel impression on me that I realised the impossibility of undertaking a piece of work where every brush-stroke would have made me burst into tears. So I gave up my plan . . .'[87]

She was thwarted in her desire to see the royal family at Mittau, where the monarch-in-waiting Louis XVIII and his dependants had settled thanks to a pension from Paul of Russia, by an illness of Julie's and by pressing commissions from her Russian patrons. The least she could do was to paint a picture of Marie-Antoinette from memory and send it to her surviving daughter Marie-Thérèse. But when she was finally free to travel to Kurland she suffered a further setback. Paul had turned against Louis and moved him on, influenced by the jealousy of his wife's *lectrice* Madame Gourbillon (whose passionate attachment to the drunken Marie-Joséphine had led Louis to forbid her joining the royal party).

But there was a far worse shock to come. On 17 November 1796, Catherine the Great died.

CHAPTER EIGHT

PAUL, JULIE AND MOSCOW: 'Such horrible fatigue'

Catherine's death did not provoke in Louise the stunned horror she had experienced at the news of Louis XVI's and Marie-Antoinette's executions, but it still upset her. Perhaps there was professional regret too. She claims – probably untruthfully – that Catherine had made a flattering request the week before her stroke.

> I went on the Sunday morning, after church, to present to Her Majesty the portrait I had done of Grand-Duchess Elizabeth. The Empress came up to me, complimented me on it, then said to me: 'They are insisting that you do my portrait; I am an old woman, but, well, since they all want it, I shall give you the first sitting a week from now'. The following Thursday she did not ring her bell at nine o'clock, as she usually did. They waited until ten and even a little later; finally the First Lady of the Bedchamber entered. Not seeing the Empress in her bedroom, she went to the little cloak-room-closet, and as soon as she opened the door Catherine's body fell to the ground.[1]

One wonders who were the 'they' who had expressed such enthusiasm for Catherine's sitting to Louise. Clearly, the idea did not come from the Tsarina herself, and it must be assumed that she still had the reservations about Louise's work which she had declared a few months before to Grimm. In any case, the whole story may be a fabrication: the timing, with the commission coming just too late for Louise to be able to act on it, is a little too convenient. Louise writes: 'Personally, I was so seized with grief and fright when someone came and whispered this terrible news to me that my daughter, who was convalescing, noticed my state and felt ill.'[2] Catherine's pulse was still beating, so there was hope; but it, and she, soon died.

Why should Louise, and according to her the people generally, have been frightened at the Empress's death? Because the reign of her son Paul, systematically repressed by Catherine for years, promised to be far more despotic. But the anticipated popular revolt did not come about. Louise implies that this was because the people were too stunned by grief to be capable of concerted action. For the time being mourning took over.

> The Empress's body lay in state for six weeks in a great hall of the palace, lit day and night and magnificently decorated. Catherine was on a 'display bed' surrounded by escutcheons bearing the arms of all the cities of the Empire. Her face was exposed, her beautiful hand resting on the bed. All the court ladies, some of whom took it in turns to watch over the body, went to kiss this hand, or pretended to. As for myself, I had not kissed it living, and did not want to do so dead. I even avoided looking at Catherine II's face, which would have stayed so sadly in my imagination.[3]

In other words, she adopted her usual blocking devices, and effectively ignored evidence of mortality and change which she found too painful to contemplate.

Paul's career up to his mother's death had been a tragedy of frustration.[4] The Tsarina had had no intention of surrendering power to him when he came of age, or, like Maria Theresa, sharing the responsibility for running the country with her son. His despotism, on which all contemporary commentators remark, had been too long suppressed. The inhabitants of St Petersburg, under Paul's draconian new regulations, were obliged to wear prescribed clothes outside, rise and go to bed at set times, get out of their coaches when they met Paul – though he graciously waived this ruling for Louise[5] – paint their houses in a particular way, dance only certain permitted dances, and avoid using words like 'club' or 'deputy', which reeked of republican France. Anyone who offended the Tsar, whether deliberately or not, was liable to be exiled to Siberia – a fate Louise feared for herself and Auguste Rivière when a fire they had lit to cook a meal by Lake Pergola flared out of control and seemed about to burn down St Petersburg itself.[6] Authoritarian though she was, Catherine had never abused imperial power in this way; but in Paul's eyes society should be taught to conduct itself as soldiers were trained to drill, with military discipline.[7]

Modern *chic* was deprecated, in part because Paul believed that years of permissiveness under female rulers of doubtful legitimacy had fostered self-indulgently 'soft' attitudes, sartorially and otherwise. The Emperor considered the informal fashions sweeping Europe to be symbolic of a more general laxity which called for correction; and so he insisted on a retention or restoration of the old styles. Everyone was to be forced to wear powder, a ruling which Louise now inconsistently regretted.

> When this decree was issued, I was doing the portrait of young Prince Bariatinsky, and as I had asked him not to come powdered, he had consented. I saw him arrive one day as pale as death. 'What is wrong?' I asked. 'I just saw the Emperor as I was coming to your house,' he replied, still trembling violently; 'I only had time to dash under a *porte-cochère*, but I am terrified that he recognised me.'[8]

Paul himself, who was excessively ugly, would have presented a challenge to any portraitist, and Louise never attempted depicting him. Portraits by Lampi and Levitsky show him as pug-like, as Catherine had complained Louise made his daughters appear, with a snub nose and doggy eyes. (He was so ashamed of his appearance that his face never appeared on coins, and he remarked that his ministers hoped to lead him by the nose, as though he had one. Perversely, though, or perhaps self-protectively, he chose the first recruits for the Pavlovsk Guards specifically for their snub noses.) Louise's memoirs add to the list of unappealing features:

> a very big mouth, adorned with very long teeth, made him look like a death's-head. His eyes were more than animated, though often he had a gentle gaze. He was neither fat nor thin; and although his whole person did not lack a kind of elegance, you had to admit that his face lent itself greatly to caricature. And however dangerous such a pastime was, a fair number of caricatures were produced. One among others showed him holding a piece of paper in each hand. On one you read: *order*, on the other: *counter-order*, and on his forehead: *disorder*.[9]

This wretched man was, however, married to an attractive woman, Maria Fedorovna, whose portrait Louise did paint. Her preliminary oil sketches show how meticulously she laid the ground for a major commission, probably submitting the studies to her sitter before broaching the definitive work. Louise describes Maria Fedorovna as very beautiful, and is diplomatic about her plumpness, which, she says, preserved the Tsarina's freshness.[10] The huge state portrait, today rolled up in the Hermitage reserve and unseen for decades, shows Paul's wife sumptuously dressed, and wearing the insignia of the orders of St Andrew and St Catherine and a diamond crown. (Louise disliked painting diamonds because it was impossible to convey their brilliance; but by using a crimson velvet curtain as background she was able to highlight the crown and make it appear to sparkle.)[11] On a stool by the Tsarina are the plans of the Smolny Institute, founded by Catherine II for the education of girls, and of which Maria Fedorovna was patron.

The contrast this elegant woman made with her husband must have been ridiculous, though Louise merely calls it striking[12] – the tall, well-endowed, majestic Empress and the nondescript Emperor. While Louise was painting Maria Fedorovna she had the opportunity to observe him and his family at closer quarters. She was grateful for the courtesy Paul habitually showed her, but noticed the embarrassment of his two eldest sons at his childish horseplay.

> During a pause, Paul began to caper about, exactly like a monkey, scratching the screen and pretending he was going to climb it. This game went on for a long time. Alexander and Constantine seemed to me to suffer watching their father fool about in this grotesque way in front of a stranger, and I myself felt ill at ease on his behalf.

But Louise painted some memorable Russian portraits of men, particularly elderly ones with expressive faces. She did two pictures of the majestic deposed King of Poland, Stanislas Augustus, both in 1797. One, which shows Stanislas Augustus in dignified half-length, wearing a red velvet cloak lined with ermine, bears a strong resemblance to the portrait she painted of Ivan Shuvalov at roughly the same time.

Stanislas Augustus and Ivan Shuvalov had much in common. Both had been an empress's favourite: the slightly older Shuvalov of Elizabeth I, and Stanislas Augustus of Catherine II. Ivan Shuvalov had a reputation for kindness and integrity (he had refused various political honours and rewards), and was known as Monsieur de Pompadour because of his devotion to the arts and to French culture. Stanislas Augustus was also an ardent Francophile and patron of painters and writers. He called on Louise soon after his arrival in St Petersburg, in March 1797, and greatly admired her work.

His life had scarcely been such as to induce the state of calm tranquillity that radiates from Louise's portrait (now at Versailles). He had first come to St Petersburg as Poland's plenipotentiary ambassador in 1756, becoming the lover of the then Grand-Duchess Catherine, but was recalled in 1758. After Catherine seized power, she had Stanislas – no longer her lover – installed as a puppet monarch in 1764. But as King of Poland he suffered only humiliations: the first partition of his country by Russia, Prussia and Austria in 1772, the degrading 'triumphal' journey with

The Sweetness of Life

Catherine and Potemkin through the Crimea in 1782, the second partition of Poland in 1793, and finally his forced abdication of November 1795 after the third partition had obliterated what was left of his country.

He had been a close friend of Madame Geoffrin, with whom he corresponded for years and whom he called *maman*, and she, in turn, tried to influence the way he ruled over Poland. Louise had first heard of him when, as a young woman in Paris, she mixed with habitués of the Geoffrin salon, which for a quarter of a century was the capital of the 'Republic of Letters'.

After Catherine II's death, Paul invited Stanislas to his coronation, but the by now elderly ex-monarch suffered further humiliation, being forced to stand throughout the ceremony. Later on, Paul was more gracious, pressing Stanislas to stay in St Petersburg and lodging him in the Marble Palace on the beautiful quay of the Neva.[13] There Stanislas entertained – mostly French expatriates and a few other foreigners – and talked about French literature.[14] He seemed particularly to distinguish Louise, at least according to the artist herself: he called her his 'good friend', as Kaunitz had done in Vienna, and retrospectively wished he could have welcomed her in Warsaw during his reign.

Louise observes that he was an exceptionally gentle and indulgent man. The proof, for her, was his forgiving acceptance of her discourtesy when he called at her studio one day:

> I was so absorbed in my work that I had a fit of temper, and at the very moment when he half-pushed open my door I cried out to him: 'I'm not in'. The King, without saying a word, put on his cloak again and went. When I had put down my palette and remembered in cold blood what I had just done, I reproached myself so sternly that that very evening I called on the King of Poland to apologize and ask for forgiveness. 'How you received me this morning!' he said to me as soon as he saw me. Then he immediately added: 'I perfectly understand that when one disturbs a busy artist, one makes her impatient; so please believe that I bear you absolutely no grudge whatsoever.'[15]

Her artistic self, if not its feverish compulsions, was made manifest on a later, sadder occasion, when her professional skill at reading faces told her that Stanislas would shortly die. He duly suffered a mortal apoplectic fit the next day.

Louise needed appreciation. She valued it in personal terms, and would have been wounded had she known Catherine's true opinion of her work, or been aware – if Rostopchin's report is reliable – that some members of St Petersburg society did not wish to receive her. But professional recognition continued to matter too. Her election to the St Petersburg Academy of Fine Arts delighted her because it showed that she enjoyed as high a professional regard in Russia as in Rome, Florence or Vienna. In gratitude she painted the Academy her self-portrait (now in the Hermitage), a rather unflattering picture in which she disguises a double chin with a discreetly tied scarf.

Louise was now in her mid-forties, and beginning to be settled. But Julie, a young woman of twenty (not seventeen, as her mother claims), was being difficult. Later on, Louise gratefully remembered the occasion of her election to the Academy because it was a bright spot in an otherwise sad and painful year. In 1800 Jeanne Le Sèvre died, and Louise seems to have felt a guilt she never expresses elsewhere at having been for so long an absentee daughter to her. But the main upset stemmed from her own daughter's wilfulness. She had fallen in love with a man Louise did not approve of, and the fact greatly distressed this doting mother. Was Julie actually headstrong? Louise suggests she was, but does so indulgently:

> when my friends said to me: 'You love your daughter so madly that it is you who obey her,' I replied: 'Don't you see that everyone loves her?' Indeed, the most distinguished people in St Petersburg appreciated her and sought her out; I was never invited anywhere without her, and I rejoiced in the successes she enjoyed in society more than I have ever done in my own.[16]

She was apparently very pretty, with large blue eyes, a delightful, slightly retroussé nose, regular teeth and a slim figure. However much she doted, Louise could not always be attending to Julie: in the mornings, for instance, she almost always had to paint. So her daughter, dangerously, spent time at the house of some friends, the Chernishevs.

Count Chernishev was director of the Imperial Theatres in St Petersburg, and Julie fell in love with his secretary Gaéten Nigris, about whom Louise is only slightly supercilious:

> This Monsieur Nigris had quite a good face and figure; he must have been thirty or so. As for his talents, he drew a little, and his handwriting was very beautiful. His gentle manners, his melancholy gaze, and even his slightly yellowish pallor gave him an interesting romantic air which seduced my daughter, and she became besotted with him.

It was distressing enough to feel that she was losing 'my daughter, my only child' to a man without talent, fortune or name. But worse was to come. Louise had always been prone to neurosis, and may have been inclined towards paranoia. Now – for no evident reason – she became convinced that she was the victim of a plot involving the Chernishevs, Julie and Madame Charrot. She nowhere specifies the nature of this supposed plot, but implies that its goal was to win Julie her freedom by turning public opinion against Louise herself as a mother. One wonders why she imagined the Russian *monde* would be concerned about a foreign mother-and-daughter relationship; but Louise's fears were not based on any rational reflection.

Her time in Russia, where she still had months to live, would be poisoned for good by this development, and Louise's sense of being victimised and misunderstood grew so obsessive that it forced her to uproot herself and move. The disappointment with Julie was a turning-point, and may have become magnified in her imagination. All Louise's old fears of being gossiped about – perhaps damagingly enough to lose public favour, and so lucrative work – resurfaced. Typically, neurosis became muddled up with new and unjustifiable worries about money.

> An unbelievable thing is that the cabal against me hoped so devoutly that I would yield to persecution that people were already talking about the dowry. As I was thought to be very rich, I remember the Neapolitan ambassador coming to see me and asking for a sum which greatly exceeded my fortune; for, as you will remember, I had left France with eighty *louis* in my pocket, and part of the savings I had made since that time had been taken from me by the Venice bank.[17]

(Why the Neapolitan ambassador should have come to ask for anything is unclear.) Most painful of all was to see her daughter turning against her. She principally blamed Julie's governess, who had – unforgivably – let her read novels without Louise's knowledge. But when Julie fell ill with distress and frustration, Louise's defences were down. She wrote to Jean-Baptiste-Pierre Le Brun asking him to give his consent to Julie's marriage, and eventually word of his agreement arrived.

Louise's authority over her daughter in this affair was moral, no more: it was the father who disposed of his children, not the mother (who legally had to justify a refusal). So if Louise expected some gratitude for 'sacrificing all my desires and all my repugnance', this would only have been because she had brought her daughter up virtually single-handed, and been doubly a parent to her. In the event, no thanks were forthcoming:

'the cruel child expressed not the least satisfaction to me for what I had done for her'.

Perhaps Julie, quite apart from having fallen in love, simply felt that the time had come to break free from a demanding and jealous mother. To judge by Louise's neglect of her twenty-five years later, when Julie was on her deathbed, the errant daughter was never quite forgiven. But in fact Julie did not break completely free from Louise at this stage: financial support seems to have been needed after the marriage, and Louise says that she provided it.

Again predictably, money matters aggravated Louise's sense of griev-ance, and combined to pitch her into the deep depression which lasted, with occasional remissions, until she left Russia. The long *cri de coeur* of a letter she sent her former husband from Moscow on 29 January 1801,[18] apparently provoked by his describing her – in a lost letter – as being 'unnaturally' happy away from her daughter and family, dwells on the generosity of her treatment both of him and of the Nigrises, whom Le Brun had accused her of leaving in destitution in St Petersburg. In fact they were living with the Chernishevs and were apparently very far from destitute.

Le Brun's letter, she told him, was 'so absurd, so dreadful that I do not know how I can find the strength to reply to it'. She then launches into an attack on him which rehearses all the old grudges, all her sense of being ill-used.

I should think I am mistress to do what I want with what I have earned through such labour. Over more than twelve years you have given me no more than 1,000 *écus*, which you still reproach me for. I have given my daughter as much for her keep during the two months I shall be away. Compare your conduct with mine. I gave you everything, I had to work like mad to support myself, my daughter, pay for her education, her maid, a servant, a carriage, a cook, a household, continual moves, travels. What would I have done without my work? If I had been ill, you would have let me die of hunger. For instead of saving you have kept women who deceived you, you have gambled and lost huge amounts. I know this from a thousand reports. You measure me by your own yard-stick, but I am not like that, I do not let strangers' hands profit from what I have. I have too much trouble earning it . . . it seems easy to you to attack me, even slander me with false suspicions introduced into your heart by vipers' tongues, and the source is a woman to whom I have done only good and who has caused all my suffering and the destruction of my health. This woman is

193

Madame Charrot, who is a harpy [*sic*] I have nourished in my bosom. I needed all the tenderness I feel for my daughter to put up with her for the last two years. I released her at the time of the marriage. She took no care of me, yet I rewarded her with a wage of nine thousand francs or three thousand roubles in cash . . . After I left, to my great regret, she stayed in St Petersburg and spread the rumour that I was not coming back for three or four years, that I was leaving my daughter in wretchedness, whereas she and her husband were supported only by me . . . Now people write to me from St Petersburg that they are sorry to hear I am leaving my daughter penniless. That is my lot, to be persecuted, slandered – when I was young and pretty it was another matter. So my heart is sick and bleeding, to the point where life is burdensome to me. I flee the world like the plague – the misanthrope is right.

It is an explosive and sometimes hysterical letter: Louise is surely untruthful, for example, in claiming that she alone supported the new ménage since Gaétan Nigris was professionally employed. It was written, paradoxically, after she had left for Moscow with Auguste Rivière to refresh her spirits in a new environment (and also, on the evidence of this letter, on an errand to sell pictures on behalf of her ex-husband, though she offers no further information on this).

Before that, though, the wedding arrangements had to be made and the marriage celebrated, and these necessities depressed her further. Louise's St Petersburg earnings provided the dowry; Le Brun's only, involuntary, contribution seems to have been to feature as a miniature portrait in a diamond bracelet Louise also gave Julie.[19]

According to Louise's account, her daughter was barely happier than herself after the ceremony.

The day after her marriage I went to see my daughter. I found her calm and unenthusiastic about her happiness. Then, a fortnight later, finding myself at her house, I said to her: 'You are quite happy, I hope, now you have married him?' Monsieur Nigris, who was chatting to someone, had his back turned to us, and as he had a streaming cold he had a heavy greatcoat on his shoulders. 'I must admit that this padded robe puts me off; how do you expect me to be in love with a get-up like that?' So a fortnight had been long enough for love to vanish.

In a footnote, though, Louise does allow that the couple lived harmoniously enough together for several years, since Nigris had a gentle, emollient character – contrasting, she implies, with her own daughter's headstrong one. Selfish and ungrateful or not, Julie had deeply upset her mother.

Who was to blame? One cannot help thinking of another mother and daughter: Madame de Sévigné and the cold, proud Françoise de Grignan, whose only answer to burning and exclusive passion was withdrawal. Was Julie's crime any more grave? Louise was prone to regard her as 'her' creation: she had taken her around civilised Europe, kept the girl by her rather than consigning her to a convent, overseen her education, and chaperoned her in the drawing-rooms of the *monde*. Intense possessiveness was a fairly natural result. Now, Julie had dared to break away, as Louise, much earlier, had broken away from a constricting and unhappy household.

More than a century before, Madame de Sévigné's daughter had tried to sum up her troubled relations with her mother: 'You cannot do me any more harm, for you no longer have me: I was the disorder of your mind, your health, your house; I am worth nothing at all to you.'[20] Her mother's response was to accuse Françoise of being part of a 'plot' against her. One thinks ahead to Louise's obsessive fears of the cabal threatening her happiness in St Petersburg. She remained convinced, as Madame de Sévigné did, that her daughter had wronged her.

> As for myself, all the charm of my life seemed irredeemably destroyed. I no longer took the same pleasure in loving my daughter, and yet heaven knows how much I still loved her, despite all her faults. Only mothers will understand me properly. Soon after her marriage, she caught smallpox. Although I had never had this dreadful illness nobody could prevent me rushing to her bedside. I found her face so swollen that I was seized with fear; but I was afraid only for her, and as long as the illness lasted I did not think for a second of myself. I was happy enough, in the end, to see her recovered without having any marks at all.[21]

The contrast with Louise's absence from her daughter's deathbed a quarter of a century later is remarkable. Either she was more stunned by Julie's last illness than seems possible, or relations between mother and daughter had become immeasurably worse in the interim. It is striking, for instance, that she refused to share her house with Julie (despite the fact that she was rich and Julie had no evident means of support) because she disapproved of her friends – a 'taste for bad company' which, at the end of her stay in England in 1805, she would blame on her former husband's influence.

The Sweetness of Life

*

Louise set off for Moscow on 15 October 1800, and stayed four months. The journey was ghastly.

> It is, I believe, impossible to experience such a hideous fatigue as the one which awaited me *en route* from St Petersburg to Moscow. The roads which I had expected to find frozen . . . were not. These roads are dreadful, and the logs which make them barely passable in extreme cold had not yet been fixed by the ice and rolled about constantly under the wheels, producing the same effect as great waves on the sea.[22]

Stopping at an inn at Novgorod – the only one they found on the journey – did not make her feel any better.

> With a desperate need to rest, dying of hunger and fatigue, I asked for a room. Barely had I settled into it when I smelt some noxious odour which turned my stomach. The landlord, whom I asked to let me change apartments, had none to give me, and I resigned myself to staying; but soon, having formed the belief that this unbearable smell was coming through a glazed door in the room, I called a boy and interrogated him about this door. 'Ah!' he replied calmly, 'The fact is that there has been a dead man behind the door since yesterday; that must be what Madame can smell.' I asked for no more details; I got up, had the horses harnessed to my carriage and left, taking with me no more than a morsel of bread to sustain me for the rest of the journey to Moscow.[23]

She must have wished again that she was a great lady, since apart from being serenaded at meals they habitually travelled, like the *grande dame* of Proust's *A l'ombre des jeunes filles en fleurs*, with their entire household retinue in tow, and never needed to use inns: bed, kitchen utensils and furniture accompanied them everywhere.[24] The torment of travelling was further increased for Louise by the fact that nothing could be seen out of the window of the carriage: thick fog enveloped everything.

The first sight of Moscow ended her disgruntlement. She was overwhelmed by the contrast between rough simplicity and stately magnificence, and by an exoticism that made her feel she was in Isfahan rather than Russia. 'I shall not attempt to describe the effect produced by these thousands of gilded domes topped by huge golden crosses,' she wrote, 'these broad streets, these superb palaces, mostly situated so far from one another that villages separate them; for to form an idea of

Moscow, one has to see it.'[25] Madame de Staël would later be struck by the simultaneous sophistication and rusticity of Muscovite life, which she thought stemmed from the blend of European civilisation and the Asiatic. Moscow was truly foreign, whereas St Petersburg could be regarded as a European colony. The fact that there was no court meant that the nobility could independently indulge their taste for monumental splendour and the luxurious existence of Eastern satraps.[26] One of the grandest of the *grands seigneurs*, Prince Alexander Kurakin, was reputed to keep a seraglio in his palace, and similar stories were told of other grandees.

Within a few days Louise had begun working at her usual furious pace, starting portraits of the Governor of Moscow and his daughter and the illegitimate child of her patron Countess Catherine Stroganova. Not that she was prepared to admit any professional activity to her ex-husband. According to the letter of 29 January 1801 she had had to take a spacious house to display Le Brun's pictures adequately, and quite apart from the trouble of moving from her original lodgings she had been distracted from painting by the need to show them to potential buyers.

> I have done four busts here in the intervals of people's visits to see your pictures, and that is all I have been able to do. I have refused requests to do more than twenty. My travelling companion will do them, for he is staying on here after me.

The *Souvenirs* give a fuller picture of Louise's housing problems. She had abandoned the palace originally lent her by Count Demidov because of the noise made by musicians rehearsing, and moved into Catherine Stroganova's property. But it was unbearably cold, not having been lived in for seven years.

> I remedied this as best I could by having all the stoves on at maximum heat. This precaution did not save me from having to have a fire burning all night in my bedroom, and I was so frozen in my bed, with the curtains hermetically drawn, to say nothing of a little lamp lit near me to take the chill off the air, that I wrapped a pillow round my head and tied it with a ribbon, at the risk of being smothered. One night when I had managed to fall asleep, I was woken up by smoke, which was asphyxiating me. I only had time to ring for my chambermaid, who assured me she had put out the fires everywhere. 'Open the door of the gallery,' I told her; barely had she obeyed me when her candle was snuffed out and my bedroom, along with the entire apartment, was filled with

thick, stinking smoke. We smashed all the window-panes as quickly as possible, but as I had no idea where this dreadful smoke was coming from, you may imagine how worried I was. I immediately summoned one of the men who lit the stoves, and he told me his workmate had forgotten to remove the cap which closes the pipes, and which is, I believe, on the roof . . . What tormented me most in this night of tribulation was the impossibility of immediately removing a collection of pictures by several masters which my husband had sent me, and which I had exhibited in a room adjoining my bedroom . . .[27]

By five in the morning the smoke had scarcely lessened; according to Louise's letter to Le Brun, it had still not cleared ten days later. In the meantime she perished with cold: the temperature was 22 degrees below freezing, and there were no windows. It all explains her outraged tone of self-pity:

I thought I would die because of the house which I only took for your pictures [she tells Le Brun slightly inaccurately], it has given me consumptive pains all over my body; the aches I had in my head have increased to the point that they are unbearable. I cover myself with cotton flannel . . . I always feel cold. My blood has been so cold for five weeks that I thought I would die . . . I was so freezing I couldn't sleep.

The portrait of the Governor of Moscow, Marshal Saltykov, was half-grilled, and had to be completely repainted. Le Brun's pictures were more or less undamaged, but moving them into new quarters took time and entailed trouble which Louise begrudged. She had 'killed' herself for his profit, she concluded.

So she might have felt less than enthusiastic about thanking Countess Stroganova for the loan of her palace; but she still produced a captivating portrait of her illegitimate daughter. The very pretty Varvara Ladomirska bore the surname of an extinct Polish family which Paul I had allowed her and her brothers and sister to assume. Louise's portrait in some ways resembles one of Julie Le Brun as Flora, at least in facial expression, and is closer still to the picture of Aniela Angélique Radziwill begun before Louise left Russia. Both show a girl in the bloom of youth, with bright dark eyes and a shy smile, and both are poetic images which illustrate Louise's evolution away from the rococo and the formal court portrait to a warm, moving and seductive romanticism. Varvara Ladomirska, dressed in a gold-trimmed tunic fastened at the shoulder with a brooch, is wearing exactly the kind of costume Catherine II had disapproved of in Grand-

Duchess Elizabeth, and which Louise congratulated herself on having introduced to Moscow society. When she attended a ball Marshal Saltykov's wife had invited her to, she found an assembly of dazzlingly beautiful young women wearing Grecian-style tunics bordered with gold fringes, and took complete responsibility for this phenomenon.[28]

The Moscow society Louise frequented was not invariably elegant: some of the fabulously rich natives she encountered were also exceptionally boorish. On one occasion she was invited to dine with a banker, a gross and unprepossessing person whose equally coarse guests seemed to her a parody of the money-making classes.

> We were eighteen at table; but never in my entire life have I seen a group of faces so ugly and above all so insignificant, real money-men's faces; when I had looked at all of them once I no longer dared to raise my eyes, fearful of meeting one of them again; there was no flow of conversation, you might have taken them for dummies if they had not eaten like ogres. Four hours went by in this way; I had reached such a point of boredom that I felt ready to be ill; finally I made my mind up: I invented an indisposition, and left them at table where perhaps they still are.[29]

Another seemingly crass acquaintance, Prince Bezborodko, had far more subtlety than outward appearances suggested. Louise did not paint his portrait, but the one by Levitsky emphasises the earthy, unbuttoned informality of this great man (whose name, meaning 'chinless', came from an ancestor whose chin had been sliced off in a swordfight).[30] His mnemonic gifts were legendary. At the age of twenty-eight, on first meeting Catherine II, he had quoted to her word for word a law she had forgotten, and told the stunned Empress on precisely what page of which volume of texts it was to be found. Bezborodko was officially in charge of petitions addressed to Catherine, which meant, according to Louise, that he was besieged by women anxious to have their pleas heard: his usual response was that he would forget a request or lose a petition.[31] In her correspondence with Grimm, Catherine called him her factotum; later he became a secretary of state in the Foreign Office. All negotiations requiring a degree of dexterity were habitually assigned to him. In 1791 the death of his protector Potemkin and the rise of Platon Zubov had conspired to push Bezborodko into the background.[32] In the meantime he had become a Count of the Holy Roman Empire and grown enormously wealthy. Louise describes him in 1800 as the richest inhabitant of Moscow, and possibly the richest man in all Russia, reputed to be able to raise an army of 30,000 soldiers simply from the serfs he owned.[33] He possessed salt mines in the Crimea and fisheries in the Caspian Sea, and was said to be the most benevolent of masters.

She slightly blunts the force of the most famous story told about Bezborodko, which highlights both his phenomenal improvisatory gifts and the debauchery for which he was also known. At weekends Bezborodko was in the habit of dressing simply and attending masked balls at which the dregs of society were present. On one of these occasions he received a summons from Catherine while dead drunk; he arranged to be taken home and doused with cold water as well as bled in both arms, was then conducted to the imperial presence in a completely lucid state, and was asked by the Empress for the text of a law she had asked him to draft. Bezborodko, who had completely forgotten to do so, pulled a blank sheet of paper from his pocket and gave her the entire *ukaze* as though it were before his eyes. When Catherine discovered the deception he begged for forgiveness, but was named Privy Councillor instead. Louise's version of the story, disappointingly, omits all reference to Bezborodko's drunkenness.[34]

He was known as a roué as well as an astute politician, and rumoured to have been one of Catherine's lovers. Although devoid of looks and grace, he adored women, and kept a harem as well as a supply of actresses and dancers. But this plebeian with rough appetites was also a connoisseur and patron of the arts.[35] He owned one of the finest galleries in Russia, and in 1796 bought the extremely valuable collection of paintings and sculpture assembled in Paris during the Revolutionary years by Count Golovkin. The Russian Revolution, like the French, would later present the authorities with the problem of nationalising and preserving works of art previously owned by the ruling families.[36] Just as the Louvre, after accumulating the royal collections, absorbed a mass of works confiscated from the *émigrés*, so the Russian museums expanded by appropriating the collections of great connoisseurs of the Empire. Eventually Bezborodko's would be assimilated, as Yusupov's and Shuvalov's had been.

Despite flattering attentions and professional success, Louise was immobilised in gloom. She is explicit about her paralysing melancholy in a letter she sent Gaétan Nigris from Moscow, which is surprisingly fond for someone who had so disliked her daughter's choice of husband:

> the bond between us is too close to my heart for anything involv-
> ing you to be alien to me, and unless I were an egoist I could not
> remain indifferent to it; those who were unjust towards me have
> put much too great a distance between us, for I am willing to

believe that neither you nor my daughter are at fault; she was well deceived! I suffered cruelly from it all, and despite time and my own efforts, the wound is still so raw that when I am alone with myself, my ideas about the happiness a mother may hope for, when she has never had anything to reproach herself with, affect me more than they console me. Circumstances have long obliged me to undertake laborious, painful work, and as a result my health is beginning to alarm me, not as far as my life is concerned, I have no desire to see it prolonged, and I have not changed in what I have often told you in that respect, but I feel a weakness which is destroying me; I am becoming so sad that the greatest misanthrope would seem too gay to me; society fatigues me, solitude kills me, and I can find no position that suits me; my only hope is in rest, sun, a warm climate, and before long I intend to go and seek them out.[37]

There is self-deception in the letter, but also a very moving suffering. The 'plot' Louise imagined seems to have dissolved, or to have undergone a change of focus, leaving only pain and incomprehension behind. Though so strong in some respects, Louise was radically affected by the loss of mental repose. She seemed to have reached an impasse. Obviously, anything was better than staying put. She had probably never heard Horace's view that *Caelum, non animum, mutant/Qui trans mare currunt*,[38] but back in St Petersburg she would be forced to acknowledge its justice. Moving would change her sky, but not her disposition.

But she did not know this, any more than she guessed the real change that would greed her back in the imperial capital. So she determinedly waved off further commissions in Moscow and left, to face intolerable travel conditions again *en route* for St Petersburg. All she wanted to do was see her daughter once more and then leave Russia for good.

En route she heard rumours that Paul had died. In fact he had been assassinated, though his death was publicly attributed to an apoplectic fit. His son Alexander probably connived at the assassination, but was not a member of the conspiracy that carried it out. This was led by Count Peter Pahlen, who is said to have remarked that to make an omelette one must break eggs, and who, according to Louise, had deliberately terrified Paul with reports of a plot the Empress and her children had hatched to seize the throne.[39] This led Paul to order that his family be imprisoned, which made it easy to persuade Alexander that his father was of unsound mind. Paul's mistrust of Maria Fedorovna in any case meant that he habitually double-locked the door separating his apartment from hers, which prevented a quick escape when his attackers were upon him.

Back in St Petersburg, Louise found the populace delirious with joy, dancing in the streets and blessing heaven for their deliverance from tyranny. But if, as she states, a golden age set in after this murder, it was still not enough to dispel her gloom. Yet circumstances seemed to be conspiring to lift her, at least if professional success had been enough to restore her equanimity. Count Stroganov came to tell her that Alexander wanted to commission a bust and an equestrian portrait of himself.

> Barely had this news circulated than a crowd of people from the court rushed to my house to ask me for copies, either of the one on horseback or the bust, they scarcely cared, provided they had the portrait of Alexander. At any other time of my life this would have been the means to make my fortune; but alas, my physical indispositions, to say nothing of the moral sufferings that still plagued me, did not permit me to profit from it; the sad state of my health grew worse every day.[40]

Gaétan Nigris was unable to understand how Louise could think of leaving St Petersburg at the time most favourable to her fortune, failing to grasp the psychological nature of her malaise. Indeed, it seemed perverse to want to obey a doctor's orders to go and take the waters at Karlsbad – as though they could cure heartbreak and despair – when Louise's intention in coming to Russia in the first place had professedly been to round off her fortune. Presumably she had been well paid in Moscow, but her St Petersburg earnings had been depleted, she does not say how greatly, by the need to provide Julie's dowry.

Since she was so clearly subordinating financial matters to emotional ones, we may believe Louise when she describes how she felt to be leaving friends:

> the Princesses Kurakina and Dolgorukova, the excellent Count Stroganov, who had given me so many proofs of attachment – it was they I regretted far more than the fortune I was renouncing. I remember that as soon as the dear Count heard that I was going to leave he came to see me; his grief was so great that he paced up and down my studio where I was painting, saying: 'No, no, she will not leave, that is impossible.' My daughter, who was present, thought that he was going mad.[41]

The unspecified 'obstructions' which her doctor had recommended taking the Karlsbad waters to clear were her pretext too when she anxiously announced her intention to the Tsar and Tsarina. The truth was obviously more complicated, but could scarcely be divulged to her patrons. Even if it could have been, would it have seemed important to them? Perhaps not. Louise was no mere 'phiz-monger', but it was as much for her technical skill as her psychological acuteness that she was valued. Courtier-artist though she was, she could not necessarily assume that her worth was seen in terms of more than mechanical virtuosity: the Romantic concept of genius had not really penetrated the Russian court of the 1800s. So to suggest that an existential malaise was gripping her and destroying her peace might have won her less comprehension than to adduce a merely physical embarrassment, or produced no more penetrating a diagnosis than Alexander's 'Don't leave, that would be too far to go to look for a remedy; I will give you the Empress's horse, and when you have ridden it for a while, you will be cured.'[42]

Besides, this time Louise does not claim that she could not work. That had been the consequence of her father's death and of her terror at the outbreak of Revolution. The problem now was that she could not live. Had she finally come to see painting as *less* necessary to her than breathing? Unlike Madame de Sévigné, she had a profession, and one might have thought that the activity it involved would help counteract the *mal d'amour* which she, like her predecessor in daughter-worship, found so devastating. But on this occasion her 'beloved art' was not enough. She had been radically affected both by the loss of her daughter and by the criticisms levelled at her as a parent. The wounds, of a kind no male artist would or could have suffered, stayed unhealed for a long time.

CHAPTER NINE

THE RETREAT FROM ST PETERSBURG:
'I march towards a tomb'

Leaving the country 'which I still regard as a second homeland'[1] would have been painful in any circumstances. Leaving when she felt ill and unpleasantly alone was worse. Auguste Rivière was accompanying her in a separate barouche, but his presence was intermittent, 'especially when we had passed the frontier and encountered the sand; for the postilions, whom he was unable to make obey him, constantly took him off on side-roads while I followed the main route.'[2] Yet Louise needed company. Solitude, as she remarked in her letter to Le Brun from Moscow, had become abhorrent to her. She had been unable to bring her chambermaid with her because of her advanced state of pregnancy, so instead she gave a lift to a poor old man who wanted to go to Prussia. She did so out of pity rather than because she thought his presence could restore her. In fact he drank himself into a stupor at every staging-post and each time had to be carried back to his seat.

She could still be lifted by fresh sights and new experiences. The Baltic peoples and Baltic lands enchanted her. From the sophistication and cosmopolitanism of St Petersburg she was transported back to an earlier age. In the small town of Narva she saw women dressed in the ancient style – but genuinely, not as examples of high society's mania for antiquity.

> They are beautiful, for in general the Livonian people are magnificent-looking; almost all the old men's heads reminded me of heads of Christ by Raphael, and the young men, whose straight hair fell to their shoulders, seem to have served as models to this great master.[3]

But in general her state of mind prevented her from seeing the world as it 'really' was. She must have been made aware of the truth of what Ruskin would call the pathetic fallacy: having hoped to see the royal family-in-exile at Mittau, but missed them, she experienced disappointment so crushing that the natural world seemed to suffer with her.

> Our state of mind and health exerts such a powerful influence on the objects around us that I remembered more than once how gaily, on my way to St Petersburg, I had travelled the road I had just followed so sadly. I remember particularly that the look of Kurland had enchanted me. These magnificent forests of ancient oaks, huge fir-trees or alders whose whitish trunks stand out so sharply against their foliage, which is like that of the weeping willow; these beautiful lakes, these charming hills, these pretty valleys – my serene, happy imagination enlivened them then with a thousand laughing, poetic ideas. In the woods I saw Diana followed by her retinue; in the prairies, dancing shepherds and shepherdesses, as I had seen them in Rome on ancient bas-reliefs: in short, I made my journey into an enchantment. But on the return there were no more fantastic figures or joyful dances. My sadness and my sufferings had depopulated this lovely countryside, which I barely looked at.[4]

Louise would write to her brother Etienne Vigée from Dresden that travel cured her of all the ills of urban living. But this time her sufferings had not been produced by life in the city. The relief she might otherwise have hoped to find in having her organism shaken up on a long journey was therefore not immediately forthcoming. And being unable to *see* things, which was the usual consequence of her feeling sad, she was simply more aware than usual of the unpleasantness of travelling in still-uncivilised lands at the start of the nineteenth century – the appalling inns, the inedible food, the dreadful roads and so on. The sight of Auguste Rivière repeatedly crossing the highway in his barouche, about to investigate yet another side-road, might have been amusing in other circumstances, but now probably just seemed provocative.

She was, in any case, hardly in a mood to be diverted. She was sinking into the kind of state which, just before her departure from France in 1789, had made her unrecognisable to family and friends.

> In my then condition of sickness, such a tiring mode of existence ought to have been fatal to me: indeed, it only took a few days for me to be reduced to a degree of depression that my courage and my earnest desire not to stop *en route* could barely overcome. I became so weak and ill that I had to be dragged to the coach, where I stayed motionless, devoid even of the faculty of thought. I experienced no other sensation than that of a sharp pain in my right side, caused by rheumatism, and which each jolt intensified. This pain was so unbearable that one day, when the coachmen

had sunk us into a road that was being repaired and which was full
of stones, I completely lost consciousness.[5]

Reaching Berlin ought to have revived her, and to an extent it did. She had
promised herself *en route* to St Petersburg that she would call on Queen
Louise of Prussia when she returned from Russia, and so had at least one
royal meeting to look forward to after being disappointed at Mittau. There
is no evidence, incidentally, that Louise was acquainted with the Queen at
the time of making this promise to herself. Perhaps knowing Prince Henry
made her feel that she already had an entrée to the Prussian court, or perhaps she had been approached about a portrait commission. Louise could
not afford to be bashful about exploiting royal contacts. She had, by this
time, an assured status, which meant that obtaining introductions to
queens and empresses was easy. The network of patronage largely followed that of family relationships: knowing one royal, one felt one knew
a host of others. The Habsburg and Bourbon connections had already
opened doors all over Europe. It was natural enough to expect the
Hohenzollern one to do the same in Prussia.

Some difficulties had to be settled before Louise could explore this
promising avenue. She had a tussle with customs officers when she
arrived. Eventually she was allowed to leave for her hotel with an official,

> a real devil, who besides was dead drunk. He undid my packages,
> my water-bags, turning everything upside down, and grabbed
> hold of a length of Indian embroidered muslin which Madame du
> Barry had given me when I left Paris. As I did not want my *Sibyl*
> or the studies I had made of the Emperor and Empress of Russia
> to be unrolled, seals were put on my carriage and I could finally
> go to bed, but seized by a dreadful trembling which did not allow
> me to sleep for a second.[6]

But she was obviously becoming more robust than she had felt at the end
of her stay in Russia, and readier to fall in with royal requests than she had
been just before leaving St Petersburg.

> Three days were enough for me to recover from my fatigue, and I
> was feeling much better when the Queen of Prussia, who was not
> in Berlin at the time, had the goodness to summon me to see her
> in Potsdam, where she wanted me to do her portrait.[7]

This was probably in part a political gesture. Frederick William III's wife
was a passionate opponent of the French Revolution and a declared

enemy of Napoleon, whose star was rising in France. It obviously suited her to give her patronage to an artist so closely associated with the pre-Revolutionary French court, and an enemy of republicanism.

Louise is not necessarily to be trusted when describing her noblest sitters in the *Souvenirs* – her pen-portraits of Marie-Antoinette and Maria Carolina show that. She rarely misses the chance of prudent flattery, any more than in her portraits proper. When the *Souvenirs* were published in the 1830s, Louise von Mecklenburg-Strelitz had been dead for over a quarter of a century, but they evoke her beauty as though it were still present:

> my pen is powerless to describe the impression I had the first time I saw this princess. The charm of her heavenly face, which expressed benevolence, goodness, and whose features were so regular and delicate; the beauty of her figure, her neck, her arms, the dazzling freshness of her complexion, everything, in short, surpassed the most ravishing vision one can imagine. She was in full mourning, wearing a crown of spikes of black jade which, far from damaging her looks, made her whiteness the more startling. One needs to have seen the Queen of Prussia to realise how spell-bound I must have been on first meeting her.

From a distance, Louise writes, she appeared sixteen, though at the time she was twenty-five. Louise's pastel studies make her an astonishingly child-like beauty, captivating and informally dressed. She probably did not exaggerate her beauty, though much of what she says about Queen Louise – her perfect complexion, her charity – matches her statements about Marie-Antoinette, whom we know she 'improved'. But Madame de Staël confirms that the Queen was ravishing as well as virtuous.[8]

Her virtue perhaps needed to be underlined, for Louise of Prussia was later accused of having had an extra-marital relationship with Tsar Alexander. Louise is unspecific about this 'infamous calumny',[9] but the accusation was as brutally levelled by the Queen's enemy Napoleon as by memorialists of the period. All Louise says is this:

> I remember that at this time, when I was sitting in Countess Potocka's box at the Paris Opera, a Polish soldier serving in the French army entered (certainly a Pole was not suspect when he was defending a Northern power): I spoke to him about the unworthy lies which people were swapping about the Queen of Prussia's relations with Emperor Alexander. The young man replied: 'Nothing is more false, people write all those things to

liven up despatches.' And yet the dear creature they made into their victim read these horrors, and the grief she felt as a result, together with so many other sources of grief, may have hastened her death.[10]

The 'other sources of grief' possibly included the allegation that she had forced her husband into a disastrous war with France, culminating in the rout at Jena in 1806.

Louise's busy activity during the weeks she spent in Berlin suggests that she had readjusted to the idea of being a working painter. She did pastel portraits of other members of the Hohenzollern family, which she reproduced in oil when she was back in Paris. She continued, as though it were necessary, to 'sell' herself, showing the appreciative Queen her portraits of Alexander and Elizabeth, and putting the inevitable Sibyl in a frame for Louise to contemplate. 'I cannot describe her graciousness as she made clear to me how greatly she admired them; she was so sweet and good that the attachment she inspired was not unlike tenderness.'[11] In the face of such flattery, Louise herself could not do less when the Queen introduced her to her surprisingly unprepossessing children. She fell back on her usual compliment in such circumstances, remarking that their faces were highly expressive ('*avaient beaucoup de physionomie*'). She could smooth blemishes with words as well as paint.

There were enough pleasures in Berlin to compensate for the fact that she felt inadequately housed – in an *hôtel garni* – and found the coffee undrinkable until the Queen took to sending her her own. There was a memorable outing to Peacock Island, which had an unassuming royal palace and a menagerie that formed the nucleus of the future Berlin Zoo. There were the Queen's many marks of favour. But Louise was beginning to feel like returning to Paris. She was not to know that the disappearance of *ancien régime* society would so blunt her pleasure at being there that she would soon be travelling once more.

It had been easy for Etienne Vigée and her friends, Louise rather inaccurately writes, to have her name deleted from the list of *émigrés*.[12] Perhaps she was unaware of the fruitless efforts which various people had made in the 1790s to do just that. An undated letter from a group of artists to the Director of the Académie de peinture – its signatories including Hubert Robert, Girodet, Duplessis, Madame Vallayer-Coster, Fragonard, Lagrenée and David – had argued that Louise's journey to Italy had been planned for several years before it was finally undertaken, but continually been postponed because of her workload. She had never been an *émigrée*, therefore, and was now needed back in France.[13] But clearly this did not help.

Louise's pleas for special treatment as an artist had fallen on deaf ears. Le Brun too had written to the authorities on her behalf, contending that her profession obliged her to consort with the (exiled) privileged classes, but that her leisure moments were spent with artists alone.[14] Perhaps sensing that this was unlikely to carry conviction, he then produced two different reasons for her emigration. It had been the simple consequence of the slanderous attacks she suffered, he wrote, and besides no artist could seriously work during a revolution.

> It is not in the midst of the clash of arms, in the tumult and agitation inseparable from the burgeoning revolution that one can cultivate the arts. The arts are friends of peace and silence; they need to recollect themselves before creation can begin, and in the instant of creation itself trouble must not be allowed to intrude, nor fear distract them.[15]

This, he observed, was true of men, and more so of women,

> whose constitution is delicate and whose organs are weakened by long periods of work and constant application. But the citizen Le Brun would not have wanted to leave France before liberty had been assured in her country, she saw its benevolent dawn, and contributed to the patriotic gift which was given to the Constituent Assembly by the women artists of Paris.

(There is no evidence, incidentally, that Louise made any such contribution.) The plea concludes with the highly inaccurate statement that Louise, once in Italy, 'marched straight towards Rome'.[16] This is imaginative stuff, but less misleading than the claim that the homeland should be allowed to reclaim 'the one who aspires only to taste the benefits of an immortal Revolution'.[17] Like his brother-in-law Etienne Vigée, Le Brun could be an adroit time-server, but sometimes his touch deserted him.

Louise's name was finally removed from the list of *émigrés* in 1800. Having officially been a *Française* again for a year, and hearing that relative calm now obtained, she determined to end her twelve-year absence and return to Paris. This meant finding a representative of the new republic to establish, without possibility of mistake, that she could re-enter France safely. She felt some repugnance at the need to have dealings with such a person, but was cheered to discover that the French ambassador to Berlin was General Beurnonville, 'a good upstanding military man . . . He gave me the most satisfying welcome and pressed me in the most flattering manner to return to my homeland, assuring me that peace and order had been completely re-established there.'[18]

Much as Louise would have preferred the cause to be otherwise, this was true. Military victories in the Rhineland and Low Countries had strengthened the Republic's hand in the early 1790s, while Napoleon's 'whiff of grapeshot' had crushed monarchist insurrections in Paris in 1795. Though the alliance of Russia, England and Austria had inflicted a series of defeats on French troops from 1798, Napoleon's star had risen so high that he had been able to overthrow the government of the Directory and assume power as First Consul. Through most of 1799 the Allies had pressed the French troops backward on several fronts, but the furious fighting had subsided by the end of the year. In 1800 Bonaparte won major victories at Marengo and Hohenlinden and gained important territorial concessions (ratified in the Treaty of Lunéville of 9 February 1801) from the Habsburgs. Within less than a year, in addition, he had effectively reconquered Italy.

Louise apparently does not hold against Beurnonville the fact that he had been involved in the Revolutionary battles of Valmy – a defeat of the Prussians in 1792 which caused Goethe to remark that a new age had dawned – and Jemmapes, where the victory of the French allowed them to annexe Belgium to the fledgling Republic. Beurnonville's favour continued under the Empire, when Napoleon named him count, and under the Bourbon Restoration he became a peer of France, a minister of state and finally a *maréchal de France.*

Beurnonville had gauged the impatience of Louise's mood accurately, but others still tried to persuade her to stay. 'A few days before I left Berlin,' she writes,

> the director-general of the Academy of Painting came with infinite graciousness to bring me personally the diploma for my admission to this Academy. So many marks of benevolence, which were showered on me at the Prussian court, would certainly have kept me longer, if my plan had not been completely settled on.[19]

She still felt 'a kind of terror' at the prospect of returning to Paris. Why? The letter (of 18 September 1801) she sent her brother from Dresden, her next stopping-place, suggests some of the answers:

> the impatience you feel to see me certainly does not exceed mine; but, dear friend, I cannot hide from you what goes on in my poor head and heart as I think about returning to Paris. As I draw closer to France, the memory of the horrors that occurred there comes back to me so vividly that I am frightened of seeing the places

which witnessed these dreadful scenes again. My imagination will bring it all back. I wish I were blind, or had drunk the waters of Lethe, so as to be able to live in this bloodstained land! It seems to me that I am walking towards a tomb, and I am not mistress of my black ideas on this subject.

On the other hand, when I think that I shall have the joy of embracing you, seeing the friends I have left, admiring master-pieces of art and interesting objects again, I feel swayed in the other direction and no longer hesitant; I tell myself I *will* go. Yes, my friend, I will come to find you all again; but alas! I will not find our poor mother. This grief is the most painful one. You will show me her tomb . . . Heavens, what sad ideas.[20]

She was still neurotically obsessed by the thought that she might again encounter slanderers in France, inaccurately adding that she had been free of them abroad.

You know what suffering this viper [i.e. slander] caused me! All my persecutors are still there; what if I fall into their poisonous clutches again! . . . As soon as you have received this letter, answer all my terrors by return. Tell me particularly if I shall enjoy free-dom of movement; for after spending the winter with you, I shall have to go on another little trip. I am not afraid of travelling, it's good for me. Living in towns kills me, and the open road cures me: the journey and a few baths have completely restored my health.[21]

So Louise was returning home with a very limited sense of commitment. The anticipated change from *ancien régime* ways must have been as potent a factor in awakening her dread as the anticipated resumption of slander. But one doubts whether the slander would actually have resumed. Most of the friends in high places she had been scurrilously associated with were in exile or had perished, and Calonne would die in Paris in October 1802. Besides, Louise herself was now middle-aged, a reasonably but not dangerously attractive woman. Nor was it at all certain that she would enjoy the same professional adulation, and hence provoke the same spiteful envy, as she had before the Revolution. She may have been in demand in Vienna, Brunswick, Munich and St Petersburg, as she tells Etienne, but a new generation of portraitists had established itself in Paris since her departure. Probably what Louise was really fearing was the ill-will of those who had been unimpressed by the alleged grounds for her emigration.

Brunswick, her next port of call, did not delay her long. This was despite the fact that the Rivière family lived there and that she was leaving Auguste, whom she would not see again. Perhaps she found the ducal court as stultifying as the young writer Benjamin Constant had done a few years before her. Brunswick generally, he wrote on 19 March 1788 to the novelist Isabelle de Charrière (author of *Lettres neuchâteloises* and *Lettres écrites de Lausanne*), was duller than anywhere in Switzerland.

> I swear to you that even supposing yourself in the middle of Neuchâtel, in a grand assembly . . . or in an assembly of Lausanne scholars . . . you would not have an adequate idea of the tedium of this town. There is something so dreary in its very aspect, something so cold about its inhabitants, something so languishing in their intercourse together, something so unsociable in their manner of seeing each other; they have neither court-intrigues nor love-intrigues nor debauchery-intrigues. There are court ladies who sleep with their lackeys; there are street-walkers for the use of soldiers and court gentlemen who want them; there are women, of course, whom the English, among others, lodge, feed and dress as a way of killing time. But all this killing of time is so glum; it takes such an effort to kill it for good, and there are moments of agony so painful for its executioner! There is an Italian opera every fortnight, of course, where three actors and three actresses, of whom one is wall-eyed and has a wooden leg, act out farces of which no one understands a word (for there are not two people who understand Italian here). There are also ramparts where there is one foot of mud, ditches where the town sewers discharge themselves from both sides, sentinels everywhere, and you can walk there and sink in knee-deep on horseback. There are also Englishmen who get drunk and play Pharaoh.[22]

Louise probably found things less stifling. She was better at being politely bored; Constant was famous for his impatience with dead routine, and did not suffer fools gladly. Because she remained a courtier-artist to her fingertips, she worried about possibly offending the Duke of Brunswick by declining to do his portrait, the more so as 'this prince had a very fine head'.[23] But she was in a hurry to move on.

She spent even less time – just one night – in Weimar, the glittering little court where Germaine de Staël and Constant would stay soon after her, talking with Schiller and Goethe and mixing with the cream of German culture. They enjoyed themselves more than Louise did, though Germaine found nothing stimulating there. Weimar was only a small town in Thuringia, but it became a literary mecca, the birthplace of German classicism. It was one of the few towns in Germany that were not dominated by French taste, as Berlin was, or the 'Klein-Paris' of Leipzig, and so perhaps lacked intrinsic interest for Louise. Thanks to its enlightened rulers, it had gained great intellectual and artistic prestige, and a fame that belied its size. Germaine would be flattered to find that 'the lowest classes of society'[24] there had read her recently published novel *Delphine*, but she actually spent all her time at the court, which showed her 'an unheard-of obligingness'.[25]

Louise, by contrast, spent no time whatsoever there. This was because she had suffered so horribly on the journey to Weimar,[26] where she did not arrive until midnight. But instead of immediately retiring she decided to worry about having overpaid toll-charges on the journey from Berlin, and sent the servant off to recover the money she was owed on the last one. This inadvertence obviously struck her more than the fact that she was in the glorious town of Wieland, Goethe and Schiller, for she says nothing about it. (Perhaps she had never heard of them.) Nor did she stay to find out more, despite the letters of introduction she had brought from the Prussian court. She left immediately the next day.

Meeting her old acquaintance Friedrich Melchior von Grimm again at Gotha was a welcome relief. After the Revolution Grimm, a friend of Diderot and the other encyclopaedists, had been obliged to leave France; and although Catherine II named him her minister in Lower Saxony, he later resigned the post. In Gotha – whose *Almanach*, published from 1764, contained the names of all the noble families Louise would paint – he helped her change money, did everything to smooth her onward progress, and was in general exceptionally obliging. But, writing less than two years later, Germaine de Staël described the ex-minister as a ridiculous figure:

> All his faults have been greatly enhanced by his eighty years: he is ponderous, slow, mocking, lacking in wit and a sense of measure, and with a stupidly aristocratic bias. All that remains of his old philosophy is a bitterness about life ... He said in my hearing: 'It's pathetic of me to live long; I wanted a good, short life, and the opposite has happened.'[27]

It seems that he had already suffered the reversals which help explain his bitterness by the time Louise visited him. His capital, furniture, library and precious possessions had all been seized in Paris, though his diplomatic status should have safeguarded them, and he was becoming almost completely blind. Yet Louise was struck only by his kindness.[28]

The Sweetness of Life

The main excitement of the next stage of the journey was an encounter with a confidence trickster in Frankfurt. Was it Louise's trained artistic eye that made her almost instantly suspicious of the man? It seems likely, though some St Petersburg friends of hers, the Divovs, were quite taken in.

> I had left my old drunkard, who had tormented me so much, in Berlin, and when I got out of the coach a young German, very well dressed, who was at the entrance to the hotel offered to carry my bags up for me. He put them on the table of the first room I was to occupy, then, as I had naturally followed him, he tried to kiss my hand, which I refused with the greatest imaginable politeness, though thanking him for his own civility.

She was pleased to find the Divovs planning to stay at the same *hôtel garni*, since the young German unsettled her. He was as eager to help the new arrivals. Elizabeth Divova, in gratitude, invited him to dine with them, and he regaled them with cock-and-bull stories about a thwarted marriage. Louise remained impatient.

> We were forced to spend six days in Frankfurt, and I was thoroughly bored there; but there was a rumour that Bonaparte had been assassinated, which would have changed all my plans to return to Paris. Finally, when we were ready to leave and our packing was done, it emerged that Madame Divova was short of several silver place-settings. I had not a moment's doubt that they had been stolen by the young German, and as soon as I arrived in Paris I read in the *Gazette* that the young man had just been arrested for theft.[29]

Quite why Napoleon's assassination would have completely changed Louise's travel plans is unclear. The assassins would presumably have been men who disliked his rise to power no less than she did herself. At any rate, her feelings of trepidation as she re-entered France were as great as they would have been had the report been true.

> I shall not try to describe what I felt inside when I reached France, this land I had left twelve years before; fear, pain, joy shook me in turn (for there was all of that in the thousand sensations which overwhelmed my soul). I wept for the friends I had lost on the scaffold; but I was going to see those who remained again. France, to which I was returning, had been the scene of dreadful crimes; but France was my homeland![30]

And, as though it had been the most natural thing in the world, she made straight for the marital home in the rue du Gros-Chenet, where Le Brun still lived, and settled in there. If she had been concerned about one possible effect of her long absence, she need not have been. She was still newsworthy. The *Journal de Paris* and other gazettes recorded her return to the city she had left in 1789, but did so without making insinuations she would have found wounding about the motives for her original departure. Le Brun, as well as Etienne and Suzanne Vigée and their daughter Caroline, seemed genuinely glad to see her.

Louise, whose Moscow letter showed how bitterly she still resented her former husband's profligacy, cannot resist a dig at him now.

> I found the staircase filled with flowers, and my apartment perfectly decorated. The hangings and curtains in my bedroom were of green cashmere, the curtains bordered with soft gold-coloured embroidered silk; Monsieur Le Brun had had the bed crowned with a canopy of gold stars; all the furniture was comfortable and tasteful; in short, every one of my desires had been anticipated. Although Monsieur Le Brun spared none of my own expense in arranging it all, I was still sensible of the care he had taken to make my living-quarters agreeable.[31]

Louise had always indignantly denied having expensive tastes, whether in furnishing or dress, and perhaps this apartment was no more showy than the one enemies like Champcenetz had criticised in the 1780s. Brifaut's *Souvenirs* remark that it was unostentatious, but made into a jewel-house by her paintings, which hung everywhere.[32] The artist Gigoux, however, later described it as part of a 'vast *hôtel*', and said it was as splendid as the Trianon at Versailles.[33]

The huge saleroom in the hôtel de Lubert was cleared for a concert on the evening Louise returned. She writes that she was flattered and moved to tears by her reception. Her painter's eye was caught by the ravishing Jeanne-Marie Tallien, as it would be on a later occasion when Hubert Robert, who knew her well, brought the two women together. Louise was dazzled by the creature who was said to be Madame Récamier's only rival in looks:

> I admit that I searched in vain for any fault in the appearance of this enchanting woman. She was both beautiful and pretty; for the regularity of her features did not rob her of what is called expressiveness. Her smile, her glance had something bewitching about them, and her figure, her arms, her shoulders were admirable.[34]

So Paris could clearly still offer examples of the dashing exquisite females Louise loved to paint. The duchesse d'Abrantès gives an even more fulsome description of her than Louise: typically, she writes,

> her dress did not contribute to the effect her beauty made, for she wore simple Indian muslin chemises, draped in antique fashion and fastened at the shoulders with two cameos. Her hair, velvet-black in colour, was short and crimped around the head; this style was then called *à la Titus*; on her fine white shoulders was a superb red cashmere shawl, an item which was still very rare at that time, and much sought-after. She draped it around herself in a way that was always gracious and visually arresting, and so formed the most ravishing picture.[35]

According to Talleyrand, no one appeared so richly *déshabillée* as she did.[36]

Louise did not, in fact, paint Madame Tallien, but she became a friend of hers, attending several of Louise's soirées in the rue du Gros-Chenet. Nor was Madame Tallien simply the owner of a pretty face: she did good, and had been called 'Our Lady of Mercy' by unfortunates she saved from the guillotine or otherwise helped by using her influence over her blood-thirsty politician husband (whom she divorced the year Louise met her). She was thought by the public to have triggered the so-called Thermidor reaction which led to Robespierre's downfall. Jeanne-Marie's circle included the politician Barras and the playwright Marie-Joseph Chénier, as well as the composers Cherubini and Méhul and the singer Garat. After tiring of Barras, with whom she had had a liaison, she had four children by the banker Ouvrard before becoming the princesse de Chimay under the Empire, and moving to the splendid house at the end of the long rue de Babylone[37] where Louise watched her and her husband's accomplished theatrical performances.

Establishing contact with old acquaintances again should have been reassuring, and to an extent it was. The elation Louise felt at returning from exile took some time to wear off, and she was initially kept so busy with visits and various kinds of entertainment that she had no time to be melancholic. Gloom descended later – partly as she became aware that she had lost far more friends under the Revolution than she had thought – and drove her to take desperate measures. She found some people very much as she had left them.

> The first visit I received the day after my arrival, as I was getting

up, was that of Greuze, who seemed quite unchanged. You would even have thought his hair had not been disarranged: his curls fell on either side of his face, just as at the time I had left. I was touched by his promptness, and very pleased to see him again.[38]

Given that Greuze lacked all the polish of the court painter, had rough manners and was extremely arrogant, this enthusiasm might seem surprising. Diderot had been sure that 'this vain man' should not be among the French artists sent to Russia, and commented on Greuze's unbearable vanity in more than one letter to Falconet: 'he is an excellent artist, but a very difficult man. One should take his drawings and pictures and leave the man.'[39] Or, 'As for the artist, he continues to be drunk with his own greatness; and so much the better, perhaps he would do less well without the enormous presumptuousness his talent gives him . . .' And this was really the point. As *Le Neveu de Rameau* puts it, 'If you throw cold water over Greuze's head, you may extinguish his talent along with his vanity.'[40]

In 1802 he was seventy-six, and had been ruined by the Revolution (and in part, allegedly, by his spendthrift shrew of a wife). Tastes, too, had changed. In 1801 Greuze wrote to Lucien Bonaparte that he was starving, and said that he had lost everything but his talent and courage. So Louise, character differences apart, had reason to feel pleased at the old man's visit. She also remembered what her painting technique owed to his lessons.

Vien was even older, and perhaps because of his age – eighty-two – Louise called on him rather than the other way around. It is hardly surprising that she should have so appreciated the work of this pioneer neo-classicist. 'One may regard Monsieur Vien,' she writes,

> as having spearheaded the move towards restoring the French school. He was the first to paint Greek and Roman costumes with style and precision. David and his pupils, Gérard, Gros, Girodet, are justly famous from this point of view, true. But it is fair to say that Monsieur Vien had given the first example of this improvement in his historical subjects.[41]

In fact Vien's style remained more wedded to the rococo mode than Louise suggests[42] – he softened the sternness of antiquity with touches of slightly effete *galanterie*, having calculated correctly that this suited the taste of the age better. All Vien said, modestly, was that he had opened a door; David had broken it down.

Vien had been the King's First Painter, and was later named Senator by Napoleon. He was still artistically active, as Louise herself would be into her eighties. Unlike Greuze, he seems to have been a model of the social graces, and as Louise delightedly reports,

> I was highly flattered by the warm welcome he was kind enough to extend to me, and by the extreme goodness he showed me. [Despite his age] he showed me two oil sketches in the style of the ancient bacchanalia which he had just done. They were charming. I was so surprised and enchanted that, though it is thirty-five years since I saw them, I remember them perfectly.[43]

Vien was without rancour towards the young Turks who had built on his beginnings and enjoyed public favour from the 1780s onward. What of Louise? The other artists she mentions first seeing in Paris were her old friends Robert and Ménageot. There is still no explicit reference to the woman who had been seen as her rival – Adélaïde Labille-Guiard had only one more year to live, and Louise, with decades of paintings ahead of her, managed to go on ignoring her. But perhaps she had more grounds to be jealous of the new school of portraitists she found flourishing on her return to the capital. Her friend, the young writer Sophie de Bawr, categorically denies that she was. Their idiom, after all, was very different from hers.

> Far from envying the success of the painters who were then dazzling Paris, her first thought was to seek out Gérard, Girodet, Guérin and Gros and invite them to her house. All four remained her friends until they died (for all four predeceased her). She went to see their pictures in their studios before seeing them in the Salon; she praised, she admired with inexpressible frankness and pleasure; and this woman, whose face was still charming and whose figure was of remarkable beauty, gave them advice like a master.[44]

And what Louise herself writes in the *Souvenirs* seems to bear out this statement. Gérard had already made a name for himself with his pictures of Belisarius and Psyche, and, she says,

> I had the utmost desire to make the acquaintance of this great artist, who was said to have as distinguished a mind as he did a rare talent. I found him deserving of his reputation in every way, and have since always numbered him among the people I like to spend time with. He had then just finished his fine portrait of Madame Bonaparte reclining on a settee, which was to add greatly to his renown in this genre.[45]

Gérard painted many of the beauties who had been Louise's clients before and after the Revolution – the Countess Zamoyska whom Louise wrongly thought she had depicted doing a shawl-dance in Vienna (but who seems to have been the subject of another, lost picture), the princesse de Talleyrand, Countess von Schönborn. He assembled as dazzling a gallery of subjects as Louise had done in her prime, and as the painter of Empresses Josephine and Marie-Louise he gradually supplanted Louise, the painter of Marie-Antoinette. Louise still had striking work to do – the portraits of Josephina Grassini, Mrs Chinnery and Madame de Staël (whom Gérard would also depict). But the new painter of women under the Consulate, and then under the Empire and Restoration, was to be Gérard.[46]

Louise does not mention David among the younger artists she saw on her return, and it is not really surprising. David may have been one of the signatories to the document calling for her name to be removed from the list of *émigrés*, but his political activities during the Revolution had filled Louise with distaste. So, although she writes of Gérard's Belisarius and Psyche pictures, she says nothing of David's; nor, when she later describes seeing Gérard's portrait of Madame Récamier, does she mention David's outstanding picture of her.

She welcomed the excuse which seeing Gérard's picture gave her to make the acquaintance of this fabled beauty. She was thrilled to meet such a 'lovely person', and Madame Récamier, though also fabled for her remoteness, seemed to have been equally pleased to meet her. Perhaps it was more that she reserved her remoteness for men: she eventually softened towards the besotted Chateaubriand, but not towards other admirers like the gangling, myopic, carrot-haired Benjamin Constant. Towards someone who possessed Louise's *cachet* she was likely to be more than welcoming. Every notability of the age – diplomat, politician, artist or writer – passed through her drawing-room, and a glamorous woman painter with a European reputation was likely to appeal to this 'muse of sociability'.[47] Louise cannot have appeared a serious rival in looks – she was twenty years older than Madame Récamier, and in any case had been pretty rather than a raving beauty – but the two women had other things in common. They had the same taste in dress, for instance, both favouring white muslin and an overall simplicity. But Louise liked diamonds, while Madame Récamier preferred pearls.

It was an important acquaintance to have made. Madame Récamier's style of entertaining was able to reassure Louise that the elegance and splendour she thought had died with the *ancien régime* was still alive. She was delighted by the ball Madame Récamier invited her to and which she attended with Princess Dolgorukova.

There were a great many people, but without any confusion, and a vast number of pretty women, a very fine hôtel – nothing was lacking. As the Peace of Amiens had just been concluded there was an indefinable air of quality and magnificence at this gathering which the younger generation had been unable to experience up to that time. This was the first time young men and women of twenty saw liveries in Paris antechambers, and ambassadors in drawing-rooms; distinguished foreigners, richly dressed, all decorated with glittering orders; and whatever people may say, such luxury is better suited to a ball than short jackets and trousers.[48]

Juliette Récamier was one of the major aesthetic attractions of consular Paris. She was twenty-five when Louise met her, and according to Mathieu Molé enjoyed a fame known by no other woman of her times. She was at the height of her comeliness and prosperity, and newspapers were filled with details of the famous guests present at her balls and receptions. The attention paid to her, and to her least physical indisposition, made her the late eighteenth-century equivalent of today's media superstars. With her simple dress and bewitching looks she seemed the very essence of femininity,[49] her charms perhaps increased by her inaccessibility. Madame Regnault de Saint-Jean-d'Angély remarked that her appearance at any social event was enough to deflect men's attention from all other women.[50]

The writer Maria Edgeworth claimed that a part of the immense enthusiasm she provoked was simply due to fashion: unlike many of the *nouvelles riches* who had entered Paris society since the Revolution, she was a gracious and *decent* beauty.[51] Madame d'Abrantès had initially been predisposed against her.

I had heard much about her, and I admit that my mother had slightly influenced my opinion, persuading herself and me (because I almost always adopted her views on the *monde*) that Madame Récamier was what was then called a *merveilleuse*, that is to say an exaggerated person from the point of view of fashion and its mad, noisy devotees. I was almost afraid of her. In short – since I must say this – by assembling in my mind the parts I thought must form a whole I created an admittedly enchanting woman, but one who completely destroyed, not only all the mediocre opposition, but also faces which ordinarily earn a decent living in society and are found pretty. How surprised I was to see this enchanting face so fresh, so child-like and yet so lovely! But how much more surprised to see the pained timidity her triumph inspired in her! . . . she suffered from the enraged glances of

many women who made themselves no more agreeable by looking daggers, and who, if only out of self-interest, should have done
like me and looked with calm and pleasure at this lovely face,
exclaiming after a proper look: 'Heavens above! how pretty she
is.'[52]

The Récamier home in the Chaussée-d'Antin area was as elegant as
Louise's description suggests, and was the object of a cult among 'amateurs' of interiors. Bertie Greatheed, staying in Paris in 1803, observed
without apparent enthusiasm that 'I hear of no French house but
Récamier's',[53] and it attracted a throng of foreign as well as French visitors.
Some admired and some sneered, but all were in a hurry to see. Madame
Récamier was married to a banker – a much older man also reputed to be
her father – and the establishment was very evidently prosperous; but it
was a small jewel rather than a vast palace, its appearance of luxury arising
as much from the novelty of its decoration as from the opulence of the
interior. Juliette lived permanently amidst the same profusion of flowers
as Jean-Baptiste-Pierre Le Brun had arranged for the special occasion of
his former wife's return to Paris, and the staircases of the house, according to one witness, were like a garden in full bloom.

The centre of attraction was the hostess's bedroom, where eager onlookers would clamber on to chairs to get a better view of Juliette reclining on
her couch; but one also visited the bathroom. There were two drawing-
rooms and – a rarity in a private house during this period, when the table
was generally set at random – a dining-room. Marble and mahogany were
everywhere, as were enormous wall-mirrors; the spirit of the antique prevailed, though its sources were imprecise – Greek, Etruscan and Pompeian
all at once. Some found the ensemble too massive for a young woman in
her twenties; others called the house a pretty bauble, and the Goncourts
described the interior as a pastiche of classicism.[54] But most of the
Récamiers' contemporaries were enchanted, and so was Louise.

Perhaps her relief at finding some standards still upheld in consular
Paris prevented her from feeling the disappointment Bertie Greatheed
declared at about the same time:

> Everyone complains of Bonaparte; everyone talks of the court.
> The old evils are returned or returning without the old elegance.
> Take away the foreigners from this town and what remains? I am
> disappointed and look with dread on the time I have to stay.[55]

This was written on New Year's Day 1803. By mid-April his negative mood
had intensified.

> There is a prodigious diet of equality both of rank and fortune produced by the revolution . . . I see neither elevation nor depression, but an ordinary Vauxhall level of pretty well-dressed *roturiers*, some considerably vulgar and some tolerably well-bred. This is miserable work for those used to refinement and elegance, and that high finish of society which must result from great advantages being perpetuated to a body of privileged families; but whether it does not produce more unhappiness in a people at large is another question.[56]

Louise was struck by the comparative bleakness of life away from havens like the Récamiers', certainly.

> The first time I went to the theatre, the appearance of the auditorium seemed to me extremely sad; used as I was to see everyone wearing powder, formerly in France and since then abroad, these black heads and men dressed in black suits were gloomy to behold. You would have thought the public had assembled to follow a funeral procession.
>
> In general, the look of Paris seemed less gay to me; the streets seemed so narrow that I was tempted to believe a double row of houses had been built. That was probably due to my recent memories of the streets in St Petersburg and Berlin, which are mostly extremely spacious. But what I disliked even more was seeing the words 'freedom, fraternity or death' still written on the walls. These words, consecrated by the Terror, awakened in me very sad thoughts about the past, and did not leave me without fear for the future.[57]

An experience she found equally unsettling was passing by the Place Louis XV – now the Place de la Concorde, but then associated with the scaffold and the guillotining of the King and Queen. It was a sad day generally, because Louise had decided to make it the occasion for visiting the loathsome old Le Sèvre:

> he still lived in Neuilly, in a little house which had been bought by my father, and where I had gone several times when I was very young. Everything there reminded me of my poor mother, the happy time I had spent with her; I found her workbasket exactly as she had left it; in short, this visit was all the sadder for me because I was already in a state to be tearful. On the way to Neuilly I had to cross the Place Louis XV, where I thought I could still see

the blood of so many noble victims! My brother, who was with me, reproached me for not having made our coachman take another route, for what I was suffering then was indescribable; even today it is still impossible for me to cross this square without remembering the horrors it witnessed, and I cannot govern the effects of my imagination.[58]

Part of the less pleasant side to Paris life which Louise had now to acquaint herself with was, of course, the new political order. She is fairly circumspect about the First Consul, whom she was able to contemplate during a performance of Racine's *Esther* at Saint-Germain-en-Laye: 'He was seated on the first bench; I sat down on the second, in a corner, but only a very short distance from him, so I could examine him at my ease. Though I was in the half-darkness, Madame Campan came to tell me that he had guessed I was there.'[59]

She had seen him earlier, in fact, at a parade in front of the Louvre, and experienced the same disappointment as she had done at first sight of Catherine the Great. The conquering hero was simply not big enough.

> I was standing at a window of the Muséum, and I remember that I was unwilling to recognise as Napoleon the skinny little man who was pointed out to me; the duc de Crillon, who was beside me, had extreme difficulty persuading me that it was really he. My imagination ... had led me to picture this famous man as a colossus in form.[60]

Her attitude towards Napoleon was slightly softened when she discovered that he approved of a bust of Marie-Antoinette – whether by Louise or another artist is unclear – which Madame Campan had in her apartment. Presumably he could afford to be generous, since this was a time of prosperity for him. Louise writes:

> at this period he seemed to have nothing to fear from past or future. His victories aroused enthusiasm among the French, and even among foreigners. He was particularly admired by the English, and I remember that one day when I was going to dine at the Duchess of Gordon's she showed me Bonaparte's portrait and said: 'He is my zero' [for *héros*]. As she spoke very bad French, I understood what she meant, and we both laughed heartily when I explained to her what a 'zero' was.[61]

Perhaps the English would have been less impressed if they had known the true extent of Napoleon's Anglophobia. According to the duchesse d'Abrantès, it was around 1802 that Napoleon started inveighing against percale and muslin on the grounds of their alleged Englishness. (Everything we know as 'whites' came from England: at that time there was no French calico or muslin.) He praised the future duchess for wearing an old-fashioned dress with a full skirt, not a neo-Greek sheath – she was slim enough not to need the cosmetic help of such confections.

> That is how you should all dress when you are *en négligé*, Mesdames, and not in these English muslins which are sold to you for a king's ransom, and which have none of the nobility of a fine piece of lawn, white and fresh; then my factories would prosper. Wear lawn, batiste and silk.[62]

According to the duchess, in any case, the English could not *like* Napoleon. They came to Paris to admire him, and appreciated his noble qualities, but that was all.[63] The more politically aware among them, in any case, must have been aware that France – still, until the Treaty of Amiens, officially at war with their country – was a dangerous neighbour. By 1803 the Treaty would have collapsed; England declared war, and Napoleon started assembling a huge invasion force around Boulogne.

Louise's attitude to Bonaparte is surely ambivalent. On the one hand she despised him for the simple reason that he had fought for the republic, and now seemed to aspire to the glory of the dead King and Queen. On the other hand, Napoleon's victories had immeasurably enriched the national art-collections, though she was loath to admit as much openly. Many of these 'conquered' works would have to be restored to their rightful owners in 1815, with Napoleon's final defeat at Waterloo and exile to St Helena, but for the time being they formed one of the glories of Paris. Louise's story of how she eagerly went to enjoy them on return to France has a sting in the tail:

> You may imagine how hurriedly I took myself to the Louvre museum, which then possessed so many masterpieces; I went there alone, to enjoy these treasures without distraction: I went first through the picture-gallery, then through the sculpture-gallery; and when, after several hours on my feet, I finally thought of returning home for dinner, I discovered that the attendants, unaware that I had not left, had locked all the doors; I ran from right to left; I cried out; it was impossible to make myself heard and get the doors opened; I was dying of hunger and cold, because it was mid-February; I could not knock on the windows, they

were far too high up; so I was imprisoned in the midst of all these beautiful statues which I was no longer at all disposed to admire; they seemed to me like ghosts; and at the thought of having to spend the evening and night with them, I was overwhelmed with fear and despair; finally, after endless detours, I saw a little door which I knocked at so loudly that someone came to open up; I left in the greatest haste, delighted to be free again and to be able to return for dinner – I really needed to eat.[64]

The story is very similar to one Chateaubriand tells of his own imprisonment in Westminster Abbey in the *Mémoires d'outre-tombe*, and no doubt it too was enhanced in the telling.

There were differing views about the propriety or otherwise of looting art from conquered countries: David disapproved, Stendhal was in favour. In any case, Napoleon's assured position meant that he hardly needed to worry about the disapproval even of trusted associates like David. But things were beginning to change at the start of the year following Louise's return. Bertie Greatheed's observation on New Year's Day about the 'complaints' against the First Consul was symptomatic. Yet he also noted that whatever the popular dislike for Bonaparte's military despotism, there was no apparent desire to return to the *ancien régime*, or any respect for sovereigns or nobility.[65] If this was true, it would surely have troubled Louise greatly. But was it true? Napoleon himself, it must be said, had a distinct liking for royalists. According to Stendhal,

> the royalist party was admired by Napoleon: *Those people are the only ones who know how to serve*, he said, when the comte de Narbonne, deputed to pass a letter over to him, presented it to him on the back of his tricorn hat. If he had dared, Napoleon would have surrounded himself exclusively with people belonging to the faubourg Saint-Germain.[66]

Again according to Stendhal, he had no real interest in the Revolutionary ideal of liberty. What he offered was despotism in a new form.

> Initially to give the French people as much freedom as it could take, then gradually increase the freedom as the factions lost their intensity and public opinion became calmer and more enlightened, was not at all what Napoleon had in mind. He did not consider how much power one could entrust to the people without imprudence, but tried to guess how little power it would be satisfied with. The constitution he gave France was calculated

– if one can talk about calculation – to bring this beautiful
country gradually back to absolute monarchy and not to finish
shaping it for liberty. Napoleon had a crown before his eyes, and
he allowed himself to be dazzled by the splendour of this super-
annuated toy. He could have established the Republic, or at least a
government with two Houses; but the sum of his ambitions was
to found a dynasty of kings.[67]

Louise may have sensed the ambition Stendhal diagnoses. Had she done
so, she would have called Napoleon's crime one of usurpation. Clearly, in
her eyes, there was nothing wrong in wanting a restoration of kingship:
the mistake was to attempt this at the expense of the legitimate pretender
to the throne, Louis XVI's brother. (His son, the uncrowned Louis XVII,
had died mysteriously in 1795.) Whatever the popular rumblings by 1803,
Napoleon still seemed to a nation tired of war and upheaval the best guar-
antee against further revolution. In that climate the return of court life
was almost as natural as a return of the monarchy itself.[68] Court life was
somehow quintessentially French, as a well-drilled army was quintessentially Prussian and a powerful navy quintessentially British. The French
owed it to themselves to return to the magnificence, gallantry and *éclat*
associated with royalty; and besides, the brilliant careers of the young
army generals and of the new political leaders seemed to call for celebration and show. Visual splendour, an essential aspect of court life, was more
and more necessary to the government around 1800; so Napoleon had the
Tuileries gorgeously restored, Josephine's apartment upholstered in purple and yellow silk, and his own filled with Old Master paintings and
Sèvres porcelain.

The new order to which Louise had returned, and to which she found
it difficult to adapt, was largely one of self-made men – *parvenus*, as the
aristocratic survivors of the *ancien régime* dismissively called them. But
they had money; and money, according to the duchesse d'Abrantès, had
started circulating again after the signing of the Treaty of Lunéville in 1801.
Luxury goods were once more manufactured and bought; Paris came to
life, and stayed alive until 1814; and all well-placed people had a dozen
invitations to choose from every evening.

None the less, English visitors who came to Paris shortly after the signing of the Treaty of Amiens in 1802 found French society more formal, less
bent on pleasure, than their own. Madame d'Abrantès, too, was struck by
the improvement of manners which the Revolution had brought and the
post-Revolutionary world continued.[69] Misfortune had injected some
seriousness into daily life, she said, and ended the libertinism of the *ancien
régime*. This sense of order perhaps reminded Parisians that a military

power was at the heart of their new society. Something Louise was later surprised to notice at a soirée of the comtesse de Ségur's under the Empire may have reflected this:

> Madame de Ségur invited me to a grand musical evening where she had assembled all the reigning powers of the day . . . I was astonished as I went in to see all the men on one side of the room and all the women on the other; you would have thought they were enemies drawn up in battle-line. Not a single man came to our side except the master of the household, the comte de Ségur, whom his old habit of gallantry impelled to come and say a few flattering words to the ladies. The arrival of Madame de Canisy, a very beautiful woman shaped like a model, was announced. We then lost our lone knight; the comte went to prostrate himself at the feet of this beauty, whom the Emperor himself was said to be paying court to at that time, and did not leave her side for the entire evening.[70]

And she reports Princess Dolgorukova's view of Napoleon's court when he was still First Consul, before being crowned Emperor in 1804: 'It is not a court, but a power.'[71] To anyone used to the St Petersburg court, Louise thought, it was an understandable reaction. At the Tuileries there were very few women, but a vast number of military men of all ranks.

In 1803 Napoleon's empire, and with it the exclusive empire of men, had not yet begun. In the salons people still listened to music, watched plays, and talked about literature and art rather than money and other concerns of a world governed by self-interest. This should have cheered Louise; so should the new keenness to spend money on non-essential goods, which ought to have led to more picture-commissions. So why was she as melancholic as she apparently was? 'In the midst of the distractions Paris offered, I was still pursued by a horde of black thoughts, which overwhelmed me even in the midst of pleasure.'[72]

She tried to restart her salon, but without great enthusiasm. She gave a supper for Princess Dolgorukova to meet the blind poet Delille, another for the leading artists of the day (at which Gérard tunelessly sang *Malbruck s'en va-t-en guerre*), and a third for political and social notabilities like Metternich. But she could not be consoled for the vanished charms of the *ancien régime*. Her disaffection anticipates that of the sufferers from *mal du siècle* under the Napoleonic empire, who were revolted by the new brutality of a system where materialism and political calculation held sway. Like these young men, Louise needed to feel that ideal principles could still triumph, in art as in life. Rightly or wrongly, the Bourbon monarchy had seemed to her to represent a world of delicate sensitivity which was now irretrievably past, and she felt that attempts to revive it under the Consulate were simply a sham. In early nineteenth-century Paris, she was a Romantic yearning for paradise lost.

She did paint, though not as much as during her years abroad. In part, she had simply been overtaken by the new school of portraiture, though the falling-off of commissions may also have arisen from what some observers saw as a deterioration in her art. According to Bertie Greatheed, who visited her studio in mid-January 1803, most of the few paintings Louise was doing were of inferior quality. He mentions her renown in pre-Revolutionary Paris and St Petersburg, but comments:

> Anything so unequal as her performances I never saw, and cannot conceive that the same artist who painted the excellent picture of Lady Hamilton as a sibyl should likewise have executed the poor, husky daubs which are now finishing or lately finished. She has very few pictures in hand.[72]

We can only conjecture what these few pictures were, for the *Souvenirs* give no precise details of paintings completed at that time,

Otherwise, she relied on past achievement. She submitted no new work to the 1802 Salon, but instead sent the portrait of Stanislas Augustus in a velvet cloak which she had painted in St Petersburg, as well as the inevitable Emma Hamilton as sibyl. The critics received her offerings kindly. The *Journal de l'Empire* considered that she had emerged with dignity from the encounter with the young artists who had established themselves during her absence,[73] though the critic's observation that the gloomy colour of the sibyl picture indicated the influence of England's foggy climate suggests a persistence of the belief that Louise had left France in 1789, or Italy in 1791, to join Calonne across the Channel. The note of broad approval is echoed in other reviews. For the *Petites Affiches* the Stanislas portrait was a compendium of all Louise's talents, and her drapery painting in the same portrait was extolled by the *Journal des Arts*. According to this journal, the *Stanislas* was the equal of the fine portraits of Paisiello and Hubert Robert, proving that Louise's exile had in no way diminished her claim to be ranked among the great French painters. Madame de Vandeul, Diderot's daughter, noted like everyone else that Louise was an unrivalled textile painter, and explained why there were so many 'recycled' pictures in the Salon: the quality of the works submitted had been so low that Napoleon ordered previously executed paintings to be exhibited as well.[74] Hence the presence of Ménageot's ten-year-old

Meleager, Gérard's *Belisarius* and *Psyche*, and Louise's *Sibyl*.

Neither the favourable reception of her works nor the remaining social pleasures of Paris really cheered her. She was deeply depressed, and became as misanthropic as she had felt in Russia. Like another famous sufferer from *Weltschmerz*, Madame du Deffand, she made the wrong decision about how best to treat it: she decided to go and live in country solitude. Her retreat was in Meudon,

> in a place called the *Capucinière*, and which had been lived in by some monks. The little house I rented, built as a retreat for one of the Capuchin superiors, looked altogether like a hermitage. It was situated in the middle of the woods, and its rural, solitary air could have persuaded me I was a thousand miles from Paris. That suited me perfectly; for my melancholy was so great I could not bear to see anyone; when I heard a carriage I rushed into the Meudon woods.[75]

Meudon, to the south-east of Paris, is perhaps best known now for Rodin's unprepossessing country house, but other artistic talents had been associated with the place before him. Rabelais was its vicar; Ronsard lived there, as did Molière's future wife Armande Béjart, of a famous acting family, Jean-Jacques Rousseau, Balzac, Wagner, Manet and Céline. In Louise's time it had a congenial aristocratic society, though she was initially unwilling to be attracted by it. Finally she was persuaded to visit the duchesse de Fleury, who had earlier been her companion on country excursions from Rome, and the two mesdames de Bellegarde, one of whom she had painted in 1774. Although she found their company restorative, the effect was not lasting; and when she returned to Paris, she felt herself sinking into depression again.

The panacea of travel seemed to be indicated, and Louise realised where she must go. She decided to reverse the tide that had brought so many English tourists to Paris after the signing of the Treaty of Amiens, and finally to do in fact what journalists had claimed she did in 1789. She would go to London, which she knew to be a thriving art market with an insatiable appetite for portraits.

CHAPTER TEN

ACROSS THE CHANNEL: 'I resigned myself to the monotony of this English life'

Louise left France on 15 April 1803, not, as she states in the *Souvenirs*, the year before. What did she expect to find apart from the amenities which Italy, Austria and Russia had already provided? Perhaps, in some ways, a less accommodating environment: as she would discover, there was a degree of native hostility to the French way of painting. On the other hand, the English were known to love phiz-mongers: portraits dominated the Royal Academy exhibitions, and the native enthusiasm for them meant that Louise was always likely to enjoy success. Few artists prospered with the 'higher' modes. James Barry, whose large and ambitious cycle of history paintings decorated the Society of Arts in the Adelphi, would die in 1806 in a state of abject poverty. Benjamin West alone enjoyed favour with this genre, but largely because of court patronage. Louise had already had some English sitters, most notably Emma Hamilton, and Sir Joshua Reynolds had valued her work highly. But perhaps he did not really admire it as much as was generally believed. Northcote's account of how Reynolds responded to Louise's portraits of Marie-Antoinette and Yolande de Polignac suggests that his praise was more the product of diplomatic tactfulness than an expression of genuine enthusiasm. When the pictures were being disposed of in the London sale of the comte d'Adhémar, Northcote writes, it 'became the fashion to admire them, and to speak of them with the utmost extravagance of praise'; but a fellow-artist who dissented from the general opinion – perhaps John Hoppner – damned the likenesses in virulent verse:

> Where burnish'd beads, silk, satin, laces, vie
> In leaden lustre with the gooseberry eye;
> Where broad cloth breathes, to talk where cushions strive,
> And all, but Sir or Madam, looks alive!

Reynolds's declaration to the doubting Northcote that Louise's portraits were as fine as and finer than Van Dyck's showed only, according to

Northcote, that he disliked opposing the popular opinion, or saying anything against the interest of a contemporary artist: 'it was not his intention to mislead me, but only to put a stop to my enquiries.' To stem the torrent of applause a fashionable artist receives from society, Northcote concludes, is impossible, and to give even a candid opinion would be to incur the charge of envy. Farington's diary gives an even less generous explanation for Reynolds's excessive praise of artists like Louise: Hoppner, Farington says, had given it as his opinion that Sir Joshua was unconvinced of his own superiority as a painter, and so became jealous of and alarmed by the success of gifted rivals, 'which caused him often to recommend the works of those who [sic] he must have despised as artists while on the contrary he would not do justice to such as created an apprehension in him.'[1]

Whether or not Louise was aware of the rapturous response her work had provoked at the Adhémar sale, she could not assume that a new clientele would be easily acquired: the English taste was for a less polished, looser manner than hers, and she would be competing with established stars who mostly charged less than she did. Yet she was famous and had a glamorous reputation. It would still be something, in the country which remained most conspicuously generous in supporting the French *émigrés*, to say that one was being painted by Marie-Antoinette's former portraitist. England and France might be old enemies, but even amidst enmity they had always admired each other's style, grudgingly or otherwise – during the Seven Years' War, for instance, English art had been slavishly French.

Many of Louise's former clients had taken refuge in England. Calonne, who had married a hugely rich Englishwoman, had returned to France in 1802 and almost immediately died, but Vaudreuil stayed longer. The comte d'Artois was based in London at the time of Louise's stay – one of the reasons for the courtier Vaudreuil's continued presence – and was no doubt a draw for Louise. But she may also have been attracted by the promise of English society.

It would not have been a bizarre attraction. England might be a democracy, not an absolutist state like that of *ancien régime* France, but it had a crowned head and a court. If the Hanoverian dynasty was more recently established on the throne than the Bourbon, the Georges were not upstart parvenus like Napoleon. The Crown's position, as far as anyone could judge, was stable. So although Louise allows herself more than one disparaging observation about English ways and the English character, she could see definite attractions in the country. Moving in the elevated circles she did, too, she was unlikely to find her ignorance of the language a handicap.

The Sweetness of Life

The crossing from Calais to Dover took anything between two and thirty-six hours depending on the weather. Louise says nothing about the prevailing conditions on the day she sailed, despite being as morbidly fascinated by the English climate as all other foreign visitors, so they were probably tolerable. She noticed a huge crowd of onlookers on the quayside as she disembarked, but herself felt no inclination to linger.

> I immediately took a chaise harnessed with three horses, and left without delay; for I felt slightly worried, given that I had been assured I could well encounter robbers *en route*. I had taken the precaution of putting my diamonds inside my stockings, and I was pleased I had when I saw two men on horseback galloping towards me. What reduced me to a state of absolute terror was seeing them separate so as to be able to ride alongside either door of my carriage, or so I imagined. I confess I was overcome with dreadful trembling; but I got off with no more than a fright.[2]

Some travellers actually went so far as to prepare a purse for highwaymen, and generally met with civil treatment in return.[3]

Despite the fear they inspired in foreigners,[4] English highwaymen enjoyed a reputation for courtesy and lack of greed. Footpads were regarded as much more uncouth and threatening. Baert's *Tableau de la Grande-Bretagne* of 1800 remarks that highway robbery was conducted with much decency in England, assailants usually satisfying themselves with what their victim was prepared to give.[5] Lévis, too, insists that highwaymen were of a better class than in mainland Europe, where nearly all were deserters and professional thugs.[6] In England their trade was usually provisional, and might be abandoned for months or years once they had made a successful haul.

Louise's travels, then, had begun fairly typically, with a mixture of exhilaration, intrepidness and panic. She no longer had the reassuring company of August Rivière or even of her daughter, though there was the compensating presence of her 'charming' maid Adélaïde. On the other hand, the political climate was benign, if only temporarily so. Yet some of Louise's compatriots were still convinced that the English felt coolly towards them, just as they had believed that Britain rejoiced in French disarray during and after the Revolution, and saw it as just retribution for the defeat they had helped inflict during the War of American Independence.[7] The comte de Tilly's memoirs would refer to the English in 1804 as a nation which execrated everything to do with France instinctively, always hostile towards the French and always wanting to see them removed from the face of the earth. Of all the great Englishmen who had praised France in speech and writing, he claimed, none had really loved it.[8]

But no one disputed that the British government behaved with exemplary generosity towards the exiled French. Many *émigrés* had left their native land virtually penniless,[9] like Louise in 1789, but as even the prickly Chateaubriand acknowledged, the English ruling class treated them more than decently.[10] Where charity was impossible to accept, the impoverished emigrants turned to their own devices for making money. Louise, a wealthy woman by the time of her stay in London, claims that she never imitated English artists in the practice of charging visitors to her studio an admission fee,[11] but Madame de Boigne caustically observes that the duchesse de Fitz-James made guests at her dinners pay a minimum of 3s. per head, while actually hoping that the rich would contribute half a guinea.[12]

Chateaubriand lists his compatriots' gainful employment a decade before Louise's arrival.

> My companions in London all had occupations: some were in the coal trade, others made straw hats with their wives, yet others taught French without knowing it properly. The fault of our nation, flippancy, had at that point become a virtue. People laughed in Fortune's face; this light-fingered lady was thoroughly sheepish about taking away what they were not concerned to have back.[13]

Given their traditions, it was unthinkable that they should not also enter the fashion trade. Mademoiselle Bertin, who had fled France with the Revolution, worked in London in 1791, 1792 and 1793, though she had frequently visited England before then; and from her base in the capital she dispatched her world-famous dolls – mannequins, as they were called – to the courts of Europe.[14] She, quite as much as Louise herself, helped further the trend towards greater simplicity in dress for which Louise sometimes claims sole responsibility. The so-called *robe à l'anglaise* Rose Bertin introduced, with its simple artistic lines – the long, full skirt issuing from a tight bodice, above which frothed a soft bunched fichu – had figured in many of Louise's pre-Revolutionary portraits, and can also be seen in her English pictures of Mrs Chinnery and the Duchess of Dorset.

Rose Bertin seemingly felt no rancour towards those members of the French royal family and court who owed her enormous sums of money at the outbreak of revolution;[15] and perhaps in order to salve their consciences, they praised her wit and social grace, calling her an extraordinary woman. She continued to serve her clients generously as an *émigrée*, supplying them with money and the credit she had acquired in England. Nor does she seem to have harboured any ill-will towards those of her former customers who became *modistes* too.

No doubt there was need for relaxation and recreation among the exiled French, though some witnesses were shocked by the frivolity which Chateaubriand saw as a temporary virtue. However eagerly some of them turned to millinery and shoemaking, they seemed less serious and industrious than those who had been driven into exile under Louis XIV. Even when they cobbled, the shoes were delicate things meant for aristocratic feet. Luxury arts and crafts, with few exceptions, were the focus of their activities. Not that they seemed at all inclined, even if they were able, to support arts like Louise's own: she soon found that commissioning a portrait was a luxury few of them felt they could afford. In spite of everything, they were insouciant – less so than ten years earlier, at the time of the *joyeuse émigration*, but still enough to appear inspiringly bold or distressingly feckless, according to the prejudices of the observer.

Their conservatism was of a piece with this defiance. So it was a shock to many of them to discover that the upper classes, in London no less than in Vienna, often supported the democratic ideals that had underpinned the Revolution. When she became acquainted with Georgiana, Duchess of Devonshire, Louise was at a loss to understand how a *grande dame* and friend of the Prince of Wales could also be known as a supporter of the Whig cause.[16] The French response was to reaffirm old values, no matter how insignificant that reaffirmation might appear. The wearing of powdered hair was one such gesture, becoming as important to the *émigré* sense of identity as more substantial assertions of commitment to the old ways. After a bad wheat harvest, Pitt the Younger imposed a tax on powder in 1795, and thousands of heads, according to Malcolm's *Anecdotes of the Manners and Customs of London*, instantly turned black and brown.[17] The painter Danloux, as much a royalist as Louise, expressed outrage. No longer could one immediately recognise an emigrant except by his inveterate habit of speaking his own language, or by an indefinable elegance. 'It is odious that in a country which calls itself free one is forced to pay twenty shillings to have the freedom to wear powder.'[18]

On arrival in London Louise put up at the Brunet Hotel in Leicester Square, an establishment which according to Sir John Papworth was considered one of the first in the city because of its elegance and the convenience of its internal arrangements, and which he called equally suitable for the reception of people of the first rank and fortune and families wanting neatness, comfort and quiet.[19] (Talma would stay there during a visit to London in 1817.) Louise did not find it as peaceful a place as it promised to be.

I was extremely tired and desperately in need of rest; but it was impossible for me to sleep; the whole night long I heard someone talking and striding about on the floor above me. The cause of the noise, which was unbearable, became clear to me the next day: on the staircase I met Monsieur de Parseval de Grandmaison, whom I had known well in Paris, and whom I was delighted to see. When he told me he was staying on the floor above, I asked him not to walk about all night, and not to choose this time to recite his poetry, given that he had a very loud voice, and such a sonorous one that it penetrated as far as my room. He gave me his word and since that day let me rest peacefully.[20]

Many French visitors stayed in Leicester Square, which was comfortably close to Soho, and most of its hotels had French names. Foreigners appeared there early in its history, the majority artists and craftsmen. In the eighteenth century the jeweller Pierre Dutens settled in nos. 19 and 53; Philippe Mercier, the portrait-painter, lived in the square, as did Danloux. But there had been many British artists among the residents too – Reynolds, Hogarth, David Allan, Lawrence and Towne. John Singleton Copley spent about seventeen years in Leicester Square, until 1812, and Arthur William Devis passed some months there in 1806. But Louise's own stay was not long. Her sights were set on the West End, where richer émigrés liked to settle.

She was visited by an obliging stranger, a Frenchman called Charmilly, who offered to help her find lodgings. As a result of his exertions she took a house in what she calls Beck Street, but which must be the Baker Street which Farington's diary for June 1803 reports her as living in then, at no. 61 (the site of the present Marks and Spencer head office).[21] According to the rate-books, the building – which has been demolished – was owned by a Mrs Susanna Beckford, who let it out to tenants. Baker Street was called by Richard Phillips's Modern London of 1804 'perhaps the handsomest street in London',[22] though in a letter of 29 August 1817 Mrs Piozzi described it as being out of town. Many celebrated people lived there – Lord Camelford, the sailor infamous for his disorderly conduct, at no. 64, the actress Mrs Siddons at the top of Upper Baker Street, and, perhaps most promisingly, the comte d'Artois.

Artois had held court at no. 46 since 1799. After spells in Turin and Coblenz he had briefly visited Austria, Prussia and Russia, turned to England in 1795, removed to Holyrood Palace in Edinburgh, then went back to London. He would stay in or near the city until the Bourbon Restoration of 1814, when he returned to France.

Louise was never to paint Artois, perhaps surprisingly, but he was apparently an admirer of her work – at least, she reports his praise of the portrait of the Prince of Wales she did while in England. Of course she was keen to consort with him. It may have been while both she and Artois were living in Baker Street that he visited her studio, but they had already met at a gathering of *émigrés*. Louise, in other words, wanted to continue keeping the kind of company she had enjoyed during her emigration: royal where possible, French where possible, but failing that aristocratic and Francophile.

Artois, whom she found plumper and 'truly very handsome',[23] had greatly changed since the 1780s, as d'Espinchal had hinted in Turin. According to Louise,

> Monsieur le comte d'Artois did not circulate in society. Having only a modest income, he made savings and used them to help the most unfortunate French emigrants; the goodness of his heart led him to sacrifice all personal pleasure to beneficence. I found proof of it myself in a circumstance it pleases me to relate. A young woman, extremely interesting, called Mademoiselle Mérel, who played the harp exquisitely, had come to London in the hope of making a living from her talent. She advertised a concert. I hurriedly bought some tickets and undertook to dispose of as many other ones as I could; but despite all my efforts there were so few people in the hall, and I was so freezing that I had to leave before the end of the concert [*sic*]. I told the comte de Vaudreuil about Mademoiselle Mérel's misfortune, and by some chance he mentioned it the same day to the prince. 'Is she a Frenchwoman?' the comte d'Artois asked. On Monsieur de Vaudreuil's affirmative answer he charged him to send ten guineas to the young artiste [who, unknown to Louise, was also a prostitute].

He showed real devotion to his mistress, Madame de Polastron, who died in 1805, and his solicitude, according to Louise, presented him in an exemplary light: he nursed her in her illness, and comforted her in the loss of her son.[24] The portrait Louise did of her shortly before she died reveals the ravages both of personal tragedy and of disease, the latter exacerbated by the privations of her life in Edinburgh and the dampness of her London house in Thayer Street. Her face is drawn with pain, and offers an image as nakedly suffering as the one Louise had depicted over a decade before in her portrait of Maria Carolina of Naples.

She may well have reckoned on capturing other such tormented faces, their lineaments and expressions a testimony to the mental pain of uprootedness from their homeland and family. But the most strikingly damaged visage she saw in London was that of no emigrant, but of Emma Hamilton, blowsy, mountainous, wrecked by drink, an enormous Andromache grieving for her dead husband, and wearing a 'Titus' coiffure which obviously suited her far less well than it did Madame Tallien.[25] Remembering the lascivious bacchante and ravishing sibyl of Italy, Louise responded with shocked disbelief to this travesty. (Gillray's 1801 drawing conveys her enormous bulk, and is careful also to show the flask of maraschino on her dressing-table.[26]) Emma had never quite persuaded Louise of her right to move in high places, and the deterioration she noted probably merely confirmed her in the view – which her acquaintance with Madame Grand/de Talleyrand had also prompted – that basic vulgarity will out sooner or later. After all, Emma's assumption of familiarity with Maria Carolina had been shocking – much more so, Louise surely thought, than her own closeness to Marie-Antoinette had been to the King – and it was vaguely gratifying to find a coarse woman reverting to type.

Louise could not stay long in Baker Street: it was too noisy, abutting on to the Royal Horseguards' barracks (or so she claims), and the house too full of boisterous children. So she moved the short distance to Portman Square. It now possesses few of the glorious buildings which graced it in Georgian England, though the most beautiful in London – Home House, or no. 20, the former headquarters of the Courtauld Institute – still stands, a sadly neglected monument to Robert Adam's genius, as do its immediate neighbours nos. 19 and 21. Once the square also contained the fabulous Portman House, designed by Adam's rival James 'Athenian' Stuart for the author Mrs Montagu, who held public breakfasts and bluestocking parties there, and on May Day entertained the sweeps of London; but the house was destroyed by bombs in the Second World War.

Construction of the square had been begun in 1764, and finished twenty years later. In *Espriella's Letters*, published in 1807, Southey describes it as lying on the outskirts of town, approached on one side by a road that was unlit, unpaved and inaccessible to carriages. None the less, it was a favoured address for members of the *haute émigration*. However great its beauty and cachet, though, it could not satisfy Louise, whose reassuring preliminary reconnaissance had failed to detect a serious drawback. The morning after she moved in, at daybreak,

> I heard earsplitting cries. I got up, stuck my head out of the window, and saw in the one nearest to me the most enormous bird you have ever seen. It was tethered to a great perch. Its gaze was furious, its beak and tail of a monstrous length: in short, I declare without fear of exaggeration that a huge eagle, set next to it, would

have looked like a little canary. From what I was told, this horrible beast must have come from India. But whatever its place of origin, I still wrote to its lady owner to ask her to keep it on the street side. The lady told me that it had been kept that way at first, but that the police had made her move it because it scared passers-by.[27]

She also discovered that the corpses of two Indian slaves had been buried in the house by their ambassador masters. All things considered, she decided to move on, and took a flat the other side of Piccadilly in Maddox Street. It was 'dreadfully damp', but had a reception-room large enough for her to entertain. In any case, she was thoroughly tired of moving.

Louise's general remarks on London architecture tell us little. Though she lived in the best areas, she says almost nothing about her various houses except that they were *belles* and spacious – and, of course, made impossible to inhabit by damp and noise. It cannot be that she was insensitive to the physical beauty of her surroundings – what she says in the *Souvenirs* about other places she lived in disproves that. It may be that, like other foreign visitors to England, she found the massed uniformity of the vernacular urban style unappealing. The barrack-like blocks of houses dyed brown or olive green by the damp and coal-smoke appeared monotonous in comparison with the variety of Paris or Rome. Ferri di San Costante's *Londres et les Anglais* of 1804 gives a gloomy view.

> The general aspect of London is sad and lugubrious. There are many contributory factors: first the architecture of the houses, which is everywhere of the most absolute and meanest simplicity, and the dullest uniformity. The thick fog which blocks the rays of the sun also makes London sombre and sad . . . The inhabitants equally cast an atmosphere of gloom on the look of London. 'You would think,' said a visitor, 'that the people you see in the street are following a funeral procession.' No public luxury strikes a visitor's eyes at the outset; there is no glint of gold and silver anywhere; people's clothes are like their faces; they look alike; you might think the whole nation was in uniform.[28]

Louise did, however, concede that the streets of London were 'handsome and clean', and that the wide pavements made them pleasant to walk along.[29] (Visitors noted, by contrast, how dangerous it was to saunter in Paris.) Streets on the new, elegant estates in the West End were up to sixty feet wide, double the width of the widest traditional Paris streets. London was, in a sense, lucky to have lost its medieval nucleus in the Great Fire.

Other European cities retained narrow labyrinthine centres, unsuitable for the *bon ton* to stroll in. Touring the city on foot was a pleasure for *flâneurs* in eighteenth- and early nineteenth-century London. It provided a contrast with the extraordinary bustle of the place.

London seemed disappointing to visitors, though, in having very few public art collections. Some people attributed this to the fact that Britain was a constitutional monarchy, saying that the show of magnificence was inherent only in absolutist regimes.[30] Artistic treasures had to be sought elsewhere. As Louise writes,

> It is not that one cannot find a wealth of precious objects in England, but most are owned by rich private citizens who adorn their estates in the country and the provinces with them. At the time I am writing of, London had no museum of painting; the one which exists at present [i.e. the National Gallery] is the product of legacies and gifts made to the nation only over the past few years.[31]

ouise visited, had acquired Sir
other antiquities, and the pro-
mpaign (including the Rosetta
eemed little to those who knew
ibitions and the acquisitions of
enthusiasm, and were generally

e connoisseurs to assemble fine
ho commented on the magnifi-
ck Castle and elsewhere, was as
e proliferation of former *émigré*
families. It seemed the harder to
ensitivity they might have devel-
only regarded as philistine. This
heir country was unfit to house
uld amass great works in order to
y dismissive of their expertise,
sh – including the Royal Family –
om London to the poet Lebrun-

Brun had living here another
fit from the chance and the
pictures being bought for

extravagant prices while others, which are sometimes worth more, are sold for nothing, he would profit greatly.[34]

This explains why, despite resolving to acquire nothing, he himself had actually bought five or six pictures and quickly been offered two or three times what he had paid for them. His prize purchase, a superb Poussin of David displaying the head of Goliath, was eventually to form part of the Prado's collection.

In the *Souvenirs* Louise comments admiringly on a comparable astuteness in Artois's son, the duc de Berri:

> He often arrived carrying under his arm little pictures he had just bought very cheaply. What proves that he was a connoisseur of painting is that these little pictures were superb Wouwermans; but you needed great sensitivity to appreciate their merit underneath the layers of grime that coated them.[35]

The English, by implication, were too boorishly ignorant to recognise such minor masterpieces for what they were. From this it was a short step to arguing that they patronised the arts more out of ostentation and self-regard than genuine love and expertise.[36] Correspondingly, foreigners said, English artists painted not as Louise claimed to do, out of inborn passion, but as a speculative endeavour. For Napoleon's 'nation of shop-keepers', covering canvas with pigment was a commercial undertaking like any other.

In fact, the accusation of philistinism is hard to sustain, at least in the case of the aristocracy. As buyers of art, the landed English then made a far better showing than the landed English now. The Orléans collection, for instance, which Louise had so admired in her girlhood, had been snapped up by the Duke of Bridgewater, Lord Carlisle and Lord Gower after the guillotining of Philippe-Egalité. The chagrin the French felt at seeing how many works once owned by *émigrés* ended up on the London art market (usually sent by dealers like Jean-Baptiste-Pierre Le Brun), and from there found their way into the town and country houses of the wealthy, must have been increased by the reflection that England's relative internal stability, at the end of an era that saw France torn apart by revolution, had helped boost the purchasing-power of these patrons of the arts. The situation would have changed by the second decade of the nineteenth century, when the bottom dropped out of the London art mar-ket. But for the time being it seemed as stable as England's constitutional monarchy.

If the English loved art more than their reputation argued, and more than the dearth of public art-collections suggested, did they love artists? Not according to Richard Phillips.

> It is not only the custom of the present day to exclude men and women of letters from the society of the high-born; that tyrannical species of oppression is also extended to painters, actors, actresses, and persons the most distinguished in art and science. The pictures of our celebrated masters are purchased at a high price, and considered as the embellishments of our most magnificent mansions; but the painter is unknown except in his works.
>
> While meditating on the want of discrimination, the discouragement, and the injustice of this neglect, to meet a peer arm in arm with a pugilist or a gambler, low of birth, vulgar in deportment, insolent in look, coarse in language, whose ignorance is only equalled by his effrontery, excites pain, indignation, and disgust . . .[37]

In that case the favour Louise enjoyed with the Prince of Wales and with the English aristocracy must have been exceptional. Not only did the future George IV sit to her – something he had refused to native portraitists, she rather inaccurately says[38] – but he attended her soirées with particular pleasure. After a concert at her Maddox Street house at which Mrs Billington and Signora Grassini sang he graciously told Louise: 'I flit about from one soirée to the next, but at yours I stay put.'[39] Besides, the Prince of Wales personally involved himself in extending Louise's stay in England, according to her.

> Shortly after my arrival in London, the Treaty of Amiens had been broken, and all the French who had not been living in England for more than a year were obliged to leave immediately. The Prince of Wales, to whom I was presented, assured me that I was not to be included in this edict, that he was opposed to it, and that he was going immediately to ask his father for permission for me to stay. This permission was granted with all the necessary details, mentioning *that I could travel all over the interior of the kingdom, staying wherever I wanted, and besides that I should be protected in the seaports where I chose to stop*, a favour which the French who had been settled in England for several years had considerable trouble obtaining at that time. The Prince of Wales put the seal on his obligingness by bringing me this paper himself.[40]

It cannot have been the fact of Louise's looks – she was now nearly fifty years old – or social gifts that procured her this entrée to the court, though according to Louise the Prince of Wales was rumoured to be attracted to her: 'I discovered that the Queen Mother [Louise means Queen Charlotte, George III's wife] said her son was paying court to me, and that he often took luncheon at my house. It was a lie; for the Prince of Wales only ever came to me in the morning for his sittings.'[41] There was, in fact, no reason why the painter of Marie-Antoinette should not have been accepted by court and nobility. Portrait painting, in England as in France, offered one of the most reliable routes to social advancement at the time.[42] As Reynolds's career demonstrated, humble beginnings did not prevent one from being patronised by the great, ennobled, and elected to the highest artistic office in the land.

Correspondingly, one needed to live up to one's elegant, worldly reputation by keeping a stylish establishment. The great actually called at artists' studios, as Artois called on Louise, which meant that the premises had to be worthy of the callers. The politician Fox came several times to her studio, paying an entry fee on each occasion (and so disproving Louise's claim that she never charged people for the privilege of seeing her work), but never managed to catch her at home. Louise regretted this, but was more fortunate with the actress Mrs Siddons, who did find her in.

> I had seen this famous actress for the first time in *The Gamester*, and I was able to tell her how enthusiastically I had applauded her. I do not believe it possible to possess more talent for acting than Mrs Siddons; all the English agreed in praising the naturalness and perfection of her diction; the sound of her voice was enchanting; only Mademoiselle Mars's seemed to me to recall it, and – something which for me defines the great actress – even her silence was admirably expressive.[43]

As an artist with an elevated clientele, Louise simply had to live where the *bon ton* was prepared to visit her. That meant the West End. Her insistence on living in the smartest parts of London, in other words, was not the product of snobbery so much as a reflection of her business acumen and entrepreneurial spirit. Even if it was true that portraiture was a buyer's market,[44] and that patrons could afford to be high-handed, painters with a sense of their own value, as Louise undoubtedly had, could maintain their importance with sitters. As well as employing promotional techniques which kept them in the fashionable public's eye, they ensured that their studios remained popular rendezvous by keeping them stylish and elegant.

Louise's pride in the fact that the Prince of Wales attended her soirées

with particular pleasure is, then, the justified pride of a woman professional assured in her acceptance by a foreign society at the highest level.
Where the heir to the throne led, others must follow; and she was welcomed by the aristocracy into their own town and country houses. Not
that she necessarily relished all the forms of hospitality they offered. But
by now, having been exposed to Austrian *Redouten* and Italian *conversazioni*, she knew how peculiar national types of social intercourse could
be. Routs were particularly baffling to her, as they were to other visitors.
Baert calls them crowds (*foules*), and sees in their dead, cramped silence
an image of the English nation itself, trapped inside its grave taciturnity.[45]

For Louise, these tiring stand-up affairs were completely devoid of
pleasure. When an Englishman remarked in the course of one solemn
evening, 'How amusing these occasions are!', she replied that what was
amusement to the English was tedium to the French.[46] Still, she writes
elsewhere, such assemblies enabled her to meet the best English society.
The vogue for routs seemed to have peaked in the early nineteenth century, and remained unfathomable to outside observers.[47] The German
Goede remarked in 1802 that all present at such assemblies complained
about the heat, noise and general discomfort, but still rejoiced in being so
divinely and fashionably squeezed.

Among the most fashionable London routs Louise attended were those
of Lady Hertford at Manchester House (at present the home of the
Wallace Collection, and known as Hertford House). Others were given by
Georgiana, Duchess of Devonshire, at Devonshire House in Piccadilly –
the splendid, now demolished, urban counterpart of Chatsworth.
Designed by Kent and built around 1737 at a cost of over £20,000, it was
the resort both of the Whig opposition and of London's *beaux esprits*.

It is a shame that Louise never painted Georgiana's portrait. Perhaps
she was less fascinated by her looks than the Duchess's world was.[48]

> She must have been forty-five years old at that time. Her features
> were very regular; but I was not struck by her beauty. Her com-
> plexion was too high, and unfortunately she had a blind eye. As
> women then wore their hair over their brows, she hid this eye
> under a mass of curls, which did not at all succeed in hiding such
> a grave defect. The Duchess of Devonshire was fairly tall, with a
> plumpness which, at her age, suited her very well, and her easy
> manners were extremely gracious.[49]

Nowadays we should probably call her a *jolie-laide*, whose attractions, as
Fanny Burney saw, were dependent on animation; according to Burney,
her countenance had an ingenuousness and openness so singular that at

243

expressive moments not even her sternest critic could deny the justice of her fame.[50] She herself described her facial shortcomings – 'a snub nose, a wide mouth and a pair of grey eyes' – but they evidently did not strike Tilly as such: he called her beautiful and graceful.[51] Walpole and others agreed that her good nature and liveliness (what one newspaper called a hoydenish affability[52]) compensated for her deficiencies of aspect, which included the sightless eye. She had long been at the centre of the fashionable world: in 1784 she was the first person to wear a chemise gown in public, attending a concert in a muslin shift with trimmings of fine lace given her by Marie-Antoinette. She enjoyed easy access to the French queen's circle, and was also an important client of Rose Bertin's. She possessed abundant energy and animal spirits, as well as a recklessness that plunged her hopelessly into debt. Louise says nothing about Georgiana's frantic gambling, which led her to borrow money from Calonne as well as from the banker Coutts;[53] perhaps by the early 1800s it had cooled. In 1791 her husband sent her into exile abroad, both because of her debts and because he believed her to be with child by the future Prime Minister Charles Grey. The latter was not alone among her close political connections. Her highly publicised support of Fox, and the famous Westminster election of May 1784, at which the Tories had moved heaven and earth to ensure that Fox was not elected, gave her the title 'Fox's Duchess', and made her notorious. Georgiana and her sister, Lady Duncannon, apparently 'beat up' voters in the outlying districts, and even caressed them in order to win their allegiance.

Louise was frightened by the vehemence of political protest in early nineteenth-century London: she witnessed what seemed to her terrifying riots, not realising that the Georgian crowd was clamouring for redress of grievances rather than the overthrow of the ruling class, or revolution *tout court*. She could not have understood that London from the seventeenth century on had been the breeding-ground of radical politics, and that its electorates were characteristically volatile and even uncontrollable. Politicians were not averse to whipping up husting mobs. Prince Bariatinsky was able to reassure Louise that 'things always happened thus when an important election was in the offing, and the tumult would have ended by the next day'.[54] All Louise was really seeing was a practical demonstration of Rousseau's dictum that the English were free only at election-time, and that the manner of their asserting such freedom proved how unworthy of it they were. Louise, who was shocked to see hordes of *hoi polloi* roaming the streets dead drunk, was no doubt unaware that at such times public houses dispensed drink freely at the expense of the vote-seeking candidates.[55]

Concerts were much more to Louise's taste than routs or politics, and were as fashionable in London as they had been in Vienna. Composers like Handel from the 1720s onwards, and Haydn in the 1790s, had orchestrated London's musical life. Subscription concerts became popular, and were regularly held between Christmas and June. At the end of the eighteenth century Carlisle House in Soho Square was a leading musical venue. According to Fanny Burney, 'the magnificence of the rooms, splendour of the illuminations and embellishments, and the brilliant appearance of the company exceeded anything I ever before saw.'[56]

Louise held grand receptions in her Maddox Street house which attempted to match the *éclat* of her pre-Revolutionary evenings in Paris. On one occasion she arranged for Emma Hamilton to perform her attitudes, something she had previously been unwilling to do in London. It was done at the request of the duc de Berri and the duc de Bourbon, and Louise invited some other French guests for the occasion:

> on the appointed day I placed in the middle of my drawing-room a very large frame with screens at either end. I had made an enormous candle which spread a great pool of light; I placed it in such a way that, invisible though it was, it lit up Lady Hamilton as one lights a picture. All the guests having arrived, Lady Hamilton assumed various attitudes with a truly admirable expression. She had brought with her a young girl who must have been seven or eight years old, and who looked very like her. People even told me that this girl was Mrs Nelson's daughter. She posed with her, and reminded me of the women pursued in Poussin's *Rape of the Sabine Women*. She passed from grief to joy, from joy to fear, so convincingly and with such speed that we were all delighted.
>
> As I had invited her to stay to supper, the duc de Bourbon, who was sitting at table next to me, pointed out to me how much porter she was drinking. She must have been well used to it, for she was not drunk after two or three bottles.[57]

Another time Josephina Grassini sang with Mrs Billington. Louise presented the Italian to all the grand ladies she had invited; 'for,' she writes, 'she was already much sought-after in London, which was entirely natural, given that to her remarkable beauty and talent was joined an extremely winning nature . . .'[58] Others confirmed the truth of Louise's remarks. The Grassini voice was so phenomenal that it actually made contraltos more popular than sopranos, which had never been the case before. Sometimes, in a spirit of mischief, she swapped rôles with her rival Mrs Billington, whom Richard Phillips called the finest female singer in Europe. (The superb full-length portrait of her by Reynolds at Covent Garden shows

her, Madame Grand-like, as St Cecilia surrounded by singing cherubs.)
However much she may have irritated opera directors by singing soprano,
Josephina Grassini was universally admired for her kindness and
intelligence.[59] She was a celebrated wit, too:[60] when she heard Napoleon
observing that all Italians were by nature thieves, she responded '*Non tutti,
ma buona parte*' (alluding to his blithe appropriation of artistic treasures
from conquered countries). She had come to London in 1804 for the
express purpose of measuring herself against Mrs Billington, a contest of
which Lord Mount-Edgcumbe remarked that the deaf would have been
charmed by the Italian, but the blind given the Englishwoman the preference. It was in 1805 that she sang the part of Zaïra in Peter von Winter's
opera at the Haymarket Theatre, and Louise painted two of her three
London portraits of her as a sultana. In these pictures the singer's pose is
inspired by the portrait of Emma Hamilton as a sibyl, and her dress by
Smith's *Eastern Costumes*: the emeralds she wears are the presents given to
Louise by Tipu Sultan's ambassadors, as is the sumptuous gold-
embroidered muslin of her dress.

Grassini had many male admirers. Prince Augustus Ferdinand of
Prussia – whom Louise had met in Venice – threw her into the sea in
Naples in a fit of jealousy, but the contralto, a strong swimmer, came to no
harm. De Quincey revered her, as did Baudelaire (whose translation of De
Quincey's line in *Confessions of an English Opium-Eater*, 'In those days
Grassini sang at the Opera: and her voice was delightful to me beyond all
that I have ever heard', rather flatly reads '*C'étaient les beaux temps de la
Grassini!*'). Napoleon, on hearing her sing in Cimarosa's *Gli Orazi*,
exclaimed: '*Elle excite en moi l'héroïsme*'. In 1806, after Louise had returned
to Paris – where she painted Josephina again – he named the contralto his
first singer, and gave her the title of countess so that she could appear at
court. She called him her 'government', and finally seduced him in Milan.
They took little trouble to conceal their liaison.

Josephina Grassini returned to the Haymarket Theatre in 1814.
Castlereagh, the Foreign Secretary, presented her to Wellington, whom she
met again when he was British Ambassador in Paris under Louis XVIII.
She continued a successful singing career on the Continent, returning to
Milan and Venice, and formed a rivalry with Angelica Catalani (whom
Louise would also paint when she returned to Paris from London).

But for all the glamour and celebrity of her person, she touched Louise
most by her sheer niceness. Her kindly nature was nowhere so well
expressed as at the time of Louise's departure.

> At the moment when I was about to climb into my post-chaise to
> go to the inn near where I was to embark, I saw the charming

Madame Grassini arrive; I thought she was simply coming to say goodbye to me, but she told me she wanted to take me to the inn, and made me climb into her coach, which I found packed with pillows and parcels. 'Why are you bringing all that?' I asked. 'Don't you know you are going to the most awful inn in the world? You may have to stay there a week or more if the winds are not favourable, and it is my intention to stay with you.'[61]

Apart from attending routs, going to concerts and arranging musical soirées, Louise went to the theatre – though her enjoyment, notwithstanding her appreciation of Mrs Siddons in *The Gamester*, must have been lessened by her ignorance of English. The theatre thrived in London. But the pleasures it offered were not available every day of the week: theatres no more opened on Sunday in the early nineteenth century than they do at the end of the twentieth. Louise found English Sundays infinitely depressing,

> as sad as the climate. No shops are open, there are no shows, no balls, no concerts. A general silence prevails everywhere; and as no one is allowed to work on that day, or even make music, without running the risk of having his windows smashed by the populace, there is nothing for it but to spend one's time promenading, which is very popular . . .[62]

The Pall Mall promenade was much favoured, and within easy reach of the parks – Green Park, Hyde Park, St James's Park and Kensington Gardens. The latter became the most exclusive green after Queen Caroline, wife of George II, had it fenced around and posted servants on the perimeter to stop 'persons meanly clad' going in.

Were things better in Paris? John Carr, a visitor there in 1803, thought so.

> A Frenchman once observed to me that a Sunday in London was horrible, on account of there being no playhouses open at night! The decorum and good manners which are even still observed in all the French places of public amusement are very impressive and agreeable.[63]

But Bertie Greatheed disagreed. 'Though Sunday is not kept as with us, as indeed it never was, yet more than half the shops are shut, and it is perfectly distinct from the other days.'[64] The strangely Puritanical attitude of the British to the sabbath must have surprised someone like Louise. Since she presumably knew that her friend Lady Mary Bentinck had been threatened by the stones of the mob for giving Sunday evening concerts and suppers at her house in Piccadilly, she perhaps concluded that violent Puritanism and over-exuberance at the hustings were just reverse sides of the same coin. Later, Nietzsche would remark that it was a masterstoke of English instinct so to hallow and begloom Sunday that the Englishman unconsciously hankered after his week- and workday again. Sunday was a kind of cleverly devised fast inserted into the calendar in order to whet the appetite for the monotonous labours to come.[65]

This was not the only gloomy aspect of England as far as Louise was concerned. For someone as sensitive as she was to light and atmosphere, the English climate was hard to endure. She understood why Reynolds had felt such frustration at the impossibility of drying canvases in the prevailing damp, and why he had been driven to desperate measures: 'He conceived the idea, I have been told, of mixing wax with his pigments, which dulled them.' (Paradoxically, towards the end of his career Reynolds grew reliant on bitumen, a tar-like substance which gave a rich and glowing effect when first applied, but which never quite dried and resulted in traction-cracks on the surface of his paintings.)

Louise was not reduced to quite such extremes, but had to take troublesome precautions:

> to dry the portraits I painted, I took the decision to leave a fire burning constantly in my studio until I went to bed; I put my pictures at a certain distance from the fireplace, and very often I left routs so as to see if I needed to draw them closer, or place them further away. This was an indispensable but very tedious necessity.[66]

Quite apart from the artistic difficulties caused by the climate, Louise felt sure it was harming her health. She took every opportunity, therefore, to escape to the country, 'where at least I saw the sun'.[67] She wrote to her brother:

> I can see you are worried about my tolerating fog and the smell of coal-smoke; as for the latter, I am completely used to it and no longer smell it; I even prefer this kind of fire to ours now; but as for the thick, heavy atmosphere that surrounds me, I could never get used to it; in the first place one sees nothing, and you cannot imagine how this gloomy black shroud obstructs one's thoughts; this dirty crêpe dulls my imagination, and I find it entirely natural that spleen was born here. But people assure me that this year is unusual, that it is one of the brightest, finest there has been for a

long time, which gives me a fair idea of what the others have been![68]

Foreigners generally were shocked by the 'impure and thick mist' caused by the burning of coal in grates, and wheezed their horror at the smuts dirtying buildings and even horses. The Frenchman Pierre-Jean Grosley complained that the smoke formed a cloud 'which envelops London like a mantle; a cloud which . . . suffers the sun to break out only now and then, which casual appearance procures the Londoners a few of what they call *glorious days*.'[69] What Lady Mary Wortley Montagu called 'this sinful sea coal town' appalled Lichtenberg when he discovered he had to write by candlelight at half past ten in the morning. The American Louis Simond would comment in 1810 that 'the smoke of fossil coals forms an atmosphere perceptible for many miles'.

The climate only a short distance from London was completely different, Louise said. Returning to town was a regular disappointment:

> Often, coming back from these different outings, I would stop on the high ground four or five miles from London, hoping to enjoy the view of this vast city; but the fog which hung over it was always so dense I could never see more than the tips of its steeples.

If it was not the fog and smoke, then it was the rain. Louise was tough, but not as tough as aristocratic English ladies, in the face of this hazard.

> English women are used to braving their climate. I often met them in driving rain, spinning along in open barouches without umbrellas. It was enough for them to pull their cloaks around them, which is not without its inconveniences for a foreigner unused to this aquatic regime.[71]

Not everyone agreed that the English weather deserved the criticism it got. Madame de La Tour du Pin was robust: 'It is my opinion . . . that the English climate outside London is much maligned. I found it no worse than the Dutch, and incomparably better and less unpredictable than the Belgian.'[72]

'I resigned myself to the monotony of this English life, which could not be to my taste after I had lived so long in Paris and St Petersburg,'[73] Louise wrote. Sometimes she blamed the English character. The fact that silence so often appeared to be *de rigueur* was mystifying to one who had been brought up to respect the art of conversation. When she visited Donnington Park, Lord Moira's seat, the hospitality offered seemed to her in some ways odd. This was despite her host's famed generosity towards *émigrés*, and their frequent presence at his table: it was said that faces there often changed, but costumes rarely, because the emigrants passed them round among themselves.[74] After a Donnington dinner, Louise wrote, 'one gathers in a beautiful gallery, where women sit apart, busy embroidering or doing tapestry work, and without exchanging a single word. For their part, the men pick up books and keep the same silence.'[75]

Louise, discovering that a moonlight stroll in the park would be frowned on, took up a portfolio of engravings to look at,

> refraining, in common with everyone else, from saying a word. In the midst of such a taciturn company, thinking I was alone one day, I let slip an exclamation at the sight of a charming engraving, which gave everyone present the surprise of their lives. But it is a fact that the complete absence of conversation does not rest on the impossibility of chatting agreeably in England; I know many English people who are very witty; I might even add that I have not met a single one who was a fool.[76]

She encountered the same taciturnity when she visited the Duchess of Dorset at Knole.

> The first time we all gathered for dinner, the Duchess said to me: 'You will be very bored, for we do not speak at table.' I reassured her on this point, telling her that that was my habit too, having for many years almost always eaten alone. She obviously set great store by this custom; for at dessert her son, aged eleven or twelve, came up to her, and she barely said a word to him, and finally sent him away without a single mark of affection.[77]

It was the general view of French visitors that the British had a particular taste for silence. According to Ferri di San Costante, the pause ensuing on an exchange of words was known as *une conversation anglaise*: the erstwhile interlocutors simply looked at one another intently and mutely for several minutes, as though reflecting profoundly on what had been said.[78] Nearly half a century before, Rousseau had presented a more positive image of such wordlessness in *La Nouvelle Héloïse*, describing the so-called *matinée à l'anglaise* enjoyed by Julie, Saint-Preux and Wolmar:

> After six days wasted on frivolous conversations with indifferent people, we today spent a *matinée à l'anglaise* [Saint-Preux writes], united and surrounded by silence, revelling at one and the same

time in the pleasure of being together and the calm of recollec-
tion. How few are the people who know the rapture of this state!
I have not met anyone in France with the least idea of it. 'The
conversation of friends never wanes,' they say. It is true, language
provides an easy chattering for those joined by an ordinary
attachment; but friendship, milord, friendship! . . . Can what one
said to one's friend ever be worth what one feels by his side? . . . It
is certain that this state of contemplation gives feeling men one of
the greatest pleasures life can offer. But I have always found that
unfortunate people prevent one from enjoying it, and that friends
have to be on their own to feel they need say nothing except when
they want to.[79]

If English women struck Louise as particularly silent, she blamed part of
their repression on another strange social habit. For this *habituée* of
European salons, it was beyond comprehension that the sexes should be
as rigidly divided as they were at English dinners. At Donnington Park 'the
women left table before dessert; the men stayed behind to drink and talk
politics.'[80] Perhaps this explained the Englishman's typical lack of *politesse*
and the Englishwoman's typical reserve. Madame de Staël's *Corinne*,
published a few years later, gives an unforgettable picture of the
institutionalised suppression of the female in English polite society.
Corinne, living with her family in Northumberland after fifteen years in
Italy, is astonished by this segregation of the sexes: 'my stepmother . . . gave
the women the signal . . . to withdraw and go and prepare the tea, leaving
the men alone at table during dessert. I understood nothing of this
custom, which surprises people greatly in Italy; there, no one can conceive
of there being any pleasure in company without women.'[81] They spend
three hours in the drawing-room, waiting for the men to join them.

Imagine what it was like for an Italian like me to have to sit round
a tea-table for several hours every day after dinner, with my stepmother's companions . . . One woman would say to the other: 'My
dear, do you think the water is boiling enough to pour on to the
tea?' 'My dear,' the other would reply, 'I think it would be too soon;
for the gentlemen are not yet ready to come.' 'Will they stay at
table long today?' a third asked. 'What do you think, my dear?' . . .
I had been inside Italian convents; they seemed to me full of life
beside this company, and I did not know where to put myself.[82]

The same regimented spirit governed English walks. There was an equal
sense of repression, according to Louise, and an equal deadness:

the women walk together on one side, all dressed in white; their silence, their perfect calm, almost persuades you they are ghosts walking; the men stand apart from them and have the same serious air. I have sometimes come across couples *tête-à-tête*, the woman giving the man her arm; when I chanced to walk some way with these two people, I amused myself waiting to see if they would say a word; I never saw the silence broken.[83]

One acquaintance who seemed not to share the standard English inhibitions was the Margravine of Anspach, who invited Louise to stay with her in the country. Louise was fearful that she would not be inhibited enough, and so would disturb her artist's routine.

I had undertaken to do the portrait of the Margravine of Anspach ... As I had been told that the Margravine was a very odd woman, who would have me woken every morning at five o'clock, and a thousand other equally unbearable things, I only accepted her invitation after setting my conditions with her. First I asked for a bedroom where I would hear no noise, as I wanted to sleep fairly late. Then I warned her that if we went on a drive together, I would never speak in the carriage, and that, besides, I liked walking alone. The excellent woman agreed to everything and kept her word religiously, so that, if by chance I met her in her park where she was often to be found digging, just like a labourer, she pretended not to see me and let me pass without saying a single word.[84]

Perhaps Louise wanted somehow to reflect this gardener's robustness in her portrait, for the Margravine remarked of it that 'even Madame Le Brun ... has made an arm and hand out of all proportion to the chest and shoulders'.

The Margravine was herself as well travelled as Louise. She had left her first husband Mr (later Lord) Craven after fourteen years of marriage and wandered around Europe with her third son Keppel, whom Louise also painted during her stay in England. (The Margravine's memoirs refer to her son's portrait having been done in France as well by an artist of Marie-Antoinette's,[85] who is probably Louise.) She spent several years at the court of Anspach, and eventually married the Margrave. In England they lived both at Brandenburg House in Hammersmith (then a riverside village) and at the much larger and finer Benham House near Newbury, where Louise was persuaded to spend three happy weeks. The Margravine loved this place, which she had built herself and where she had laid out the grounds according to her own taste: landscape gardeners like Capability Brown were not invited to help.[86] It was a source of great unhappiness to her that her son later sold Benham, and that the seventeenth-century Brandenburg House – whose gardens she had also designed and cultivated – had to be completely levelled after dry rot attacked the timbers.[87]

Notwithstanding the warnings she had been given about the Margravine's troublesome character, Louise enjoyed her company enough to undertake several voyages by sea with her. The most exciting was to the Isle of Wight, which Louise liked because it made her think of Switzerland, and because its natives seemed so tranquil and gentle. (She obviously never discovered the smuggling that was rife on the far side of the island.) It inspired her to flights of Rousseauist eloquence:

> everyone who lived there was well dressed, looked affable and kindly and did not seem affected by the immoral contagion of big cities. Besides the amiability I noticed in the population, the landscape was so ravishing that I could have spent my life in this beautiful place: only the Isle of Wight and the island of Ischia, near Naples, have given me this desire.[88]

When London was passing through its dead season, she thought, one could do nothing better than explore the countryside, 'which is truly superb'.[89] So she accepted all the invitations she received to visit the aristocracy on their estates. According to Baert's *Tableau de la Grande-Bretagne* (1800), 'the rich only think of themselves as *camping* in town; their establishment is in the country, and it is only there that they are thought to keep house stylishly.'[90] Louise duly went to Blenheim ('called Marlborough'), which Voltaire called 'a great mass of stone, devoid of charm or taste', and Stowe. Unlike Saint-Preux in *La Nouvelle Héloïse*, she liked Capability Brown's gardens there: 'The park at Stowe, adorned with a temple, monuments, constructions of every kind, is of the greatest beauty.'[91] Knole, which she spells 'Knowles', seemed to her sad. The Duchess's descendant Vita Sackville-West, who was born there and wrote its history, disagreed: Knole, she says,

> has the deep inward gaiety of some very old woman who has always been beautiful, who has had many lovers and seen many generations come and go, smiled wisely over their sorrows and their joys and learnt an imperishable secret of tolerance and humour.[92]

But the mood which met Louise was far from being one of gaiety.

According to Farington, Opie described the portrait Louise did there of the Duchess of Dorset as a 'pretty head, and well set on the shoulders.'[93] In fact Louise's portrait is less of a pretty head than of a regular and comfortably plain one, which sits on a body dressed without show in a plain black redingote with frilled collar and demure fichu. She wears a puce-coloured beret which is too close-fitting to be dashing, and altogether cuts a discreet figure, plumply round and almost bourgeoise in appearance. Hoppner's full-length, like Louise's portrait still hanging at Knole, makes her look more handsome, as does a later and rather dramatic portrait of the Duchess, attributed to Louise and now relegated to the private rooms. Curiously, Louise nowhere mentions this second picture in the *Souvenirs*.

Louise liked outings as much as native Londoners did. Not that she always seems to have been aware, at least retrospectively, of quite what an outing to a particular destination represented. The fashionable spas frequented by the quality – Matlock, Tunbridge Wells, Brighton – are described by her as being in the vicinity of London. She particularly liked Matlock because it 'altogether has the look of a Swiss landscape.'[94] Tunbridge Wells, where the *monde* went as much for the diversion of the season as for the medicinal chalybeate waters, was rather a disappointment. True, like Matlock it was 'a very picturesque spot'. But

> if one rejoices in the morning, wandering through the beautiful environs, in the evening one is thoroughly bored in the assemblies, which are very numerous; we foregathered for meals, and after supper, as after dinner, everyone got up to sing *God Save The King*, a prayer for the King which moved me to tears because of the sad comparison it made me draw between England and France.[95]

If Brighton could not be missed – particularly by someone who counted the Prince Regent among her enthusiastic admirers – Bath was even more essential. Louise spent three almost entirely sodden weeks there, and sounds very like the young Catherine Morland in her excited references to the city. Like the heroine of *Northanger Abbey* too, she found the Assembly Rooms unpleasantly packed. Catherine, as well as Louise, 'was tired of being continually pressed against by people, the generality of whose faces possessed nothing to interest, and with all of whom she was so wholly unacquainted that she could not relieve the irksomeness of imprisonment by the exchange of a syllable with any of her fellow-captives.'[96] Louise suffered as much as Catherine from knowing almost no one, and enduring the silence and 'insolence' of unpolished provincials. This scene, in particular, is worthy of Jane Austen:

I was with Madame de Beaurepaire, and we sat down next to some very old and very ugly Englishwomen; I correctly assumed that they belonged to the number of those who never leave their province, where they retain their gothic pride, for grand ladies in London and Englishwomen who have travelled are amiable and polite, whereas our neighbours, as soon as we had sat down, turned their backs to us with a certain air of contempt. We were resigned to enduring the disdain of these old women when an Englishman who knew them went up to them and whispered a few words in their ear, which made them immediately turn round and behave more pleasantly towards us.[97]

Louise seems not to have encountered Jane Austen, who was living in Sydney Place at the time of her stay, but shared her sharp eye for provincial inconsequence.

She would have enjoyed Bath more but for the 'toiling' walks up steep hills – she calls them 'towering mountains'[98] – in the pouring rain. She found the architecture in poor taste, an astonishing judgement which suggests that it was the uniformity of the English urban style which she saw as unappealing. Otherwise her views were entirely enthusiastic:

> it is a superb town, with a noble, picturesque aspect; as you arrive, a mile outside the city walls, you see very lofty mountains on both sides of the road; Bath is spread out on the left and you see the outlines of houses, palaces, grandiose circuses, all built on the highest hill. The view is truly magnificent, theatrical; I thought I was dreaming, and I thought of Ménageot; he would have loved this sight . . . The only inconvenience of a town built in this way is that you cannot go anywhere without climbing or going down hills; but you have to suffer a little for enjoying such a visual feast.[99]

She was delighted, too, to be in the world of 'fashionable coryphaeuses'.[100] Had she visited England fifteen years later and been able to read *Northanger Abbey*, she would probably have delighted even more in Henry Tilney's expert understanding of her favourite cloth, muslin.

> 'Do you understand muslins, sir?'
> 'Particularly well. I always buy my own cravats, and am allowed to be an excellent judge; and my sister has often trusted me in the choice of a gown. I bought one for her the other day, and it was pronounced to be a prodigious bargain by every lady who saw it.

I gave but five shillings a yard for it, and a true Indian muslin.'

Mrs Allen was quite stuck by his genius. 'Men commonly take so little notice of those things,' said she.[101]

Louise must have liked London itself more than her memoirs sometimes suggest. She became so busy that she regretted having applied for permission to stay only three or four months, and wrote to the banker Perrégaux (the very wealthy Swiss husband of the Madame Perrégaux whose 1789 portrait by Louise is in the Wallace Collection, and who himself became the first *Régent* of the Banque de France) asking him to help her get an extension.[102] She would never have undertaken the trip to England had she realised that the peace treaty of Amiens would be so fragile, she explained, but now she needed time to finish the various portraits she had begun: she intended to stay in England until the following year if she could, and if not to book a passage on a neutral ship and return to Paris, where her daughter was expected shortly. (Julie was now estranged from her husband, who would himself come to Paris in 1807–8 to hire more French actors for St Petersburg.) In the event Louise remained. One wonders why she needed to apply to Perrégaux at all when the Prince Regent had already obtained permission for her to stay on for as long as she liked. Could the story of this royal intervention be a fabrication, in line with some of the other stories about monarchs Louise tells in the *Souvenirs*?

The portrait she painted of the future George IV seems to have been the only one she did of him, though some puzzling references suggest otherwise. Mrs Papendiek's *Court and Private Life in the Time of Queen Charlotte* reports of the year 1791 that 'Madame Le Brun had lately come to England'[103] and painted the Prince of Wales in return for the 'vile fellow'[104] the duc d'Orléans, of whom Reynolds did a full-length portrait. Orléans was said to have commissioned the portrait of his friend. Since Philippe-Egalité was guillotined in 1793 this can hardly be Louise's London picture. In any case, she was in Italy in 1791. Or was she? We may remember the claim made in Roman journals that she had left Italy to join Calonne in London. But if Louise did swap Italy for England in the early 1790s, her stay would necessarily have been a brief one, given the commissions she had undertaken in Rome and Naples. Tempting as it may be to suspect the *Souvenirs* of covering up a liaison and a secret journey of Louise's for the sake of propriety, the dates do not seem to fit. Nor does that of the alleged passage to England in 1789, when Louise was rumoured to have joined Calonne over the Channel. What are we to make of Mrs Papendiek's assertion? It is possible that, writing at several years' distance, she is simply confused about the date of Louise's visit to England, or that she half-remembered the story of her having fled there on leaving France.

Louise, who lists only the 1804 portrait of the Prince of Wales in the *Souvenirs*, would scarcely have failed to mention also painting him earlier. If the London portrait was indeed an exchange for the Reynolds one, it was done belatedly, for the duc d'Orléans had sat to Reynolds in 1785 (which makes the notion that a *1791* portrait might have been done in exchange for it more comprehensible). In any case, in 1785 it seems to have been intended that Reynolds himself should paint the portrait of the Prince of Wales. When she painted him, Louise writes,

> The Prince of Wales must have been about forty, but he looked older, given that he had already become too plump. Tall and well-shaped, he had a handsome face; all his features were noble and regular. He wore a wig arranged very artfully, with the hair parted at the front, like the Apollo Belvedere's, which suited him wonderfully well. He was very good at all physical exercises; he spoke French excellently, and with the greatest ease. He had an exquisite elegance, a magnificence that went as far as prodigality; for at one point, it was said, he had debts of 300,000 *louis*, which his father and Parliament ended up paying.
>
> As he was for a long time one of the handsomest men in the three Kingdoms, he was idolised by women.[105]

Louise's picture, which she did shortly before leaving England, does not much disguise his plumpness, but it does capture his dash: it is a three-quarter-length oil showing the Prince in hussar costume, arrestingly posed. He gave the portrait to his 'extremely beautiful' morganatic wife Mrs Fitzherbert, whom Louise wrongly states never to have been married to him. She won Louise's heart by flattering her artistic vanity: 'She put it [the portrait] in a wheeled frame, like a cheval mirror, so that she could move it into all the rooms she occupied, which I found highly ingenious.'[106]

Louise painted some foreign subjects in England – Prince Bariatinsky, Prince Biron of Kurland (wrongly listed as 'Lord Byron' in the *Souvenirs*), Signora Grassini. But most of her sitters were native. She was more successful in gaining their patronage than Danloux, who returned to France just before her arrival. Hoping to attract an English clientele to replace the one he had lost to the vindictive hatred of David, he found to his chagrin that most of the aristocracy preferred to be painted by Romney, Hoppner and Copley. But Louise's reputation was more firmly established in the *monde*, and she had better contacts. This is not to say that her work was universally liked. Benjamin West, for instance, thought she was a lesser painter than Labille-Guiard.[107] Farington's diary entry for 7 June 1803 reports Opie's rather double-edged comments on inspecting her pictures at 61 Baker Street:

> They are painted in the present French manner, but better than any he saw in Paris. The imitation of particular things, velvet, silk &c.&c. very good. Perhaps the care and correctness might be considered by the English painters with some attention and to their advantage. But with all their merit they afforded him no high pleasure as works of art. He would not desire to hang them up in his house.[108]

On 1 April 1804, Farington dined at Sir George Beaumont's house. The talk was again of Louise's pictures. Sir George 'thought that *imitative* kind of painting resembled wax-work, and seemed to be rather copying such imitations of nature as are made in that way than real life.'[109]

But the real, stinging (and anonymous) attack came from Hoppner, in the preface to his 1805 translation of the *Oriental Tales*. It begins as a broadside on the French school generally, but then narrows its focus onto Louise. Her chief fault is seen as *polish*.

> Smoothness and finishing, whatever the young connoisseur may think, are not convertible terms! A piece of drapery by the pencil of Rembrandt, who was certainly not remarkable for the polish of his surface, differs from the piece in the woollen-draper's or in Madame Le Brun's shop, as much in appearance as in value . . .[110]

Few things, according to Hoppner,

> have tended to produce more error in judgment passed on pictures than the imposing quality of smoothness, which is generally conceived to be the effect of successful labour and close attention to finishing; and appears to have been spread over the works of the insipid, as a kind of snare to catch the ignorant. On the art of spreading these toils, and on a feeble, vulgar and detailed imitation of articles of furniture and dress, rests the whole of Madame Le Brun's reputation.[111]

But true art, as Reynolds saw, has nothing to do with high finishing or minute attention to detail. It has to do with an enlarged comprehension that sees the whole object at once.

Whenever a spurious art appears among us, powerful enough in its patronage, not in its inherent strength, to do mischief, I trust that I shall neither want patriotism nor courage openly to meet, and cordially to assist in its defeat and extermination.[112]

Hoppner momentarily wonders whether he should have spared Louise on grounds of chivalry, but says that her 'overweening presumption' means she has waived the privilege of her sex.

She has challenged hostility, when she might have escaped with impunity by falling into that rank which the mediocrity of her talents, and the state of the arts in this country, rendered it decent for her to take.

Luckily, Louise could still read no English. She caught the general drift of Hoppner's attack, however, and was driven to defend herself. Perhaps Hoppner, who insisted that he did not write out of spite, was one of the 'many English painters who became furious with me' when they discovered that she was doing a portrait of the Prince of Wales. She conceded that 'I find it difficult to leave my works; I never think them finished enough, and for fear of leaving them too imperfect my nature forces me to think about them for a long time and keep retouching them'. But

as for these fabrics, these *speaking* cushions, these velvets on display *in my shop*, my view is that one should pay as much attention to all these accessories as possible, but without detriment to the heads. On this point I have the authority of Raphael, who never neglected anything of this kind.[113]

She was most offended of all by the gratuitous and insulting reference to her *shop*, which she called

scarcely worthy of an artist's language. I show my pictures without anyone having to pay at the door. I have even, to distance myself from this practice, indicated the one day every week when I receive people known to me, and any others they are pleased to present; so I must observe to you that the word 'shop' is out of place, and that severity never dispenses a man from being polite.

To which one might add that anger never dispenses a woman from being truthful. Reading Hoppner's description of Louise's paintings as '*expensive* trash',[114] we may remember her claim earlier in the *Souvenirs* never to

259

have understood French–English exchange rates properly, and constantly to have undercharged for her portraits in London.

This last does not seem particularly likely. Opie said that her price for a three-quarter-length was 200 guineas and for a full-length 500.[115] In 1803 Bertie Greatheed called Gérard's price of £250 for a full-length 'prodigious', though he liked his work.[116] There seems little reason to dissent from Madame Ancelot's verdict that Louise's 'innumerable' portraits were almost all '*magnifiquement payés*'.[117] Louise presumably knew the dealers with whom her former husband still did business,[118] and was certainly interested enough in money to discover what the generally prevailing prices for portraits were. (She then, equally certainly, overshot them.) So to be told that she ran a 'shop' was offensive only in that it demeaned her sacred art, and made her sound more mercenary towards the viewing public than she liked to claim she was.[119] As she well knew, she was in a commercial centre, unsentimental and pragmatic in its attitude to money. There is no evidence that she thought the Londoner's devotion to the business of lining his pocket distasteful. Indeed, she may have felt his commitment to the practical arts of calculation and gain to be refreshingly unhypocritical.

Whatever the doubts some entertained about her competence, Louise felt appreciated and happy enough to spend over two years in a country she had originally meant to stay in for four or five months. But did she herself admire English portraiture, or learn anything from her exposure to it? The smooth style Hoppner attacked her for, and which she practised partly because she disliked impasto, was not very English. She disapproved of the loose facture characteristic of much native work, and even criticised Reynolds on this score:

> In London I saw many of the famous Reynolds's pictures; their colour is excellent, and recalls Titian's, but in general they are barely completed, apart from the heads.[120]

This seemed to be a general feature of English portraiture. At least, painters were in no hurry to finish their canvases.

> I went . . . to visit the principal artists, and I was extremely surprised to see that all of them had a great room full of portraits with only the heads finished. I asked them why they exhibited these portraits before they were completed; all replied that the sitters were happy just to be seen and identified; besides, once the sketch had been done they paid half the total agreed in advance, so that the painter was satisfied.

Certainly, most British portraitists contemporary with Louise lacked a neat touch. Like Reynolds, they felt that the unfinished had the virtue of appealing to the spectators' imagination, encouraging them to 'complete' the work for themselves. Reynolds had remarked in his fourteenth *Discourse* that the likeness of a portrait lay more in preserving the general effect of a countenance than in minute finishing of the features of the particular parts. As a corollary to this, painters who worked fast were encouraged, especially those who captured likenesses by daring leaps. Portraiture was in a certain sense a performing art, and leaving traces of the painterly process was far from deprecated.[121] But such enthusiasm for the *non finito* was something imperfectly understood, or at least appreciated, by Louise herself.

Yet there is surely some regret in her acknowledgement to the anonymous Hoppner that she found it difficult ever to leave her works, and that she never thought them sufficiently completed. Her propensity for constantly retouching rather than boldly preserving a moment's striking effect may simply show that Louise was a victim of her sex, lacking the confidence that comes with institutional support and time-honoured social sanction. Whatever the 'overweening presumption' Hoppner detected, and whatever the scale of Louise's international success, she still felt occasional doubts about her talent. As she wrote to Hoppner,

> you may denigrate my pictures as much as you please, all your criticism will still fall short of what I think of them . . . I have never been completely happy with a single one of my works.[122]

The English interlude was clearly a success for Louise, both from the point of view of 'my financial interests as a painter'[123] and because it enabled her to shake off melancholy again. But the news that Julie Nigris was in Paris decided her to return, more particularly as she had heard that Jean-Baptiste-Pierre Le Brun was allowing her daughter to form all kinds of unsuitable friendships. She had not seen Julie for five years, and seems to have been apprehensive about their reunion. She felt both distanced from her daughter and anxious for renewed proximity to her, as this passage from the *Souvenirs* reveals:

> For her misfortune and mine, my poor child was extremely headstrong; besides, I had not succeeded in giving her all the distaste I personally felt for bad company. Add to this – whether through my own fault or not – that however much influence she had over my mind, I had none whatsoever over hers, and you may imagine that she sometimes made me weep bitter tears.

But she was still my daughter; her beauty, her talents, her mind made her as enchanting as can be, and although I could sadly not decide her to come and live with me, given that she insisted on seeing several people I could not receive, at least I saw her every day, and that was still a great joy to me.[124]

So despite the entreaties of her English acquaintances, and after an unspecified period at the inn to which Josephina Grassini accompanied her, she set sail for Rotterdam. (The Channel routes were closed because of the renewed enmity between France and England.) After ten days at large in Holland, where the Spanish ambassador, a friend from St Petersburg days, arranged for her to go on consoling outings to The Hague, she was given a passport and told she could proceed to Antwerp. Here she was shown the city's treasures by the obliging prefect, Monsieur Hédouville, and visited a sick young artist who greatly admired her, and whom her mere presence was apparently enough to cure. The following day she continued her journey to Paris, and arrived there in July 1805.

CHAPTER ELEVEN

EMPIRE AND RESTORATION: 'I resumed my musical evenings'

On Louise's return, Madame de Ségur's husband told her – and the news can hardly have come as a surprise – that Napoleon, now Emperor, both mistrusted her and resented the fact that she had gone to visit 'her English friends'.[1] But apparently his annoyance was less than it seemed, for in March 1806 he would commission a portrait of his sister Caroline Murat – wife of Joachim Murat, the future King of Naples – whom Louise felt no enthusiasm about painting. Part of her reluctance, aside from the implied association with a new political order she did not care for, may have arisen from her feeling that she had struck an uncharacteristically bad financial bargain. Or had she? Although she says that she was paid only 1,800 francs for the picture, less than half what she normally charged for a full-length portrait, records suggest that the real amount was 4,000 francs;[2] so perhaps we should assume that she is, consciously or not, belittling the commission because it came from Bonaparte. Since she adds that she included the figure of Madame Murat's daughter Laetitia for nothing, what she may really mean is that her standard charge was in this instance too low.

Her main objection, however, stemmed from Caroline Murat's bad manners:

> she constantly cancelled the sittings she gave me, so that, despite my desire to finish the job, she made me spend nearly the whole summer in Paris, usually waiting for her in vain, which made me more impatient than I can say. Besides, the intervals between sittings were so long that she changed her hairstyle. The first days, for instance, she had curls tumbling onto her cheeks, and I painted them as I saw them; but some time later, as this hairstyle became old-fashioned, she came looking quite different, so that I had to scrub out the hair I had painted falling onto her face, as well as painting out the pearls of her hairband and replacing them with cameos. The same thing happened with dresses. The one I

had painted initially was quite décolleté, as one wore them then, and with a wide band of embroidery at the neck; this fashion having changed, I was obliged to give the dress a higher neck and redo the embroidery, which was set much too widely.[3]

She could not contain her exasperation. She may not have passed the remark to Vivant Denon – 'I have known true princesses who never tormented me or kept me waiting' – as audibly as she says she did apropos of Madame Murat's behaviour, but there can be no doubt of her real annoyance. She was in general impatiently dismissive towards the new Napoleonic aristocracy. Despite her status, Caroline Murat remained for Louise a parvenue. The attempted fusion of the old nobility and a new *noblesse d'Empire* was never really a success, and in 1812 Napoleon would admit that the bonding of the two élites had failed to come up to his original expectations.[4] Two years later, with the restoration of the monarchy, the old aristocracy resumed their time-honoured titles and the new *noblesse* busily forgot about Napoleon.

Louise's portrait of Caroline Murat is undoubtedly regal, whatever her opinion of the subject's lack of royal mannerliness; but overall it is a feeble work. Caroline appears in the picture – now at Versailles – as a woman of grace and poise, though contemporaries varied in their assessment of her looks. Elizabeth Divova, who was habitually rhapsodic, describes her as very pretty, as well as good-natured and polite,[5] but according to the duchesse d'Abrantès, 'She had grace but no bearing, and beauty but no attractiveness, and somehow all that found expression on her face.'[6]

In Louise's portrait Madame Murat is both queenly and *chic*; a diadem pushes her wavy hair modishly off her cheeks, and her rich brocade dress, which with its velvet train epitomises the 'Empire' line (a fashion actually dating from the late eighteenth century), has a pearl-encrusted bodice. Her face is slightly complacent, suggesting a sense of superiority; but she is as dignified as any of the genuinely grand ladies Louise had painted under the *ancien régime*, and her daughter no less winning than Louise's earlier children. The overall effect, however, is flat.

The evidence of a new world governed by different niceties from the ones Louise remembered could scarcely be denied. If she resisted the temptation to show Madame Murat as the vulgarian the duchess d'Abrantès took her to be, she was still conscious that the capital was home to a less refined set than she had previously known. When this concerned her daughter Julie, it particularly mattered: hence, it would appear, the physical distance Louise kept from her. Perhaps Julie's crime was simply to prefer mixing with people who were not wedded to the ways of the *ancien régime*.

The first friend Louise made on returning from London seemed to complement the one who had seen her off. Angelica Catalani was a young and beautiful soprano: she lacked the expressiveness of Josephina Grassini, but her voice had other strengths. Then the toast of Paris (where she was to die of cholera in 1849), she had enjoyed early success in her native Italy, a success due to her looks as well as to her musical gifts. After performing around Italy she sang in Portugal and Spain before moving on to Paris, where she gave several concerts. There and in London, where she was to be seen in 1806, she earned enormous sums, but was also wildly extravagant. She spent seven years in England, where her house was the rendezvous for many French *émigrés*, tried unsuccessfully to buy the King's Theatre, returned to Paris to take over the Italian Opera, left France during the Hundred Days in 1815, and returned after Napoleon's exile. In keeping with her general extravagance, she ran her opera company with ruinous abandon.

Her singing electrified audiences. 'Her voice,' Louise writes, 'one of the most astonishing you could imagine, united phenomenal range and an agility which seemed almost miraculous . . . she charmed you as a nightingale does.'[7] Lord Mount-Edgcumbe, admittedly, said that she spoilt her performances with excessive ornament, and lacked restraint. Louise's portrait of this beautiful creature suggests no such wantonness, still less the stoutness which later overtook her. Looking like a cherubic *ingénue*, she is dressed in a simple white costume, and has dark hair curling as naturally and freely as Isabella Marini's. She seems enraptured by the heavenly sound she is making (presumably an aria from the opera *Sémiramis*, whose libretto is open on the piano), and anxious to please. During her own lifetime Louise kept this enchanting picture in her own home, hanging it as a pendant to one of her portraits of Josephina Grassini as a sultana.

Angelica Catalani was gracious enough to perform at the musical soirées Louise began to hold again. These were evenings devoted principally to song, for she had lost the violinist Viotti: he may still have been in England, where Louise had met him during her stay, but in any case financial difficulties were drawing him further and further from his musical career. (Later on Louise would attract the virtuoso violinist Lafont to her drawing-room instead.) She and her guests sometimes contented themselves with non-musical pleasures too. The society game of *tableaux vivants* was revived from Louise's St Petersburg days. She felt that the pleasure of this innocent pastime far exceeded that provided by the card-tables of Paris and the stifling routs of London, however trivial it might seem to a modern age obsessed with politics and gambling. And she was happy to enjoy the company of faithful old friends, particularly the still schoolboyish Hubert Robert.[8]

Louise's frustrations with the Murat commission were to some extent soothed by her resumption of her usual calm life. But after a while she felt the familiar urge to unsettle herself again – not by enduring the slights of insolent patrons, but by freeing herself from the whole stifling world of Parisian etiquette. The lure of travel was too strong to resist. So in 1807 (not 1808, as she says) she set off to experience elemental nature in Switzerland. The trip is described in a series of letters to the slightly scandalous Countess Helen Potocka, formerly married to the prince de Ligne's son Charles.

Perhaps Louise was still remembering 'Swiss' Matlock. At any rate, she wanted to enjoy the Alpine sublimity of a world which other intrepid women had discovered before her – in 1773 the comtesse de Brionne had crossed the mountainous Jura region, whle in 1774 Mrs Schwellenberg, Queen Charlotte's lady-in-waiting, in turn visited Grindelwald (then as now obviously a favourite for middle-aged lovers of peaks and spectacular views). Four years later Madame de Sabran and comtesse Diane de Polignac journeyed to Bâle, Soleure, Lucerne and Geneva, and Madame de Sabran wrote to the chevalier de Boufflers of her rapture amidst the terrifying mountains, whose peaks seemed to challenge the heavens: she cursed fate, she informed her lover, for not having made her a *Suissesse* by birth.[9]

Not all the visitors had come to worship nature. In 1789 the Polignacs were being forced to leave their retreat in Bâle for political reasons, and the comte d'Artois and Condé were obliged to take the Tyrol route from Berne to Turin in order to avoid French Revolutionary forces.[10] In 1790 the Swiss began increasingly to notice French aristocrats travelling across their territory, their *villeggiatura* having become an exile; and in 1792 the author Sophie von La Roche found the Swiss roads littered with *émigré* carriages.[11] The Switzerland Louise encountered fifteen years later presented no political dangers to the traveller, though its physical perils were ever-present. She entered via Bâle, and set out for Bienne on a road recommended to her as spectacularly beautiful. Its beauty was matched only by the horror of its precipices, endless plummeting drops with no barriers or parapets to guard the traveller's safety. Louise herself nearly fell into an abyss when the horse drawing her carriage stumbled and then reared up in fright, blood coursing from its nostrils and spattering the windows of the vehicle.

> I admit I was extremely frightened; I hid my fear so as not to increase that of my dear companion Adélaïde [her maid]; finally heaven took pity on us. At the very moment when we were going to be swallowed up in the precipices, a man (the only one we met

on this road) came up to us, opened the carriage door and helped us down; then he immediately joined with the coachman to hold up the horse and loosen its harness: the poor animal's collar was too tight, and it had had a rush of blood to the head.[12]

This scare decided Louise to continue her journey on foot. She reached Bienne safely, but was in too much of a hurry to see the île de Saint-Pierre to stay more than a night there.[13]

The île de Saint-Pierre was where Rousseau had found refuge in the midst of persecution, and briefly enjoyed perfect happiness.

> Of all the dwelling-places I have known (and there have been some charming ones), none has made me so truly happy or left me with such tender regrets as the île de Saint-Pierre in the middle of Lake Bienne . . . I found staying there so delightful, I led a life so in tune with my mood that, determined as I was to end my days there, my sole worry was that I would not be allowed to execute this project . . . I was only permitted to spend two months on the island, but I would have spent all of eternity, without being bored for an instant . . . I count these two months as the happiest time in my life, so happy that they would have sufficed for all my days without making me desire another state for a single second.[14]

It was hardly surprising that Louise should have been moved to go on this pilgrimage. *La Nouvelle Héloïse* had made Rousseau the literary darling of the later eighteenth century, and Louise had read it along with everyone else. She shared many of Rousseau's enthusiasms. She was not as hostile to the city as he was, but thought like him that country living put man back in touch with himself. Rousseau's sentimental style, his 'feeling' expansiveness, chimed with the easy emotionality of Louise's painting. Both favoured naturalness of dress, Rousseau because he disliked sophistication (and also because he suffered from a painful urinary complaint and could not bear to wear tight clothing), and Louise because she found the flowing lines of the neo-classical style more elegant than fitted garments. Both thought that children should be lovingly brought up by their own mothers, even if Rousseau abandoned the five children he apparently fathered to a foundling's home. Only Louise's feisty female independence jarred with the master's doctrine, for Rousseau's *Emile* – a pedagogical novel – will have no truck with woman's liberation (which is why Mary Wollstonecraft despised it).[15]

In the course of her first Swiss trip Louise could not resist visiting some of the sites made famous by *La Nouvelle Héloïse*. Vevey in the Vaud, 'the little town at the foot of the Alps' of the novel's subtitle, is the scene of the romance, and she duly went there. To the modern mind it may spell condensed milk, chocolate and baby food, but to romantic souls of the late eighteenth and early nineteenth centuries it meant a great deal more. For Louise it was a place of dreams, a spot where she could happily have spent the rest of her life. Its climate and site were superb, and

> The environs of Vevey offer delicious opportunities for walking. Following the left-hand side of the lake, one arrives at the Château de Chillon via wooded slopes interrupted by villages. At their foot, by the path, a limpid stream flows swiftly on, and enchants you with its gurgling; on the right, mature trees border the lake, which you glimpse through the branches.[16]

She went at dawn to Clarens, where Julie and her husband Wolmar had their estate (and where Byron would settle a few years later), and felt filled with novelistic memories. She saw the high mountains of Meillerie, the scene of memorable episodes marking the frustrated love of Saint-Preux, and went boating on Lake Geneva as he had done with Julie. Louise, though, had to be satisfied with a less seductive companion: the innkeeper at Vevey offered to take her in his own boat.

> He looked such a decent man that I accepted his proposal, at least on condition that he would not say a word during the trip, since I wanted as always to admire the effects of beautiful nature and silence. Since Adélaïde was too tired to follow me, I left alone with the hefty innkeeper; he was not Saint-Preux, I was not Julie, but I was no less happy.[17]

Louise completed various landscape studies while she was in Switzerland, both on the first trip and during her second visit a year later. Nearly all of them seem to have been lost. She sketched water – the lakes of Brienz, Zug and Bienne, the famous Goldau waterfall[18] – and mountains. Mont Blanc particularly excited her, and she did several pastel drawings of it.[19] But she was never satisfied with her efforts:

> The sunset cast golden tints on the upper reaches of this enormous mass; the lower regions of the chain were the colour of irises and opals; this part of the glacier had no colour but the reflection of the sky. Finally this grandiose mass was interrupted on the left by high mountains of firs, completely in the shadow; below, the plains were in shadow too, making a contrast and a foil which the

effect of Mont Blanc did not at all need; but this contrast rounded off the picture. I wanted to capture the reflection; but alas, it was impossible; no palette or pastels could render these radiant tones.[20]

One large picture of Mont Blanc is extant, a very Romantic image executed with a free technique. All the evidence suggests that Louise was still an inferior landscapist. The story she tells at one point of the ten-year-old son of her Dutch travelling-companions, the van Brachs, copying one of her 'living' scenes as competently as the original had been executed may not, in fact, describe a particularly impressive feat.[21] But she needed a rest from what she did best, and sketching sublime landscapes provided that.[22]

The attraction of Switzerland was its spectacular wildness. So it annoyed her to have to share the sights with other people. This was the trouble with the glacier at Mont Blanc.

> I must tell you that there were crowds of tourists heading there at the same time as us; to avoid this throng, who were talking and shouting, I let them draw slightly ahead. So I spoke alone to my guide in order to avoid the bustle and the endless parlying of this whole band. We advanced to climb up to the glacier. After half an hour's walk, I was moving onto a very narrow path at the top of an enormous precipice when, having arrived there, I heard Monsieur van Brach shout to me: 'In heaven's name, Madame Le Brun, don't go higher, I beg of you.' But he, his wife and his son continued their climb.[23]

So Louise obediently went down to a smaller glacier, and began to sketch it, 'leaning my portfolio on my guide's back'. Finally she returned to her inn, only to find that van Brach himself had been overwhelmed by the ascent of Mont Blanc, and fallen into a cataleptic state which lasted for days.

Chamonix seemed to her a God-forsaken place 'which should be inhabited only by goats and chamois'.[24] Still she did not waste her time there: she painted the range of mountains broken by glaciers, and the entire valley (which she found sad, bare except for the marigolds which young shepherdesses made into nosegays for visitors). She vowed never to return; but Geneva made an altogether happier impression. Louise was inevitably shocked at the citizens' detestation of Rousseau – whose books had been burnt there during his lifetime – and by the lengths to which the city had gone to prevent a statue of the great man being erected. But she was flattered at being made a member of the Genevan Société pour l'avancement des arts in November that year.[25]

Another landmark of Louise's first Swiss trip was the September visit to Madame de Staël at Coppet, where she spent a week and abandoned landscapes for portraiture. According to the secretary of the Genevan Société, she had come unprepared to do anything but pastel sketches, could not buy paints in Lausanne or Geneva, and had to improvise her medium by pounding pastels and mixing them with oil.[26] The end result, he wrote, left something to be desired, but the portrait of Madame de Staël was still a more than recognisable likeness.

Germaine de Staël presented Louise with an artistic challenge. Not everyone agreed on her want of beauty – Goethe, for instance, found her attractive – but most called her looks coarse.[27] She had protuberant eyes, thick lips and a double chin,[28] and her lover Benjamin Constant (whose relationship with her dragged on unsatisfactorily for years) described her as a man-woman. Yet she contrived to secure a string of lovers in the course of her career. If Constant, however intellectually brilliant, was no more physically appealing than Germaine herself, other men in her life were: Fanny Burney found herself unable to believe in Germaine's affair with Louis de Narbonne because he was so handsome,[29] and her last love, Jean Rocca, was also an unusually attractive man. Louise herself remarks that 'Madame de Staël was not at all pretty, but the animation of her face made up for her want of beauty.'[30]

In Louise's portrait Germaine is shown determinedly, even ferociously, smiling. In 1807 this was quite an achievement. It was a year of outward glory – *Corinne*, which Louise had just read, had been published to great acclaim in the spring – but inner turmoil, in which she had perpetually to face the problem of Constant's irresoluteness. (His desire to end their relationship was so perennial that he simply referred to it in his journal by numerical code.) Constant was present at Coppet during Louise's stay, but previously Germaine had had to retrieve him from a refuge he had sought with his cousin Rosalie.

Whether or not Germaine felt happy to be sitting to Louise, she does appear powerfully animated. As Louise had chosen to depict her in the character of Corinne, inspirationally singing or improvising to her lyre,[31] such liveliness was essential; and Louise ensured the desired effect by having Germaine recite speeches from Corneille or Racine, 'which I barely listened to', during the sessions.

> When she had finished her tirades, I said to her: 'Carry on reciting;' she retorted: 'But you are not listening,' and I replied: 'Recite anyway.' Finally understanding what I meant, she went on declaiming passages from Corneille and Racine.[32]

Perhaps it was just as well that Louise was too busy to pay much attention. Germaine's incompetence as a tragic actress was widely acknowledged. Roger de Damas called her detestable,[33] and Madame d'Abrantès said that she was more convincing in *soubrette* rôles.[34] Louise remarks that she saw Germaine and Madame Récamier perform in Voltaire's tragedy *Sémiramis* that summer at Coppet, but seems to be confusing it with Racine's *Andromaque*.

Her portrait, like Gérard's later one, shows off Germaine's arms and shoulders, of which she was exceptionally proud. It was on their account that she favoured décolleté dresses and, perhaps, that she cultivated the habit Louise comments on:

> it was only after dinner that one could chat to her. One then saw her walking around her drawing-room, holding in her hand a little branch of greenery; when she spoke she shook this branch, and her words had a warmth which was hers alone; it was impossible to interrupt her.[35]

(Gérard's portrait reproduces the greenery.) Louise also shows her subject in a simple Grecian tunic, possibly assumed for the purposes of the sitting, but possibly also Germaine's habitual garb.[36] Madame de Boigne once met her in a Lyons inn on her way to Savoy, trailing Constant, Talma and the German critic August von Schlegel after her: she was wearing a white muslin dress with bare arms and shoulders, and seemed to Madame de Boigne to be presenting an odd appearance at midday in an inn. She was holding a small branch of foliage which she constantly twisted in her fingers, probably to show off her fine hands. It all added to the strangeness of her aspect, which was increased when she returned from a trip to the mountains with sunburn. But later Madame de Boigne claimed to be charmed by her looks and to find her almost beautiful.[37]

The dating of the Staël picture has confused critics, probably because the *Souvenirs'* account is itself muddled. Although Louise places the stay at Coppet in 1808, it actually occurred the year before. There was a second trip to Switzerland in 1808, and Louise's memoirs amalgamate the two trips indiscriminately. She describes having met Prince Augustus Ferdinand of Prussia at Coppet, which sets her time there firmly in 1807: the Prince was staying at the château because he was in love with Juliette Récamier, a fellow-guest, and did not return to Coppet the following year. There is another confusion in the dating of a letter from Germaine about the engraving of the portrait, quoted in the *Souvenirs*. Louise marks the letter which mentions Germaine's imminent departure to spend the winter in Vienna as having been written on 16 September 1808, but the stay in

Austria really occurred in 1807.[38] Additionally, Germaine herself writes of the portrait in a letter of 18 September 1807, and says that Louise is taking it to Paris to complete. The earlier letter from Germaine is diplomatic.

> I should be truly ashamed, Madame, at having delayed so long in replying to you if I had not been so ill for some time that everything was difficult for me. I put myself in your hands for the exhibition at the Salon [Louise apparently never did show the portrait there], and I flatter myself that your talent will succeed in getting what is lacking in the original excused. As for the engraving, I will take responsibility for it here; otherwise there would be too long a delay before I took delivery of the portrait . . .[39]

Later Germaine wrote to Julie Nigris that she had given up the idea of having the portrait engraved – 'it is too expensive for a whim, and I have just been involved in a complex court-case which obliges me to be careful about money.'[40] When she finally received the picture, which she called 'magnificent', Germaine implied with rare self-effacement that Louise had greatly improved on the original: 'Without thinking of my portrait, I have admired your work'. Perhaps this is no more than conventional flattery, though: 'All your talent is there, and I should like to think that mine could be encouraged by your example; but I fear that it is merely in the gaze you have given me'. This letter is dated 14 July 1809. One sent to Prosper Barante on 27 July reveals that Germaine initially disliked the picture, however,[41] and on 25 June she had written to Juliette Récamier expressing the hope that Louise would not exhibit it at the Salon.[42]

Was this because she wanted to take possession of it as quickly as possible, or because Germaine was not, in fact, as pleased with it as she declares to Louise? There is a much more flattering replica originally given to Germaine's young lover Jean Rocca, and now at Coppet, which closes the subject's open mouth, slims down her figure, and mends her cow-like expression. Its date is unknown, but perhaps this is the version Germaine wanted to have engraved.

In any case, words counted far more for than pictures. Words, and the art of talking, reigned supreme at Coppet. Germaine had offered so many victims of proscription refuge there that the old traditions of French hospitality, including the cultivation of conversation – what many *émigrés* missed above all in their exile – were eagerly preserved.[43] As Lamartine noted in his history of the Restoration, in Germaine's salon

> conversation was an ode without end. People crowded round her
> to be present at this eternal explosion of lofty ideas and magnan-

imous sentiment expressed with the inoffensive eloquence of a woman . . . The modern world had not, since the sibyls, seen the incarnation of virile genius in a woman. She was, at one and the same time, the sybil of two centuries, the eighteenth and the nineteenth.[44]

'What is called homesickness,' Germaine de Staël would write in *De l'Allemagne*,

this indefinable regret for one's native land, which is independent even of the friends one has left behind, applies particularly to the pleasure of conversation which the French nowhere find as well developed as in their own country . . . In all classes, in France, people feel the need to chat: the word is not so much, as elsewhere, a means of communicating one's ideas, feelings and affairs as an instrument to play for pleasure, and which revives the spirits, as music does for some races and strong liquor for others.[45]

This nostalgia seems prophetic, because Napoleon's displeasure – already expressed at the time Germaine's novel *Delphine* was published by his banning her from the vicinity of Paris, on account of some free-thinking episodes in the book – would be so provoked by *De l'Allemagne* (1810) that she was exiled from France. He was enraged by her glorifying of a race whose growing nationalism was already causing him trouble. So Germaine, regretfully, took up permanent residence at Coppet, the château on Lake Geneva which her father Necker had bought and where the bodies of both her parents lay pickled in spirits in the family mausoleum.

However much Germaine may have admired German culture, she thought the art of conversation alien to the Germanic character. Germans, she said, want to have seriousness in everything;[46] so they prefer discussion, a useful occupation rather than an agreeable art. The essence of conversation for her lay less in the ideas it developed or the knowledge it allowed speakers to display than in an indefinable way of responding to an interlocutor and of speaking, in Richardsonian fashion, 'to the moment'.[47] In conversation one was applauded for what had cost no effort, and showed one's wit in a multiplicity of ways, through accent, gesture and look; in short, one produced a sort of electricity, sparking off thoughts in others. As a Swiss, Rousseau thoroughly disapproved of this Gallic fizz. However delightful it might appear to others, he thought, it was insubstantial, a quintessentially French way of weaving gossamer into intricate but useless forms. Conversation taught nothing, neither how to judge others rightly nor how to assess things at their true worth. It was simply an art of dissimulation.

He would surely have rejoiced at the fact that from roughly 1792 to 1815, by all accounts, silence reigned.[48] But not at Coppet: what Louise says about life there makes it clear that the same sort of verbal torrent surged as in Germaine's Paris drawing-room. Yet the hostess was also conscious of her guests' claim to attention. She was, it seems, a superb *salonnière*, gracious and without affectation. She left people free to pursue their own interests during the day; the company assembled in the evening, and only after dinner could they talk with Madame de Staël. Then she was to be seen walking up and down the drawing-room, shaking her branch of foliage excitedly as the spirit moved her. It was, Louise says, impossible to interrupt her at such moments:[49] she seemed, like her heroine Corinne, in the grip of divine enthusiasm. Germaine was a blazing egocentric, but also a creature of seductive human warmth. One was either allergic or addicted: Louise, though less dangerously than Constant, was among those who were positively drawn to her.

Madame de Staël features in another work by Louise, but as bystander rather than principal subject. This is the large picture of the Alpine shepherds' festival near Interlaken, a celebration to commemorate the Swiss national character and customs in which different classes of the various cantons paraded, made music and played games.[50] One writer reported that Louise's main reason for returning to Switzerland in 1808 had been to attend the festival, and that she had pressed other Parisians to accompany her.[51] 'The Swiss,' Madame de Staël remarks in *De l'Allemagne*, 'are not a poetic nation, and one is understandably amazed that the admirable aspect of their country has not fired their imagination more.'[52] But the Alpine shepherds' festival at Unspunnen, in the canton of Untersee, did seem to show an imaginative pride in the national identity. The journey there correspondingly excited both Germaine and Louise, who was perhaps influenced in the *Souvenirs* by her friend's written account. 'To go to the festival,' Germaine noted,

> one had to sail across one of those lakes in which the beauties of nature are reflected, and which seem to have been placed at the foot of the Alps to multiply their ravishing appearance. Stormy weather made the mountains look less distinct to us, but they were all the more fearsome mingled with the clouds. The storm intensified, and although I was seized with a feeling of terror I liked the rolling thunder which confounded man's pride.[53]

Not everyone was so moved. The elegant young Parisians who had been

'Romantically' drawn to the festival wondered what sort of bargain they had made. According to Germaine,

> suddenly transported to the Swiss valleys, they could hear nothing but the roar of torrents, they could see nothing but mountains, and they asked themselves whether they could get bored enough in these solitary places to return to the *monde* with still keener pleasure.[54]

Louise stayed with the artist Franz Niklaus König and his wife, who gave her a 'charming room' and a 'brand-new bed with green curtains'.[55] The Königs offered a *table d'hôte* at their house for all the visitors of distinction, and Louise was unable to make them take anything for the fortnight she spent with them, apart from her self-portrait in oils, which she sent later from Paris.

The day of the *Alphirtenfest* dawned mild and misty. Arriving at half past ten, Louise found the sight of the natural amphitheatre ravishing. Above it towered the castle, a half-tone against the mountain of pine trees interspersed with cultivated fields. Germaine recorded that 6,000 people were present at the festival. When Louise arrived the whole area was full, and the sun which broke through picked out every colour of the participants' costumes. She sat down next to Germaine.

> A few seconds later, we heard sacred music sung perfectly by young shepherdesses, then the famous air of the *ranz des vaches*. The shepherdesses were preceded by the bailiff and magistrates. Then came peasants from the various cantons, all dressed in different costumes; white-haired old men carried the banners and halberds of each valley. They were dressed as they would have been five centuries ago, at the time of the Rütli oath . . . Madame de Staël and I were so moved, so filled with emotion at this solemn procession, this rustic music, that we clasped each other's hands without being able to say a single word; but our eyes filled with gentle tears. I shall never forget this moment of mutual sensibility.[56]

Perhaps Germaine was less romantically moved than she chose to suggest to Louise. Her remarks in *De l'Allemagne* about the *ranz des vaches* hints at a more prosaic response:

> People talk a great deal about an air played on alpine horns, and which made such a powerful impression on the Swiss that they

would leave their regiments when they heard it to return to their homeland. You may imagine the effect this air can produce when it echoes off the mountains; but it has to resound in the distance; close to, it does not create a very pleasant sensation. If it were sung by Italian voices, one's imagination would be quite intoxicated by it; but perhaps such a pleasure would generate ideas which were foreign to the simplicity of the country. One would start wanting arts, poetry, love, whereas one actually needs to be satisfied with rest and rustic life.[57]

By this time things that epitomised Swissness perhaps reminded her unpleasantly of the more stimulating life she had led in other countries. Like her heroine Corinne in the north of England, she probably felt constricted by provincial environments. But for Louise the sublime wildness of Swiss scenery enlarged everything.

The festival gave her a sense of life, and appealed to her feeling for the *pittoresque*. Sigmund Wagner, who wrote for a Swiss journal, noted that the *Alphirtenfest* offered both Germaine and Louise rich material for their respective talents. Touring the countryside before the festival, according to Wagner, Louise 'was in a continual state of rapture, and chose several views she wanted to paint'.[58] In a letter of 16 August 1808 to Maurice O'Donnell, Germaine wrote that 'Madame Le Brun draws views and I read or write to you.' And according to a footnote in the *Souvenirs*,

> After the festival, Madame de Staël went walking with the duc de Montmorency; I found a spot in the meadow and settled there to paint the site and the massed groups. The comte de Grammont held my box of pastels. This view of the festival is painted in oils; Monsieur le prince de Talleyrand owns the picture.[59]

This work is important both as a documentary record and because it is the only one of Louise's few surviving landscapes to contain human figures – that is, if Louise herself was responsible for it. The account given in her memoirs says unequivocally only that Louise did pastel studies on the spot. It does not state that she was the author of the oil owned in the 1830s by Talleyrand, but which is now in the Berne Kunstmuseum.

Certainly, Louise herself is identifiable in the oil, sketching on her knee with the top-hatted comte de Grammont holding her box of pastels. Other figures can be named with a fair degree of certainty (Germaine on the arm of Mathieu de Montmorency, both of them viewed from behind). But most of those present are the anonymous peasants, either looking on or taking an active part in the festival. It has sometimes been suggested that Franz Niklaus König painted the entire picture, or that he collaborated on it with the landscape painter Georg Volmar.[60] (König is known to have painted and engraved other scenes from the *Alphirtenfest*.) But there are strong arguments for attributing it to a non-native, for local detail is often lacking or defective: the alpine horns, for instance, are incorrectly drawn, and pointing upwards rather than resting on the ground. The drawing of the trees seems more skilful than comparable work by König, as does the handling of the colours. On the other hand, König's studies of costumed Swiss characters, such as the collection published in 1801, were unquestionably sources for the depiction of dress and the groupings of peasants in the picture, and in the *Souvenirs* Louise praises work of this kind which he had done:

> Monsieur König drew landscapes; his Swiss men and women in costume acquire added interest from the way he grouped them, which makes them superior to those which many other artists did before him. I often went round the country surrounding Untersee with Monsieur König; he drew the landscape with great facility, and also with talent.[61]

Of the two hundred or so landscapes which Louise did over her career,[62] a considerable proportion must date from her two Swiss trips. She seems to have sketched because she was happy. As she wrote from Coppet to Julie Nigris, whom she had presumably left behind in Paris,

> The spectacle of nature consoles one for a great many things, or distracts one from torment; I have just been made especially aware of this. You cannot imagine the pleasure I felt during our travels over Switzerland; you cannot conceive of all the pictures, all the views, all the sites – so varied and so picturesque. How many things I shall have to tell you about on return! I feel as though I have lived ten years in two-and-a-half months; it is not that time has dragged, but every hour has been so interesting and packed so full that I have fixed it, as it were, or noted its distance from the next.[63]

Partly, no doubt, the Alpine air has been responsible for lifting her spirits. Louise remained as impressionable as ever to atmospheric purity.

This is one of the reasons why, when she returned from Switzerland in 1808, she decided to revise her way of life:

no longer wanting to live in Paris during the summer, I bought
the Louveciennes country house I still own. I was won over by
the view, so extensive that the eye can follow the course of the
Seine for a great distance; by the magnificent woods at Marly, by
the delicious orchards, so well tended that one believes oneself
in the Promised Land; in short, by everything which makes
Louveciennes one of the most charming spots around Paris.[64]

The house which Louise would keep until her death no longer exists. It
was demolished in 1868 to clear space for the construction of the château
des Sources, an imposing building which still stands. It was situated
between the rue de la Croix-Rouge, the Grand-Rue, the rue des Voisins
and, on the south-east side, the ruelle des Regards, the insalubrious haunt
of thieves and malingerers who thought nothing, Louise writes, of sidling
threateningly up to her own property. She tried to purchase rights to this
passage in 1817, but her request was refused on the grounds that the alley-
way had always existed and greatly facilitated access to the village fields
and the transport of crops. Louise's boundary walls, besides, were deemed
to be the real culprits: they were simply too low. So, reluctantly, she built
higher ones.[65] She also set about beautifying the house, or rather encouraging others to beautify it.

I had often expressed the desire that my friends should put
their imprint on the panels in my drawing-room at
Louveciennes, to leave me a souvenir. One fine summer's day,
at four in the morning, and while I slept, Monsieur Le Prince
de Crespy [sic], the baron de Festhamel, Monsieur Rivière and
my niece Eugénie Le Brun silently set to work; by ten o'clock
everyone had completed his frame. You can imagine my surprise when, having come downstairs for breakfast, I went into
my drawing-room and found it adorned with these charming
paintings as well as bouquets of flowers; it was my birthday. I
was overcome with tears; it was the only thanks my friends
received.[66]

She had not given up her Paris social life: her Saturday soirées continued,
though old friends were dying. If she had lost Delille and other literary
acquaintances, new contacts helped fill the gap. But Louveciennes, about
fifteen miles from Paris, was now her preferred base. 'Having at last
acquired a taste for repose',[67] she left for the country before the new leaves
were on the trees.

There, my life passed by as peacefully as could be. I painted, I busied myself in my garden, I went on long solitary walks, and on Sundays I entertained my friends.[68]

Her only regret seems to have been for the despoilment or loss of cherished landmarks of the *ancien régime*, particularly Ledoux's exquisite pavilion at Louveciennes. On first settling there,

> I had hastened to go and visit the pavilion which I had seen in all its beauty in September 1789. It had been entirely stripped of its furnishings, and everything which adorned it in Madame du Barry's time had disappeared. Not only had the statues and busts been removed, but also the bronzes on the fireplace, the locks as finely tooled as a goldsmith's work; in short, the Revolution had been there as everywhere else. But at least the four walls were standing, whereas at Marly, Sceaux, Belle-Vue and so many other places, only the site remained.[69]

There were still political shocks to sustain, but none as powerful as those of 1789 and its aftermath. After the Grand Army's retreat from Moscow, Prussia had declared war on a weakened France and its allies in 1813, and a coalition of other countries followed suit. On 21 December the allied armies crossed the Rhine and penetrated northern France, and on 31 March 1814 they entered Paris. The Prussian troops had devastated whole areas of the French countryside as they advanced towards the capital, and Louise found herself caught in their path. Louveciennes was invaded, and the houses and church pillaged. (Two years later Louise would generously offer the curé a ciborium and chalice to replace the ones the Prussians had stolen.) Louise's Swiss manservant Joseph, who spoke German, came into her bedroom at eleven o'clock at night to protect her, but was closely followed by three soldiers 'with hideous faces, who drew close to my bed with sabres in their hands'.

> Joseph shouted himself hoarse trying to tell them in German that I was Swiss and ill; but without replying, they began by taking my gold snuffbox which was on my bedside table. Then they poked around to see if there was any money beneath my bedspread, which one soldier calmly started to cut a piece off with his sabre. One of them, who seemed to be French, or at least spoke the language perfectly, said to them: 'Give her her box back'; but, far from obeying this invitation, they went to my desk and seized everything there, and my cupboards were ransacked. Finally, after

making me spend four hours in the most dreadful fear, these terrible people left my house, which I no longer wanted to stay in.[70]

Unable to trust the road to Saint-Germain-en-Laye, she went to lodge in a house near the du Barry pavilion, above the Marly machine. Several other women in a similar state of panic had already taken refuge there. They ate and slept together, at least where sleep was possible;

> but I could not sleep, since there were continual alerts during the night, besides which I was extremely anxious about my poor servant, who had saved my life. This brave fellow had wanted to stay in my house, to stand up to the soldiers and answer their demands, which made me tremble for him, because the village had been given over to looting. The peasants bivouacked in the vineyards and slept on straw in the open air, after being stripped of everything they owned. Several of them came to find us, lamenting their misfortunes, and these sad stories, accompanied by the sinister noise of the machine, were told to us in Madame du Barry's magnificent garden, near the *Temple of Love* surrounded by flowers, and in the most beautiful weather imaginable!
>
> I was so terrified by everything we had been told, as I was by the non-stop cannon or rifle fire we heard, that one evening I tried to go down into a basement, where I wanted to stay put; but I hurt my leg and had to go up again.[71]

News from Paris was patchy. It was clear to Louise that the inhabitants of Louveciennes, who met every evening in the house the women occupied, hoped for the return of the Bourbon monarchy. They were not immediately aware that Napoleon had abdicated at the beginning of April, accepting sovereignity of the tiny island of Elba and keeping the title of Emperor as consolation. But within a few days the arrival of Artois in France was announced. Louise, overjoyed, immediately departed for Paris, leaving Joseph to guard the Louveciennes house. During her absence he sent her plaintive letters describing the ruination of her garden, the emptying of her cellar, the destruction of her courtyard and the ransacking of her rooms. '"I beg them," he wrote to me, "not to be so wicked, to make do with what I give them"; but they reply: "The French did far worse things in our country." The Prussians were right about that; my poor Joseph and I were victims of a bad example.'[72]

On 12 April 1814 Louise saw Artois enter Paris, and wept with joy. Artois, who had preceded his brother in the march to the capital, told the

After 'Countess Skavronskaya' (1790).
Private Collection

Lord Hervey, the Bishop of Derry (1791).
The National Trust, Ickworth (Bristol Collection)

Head of a young woman
('Lady Hamilton'
c. 1790).
The Earl of Warwick.
Photograph: The
Courtauld Institute of Art

Emma Hamilton
as sybil (1791-2).
Courtesy of Derek
Johns Ltd.

Giovanni Paisiello (1791)
*Musée National du Château de
Versailles, copyright © RMN*

Hubert Robert (1788).
*Musée du Louvre,
copyright © RMN*

Grand-Duchess Elizabeth (*c.* 1795).
The Hermitage, St Petersburg

Stanislas Augustus II, King of Poland (1797).
*Musée National du Château de Versailles,
copyright © RMN*

Julie Le Brun (1798).
*Collection Tatiana
Zoubov, Geneva*

Varvara Ivanovna Narishkin, *née* Ladomirsky (1800).
Columbus Museum of Art, Ohio

The Alphirtenfest at
Unspunnen (1808).
*Kunstmuseum, Bern,
Gottfried-Keller-
Stiftung*

Mrs William
Chinnery (1803).
*Indiana University
Art Museum*

anxious crowds, 'He still has painful legs, but his head is in excellent working order; we will march for him, and he will think for us.' (Louis XVIII was gouty and immensely fat, and generally had to be wheeled about in a bath-chair, but his mental capacities were far superior to his brother's.) According to Louise, 'Experience proved all the applicability of these words, for the mind, and above all the reason of Louis XVIII were sorely needed to stabilise the Restoration at the time when the Bonapartist faction was still quite numerous.'

Finally the King himself entered his capital. Louise watched him pass in a coach along the quai des Orfèvres, sitting beside his niece the duchesse d'Angoulême. The ill-nature and peevishness which others saw in Louis XVI's daughter seems not to have struck Louise: after all, her beloved Marie-Antoinette had brought up Madame Royale 'perfectly', and Louise sympathised with her mixed emotions –

> the satisfaction she experienced at such a welcome and the painful expression of memories which must be flooding back; her smile was sweet, but sad; a natural enough thing, for she was following the same route as her mother had followed to the scaffold, and she knew it; but the cheers which met the appearance of the King, and her own presence, must have consoled this grieving heart.[73]

Louise would hardly have admitted the possibility that the French nation could greet the restoration of the Bourbons with anything but joy; but in fact the *Souvenirs* seem to reflect the prevailing mood accurately. The catastrophic Russian campaign had galvanised opinion against Napoleon across the Empire: Louise writes of the horror she had felt at reading bulletins which detailed French casualties, and which invariably ended with a sickening footnote on Napoleon's good health. Despite remarkable victories in the first three months of 1814, Bonaparte had no more been able to win back the enthusiastic support of the majority of Frenchmen than defeat the superior power of the Grand Alliance. When Talleyrand, having proclaimed the fall of the Emperor, called upon Louis XVIII to return from England to France, he did so without consulting the nation but simply in his capacity as head of the provisional government. This time the people *en masse* felt no resentment at an autocrat's behaviour.

Louis XVIII proceeded tactfully in his resumption of power. The Senate had adopted a constitution which made provision for popular sovereignty – that is, not accepting the divine right of kings, but ordaining that kings ruled with the authority delegated by the nation. Louis XVIII was no constitutionalist, but the intelligence Artois had remarked on led him to preserve appearances even when his will dictated a different course of action. His will was cleverly asserted in his refusal to follow Artois quickly from exile: he was apparently in no hurry to leave Hartwell House in Buckinghamshire, his English base, and arrived in France only on 24 April. The rapturous welcome of the people then put him in a strong bargaining position.

Louise was flattered by the attentions Louis XVIII showed her.

> As I was extremely desirous of seeing Louis XVIII close up, I went and mingled with the crowd thronging the gallery on Sunday to see him pass as he went to Mass; I was standing with everyone else opposite the windows, so that the King could see us perfectly: as soon as he caught sight of me, he came up to me, gave me his hand in the friendliest manner, and said countless flattering things to me about his joy at seeing me again; as he stood like this for a few moments, still holding my hand, and did not go up to any other woman, people looking at us no doubt took me for a very grand lady, for as soon as the King had passed by, a young officer who saw me alone came and offered me his arm, and refused to leave me until he had conducted me to my carriage.

Her joy, though, was not to last. Less than a year after his return, Louis XVIII had to flee before Napoleon, who returned from Elba on 1 March 1815 and began assembling troops among the disaffected French (whose enthusiasm for him had been rekindled by the White Terror's persecution of anti-monarchists). The Hundred Days began. If the nation as a whole seemed to accept the turnaround with ease, or at least indifference, Louise carefully plays down the popular rejoicing at Napoleon's arrival in Paris on 20 March:

> though he was brought back by the army, supported by bayonets, Parisians still seemed in a state of stupor. People were all too well aware that he was bringing back war and ruin to France; and so the cries of 'Long live the Emperor!' were very rare. Whether by chance or intention, he did not enter by day; it was at eight o'clock at night that he regained possession of the Tuileries, surrounded by high-ranking military men and a whole sad, gloomy population. The courtyards filled with troops gave the palace of our rulers the look of a castle taken by siege.
>
> Meanwhile the King had retreated to Ghent, and I remember that the populace sang out loud in the streets of Paris: 'Rendez-nous notre paire de gants, rendez-nous notre paire' [Give us back our pair of gloves/our father from Ghent] . . .[74]

During the Hundred Days, it is true, many continued to deny Napoleon their moral support, failing to cheer him when he appeared at the windows of the Tuileries and abstaining *en masse* from voting in elections to the new legislative body. On 18 June Wellington's forces and the Prussian reserves destroyed over half of the French army at Waterloo, and it was clear that the French would have Napoleon no longer. He abdicated for the second time on 22 June 1815, and in October was taken to his final place of captivity on St Helena. Louis XVIII returned to Paris on 8 July, and according to Louise did so to almost universal acclaim. But if the people believed that in him peace was being restored, they were wrong. It was certainly the case that the royalist party was now large; but those who had broken faith and followed Napoleon, finding themselves compromised, were filled with unease, and a section of the ordinary people was still passionately devoted to Bonaparte. Louis XVIII would have needed more of the common touch to overcome these problems.

It is significant that Louise, who calls the 'wise and skilful' King precisely the monarch for the times, can find no very convincing evidence to support her belief:

> together with a great deal of courage and sang-froid he possessed moral elevation and much subtlety of mind; all his manners were regal; he gave readily and generously; he liked protecting literature and the arts, and practised them himself; his features were not devoid of beauty, and their expression had such nobility that, infirm as he was, one felt an involuntary respect on first meeting him.[75]

The truth is, more simply, that she liked kings. That being the case, she easily elevated their occasional qualities into essential and timely ones. But France needed more. It faced real difficulties after the signing of the second Treaty of Paris on 20 November 1815, which obliged it to surrender territories, relinquish art treasures and pay a huge cash indemnity to its conquerors. The 1814 Treaty had granted lenient peace terms, but this time the Allies were determined to recover at least part of the cost of the campaign that had culminated in Napoleon's defeat.

For a people which felt the weight of national humiliation – for there was a widespread view that the Bourbons had returned 'in the foreigners' baggage' – it cannot have been reassuring to know that the ruling family lived elegantly, if less luxuriously than before 1789, or enjoyed courtly pleasures. But for Louise these things were of the essence, because they represented a reconstituted *douceur de vivre*. Louis XVIII's favourite relaxation, she writes, was talking about literature with cultivated men; in his youth he had written verse very prettily, and his style was that of a witty man of letters; as he knew Latin perfectly, he liked conversing in this language with our most learned Latinists . . . he could always quote the most remarkable parts of a book he had read quickly, or a play he had seen once.

Among actors, Louis XVIII particularly favoured Talma, despite the latter's known support for the republican cause; aware that Talma had lived in London with his dentist father as a boy, and had a perfect command of the language, the King always spoke English with him. Talma was said to be more deeply moved by Louis XVIII's graciousness than he had been by Napoleon's granting him a pension.[76] The only criticism of the monarch Louise ever voices, early in the *Souvenirs*, is that he had a deplorable liking for popular songs, and sang them completely tunelessly. All she could bring herself to tell him, though, was that he sang 'like a prince'.[77]

She considered graciousness to be the principal charm of royalty, as punctuality is the *politesse* of kings. Artois had it in equal measure, she writes.[78] When he succeeded as Charles X after Louis's death on 16 September 1824, he appeared keen to be an effective monarch and to win the trust and support of his subjects. Apparently this included artists, to judge by a story Louise tells:

> I happened to be at the Louvre on the day he was distributing medals to painters and sculptors. Before giving them out he said in the most gracious manner: 'They are not encouragements, but rewards'. All the artists were touched by the subtle and flattering nature of these words.
>
> He caught sight of me in the crowd, came up to me, and so emphatically declared his joy at seeing me again and finding me in good health that it was difficult to hold back tears of gratitude; for nobody knew better than he did how to find the words that touched your heart.

It is true that Charles X never commissioned his own portrait from Louise. Still she felt at ease with him, as she had done with his brother, Louis XVIII, though neither made her his court artist: perhaps she seemed too indelibly associated with the *ancien régime* for this to be politic, or perhaps she appeared too old. Charles's court might appear staid – he was elderly when he became king, as Louis XVIII had been – but that was perhaps an advantage in the post-Revolutionary, post-imperial world.[79] The killjoy duchesse d'Angoulême cast the heaviest pall on court life (Louis

XVIII had likened her to Goneril and Regan), and the effect of her moroseness was to drive courtiers away to the salons of the faubourg Saint-Germain. Only the duchesse de Berri, Charles X's daughter-in-law, introduced real gaiety to the Tuileries, giving occasional balls that recalled the splendid days of pre-Revolutionary France; but she was alone. Like her husband the duc, whose knowledge of painting had impressed Louise in London, she was a patroness of the arts. According to Louise,

> she took pleasure in encouraging young artists; she bought their pictures and often commissioned work from them. The generosity with which she paid them never prevented her from displaying a perfect grace in her dealings with men of talent.[80]

But if the Bourbons were too cautious to betray any ambitions towards the restoration of the pre-Revolutionary political situation, Charles X still hankered after the old style of monarchy, not the constitutional kind he had had leisure to observe in England. His willingness to please his subjects was limited, always conditional on the assumption that the new France was a second-best affair likely to be improved only by the strengthening of his own position; and he seems to have believed that he could restore the country, albeit obliquely, to absolutism.

He was, unsurprisingly, the darling of the *Ultras*, or extreme monarchists, and to Liberals seemed to epitomise the charge against the Bourbon dynasty that they had 'learnt nothing and forgotten nothing'. He temporised in the face of Liberal victories at the polls, and then, in May 1829, in a blind assertion of absolutist power, appointed prince Jules de Polignac as head of an ultra-royalist government. In May 1830 he was rebuffed by a fresh Liberal victory in the elections, and by 27 July Paris was under rebel control. Nine days later the Liberals proclaimed a new King, Louis-Philippe of the house of Bourbon-Orléans.

Louise professes not to understand how it was that Charles's paternalistic benevolence could none the less have culminated in the July Revolution and the abdication of 2 August. 'It is for politicians to explain why so many virtues, such goodness, were insufficient to keep him on the throne; my grateful heart can only regret it.' The truth is that Charles X, weak-willed and vain, lacked the political skill to resolve the deep social and moral conflict between the old ruling classes seeking to recover the ground they had lost and a bourgeoisie determined to retain what it had won in the Revolution and after. Louise had nothing to say about the succession of the Citizen-King, no doubt because she thoroughly disliked his anti-royal ways: within months of his succession he had abolished nearly every branch of the Maison du Roi, including the Royal Music and the

Royal Hunt.[81] His desire, and achievement, was to reign without a court, and his reign consequently lacked charisma and colour. The old dynasty was Louise's chief concern, and she must have been reassured by the fact that most nobles refused to serve under the new King. But after the disgrace of Charles X's daughter-in-law, the duchesse de Berri – found in 1832 to be pregnant despite having been a widow for twelve years – a legitimist comeback was clearly impossible. By the time of the next upheaval, the 1848 Revolution, the *Souvenirs* had been written and Louise was dead.

CHAPTER TWELVE

THE LAST YEARS: 'She is . . . better worth seeing than any of her pictures'

With the 1815 Restoration, the centre of social life was once more to be found in the salons of Paris. Most of the positions in court were filled by the inhabitants of the faubourg Saint-Germain, while the new financial aristocracy lived in the sumptuous hôtels of the Chaussée d'Antin quarter.[1] In such surroundings, perhaps against a background of music or song, or in the interludes of amateur theatricals, something of the flavour of pre-Revolutionary society could be recaptured.

Conversation, again, was the chief delicacy, for the fall of Napoleon meant the return of the old lightness and verve.[2] The constitutional regime of the monarchy freed tongues which had been frozen by years of despotism. According to Lamartine,

> Conversation came back with the Restoration, with the court, with the nobility, with the emigration, with leisure and liberty. The constitution, which furnishes a continual text to party controversy, the security of opinions, the animation and licence of speech, even the novelty of this political regime, which allowed people to think and speak aloud in a country that had just endured ten years of silence, accelerated . . . the current of ideas and the regular, living murmur of Paris society.[3]

The French language was still as Voltaire had described it in his *Dictionnaire philosophique*, infused with

> a delicacy of expression and a refinement full of naturalness which are scarcely found elsewhere. This refinement has sometimes been exaggerated; but people of taste have always been able to keep it within appropriate limits.[4]

Not everyone was impressed by the restoration of *bon ton*, especially at court, or thought that life had a new sparkle. Maria Edgeworth's stepsister

Harriet, who accompanied her to France in 1820, wrote about the seat of the court:

> Go to Versailles, where everything and everybody seems unaltered by revolution, ruin and exile. The whole society is old croaking dowagers and rheumatic battered old counts.[5]

Louise herself was regarded as anything but dull. Maria Edgeworth called her a woman of great vivacity, and said of her that she 'is I think better worth seeing than any of her pictures because though they are *speaking* she speaks, and speaks uncommonly well.'[6]

Louise made a special trip from Louveciennes to the rue Saint-Lazare – now her Paris base, since the rue du Gros-Chenet property had evidently been disposed of after her ex-husband's death – and showed the Edgeworths the work in progress – a portrait of Princess Potemkin, who although Russian had all the grace, softness and winning manners of a Polish woman, a pale, oval face with soft and expressive dark brown eyes, and in her person showed 'the sort of politeness which especially pleases'. She also let them see other paintings, like the one of Emma Hamilton as a bacchante and Josephina Grassini [sic] like Madame de Staël's Corinne, improvising on the Capitol. Maria's stepsister Fanny was full of praise for Louise. She wrote on 10 July 1820 to Harriet Beaufort that 'Madame Le Brun is well worth seeing . . . She seems to enjoy all she does with enthusiasm and not as a triste devoir.'[7] The artist Jean Gigoux confirmed that Louise's liveliness and zest continued into old age. If 'her painting, at the end of her life, had lost much of its former appeal, her person had remained quite charming, gracious and even frisky, as she must have appeared to the friends of her youth.'[8] He added that 'Madame Le Brun was very chatty and communicative; after painting, her favourite subject of conversation was Queen Marie-Antoinette.'[9]

Louise had rediscovered her old *joie de vivre*, or so it appeared. She was content to be back in France and happy with the restoration of monarchy, even if she seemed artistically to have outlived herself. Socially, she was popular and appreciated, and the establishment gave every sign of valuing her as she had been valued in the days of her beloved Marie-Antoinette. Her soirées were enjoyed as they had been before the Revolution. The painter Georges Michel, unsociable by nature, avoided them because nobility and court were much in evidence; he preferred her small, intimate receptions.[10] But others attended her salon for the warmth she projected, not caring too much about who their fellow-guests were. Brifaut, who met Louise only after her return to Paris, praised her enthusiastically.

Madame Le Brun was the child of nature, but her most spoiled child. Art had nothing to do with it. People say that love was a constant presence around her; I can well believe it. An enchanting face and figure, a talent which announced itself only with master-pieces, an uncultivated but far from barren mind, for it did not wait to be asked before it lavished riches from an inexhaustible store, was all this needed to turn the heads of her contemporaries, who often lost their reason for much less? Madame Le Brun was the idol of her century, and became the oracle of ours. All this might have made her proud; she contented herself with being good.[11]

There were more glittering houses to visit than hers; but, Brifaut wrote, they were peopled by 'gilded nonentities', and 'This whole magnificent world did not turn me away from the modest salon of Madame Le Brun, where one also met grand people, but with a grandeur that concealed itself behind a wealth of talent.'[12]

The 'banquet' at which Louise introduced Brifaut to Vaudreuil was, according to Brifaut, less splendid than agreeable. Vaudreuil, who might have been thought to epitomise the type of the 'rheumatic battered old count' Harriet Edgeworth met at Versailles, charmed Brifaut, who had been born a mere eight years before the storming of the Bastille. The vicomte never missed the concerts Louise gave under the Restoration, but attended them primarily for the accompanying conversation. He also held forth himself, and Brifaut was spellbound.

I listened to him like a beatific soul in the presence of his director of conscience. The stories of the old court, which he told for the thousandth time with perfect grace and a great air of naturalness, as though he had never told them before, acquainted me with all that joyous past from which our lugubrious present has issued.[13]

It was the *ana* of the court and the *memento* of the Revolution. The Paris house of this celebrated connoisseur was itself a veritable caravanserai for artists, scholars and writers, 'but they had to be good company; without the distinguishing mark of *politesse*, they were not received.'[14]

Not everyone was so positive about Vaudreuil. When Natalya Kurakina spent the evening at Louise's apartment in November 1816, and heard a short concert 'which failed to please', she met a courtier who was 'once the most agreeable man in Paris, but now very old and very deaf, yet still sac-rificing himself to be sociable.'[15] He had been named a governor of the Louvre, and must have felt that this was a fitting reward for such a noted patron of the arts. But at the end, according to Louise,

> His tender soul felt the need to elevate its affections above the earthly plane; he became very pious, but without a trace of bigotry. These feelings lightened his last years, and he died surrounded by friends, in the arms of a beloved prince who never abandoned him.[16]

It might have been juster to say that Vaudreuil never abandoned his prince. According to Brifaut, his indulgence of Artois was a weakness, but one which did not prevent him from admonishing his master.[17] The writer Madame Ancelot said that Vaudreuil had been as handsome as he was agreeable, and the grace of his mind and person had made him a charming man.[18] But the comtesse de Boigne, who had known him in London, was never able to discover the distinction Vaudreuil was credited with.

> He had been the coryphaeus of this school of exaggeration which reigned before the Revolution, passionately keen on all the little things and quite unmoved by the big ones. With the help of the money he milked from the royal coffers, he had made himself the patron of some tiny Virgils who praised him in couplets. At Madame Le Brun's house he swooned at pictures and protected artists ... As an *émigré* and when he had become old, he had nothing left but seeing all his pretensions ridiculed and suffering the humiliation of witnessing his wife's lovers contributing to the upkeep of his house by the presents *she* allegedly won on the lottery.[19]

Louise, though, was kinder about this 'very young and very pretty' wife,[20] to whom she says Vaudreuil was a perfect husband.

How did the rue Saint-Lazare soirées match up to the salon ideal formulated by Madame Ancelot? They had their attractions, but also appeared embarrassingly *passé* to younger guests. 'A salon,' Madame Ancelot begins in her study of the institution,

> is an intimate gathering which has lasted several years, where people know one another and seek each other's company, where they have some reason to be happy to meet. The hostess is a link between the various guests, and this link is closer when the acknowledged merit of a woman of wit and learning has formed it; but other qualities are needed to form a salon: urbanity is

required, to establish relationships quickly and allow people to converse with everyone without already knowing them (which used to be proof of a good education and of familiarity with a world to which none were admitted except on condition that they were worthy of proximity to the great and good) . . . The person who was most agreeable was the most welcome, irrespective of rank or fortune . . . the real king in this kind of republic . . . was wit! . . . if these gatherings have been less numerous in our own day, less in evidence, it is because people have generally set more practical store by intelligence, and also because politics has made so much noise it has prevented anything else being heard.[21]

According to Madame Ancelot, Louise was as ready to receive bourgeois philosophers and men of letters as the nobility. 'Equality may not then have been legislated for, but it was much more a part of everyday life than it is now the law has proclaimed it so insistently.'[22] But notwithstanding her enthusiasm for Greek suppers and Greek costume, Louise preferred republics in fiction to real ones. At the first whiff of a republican constitution for France, after all, she had left the country.

Madame Ancelot first met Louise when the painter of Marie-Antoinette was in her seventies. She seemed younger than her years, though,

so lively, gay and animated was she; and if, in the midst of the salon she had started up again, she sometimes spoke grievingly about the friends who had died in the Revolutionary turmoil, it was an interruption without bitterness to her customary good humour, which had not deserted her.[23]

On these Saturday evenings one met Josephina Grassini,

welcomed everywhere, loved by everyone, with her kindly, spontaneous, true and original nature, talking a kind of half-Italian, half-French jargon which was peculiar to her, which enabled her to say everything, and of which she availed herself to make the funniest remarks and the funniest confidences.

At her salons Louise assembled the débris of the old court thirty years on – the marquis (formerly chevalier) de Boufflers, now run to fat, his stepson the marquis de Sabran, the comte de Langeron, finally returned from Russia. There were also some new faces, among them the young marquis de Custine.

The Sweetness of Life

Astolphe de Custine's anti-democratic convictions and nostalgia for the *ancien régime*, expressed in various travel writings, must have made him sympathetic to Louise. His mother Delphine, the sister of the marquis de Sabran, had been a great friend of hers. She was, Louise writes in the *Souvenirs*, a beautiful woman,[24] and she was known to have had many lovers after her husband was guillotined. She smothered Astolphe with love, and apparently did the same to Chateaubriand. Mad about painting,

> [she] copied the works of the old masters perfectly, imitating their colour and vigour so exactly that one day, going into her study, I took the copy for the original. She did not conceal from me the pleasure my mistake gave her; for she was as natural as she was amiable and beautiful.

But it is Madame Ancelot, not Louise herself, who tells us that her son was an *habitué* of the rue Saint-Lazare salon under the Restoration. He was young and witty, according to Virginie Ancelot, and since those days had travelled widely in Europe and written books about his travels.[25] This helps to date the time of his attendance at Louise's salon, for Custine's travel writings were published from 1830 onward. In 1829 he published *Aloys, ou le religieux du Mont Saint-Bernard*, and its autobiographical background perhaps provides a clue to Louise's silence about him.

Aloys is the *récit* of a young man who falls in love with the mother of the girl he is supposed to marry, and chooses to bury his grief at the impossibility of his love in a remote monastery. It is fairly obvious that this is actually a disguised story about homosexuality (the hero's and the author's). Aloys needs an excuse for not marrying, and loving the wrong person – the unattainable mother – provides one. When Custine had himself broken off an engagement, wagging tongues hinted that it was because of impotence, but in fact meant something less mentionable. In 1824, a year after the death of the young woman he had eventually married, Custine had been beaten up by three soldiers after an assignation in a stable with a guardsman on the road from Saint-Denis to Epinay. Asked what he had been doing at nine in the evening on this deserted stretch of road, he claimed to have been visiting the Saint-Denis basilica to see the preparations for Louis XVIII's funeral there. The faubourg Saint-Germain was not taken in but according to Sophie Swetchin was less shocked by the crime than by Custine's affectation of insouciance.

> Never have I seen a more general outburst of fury, a livelier or more vocal indignation; society *en masse* is furious, as one would feel at personal betrayal. People are particularly aggrieved because

of the consideration they did have for him; and the pique at having been deceived counts for something in the homage they pay to
morality. What surprises me as much as the blame, which he has
deserved, is the way he puts up with it; even if he is the victim of
odious slander, I cannot understand how one can live in the midst
of people who think they have the right to shower contempt on
you; a Trappist desert would seem like paradise in comparison.[26]

But Custine's uncaring attitude was certainly assumed. Before the Saint-
Denis episode, and when he had merely fallen unrequitedly in love with
young men, he had written tormented and sibylline letters to them about
his sexual nature. In any case, he soon discovered he had to leave Paris,
unable to endure the weight of the *monde*'s disapproval. Unlike his hero
Aloys he did not actually withdraw into a Pyrenean monastery, as he was
rumoured to be about to do in 1825, but he travelled.

This was in 1826, after his mother's death, and Sophie Swetchin's letter
about the 'general outburst of fury' is dated 30 July 1825. Perhaps Louise
was one of those who felt enraged by Custine's 'betrayal'. Since Virginie
Ancelot does not specify when she met Custine in the rue Saint-Lazare
salon, it is unclear whether the events of 1824 had yet occurred. But if they
had, Louise might have felt torn between her loyalty to the faubourg
Saint-Germain and her sympathy for a charming and attractive man who
was being made to suffer on account of an alleged sexual misdemeanour,
as she had been at the time of her claimed involvement with Calonne in
the 1780s.

Whether or not Louise's salon was filled with the sort of people who made
Georges Michel feel uncomfortable, Virginie Ancelot thought that her
efforts to give it an *ancien régime* tone were unavailing. Certainly, there
were still *grands seigneurs*, as there were distinguished artists and writers;
but just as the power of the monarchy was now qualified by charters and
constitutions, so salons had been infected by a new philosophy which
destroyed their former ambience. It was all part of a prevailing *lourdeur*
which meant, in effect, that woman's distinctive contribution to social living was neither acknowledged nor permitted. Virginie Ancelot writes in
these terms in *Un Salon de Paris* (whose epigraph is *Et in Arcadia ego*):
women, she says, have let the *club* take the place of the *salon*.

It has been a complete abdication. Thus the evening amusements
which were their domain, the conversations of leisured, wealthy
people, where they were once entitled to shine, have all been luxuriously organised in magnificent apartments where they no

293

longer even have the right to enter. Banished from the meeting-
places of which they were queens, they did not revolt. They did
not even protest against this usurpation of their old royal status,
and the emblem, the last vestige of their vanished power was able
to disappear without their even seeming to pay attention, when
for the glorious cry in which they had their part, *My God, my king,
my lady!* were substituted these words in which they are forgotten:
God, the Empire and liberty![27]

According to Madame Ancelot, Louise's efforts were also doomed to failure because youth was lacking from her gatherings. She and a few others
were the only young guests present.

> Our political, literary and artistic sympathies made us appreciate
> all these people, but without understanding them completely;
> they had lived amidst other ideas, other habits, and society no
> longer had any unity. Then joy was extinguished amidst these
> elderly people, as the rays of the wintry sun grow cold, shining
> onto ice; then they spoke seriously about the past, about those
> who were no more, and we preferred that to the infantile games
> played by the old folk.[28]

Others who were closer to the *ancien régime*, like Natalya Kurakina,
savoured 'the delights of a choice society'[29] in the rue Saint-Lazare, and
said that one always met someone or something pleasing there. Louise's
qualities as a self-effacing *salonnière* were still much in evidence.

> I have never in my life seen a woman more amiable in the broad-
> est sense of the term, besides her personal qualities which make
> her so; but she is amiable above all in wanting to draw out others,
> in forgetting herself; and then the contrast between her and the
> society of big business makes her truly precious.[30]

No one else's dinners, Natalya Kurakina thought, matched Louise's.[31] It
was hardly surprising that the rising generation of writers and artists
should often have been visitors – Balzac, Gavarni, Horace Vernet and
others.[32]

The house where Louise received, in a street now fronting the railway
terminus, was in a commercial area typical of all the *quartiers* of Paris she
had inhabited. Her home formed part of a large house with a garden, subsequently replaced by a concert-hall. The original *hôtel* had been built on
the site of the château de Coq, where Henri IV slept on the eve of his

triumphant entry into Paris. The duc d'Aumale had bought the whole building in 1738, and it was later transformed by the duc de Brancas into a *petite maison*, or love-nest, the 'folie Brancas'. In 1758 he left it to the marquis de Polignac, and during the Revolution the *conventionnel* Lacroix, an enemy of the *émigrés*, settled there. In 1854 the last château de Coq was demolished.[33]

With the advent of the July Monarchy, some of the elderly loyalists chose to follow the Bourbons into exile again. 'From this moment on,' according to Virginie Ancelot, 'Madame Le Brun's society was no more than a little intimate circle of people who had stayed faithful, despite their differences in age.'[34] Louise's large drawing-room was decorated with some of her best portraits, she said – the picture of Lady Hamilton as a bacchante next to Calonne, 'the minister who found nothing impossible except to prevent the Revolution', Paisiello 'with the admirable expression of an inspired artist', Catherine the Great – who was never in fact painted by Louise – 'and as a pendant to her the handsome face of the King of Poland Poniatowski.'[35] There was also Boutin, who had died in the Revolution and whose property had been seized by the state: first fêtes had been given in the grounds of his town house, then a bathing-establishment was set up, along with a house 'where people who like being in good company and in society live communally'. Finally there was the portrait of the benevolent Beaujon.

A work Louise initially also kept in her own possession was the picture of Marie-Antoinette ascending to heaven, with a cloud bearing Louis XVIII (she says, but must mean Louis XVI) and two angels signifying the two children she had lost. This *Apotheosis of the Queen* is the portrait Natalya Kurakina reports seeing at Louise's house in February 1817, and which, she claims, the artist had just painted;[36] according to the *Souvenirs*, however, it was completed during the reign of Bonaparte. Subsequently Louise sent it to the vicomtesse de Chateaubriand to be hung in the charitable institution she had founded, a hospital for infirm priests and distressed gentlewomen in the present rue Denfert-Rochereau.

Chateaubriand's ill-used wife took this foundation, the Marie-Thérèse Hospital, very seriously. She obtained pictures by other celebrated artists for the decoration of the chapel – a *Virgin* by Guérin and a *St Teresa* by Gérard. Louise consulted Gérard about the painting of Marie-Antoinette's apotheosis,[37] possibly aware that he too was contributing a work to the institution. An undated response of his calls Louise's picture 'the dream of a beautiful soul, depicted by a fine talent'.[38] Louise's *Dream*, as it was also called, was hung in what Madame de Chateaubriand described as 'the best spot in this poor establishment, which owed to you a masterpiece'.[39] But having founded and decorated her establishment, in a style verging on the luxurious, the vicomtesse needed to make it pay for itself. So she set up a small chocolate-factory in the basement, and had it run by a nun, a maid-servant and a workman. Chateaubriand, who describes the hospital in the *Mémoires d'outre-tombe*, also describes his wife as the viscountess of chocolate. The factory closed only in 1925, and between 1822 and 1890 earned 23,090 francs from sales of its product.

Louise still painted, though at a gentler pace than before. Some admir-ers insisted that she was as competent as she had ever been. Brifaut wrote that the 'smooth productions of her brush' proved her talent had suffered 'no impoverishment at all':[40] the recent portraits of the comte de Coëtlosquet, the comtesse de Lostange, the Countess Davidova and twenty others, all done since her definitive return to Paris, were testimony to that. If others, like Gigoux, were less sure,[41] it was certainly the case that Louise still had a following and a clientele. She accepted a number of com-missions and had not been altogether displaced by the artists who had come to prominence during her emigration.[42]

She remained serene when Gros, whom she had first known as a little boy in 1776, was named official portraitist to Louis XVIII, and responded with generosity.

> None the less, I was astonished on my return to France to find the child become a man of genius and the head of a school. From then dates a friendship between us which time has only strengthened; for I found in Gros a noble and sincere friend. His frank, original character gave charm to our relationship, since one could count on the sincerity of his praise, as on the usefulness of his criticism. I appreciated the friendship he showed me, while enjoying all his successes to the utmost.[43]

Gros had to be seen in private to be valued at his true worth.

> Then his heart revealed itself fully, and this heart was noble and good; a certain roughness of tone, which he was sometimes reproached for, disappeared altogether. His conversation was all the more striking as he did not express himself like other men; he always found images that were full of originality and force to con-vey his thought, and one can say of him that he painted as he spoke.

His suicide by drowning in 1835 affected Louise deeply.

> A few days before our last farewell, he had come to dine at the

house, and I noticed with distress that he was taking some misplaced criticisms which he should have ignored to heart. As an
artist, as a friend of his, I shall always regret this great painter, and
the sad memory of his violent death makes my regret all the more
bitter.[44]

Gros had closed his studio, saying that he knew of no misfortune greater
than outliving oneself. Shortly afterwards his body was found in the Seine
near Meudon.

At the 1824 Salon Delacroix showed the *Scio Massacre* (which Gros
called a 'massacre of painting'); Ingres, who had stayed in Italy much
longer than was usual for winners of the Prix de Rome, won a brilliant
success with his *Oath of Louis XIII*, on which he had been working for
three years. During his visit to the exhibition Louis XVIII decorated him
with the cross of the Légion d'honneur, as he also did Sir Thomas
Lawrence. Lawrence showed several portraits at the same Salon, which
some critics contrasted unfavourably with the work of Girodet:
Lawrence's technique was deemed rough and unfinished in comparison
with the polish of the Frenchman's style, a predictable verdict which
recalls Louise's reaction to native art on her visit to England, and
Hoppner's attack on her. Gérard showed a scaled-down version of his picture of *Corinne at Cape Miseno*, along with a portrait of Louis XVIII, and
Constable exhibited some landscapes which Stendhal called magnificent.
Louise offered nothing after this year, and spent increasing amounts of
time at Louveciennes. But she did not abandon painting. She was eighty
when she did the portrait of her niece Caroline de Rivière, and past that
age when she painted the legitimist Poujoulat.

The Restoration had legitimised Louise's own pride and contentment in
her royal connections. But before it came about she had faced personal
sadness, and after it suffered a personal tragedy. First, in 1813 Jean-
Baptiste-Pierre Le Brun died. Louise had been divorced from him since
1794, but they had lived in the same house since her return from abroad:

> for a long time, it is true, I had had no kind of relations with him,
> but I was still painfully afflicted by his death: one cannot without
> regret find oneself separated forever from the person to whom
> one has been joined by such a holy bond as matrimony.[45]

This is perhaps a little strong. Louise had given no appearance of missing
Le Brun during her self-imposed exile, and had complained bitterly about
being asked to help support him and bring up Julie without assistance, not

to mention paying a generous share of the costs of the rue du Gros-Chenet house which their divorce had helped him retain.

But Le Brun had in some respects been the right partner for her, despite his unreliability. He had allowed this strong-willed woman a remarkable degree of freedom, letting her lead her life very much as she wanted to. As a dealer, he had fallen on relatively hard times under the Empire. His busiest and most lucrative periods were between 1780 and 1797; thereafter there was a decline, with only twenty-one sales between 1804 and 1813.[46] (Other dealers experienced a similar falling-off in business.) His two-year Grand Tour to the South of France, Spain and Italy between 1807 and 1809 had resulted, however, in the acquisition of over 600 works of art, many of which he offered to the public in one great sale in 1810.[47] But since he remained a dealer to his fingertips – whatever his profligacy in private life – he sent the cream of the collection for sale to an English colleague because prices over the Channel were higher. (Le Brun had been despatching Old Masters to London since the 1770s.) This was despite the continental blockade instituted by Napoleon, which theoretically prohibited commerce with Great Britain. But by 1812 the boom was over. Economic crisis had hit England too, and London prices were no longer necessarily higher than those of Paris.

So it might have been predicted that Le Brun, never to be trusted where money was concerned, would leave his surviving family and associates with obligations to meet. Admittedly, he also left wonderful pictures; but their number was equalled, if not exceeded, by the number of unsettled bills from painters, decorators, clock-makers, engravers, wine merchants, picture-restorers, printers and many others.[48] His heir Julie Nigris, then living near her mother at 83 rue Saint-Lazare, inherited heavy debts on the house in the rue du Gros-Chenet.[49] One was the sum of 10,468 francs, described in the relevant legal document as money owed to Louise herself[50] – an 'obligation' which Louise evidently waived. Had she not done so, Julie would have been ruined. But when, subsequently, Louise also waived all claims on the estate of her daughter[51] (who predeceased her), the action undoubtedly worked to her own financial advantage. According to a note dated 27 March 1820, the loan outstanding on the Gros-Chenet house had not been included in the sale of the property to her (at an unspecified date) by her former husband; so the sum had to be repaid by Julie Nigris's own heir, Jean-Baptiste-Pierre Le Brun's brother.

Le Brun's death grieved but in no sense devastated his former wife. Julie's, in 1819, apparently did. 'Apparently', because there remains considerable ambiguity in Louise's behaviour and in the account of events she gives. There is, for example, an obsessive concern with her own reactions:

I had rushed to her side as soon as I learned she was unwell; but the illness advanced quickly, and I cannot express what I felt when I lost all hope of saving her: when I went to see her on the last day, alas, and my gaze was transfixed by this pretty face, completely distorted, I felt ill; Madame de Noisville, my old friend, who had accompanied me, managed to drag me away from this bed of sorrows; she supported me, for my legs refused to carry me, and took me back to my house. By the next day I had lost my child! Madame de Verdun came to give me the news, trying in vain to soothe my despair; for the poor little thing's faults were quite forgotten, I saw her once more, I see her still, as she was in her childhood . . . Alas, she was so young! Should she not have outlived me?[52]

There is no surviving evidence to give Julie's side of the story. Did she refuse help from her mother? If she did not, Louise should surely have done more than 'rush to her side' when she heard of Julie's illness. She could have supported her daughter, instead of seeing her reduced to selling her linen to pay bills:[53] there is almost no evidence to suggest how Julie supported herself after the collapse of her marriage, though it seems that she may have done some engravings. The emphasis on Louise's prostrated grief perhaps suggests, rather unpleasantly, that she feels the need to prove how genuine her devastation was. And what was this paragon of motherly love thinking of in abandoning her daughter to the attention of others at the end?

Perhaps her love had become fixed at the stage of childhood and adolescent adoration. The Julie she worshipped was the model of picture-book prettiness 'as she was in her childhood', not the thirty-nine-year-old with a dramatically changed face. Louise had never painted her since they fell out in Russia. It was, one might have thought, an opportunity missed – the artist-parent, no longer doting but critically distanced, traces the transition from fresh youthfulness to maturity. Perhaps Julie forbade any more sittings. The *Souvenirs* give no further information, and we shall probably never know. But Louise's stress on her reappropriation of the *child* Julie, not the grown woman with a dubious set of acquaintances, suggests the limitations to her love. She admired, and wanted, someone who had ceased to exist, and whose only continuing reality was in the besotted images of her canvases.

Perhaps, though, Louise was a responsible mother in other ways – ways Rousseau would have approved of. At least she kept her child by her instead of consigning her to the distant care of others while she travelled and worked. Many of the aristocratic women she painted, if contemporary reports and the evidence of novels like Laclos's *Les Liaisons dangereuses* are to be believed, would have failed to recognise any such moral duty. But she contravened another basic Rousseauist doctrine in being such an intensely professional woman; and her devotion to that profession must have entailed some neglect of her daughter, which she over-compensated for with a jealous protectiveness and a Sévigné-like exclusiveness. One cannot forget her indignation at being accused of vindictive and mean-spirited behaviour towards Julie at the time of the Nigrises' marriage in Russia. It would surely have been matched by the fury of her reaction to a much later attack launched by Calonne's former secretary sometime after the publication of her *Souvenirs*, had she been aware of it.

According to this undated manuscript by the abbé Géralde, a review (unnamed) of the *Souvenirs* had called Louise a self-seeking woman and heartless mother. In the same spirit, Géralde advises her to repair the wrong she did Julie during her lifetime. She must found a painting-prize in her memory, and

> the artist who wins the medal you award should every year lay his wreath on the tomb that has so long been neglected, and which was erected during your lifetime expressly to serve as an expiatory monument. You must also establish a charitable fund in your own name and that of your poor child as a form of reconciliation in this world, if you do not want her to refuse to acknowledge you in a better one. Only thus . . . will you cleanse your life of the stain which disfigures even your finest works.
>
> Do good *now* towards those who have devoted their lives to you. Do not wait to be bent by infirmity before doing your duty and paying penance for great wrongs.[54]

(There is no evidence, incidentally, of Louise having had Julie's tomb built 'expressly' in expiation.)

She stands accused in the 1830s of neglecting her daughter's grave 'too long', of having 'stained' her own life by her treatment – hostile or merely neglectful? – of Julie, and of behaving unreasonably towards some unspecified women (*celles*) who have selflessly attended to her needs. These women are presumably the nieces who looked after Louise in old age, and whether their behaviour was really selfless must be considered in due course. But one wonders whether Géralde is a reliable source. The next allegation suggests that we should be cautious about accepting his word uncritically:

I say nothing about your love-affair with a young man. At ninety years of age, it is an unparalleled example of absurdity; but at least absurdity is not dishonourable, it merely amuses the world, which is always so inclined to laugh. Make yourself decent and worthy if you wish to be esteemed.

Louise was certainly long-lived, but never reached the age of ninety: she was eighty-two when the third and final volume of the *Souvenirs* was published in 1837, and the notion that she might have taken a young lover so late in life seems implausible. What provoked Géralde's animosity is altogether unclear. Apparently Louise never fell out with Calonne, who had long been dead, and there was no obvious reason for his former secretary to attack her.

What is certain, though, is that Louise did little to alleviate Julie's distress before she died. Julie had moved from the house in the rue Saint-Lazare, near to her mother, and at the time of her death was living a considerable distance away at 39 rue de Sèvres. She was buried on the morning of 10 December 1819, the funeral service being conducted at the church of l'Abbaye-aux-Bois. The funeral expenses amounted to over 90 *livres*:[55] whether Louise or Julie's heir settled them is unknown, but some if not all of her medical treatment in her last illness was paid for by her mother. On 13 December, five days after her death, Louise paid an outstanding bill of 154 francs to the doctor,[56] and the next day one of 38 francs to the nurse.[57] Without any reliable source of income since her separation, Julie had certainly suffered financial hardship, and her difficulties were exacerbated when she inherited her father's debts. Her relations with her mother had unquestionably soured, despite the fact that Louise says she saw her daughter daily (which can hardly have applied to the lengthy periods she spent in Louveciennes). The clear and irrefutable fact is that Louise was rich, and Julie died a pauper. Perhaps she rejected her mother's help, or perhaps certain forms of help were never forthcoming.

Less than a year after Julie's death, Louise lost her brother Etienne. The *Souvenirs* say little about his presence in her life after her return from exile, beyond remarking that he wept with joy to see her back in Paris, as did his wife Suzanne and daughter Caroline. Whatever the defects of his personality, Louise could not help being saddened by his death. Her friends now worried about her state of mind. They know her well enough to realise what the most practical treatment would be: 'they . . . advised me to try the effects of distraction and go on a trip. I resolved to leave for Bordeaux. I knew nothing about this town, and the route I should have to follow to get there would be a tonic for my eyes.'[58] So the 65-year-old Louise obediently set off. This would be the last time she travelled.

The Sweetness of Life

*

It was not a reassuring trip in all respects. The actual process of travelling was pleasant, because

> from Paris to the outskirts of Bordeaux the road is like a garden path; it is metalled and levelled in such a way that one feels no fatigue. My carriage, which was very comfortable, rounded off the pleasure of my journey. I felt as though I was crossing a great park where I painted everything with my eyes; so I simply fidgeted in inns. I went to bed at eight in the evening and was wide awake at half past four in the morning, waiting with great impatience for daybreak so I could resume travelling: Adélaïde said I was like a child always wanting to ride its gee-gee.[59]

But the evidence of ruination over the length of the journey was a depressing reminder of how unpleasantly destructive humans could be. Some ruins, of course, had been artistically intended. The park at Méréville, her former patron Laborde's property, had been laid out by Hubert Robert, whose stay in Rome had given him a great liking for melancholy decay. But even he had drawn the line at actually reproducing it in his copy of the Tivoli Temple of the Sibyl – he had 'restored it completely, with perfect tact and taste'.[60] Seeing sacked monasteries in any case jolted Louise out of a sense of the '*poétique des ruines*'. She wanted to sketch the remains of the Marmoutier monastery; but

> An infernal band of boilermakers was destroying all these beautiful things. A company of Dutch businessmen had proposed buying this monastery to make a factory out of it; they offered 300,000 francs, which was turned down, and later on the wretched boilermakers had it for 20,000 on condition that this superb building was demolished! The Vandals would not have done worse! Well, everywhere on my journey I heard of similar deeds.[61]

It did not dampen her enthusiasm for sketching, but simply gave her activity poignancy. Her élitist self was also flattered by some of the reactions she provoked:

> Often, when I began to sketch, some locals would gather round me. One day, as I was lamenting all this destruction with the worthy people, one of them said to me: 'I can see that Madame la comtesse had castles in these parts'. 'No', I replied 'my castles are in the air.' The title of countess which had been bestowed on me did

302

not surprise me at all, I was used to being treated like a grand lady; in all the inns I stopped at every kind of title was lavished on me. But as I owed this honour to my carriage, which was *fashionable*, it made me none the prouder, I simply paid more as a result.

She was also sadly reminded of the human cost of revolution. When she went to Chanteloup, the duc de Choiseul's seat, she found a monument erected in memory of all the friends who had come to see him during his exile.

As all the names which had been inscribed there were nobles, the revolution, with its great feather-duster, had swept them away, though they were engraved in marble.[62]

In Bordeaux itself she lived as the locals who admired her style *en route* would have expected:

I lodged in the best inn, in the Fumel hotel, which before the Revolution belonged to the marquis of the same name. This hotel is admirably situated right opposite the port, which sometimes has thousands of vessels; the other bank which one looks out onto is bounded by a beautifully verdant hill, with some houses scattered here and there on it, and in the middle distance a great mountain on whose slopes one could see some châteaux. Words fail me to describe the ecstasy, the rapture I felt at the sight of the magnificent picture which met my gaze when I opened my window; I thought I was having a delightful dream. All the vessels in the harbour, thousands of boats and small craft coming and going in every direction, while the ships remained immobile, the silence which hung over this huge sheet of water, everything combined to give you the impression of a fairy-tale. Though I stayed nearly a week in Bordeaux and enjoyed this prospect night and day, I could never have tired of it, especially by moonlight; then one sees little lights from the houses on the hillside, and everything becomes magical.

The pleasure of looking out from my window would itself have made the journey worthwhile, and I had no regrets at all about coming to Bordeaux.[63]

There were other pleasures too, and when she took stock of them all it was clear that uprooting herself, even in old age, had had its usual effect. 'My health had improved somewhat, and I returned to Paris feeling much less depressed.'[64] She still, in any case, had some family left. One niece, Etienne Vigée's daughter Caroline de Rivière, 'with her tenderness and care [became] the delight of my life'. Eugénie Le Brun, the daughter of Jean-Baptiste-Pierre Le Brun's brother, grew equally precious. According to Louise,

> Her studies initially prevented my seeing her as much as I should have liked; for from her tenderest youth she promised, by her character, her mind and her great gifts as a painter, to add to my happiness. I took pleasure in guiding her, showering her with my advice and following her progress. I am more than adequately rewarded today, now she has fulfilled all my hopes, by her sweet character and by a quite remarkable talent for painting. She has followed the same route as me in adopting the genre of portraiture, in which she is enjoying a success fully merited by her fine use of colour, her truth to life and the perfect resemblance she captures. Young as she still is, she can only add to a reputation which her initial timidity and modesty barely allowed one to believe possible.[65]

Louise's reference to having seen little of Eugénie early on is rather disingenuous. It is true that Eugénie was a pupil of Regnault's, but presumably she might also, or alternatively, have been a pupil of Louise's if her aunt had not been so averse to teaching. Louise did rather belatedly give her some instructions about painting which are reproduced at the end of the *Souvenirs*, but the advice could usefully have come at Eugénie's formative stage.

Whether or not she was actually as exploitative an aunt as abbé Géralde claims, or as she seems ultimately to have been a neglectful mother, Louise declares that her two nieces became like daughters to her – 'They make me experience anew all the feelings of a mother, and their tender devotion gives great charm to my existence.'[66] She was, however, as exacting a parent as ever, and the relationships must in some ways have resembled that between Madame du Deffand and her niece Julie de Lespinasse. The aunt provided the ambience and conferred the prestige, and the nieces were expected to minister. Caroline seems to have considered this more burdensome than Eugénie. While there was an assumption that she would be Louise's sole heir, this was found just tolerable. (Independent witnesses suspected her of financial greed: Louise's friend Hervé de Jonville wrote to Eugénie on 26 February 1842 on the subject of Caroline that 'I had been in the position to detect in her the manifestation of pecuniary interest, which attained passionate proportions.'[67]) But when she had to fear otherwise, her impatience exploded. She was less prepared than the more emollient and loving Eugénie to be stage manager to a star.

For Louise does not appear to have been as unselfish and sweet-natured in old age as some of her salon guests believed. In the eyes of the dramatist and novelist Sophie de Bawr, a relatively late acquaintance, she had been quite unspoilt by a lifetime of adulation.

> All of us who came to know her only when she was old, and who loved her so much, are quite certain that she never ceased to be simple and natural. More passionate about her art than proud of her success, she was as much a stranger to vanity as to envy. She painted, driven by need, paid by the pleasure of painting. She sometimes spoke of all the homages and consideration her talent had won for her, but without the least desire to show off . . . the goodness of her heart, the absence of all envy kept her constantly in that state of calm which happiness confers. Her health was always perfect.[68]

This happy picture did not reflect Caroline de Rivière's experience. A number of brief notes she sent Eugénie, probably in the 1830s, refer to the 'torment' Louise is inflicting on her,[69] and their tone is one of impassioned complaint. Hervé de Jonville observed that in the early days of the July Revolution of 1830 Caroline would arrive 'furious' at her aunt's house, though whether this was because of general annoyance with Louise or unspecific bad temper is unclear. When, in 1839, Caroline suspected that Louise was revising her will in favour of Eugénie, she forgot herself to the extent of complaining to Adélaïde: 'Look how wretched I am, my aunt has just deprived me of a portion of her fortune. She has given 50,000 francs in her will to Madame Le Franc [Eugénie].'[70]

It seems bizarre for Louise to have made this seemingly ungrateful niece her heir, rather than Eugénie. Family politics may partly explain it, and snobbery. Caroline became a baroness when her husband Louis de Rivière inherited an uncle's title in 1828, and Louise was always susceptible to the seductions of nobility. Eugénie, on the other hand, had been born a Le Brun. The divorce of 1794 had created a certain coldness between the Le Bruns and the Vigées, and this was apparently increased by Jean-Baptiste-Pierre Le Brun's death in 1813. But gradually Louise seems to have wanted to draw closer to a niece whose talents as a painter were blossoming, especially after Julie's death in 1819. She became increasingly fond of Eugénie, engineered her marriage to Justin Tripier Le Franc, and developed an almost obsessive desire for her company. Many notes she sent her in the 1830s refer to her 'urgent need' to see Eugénie, and the difficulty of enduring her absence. Friends like Brifaut, the actress Mademoiselle

Duchesnois, Gérard, Sophie de Bawr and Delphine de Custine's brother the marquis de Sabran all refer to the 'maternal' love Louise felt for her. Eugénie gradually became an essential presence in Louise's house. Brifaut wrote to her that 'You do the honours of her table and salon so beautifully that nothing would be complete without you.'[71]

Perhaps, in fact, Eugénie's devotion was excessive. In February 1842, a month before Louise's death, her friend Hervé de Jonville was writing to her niece to tell her to take better care of her health:

> You could have taken . . . a leaf out of your aunt's book, so active at your age, so well travelled, doing masses of portraits, so to speak, darting between the courts of Europe; and it is clear to me that with good health and peace of soul you could like her have turned your palette to account, for it might serve you just as well as hers did, if you had leisure, a modicum of health and no grief.[72]

By 1842 Eugénie had actually enjoyed far greater artistic success than Jonville implies. But obviously she was a less single-minded painter than Louise, and prepared to tolerate interruptions in a way her aunt had never been. The Louise who had refused to let even royalty interrupt her in her studio, in her obsession with her beloved art, was apparently happy to intrude upon the artistic careers of others when it suited her; and she was lucky enough to find a self-sacrificial ministrant in her niece.

Eugénie suffered terribly from Louise's mood-swings and variable health, but Louise still apparently felt she wanted more attention than Eugénie could give her. A letter she sent her niece on 19 July 1831 declared that she needed someone to take better care of her – specifically 'a young person, well brought up but with no future . . . or a young widow', but not a music-lover, since Louise herself was so sad that 'music would hurt me more than console me'.[73] And yet, as the 1869 editors of the *Souvenirs* point out, Eugénie surrounded Louise with loving care in her old age, and put up with all her aunt's fluctuations of temper. Louise probably did not mean to appear selfish, but there is something slightly opportunistic about the way she turned to Eugénie – her Le Brun niece – only as old age approached. Eugénie, however, seems to have had no vanity, and never expresses the belief that she has been exploited.

Given that she had essentially been an unpaid companion to Louise, and had to juggle her commitment to her with her commitments to a husband and family, she might have expected more generous recognition from her aunt in the end. But Louise's 1829 will, drawn up nine years after the start of her close friendship with Eugénie, still makes Caroline the main beneficiary.[74] She was to inherit her aunt's various effects, including the Louveciennes house, while Eugénie would receive an 'individual' bequest which Louise promised to increase if she had children. (Two were born, in 1830 and 1832.) Louise often gave Eugénie gifts, and with the passage of time came to appreciate her qualities more and more deeply. In 1839, as a consequence, she made a new will which gave Eugénie an annuity of 2,500 francs, along with various jewels and personal items.[75] She asked Eugénie not to inform Caroline de Rivière of the change, because she feared her anger. Eugénie might still have had some grounds for believing that she had been shabbily treated in comparison with her cousin, because the revised will only modestly increased her share of the estate; but she did not complain.

Caroline none the less tried to get the 1839 will, which she had found out about, declared void. It is alleged that in June 1841 she had Louise taken to a notary, Monsieur Bertinot, for this purpose, but without Louise realising what was happening. When Eugénie discovered the deception, she told the indignant Louise, who informed her that her own signature had been forged on the new documents. She added that she loved Eugénie more than ever, and wished to disinherit Madame de Rivière. Eugénie persuaded her not to do so, but to reinstate the 1839 will, to which Louise agreed. When Caroline subsequently tried to make Eugénie renounce some of her rights,[76] Louise successfully urged her to stand her ground. The modified will of 29 January 1842 left Eugénie 60,000 francs and six pictures of her own choice (two of which, a self-portrait with Julie and a portrait of Madame Molé-Raymond, she donated to the Louvre during her lifetime). In February that year Hervé de Jonville was still concerned that Eugénie, the deserving recipient, might not inherit the things she should.

> I intend to write her [Louise] a few lines one of these days, and very indirectly I shall talk to her about her pictures, her sketches, which will no doubt be precious to you, as well as very useful . . . if you find her in the mood to open her heart to you, remind her that her pictures, her sketches, virtually useless to Madame de Rivière, will be precious pledges to you, and an invaluable support for your art.[77]

As well as being provoked by the greed and duplicity of Caroline de Rivière, Louise was aggrieved to find her proposed burial arrangements thwarted. She had originally hoped for a place on the Calvary of Mont-Valérien in Paris, where the old cemetery of the Congregation of the Calvary (an order dissolved during the Revolution) had been reinstated under the Bourbon Restoration.[78] Despite the high prices charged, the

Parisian *monde*, with its taste for pious romanticism, flocked to reserve burial-plots there, and Louise wanted to follow suit. There was nothing particularly devout about this urge, and she was not a particularly devout woman. Early in her memoirs she comments on her mother's extreme piety, and adds that she was pious too 'from the heart',[79] which seems to mean that she *felt* but did not trouble to *profess* a religious faith. Her feeling for religion, it appears, was more aesthetic than anything else, feeding on the beauties of sacred music and the sound of organs playing.

She was especially drawn by the rusticity and picturesque calm of the cemetery, for her always conducive to spiritual feelings. 'I confess that rural churches have always made me pray with more fervour than other ones,'[80] she writes in the *Souvenirs*;

> I recall that my friend Madame de Verdun often criticised me for not attending services regularly enough . . . [but] in Paris churches, where there are throngs of people, I am not sufficiently alone with God . . . I cannot pray as well as I do in a village church.

Friends of hers had already been buried on Mont-Valérien: Anne Tolstoy, née Princess Bariatinskaya, in 1825, and baron de Rivière (the uncle of Caroline's husband) in 1828. But with the 1830 Revolution the missionary congregation of Mont-Valérien was again dispersed, new 'concessions' at the cemetery were prohibited, and burials there became increasingly rare.

Louise therefore had to change the terms of her will, and on 17 September 1831 she added a codicil to the effect that she was now to be buried at Louveciennes. She seems, not uncharacteristically, to have feared that some intrigue might prevent her instructions from being followed, and therefore took the step of writing to the mayor of Louveciennes to repeat her request, which she justified with the assertion that she had always had a 'true predilection' for the place.

Sophie de Bawr, perhaps unaware of these frustrations, reports that Louise continued blessed to the end. 'This happy destiny was never belied, even at her last moments, since in her eighty-seventh year she expired gently, quickly and without any suffering.'[81]

It was five o'clock in the evening on 30 March 1842. Her two nieces and their husbands, her doctor Monsieur Tournié, and her devoted servants were in attendance.[82] Justin Tripier Le Franc had her death-mask moulded with her head propped up on the first volume of Félibien's *Entretiens sur les vies et les ouvrages des plus excellents peintres*, which contained a section on her former husband's great-uncle Charles Le Brun.

Since she had died in Paris, not Louveciennes, Louise's funeral convoy assembled there. The procession marched from 99 rue Saint-Lazare (where her friends and relatives gathered at half past nine on the morning of 2 April) to the church of Saint-Louis-d'Antin.[83] After the religious service Louise's remains were transported to Louveciennes and provisionally buried. The burial was simple, as her will had stipulated. The permanent plot – in the old cemetery, on the site of the present place des Combattants – was purchased by Caroline de Rivière and her husband only two years later, on 31 March 1844, probably because of disputes over the execution of Louise's will.

But her body was not to be left in peace, despite the firm message of her tombstone ('Here at last I rest'). After the end of the Franco-Prussian War in 1870 it was removed along with everything else there to the new cemetery of Louveciennes at the foot of the imposing Marly aqueduct, an altogether less poetic place where Louise's grave was no longer surrounded by trees, as her will had directed that it should be. Nor could she rest tranquilly; for the site was strategically important, and a fort would be built there in 1872. Meanwhile, the old Louveciennes cemetery was secularised, and became a public square.

Louise's present grave is at the far end of the new cemetery, against the boundary wall. There are no bronze railings around it (a second breach of the provisions she had so carefully made), and trees were planted round it only in the mid-1980s. But the tombstone is more or less as she wanted it, though it is not of marble. In accordance with her instructions, it is carved with a medallion showing a laurel wreath surrounding a pedestal on which a palette and some paintbrushes rest, with the sun's rays shining down from above. The full inscription reads 'Here at last I rest: Louise Elisabeth Vigée Le Brun, died 30 March 1842. De profundis'.

What is the meaning of the first line? At the end of her memoirs Louise describes her life as having been 'wandering but calm, hard-working but honourable'.[84] Do the words suggest a welcome end to a life of sorrows – familial and other – and rootlessness? Surely the allusion is, rather, to her driven life as an artist, pursuing a vocation which, according to everything she said, procured for her the profoundest happiness imaginable, but which also led to suffering and a degree of dissatisfaction bordering on self-disgust.

After Louise's death 'differences' between her two nieces exploded. Once a respectable period of mourning had passed, Eugénie attempted to have the wills of 1829 and 1842 executed. At this point Caroline contested the 1842 will, claiming that at the time of making it Louise had been senile. This assertion was roundly denied by Louise's friends and acquaintances.[85] The comte de Belisle, who saw her a week before her death – and thus two months after the making of the last will – consulted her at that time about some object of art on which she was able to advise him collectedly, and had an intelligent conversation lasting an hour with her.[86] Poujoulat spoke with Louise the day before she died, and found her *compos mentis*, and a Madame Reiset d'Arques confirmed that her wits at the end had been intact. The baronne de Crespy le Prince painted a similar picture of her last visit to Louise in February of 1842, and her confessor denied that her final words had been confused. The most one could say, according to Madame de Bailly, was that Louise could not remember the recent past, and often in a short space of time asked a question to which she had already received the answer.[87] Possibly, Hervé de Jonville thought, the hard work of preparing her memoirs had been responsible for her mental deterioration. But in no sense could it be called senility.[88]

So the 1842 will was allowed to stand. Caroline de Rivière still inherited Louise's property and household effects. Some special instructions were attached to the disposal of certain items. Caroline's daughter Léonie was to inherit the jewel-encrusted brooch Maria Carolina of Naples had given Louise. For as long as she wished, Caroline was to be allowed to wear the diamond bracelets which had been a gift to Louise from the Queen of Prussia, then pass them on to Léonie. Caroline's second daughter Zaza was left other trinkets. The will provided for a charitable donation to be made towards the support of four old and infirm women, who were to be given fifty francs each every six months. A belt-clasp made out of a cameo of Stanislas Augustus of Poland was bequeathed to another niece, Françoise Elisabeth Le Brun (possibly Eugénie Le Brun is meant), as were a vermeil coffee-service, the sketchbooks she had filled during her travels, her painting implements, her largest silver cafetière and other silverware, and the 'Sévigné' with a portrait of Louis XIV painted by Petitot. Louise's travelling-companion Auguste Rivière was left a gold box set with a lock of the vicomte de Vaudreuil's hair. A more recent friend, Aimé-Martin (who married the widow of Bernardin de Saint-Pierre, and edited his works), received her seal. Monsieur and Madame de Bailly, Lord Trimlestown and Hervé de Jonville were each given one of Louise's Swiss landscapes – but not, Louise specified, the big picture showing glaciers.

The Musée royal – that is, the Louvre – was left the self-portrait with her daughter Louise had painted in 1786, the picture of Paisiello and the portrait of Hubert Robert holding a palette. She gave the Berlin Academy her picture of Countess Kinsky in a red shawl and wearing a turban, and the Rouen Musée des beaux-arts the portrait of Angelica Catalani ('if I still have it') – if not, the larger portrait of Josephina Grassini as a sultana. (In fact she bequeathed the Catalani picture to Caroline de Rivière, and Rouen acquired Grassini.) The bust-length picture of Josephina was left to the Vaucluse Academy in Avignon, which had made Louise an honorary member in 1827. Remembering the honours which various academies all over Europe had done her, but particularly the favours shown her in Russia, she made provision for a prize of one hundred francs to be established at the St Petersburg Academy of Fine Arts, for a *tête d'expression* in oil like the one for which the comte de Caylus had established a competition at the Académie royale de peinture et de sculpture in Paris nearly half a century before. She also laid down instructions for the medal to be given with the prize: one side was to bear the inscription 'In grateful memory of Madame Le Brun', and the other – like her tombstone – would show the sun's rays shining above a palette and paintbrushes.

Her faithful maid Adélaïde inherited Louise's dresses, except for the velvet ones and the ornate robes, which she gave to Caroline (along with her muslins). Hervé de Jonville inherited two or three Swiss landscapes, not the single one specified in Louise's will, and the pastel head of a child.

No doubt Louise genuinely regretted the fact that there was no longer a real daughter to inherit her property, however sincerely she meant the statement that Eugénie and Caroline had become her children. But perhaps she felt again as she had felt describing her time in Naples, that her life had been too much driven by considerations of material gain, and insufficiently directed towards affairs of the spirit. There was probably more than a touch of defensiveness in the remark she made to Madame de Verdun – the friend who came to report Julie's death to her – about her attitude to religion. And there may have been a different kind of defensiveness in her decision to present a religious painting to the Louveciennes church, for this picture of St Genevieve, painted in 1821 and installed in the church on Palm Sunday the following year, appears to be a commemoration of the daughter she had lost in December 1819.

In many respects the work, now in the Louveciennes museum, is a feeble one. The tone is cheaply sentimental in a Greuzian way, and St Genevieve herself is theatrical. The landscape against which she is portrayed is ineptly sketched in, and the sheep standing by her is ludicrous. The whole is in part saved by Louise's expert colour-sense, but it is also redeemed by the contrition that seems to inform it. For the face of St Genevieve, rapt like one of Greuze's *têtes d'expression*, has Julie Le Brun's features – the fourteen-year-old Julie whom Louise had painted in Italy, and whose picture now hangs in the Pinacoteca of Bologna. This, Louise's only religious painting, is also perhaps her only official act of regret along with the *de profundis* of her tombstone, a line from the psalm of penitence.

Whether the contrition is for a life lived too single-mindedly to allow for deep fellow-feeling we may only speculate. It is certainly a clumsy gesture, both artistically and morally. But it is possibly a mother's last statement on an affair which earned her as little credit as her artistic activity earned her much; and in that case it is fitting that the statement should have been painted, not said.

CONCLUSION: 'She painted, driven by need'

It had been a very long life, driven or otherwise, sorrowful or not towards its end. Did Louise outlive herself – as Gros said he had outlived himself, just before committing suicide – by forty years? Would she have done better, as far as her reputation is concerned, to have died like Julie Nigris at thirty-nine or so? If she had, we should have been without the Russian pictures and many worthwhile things that came after them – the work done in London, and in Paris after her return from exile. The Russian pictures are anything but tired: in some of them, indeed, Louise seems to have gained a new energy. And a few of the portraits painted during her stay in England are too good to be happily foregone – the *Josephina Grassinis*, for instance, and the picture of the society hostess *Mrs Chinnery*. Bertie Greatheed may have thought that Louise was capable of little but 'husky daubs' after 1800, but much of her production suggests otherwise.

If she had died at about Julie's age, Louise would still have been the portraitist of the *ancien régime*. But that might have led to as much obloquy and disparagement as the evidence of decline did. Part of the problem in this respect is that it rarely occurred to her to present *ancien régime* values other than affirmatively. Perhaps there is a critical undertone to the prettily vacuous look she gives to some society women, or the elegant insubstantiality she suggests in a courtier like Vaudreuil, but mostly she refuses to dissent from the ways of her adoptive world. Courtier-artists could not decently dissent.

Louise was not a moralist either. She did not wish to hint that the *monde* from which she earned a living needed changing. She was no Laclos, and still less – for all her enthusiastic embracing of 'natural' doctrines – was she a Rousseau. To put it bluntly, she saw no need for a Revolution which would destroy most of her clientele.

In keeping with this conservative conviction, she found no reason to question the ethos of worldliness. She may have painted women who toyed with the simple life (though she drew the line at portraying

313

Marie-Antoinette as a peasant), but she believed as fervently as they did that sociability in an elevated sense was a source of pride, not shame. The wild and uncultivated world of nature which so thrilled eighteenth-century sensibilities was tolerable only when it co-existed with the world of culture. And culture, for the portraitist and her sitters, was best expressed in terms of decorous charm, *chic* and sophistication. Even Louise's often-criticised polish, the 'finish' of her facture, was a statement of value, as was her devotion to detail. They meant that fineness mattered, and that the incomplete or the roughly sketched was a reprehensible concession to slovenliness. Immaculateness of painting technique, on the other hand, signifies that one upheld standards – the more vigorously, perhaps, in that one had had to fight to acquire the technique and meet the standards – and that one was determined to keep the barbarian at bay.

So critics like Hoppner, arguing the superior merits of a different, rougher painting idiom, were in her eyes simply wrong. Besides, there was something wholesome in the positiveness of Louise's *faire*. It was, Justin Tripier Le Franc, wrote, at the opposite pole from the murky gloom of her English counterparts.

> The portraits of Madame Le Brun do not have the afflicted character of almost all the work of English artists; on the contrary, her productions express the gaiety, the smiling happiness, which make all her pictures able to sustain the most prolonged scrutiny without losing anything of their charm.[1]

Louise, in other words, paints in a way that confidently upholds values, rather than calls them into question. When she depicts women as beautiful almost beyond belief (and describes them as such in her memoirs), she does so less because they were than because it was important to her both morally and politically that the ideal of perfection should be preserved. Painting 'fixes' a beauty that in real life fades, and so is a supremely apt instrument for halting the advance of time. Louise's painting is a metaphor for the seizing of the moment which all who would regret the loss of the old *douceur de vivre* desired – a wonderfully counter-Revolutionary enterprise.

In denying the forces of change (except those of fashion), Louise stood apart from other portraitists of the time – David, of course, but also her so-called rival Adélaïde Labille-Guiard. Nothing in Louise's work reflects the new political ideologies, whereas Madame Labille-Guiard, who stayed in Paris while Louise left for less revolutionary societies, directly deals with the architects of the new order. Correspondingly, she is more of a realist than Louise, in the sense that she is readier to show what *is* rather than what *was* (or *is* only at a remove from Paris). In keeping with this is her comparative reluctance to idealise her clients, or to portray herself in self-portraits as ageless and flawlessly beautiful. In contrast, Louise – by all accounts a strikingly attractive woman – cannot forebear to improve her own looks along with those of her sitters.

Labille-Guiard's work, a product of her uncompromising attitude to the real world, tends also to appear more individualistic than Louise's. There is often great drama in Louise's pictures, particularly, perhaps, when her subjects are artists or Russian men and women (she viewed the Russian race romantically), but there can equally be a rather tame uniformity. This is less because she repeated poses and props – all portraiture relies on formulas and patterns[2] – than because beauty, for her, precluded irregularity, and irregularity confers character.

There are some exceptions to this rule, of course. She does not disguise the bump on Countess Golovina's nose, for instance, or particularly flatter Germaine de Staël. But in general she prefers conformity to what is exceptional. She is easier about portraying non-conformity in men, both because she does not feel obliged to beautify them and because many of her male sitters were themselves out of the common run – rapt artists, composers in the grip of enthusiasm and so on. She occasionally painted women who were distinguished by something other than their looks (Isabella Marini, Countess Golovina, Josephina Grassini), but her usual practice is to suggest that her female sitters are exceptional in their beauty above all else.

If Justin Tripier Le Franc highlights Louise's avoidance of the 'affliction' characterising English work, she herself comes close to admitting the extent of her transforming flattery. She would not dream of doing so in connection with the adored Marie-Antoinette, but she is altogether franker in the case of the princesse de Lamballe: 'Without being pretty, she seemed so at the right distance; she had small features, a dazzling fresh complexion, magnificent blond hair and a great deal of personal elegance.'[3] But Louise's portrait makes her ravishing. Perhaps it was only fair, given the horror of the princess's end: another woman who adored Marie-Antoinette, she returned to France in 1793 when she heard the Queen was in danger, was decapitated, had her breasts sliced off and her heart torn from her body. Along with her head, it was paraded on a pike through the streets of Paris until one of her murderers could find someone to cook it for him.

So Louise's portraits are works of art as much as they are documents: they represent real people, but as aesthetic objects.[4] Personality is in part a function of other people's perceptions, and Louise's perceptions were those of the artist and <u>lover of beauty</u>. It is natural, then, that her portraits should also be evaluations. But should they have been more critical evaluations? Almost without exception, her judgements concur with those of the society she depicts, which is why her work is often found unchallenging. Yet she does permit herself occasional ironies – emphasising the sensuous invitation of Emma Hamilton's far-from-desolate Ariadne, or the faint ridiculousness of Madame de Staël. To that extent her portraits are also expressions of attitude.

Whether her distinctive style is an essentially female one has been much debated, but it is as difficult to pinpoint stylistic femininity in painting as it is in literature. To say that Louise's portraits convey a woman's sensibilities is actually to say very little. Men have painted delicate mother-and-child pictures and seductive women wearing gorgeous or skimpy clothes; equally, women have produced the kind of erotic images of other women which one might more readily associate with male artists.[5] Louise painted her bacchantes and nymphs – possibly because she was commissioned to do so by male clients – and Labille-Guiard did at least one picture of the same sort. Sensibility appears to be a quality common to artists, not monopolised by women; and though the love of beauty may be sexually conditioned, it is not in an exclusive sense sexually determined. To claim, as has recently been done, that only a woman could have depicted Countess Golovina is to assert the unprovable.[6]

None the less, the fact that she was female manifestly affected Louise as an artist. Her exclusion from the apprenticeship system to which the opposite sex was admitted helps explain why her early work lacks a truly personal stamp, seeming, rather, a motley reflection of various artists from La Tour to Greuze. But she developed distinctiveness and her own mastery of technique. Her colour-sense is breathtaking, infinitely subtle in its combinations, and seeming almost to anticipate Ingres. In a way, it surpasses form, or rather form in Louise's work is a function of colour. Perhaps this is no more than a reflection of her early training as a pastellist, for her work often lacks the solidity and clarity of outline which we find in some of her contemporaries.

She was always her own woman. To be called a 'great man' (Lebrun-Pindare's description of her) probably offended her as little as it did Catherine *le Grand*, or as little as she was offended by hearing David call her Paisiello portrait the equal of a man's work. She liked emphasising her tenderness as much as her toughness, and showing how successfully they co-existed. She resented society's criticism of her single-mindedness because, in her own eyes, she so effectively combined the two professions of artist and mother. No other woman painter of comparable achievement, she knew, had done as much. She inevitably encountered disapproval from a world which, though it loved her work, thought it somehow indecent (or impossible) for a woman to have done it. Like Staël's Corinne, she suffered from the conflict between what seemed to be expected of a woman and what the woman of ambition expected of herself.

She found it outrageous that under the misogynistic Napoleon there should be no place for her as a woman artist in the newly established Institut de France, which replaced the academies of the *ancien régime*. And had she been in France to hear it, she would have been infuriated by a debate at the end of 1793 on the question whether women should be admitted to membership of the Société populaire et républicaine des arts.[7] It was argued on this occasion that they could not be allowed to join because they were 'in all respects different from men', and because a current law anyway prohibited them from gathering and deliberating on any subject. According to one speaker, though it was possible to live happily with a woman who possessed artistic talent, to do so was to act against the laws of nature. In his opinion, it was because a famous woman, 'the *citoyenne* Le Brun', showed an aptitude for painting that hordes of other females wanted to dabble in the art, whereas their true destiny was to embroider belts and bonnets. It is hardly surprising, given the prevalence of such views, that Louise should have blamed the new regime for diminishing the status of her sex. Women had reigned in the old France, she writes nostalgically in the *Souvenirs*, but no longer.

Louise's *maternités* with Julie are most quintessentially a 'female' artistic statement in defending her seemingly successful combination of a professional and a domestic life. To show herself clasping a child rather than paintbrushes – the paintbrushes she holds in various self-portraits, as Hubert Robert does in the picture Louise intended to hang as a pendant to the self-portrait with Julie – was to demonstrate that she was more than a man-artist: she was a mother as well as a painter.[8] It was a way of answering those who criticised her, by implication, for having produced some 700 portraits but only one child; for having subordinated the (woman's) duty to procreate to the (man's) urge to create.

She was keen to defend herself as a good mother, though there was clearly extraordinary neglect as well as suffocating closeness in her relationship with her daughter. That she had a bad conscience about it seems clear. Hence her outrage at being blamed by her former husband and St Petersburg society for her treatment of Julie, and hence her recurrent mentioning in the *Souvenirs* of the fact that Julie accompanied her into society drawing-rooms all over Europe, and that she could refuse her nothing.[9] In the letter to Julie on 12 September 1807 concerning her portrait '*en Corinne*', Madame de Staël is at pains to underline Louise's real feelings of tenderness towards her daughter: 'it is to you that she likes to report her successes.'[10]

For her own part, Louise felt she had to set the record straight in various ways. There was not just the matter of her alleged mistreatment of Julie Nigris in Russia; there were the other kinds of personality-attack she had suffered in the course of her career. She decided to publish her memoirs because she wanted to answer her critics: like Rousseau before her, she felt that she had been persecuted and misunderstood. Since her painting could not fully argue her case, she had to write.

She explains her position in a letter to Louis Amié-Martin:

> Well, my dear friend, I have begun what you have been advising me to do for years; you know the distaste I felt for writing what you call my memoirs, for despite all the events I have witnessed I shall have . . . to talk about myself; this *self*, though, is so tedious to other people that it made me give up the idea. But Monsieur de Gaspériny, who like you pressed me to write them, decided me on it by saying: Well, Madame, if you do not do it yourself, others will do it after you, and heaven knows what they will write. I could follow this reasoning . . . having been misunderstood and slandered so often, and made up my mind. For six months I have been jotting down as I go along everything I remember about all the different periods and places in my life; you will not find any style in it, no rolling phrases or periods. I am simply transcribing the facts, plainly and truthfully, as one writes a letter to one's friend.
>
> You have already given a very good picture in your biographical note of some of the main events of my life; people may have assumed from this happy account that I was the most fortunate of women; well, my friend, this homage, these honourable and flattering distinctions were admixed with cruel suffering . . . caused by what was closest and dearest to me; and it is that which has often made me think that one should never envy the fate of anyone, even those one believes to be most fortunate.
>
> I do not include among these emotional sufferings the poisoned shafts of calumny, which has always pursued me; I have disdained them, because they came only from enemies, whom I certainly never knew.
>
> The most interesting thing I can do is focus on the remarkable events which my position in the world enabled me to see close up, as well as the most celebrated and distinguished citizens of Europe.[11]

This letter, as well as some surviving manuscript sections of the *Souvenirs*, demonstrates that Louise was indeed the author of her memoirs, though her authorship has sometimes been disputed. Friends like Aimé-Martin, Brifaut and Sophie de Bawr, and particularly her nieces, may have helped polish and edit them, but they are essentially Louise's work: self-congratulatory, selective and snobbish, but moving in their documentation of a life lived with single-mindedness and resolve, and fascinating in their recording of a woman artist's struggles in a changing world.

Are they, then, a whitewash? Not completely, though they are certainly untrustworthy. Louise did not have too much to hide – she had not, like Rousseau, abandoned her offspring to a foundling's home – and she had a great deal to glory in. She can scarcely be criticised for priding herself on combining professional activity and motherhood, even if she failed to strike the perfect balance. Who else had tried as much? Madame de Genlis says that Louise was quite justified in being determined to do more than what a Rousseau wanted women to do, that is, be a good housekeeper and mother. 'Would it not be a pity if Mesdames de Grollier and Le Brun, or Mademoiselle Lescot, had never painted?'[12]

It is unthinkable, of course, that Louise might never have painted. Her love for the art was inborn, she claimed, and instinct taught her all she knew. She had an instinctive sense of grace, it is true, which is why she is such a mistress of pose;[13] few painters have so convincingly and comfortably 'sat' their models, or had them stride so exuberantly across a landscape. Her lack of academic training may in a curious way have been an advantage, for it meant that she could focus on what her early master Vernet called nature. According to a late eighteenth-century commentator, Louise was supremely skilled at preserving 'la naïveté de la nature'.[14]

Yet in a way this seems paradoxical. Louise's most characteristic portraits are highly polished images of women who, relaxed as they may appear, are generally well aware of the impression they are making, and who exude sophistication. Nature in its other sense, of course, is conveyed in different works of hers – her rough sketches of mountain crags, avalanches, waterfalls and the like. For she was also a child of the age of sensibility, spurning society as much as she courted it, delighting in the sublime as well as the picturesque, and periodically standing apart from the tinsel and glitter of the *monde*. There is, in fact, a multiplicity of natures. If the nature of Louise's society portraits is sentimental in the Schillerian sense – that is, the product of self-conscious desire rather than spontaneity, knowing rather than naïve – then that too is a mark of its time. Louise could no more free herself from her times than any image-maker can, and in her case the urge to crystallise and so preserve the moment was particularly strong.

The Sweetness of Life

How should we see her now? Surely as more than the caprice of a half-century, from the 1770s to the 1820s. She was – generously – called 'Madame Van Dyck' and 'Madame Rubens' in Rome, and tells us so complacently in the *Souvenirs*. There are examples of such immodesty, or the lack of false modesty, throughout Louise's memoirs, which suggest that she was a more self-regarding woman than she and her friends sometimes claimed. If Reynolds thought that she had actually outpainted Van Dyck, her 1869 editors claimed that she had had no rivals during her lifetime or since. This is a preposterous assertion, but she was on any reckoning a very gifted and accomplished painter.

She enjoyed astonishing success at a time when it was still rare for women artists to make their way in the world. She has left a visual portrait of her age which may seem unchallenging – because it confirms values which a part of contemporary society was attempting to uproot – but which has more than the faded charm Balzac describes in *Ursule Mirouët*. David cruelly called her a 'servant of quality', and she was certainly more snobbish than her angry statement 'titles are a matter of complete indifference to me' implies. Like the gourmand Grimod de la Reynière's wife, she was *attaquée de noblesse*; but her splendid connections made for a gallery of sitters who epitomise the old order at a time of sharp political and social change, as well, occasionally, as pointing forward to the new.

Her span was longer than Voltaire's. She bore out at least the first of the marquis de Montesquiou's early predictions about the course her life would take: 'He told me that I would be long-lived, and that I would be a pleasant old woman because I was not coquettish.'[15] She also had all the assurance of long experience and conservative conviction: born under Louis XV and surviving to the reign of Louis-Philippe, she knew – as adamant old women generally do – exactly where she stood. Because she was someone who consorted with, and either painted or described, most of the people who mattered in art, politics and society across civilised Europe, her life is of enduring interest. She will always have her denigrators, whether for ideological reasons or on artistic grounds. But she was deservedly a crowd-puller in her own lifetime, a female icon, and a creator of images whose lasting quality is beginning to be acknowledged again.

She is to be remembered too for the scale of her achievements as a woman in a predominantly male professional world. Not that she showed any great solidarity with her own sex, though she did admire female artists like Rosalba Carriera, Angelica Kauffman and the marquise de Grollier. She did as little teaching of women as she decently could, and says nothing about the work of Adélaïde Labille-Guiard. But she resented Hoppner's misogyny as much as the scandal which attached to her because of her success and attractiveness, and deplored the anti-female prejudice of the Napoleonic world.

She probably felt, with some justice, that women writers had things easier than women artists. Since writers needed no academic training or sanction, so the argument went, they did not suffer from being denied it. But Louise cannot have considered that she was outshone by the *femmes-écrivains* she knew – Madame de Flahaut/Souza, Madame de Genlis, Madame de Krüdener or Sophie de Bawr – and despite their mutual exchange of extravagant compliments she and Germaine de Staël probably regarded themselves as at least the other's equal. In any case, the officially-exiled Madame de Staël suffered sanctions on account of her art in a way the self-exiled Louise did not.

Not all these women needed to earn a living, but some did. Louise, who was probably the most highly paid, found that her financial success was resented because of the belief – still a prevalent one – that it is more proper for men to be expensive professionals than women. She could have responded that she was, in a sense, a male by adoption: she supported a household, a child and periodically a husband, and as critics often commented, she wielded a competently male brush. She even painted women erotically. Interestingly, though, none of the sexual innuendo directed at her included accusations of lesbianism, as it did in the cases of Marie-Antoinette, the duchesse de Polignac, the princesse de Lamballe, Louis XVIII's wife Marie-Joséphine, Maria Carolina of Naples and Countess Golovina, all clients of hers.

We may regret the fact that Louise so rarely *depicts* female professionalism, or does so with any intensity. When she paints herself painting, it is usually in the image of a well-dressed and unimpassioned lady, or the poised coquette of the 'straw hat' portrait. It is not as a rough and inspired creator in the Hubert Robert or Paisiello mould. The marquise de Grollier is shown painting as decorously and controlledly as she apparently lived, though Louise's female singers – Josephina Grassini, Angelica Catalani – are allowed to display more enthusiasm. Showing writers in the act of writing is more difficult, and she does not attempt it with Germaine de Staël. But the image of this *homme-femme* striding out, scribbling on her famous tablets and furiously brandishing greenery, would surely have been more arresting than the overblown classicising one of Madame de Staël in a state of sibylline rapture.

Matching herself against males, Louise also wanted to prove that she surpassed them in her ability to combine practical competence with maternal essence. This entailed some rewriting of the truth. So too, no doubt, did the projected image of herself as husband-father as well as mother-wife. She needed to show Jean-Baptiste-Pierre Le Brun as improvident in order to emphasise her own contrasting ability to provide. There were times when it suited her to admit his own earning-power, as when she wanted to show that both she and her husband could well afford the house in the rue du Gros-Chenet for which Calonne was said to have paid. But mostly she told a different story.

Undoubtedly her memoirs propagate other myths too, retailed with the same self-presentational skill as Louise deployed throughout her career as an artist. Of these the most obvious is the myth of innateness, Louise's claim that she had no master but her own instinct – as though Vernet, La Tour, even her own father had taught her nothing. There is the linked assertion that she was driven to create by her love of art alone, which does not quite ring true. It may have suited this courtier-artist to claim that she painted for the sheer joy of it, but the joy frequently dimmed at times of stress or threat. And whether or not her husband pocketed the proceeds, she also painted for money. She was more self-conscious, and consciously professional, than she liked to admit, and we surely have to adopt the same (psychological) distance when reading her memoirs as the (aesthetic) distance we adopt when viewing her pictures.

But she was patently no fraud. She was, rather, a mistress of the artful transposition, in her sometimes devious and fawning *Souvenirs* as in her painting – a teller, like Rousseau, of 'true lies'. She was as entitled to peddle agreeable fiction in the one as the other, at least where her modern audience is concerned. Exact resemblance stops mattering with the passage of years; what remains, and what counts, is the flavour of a life and time.

Louise has left many monuments, and one has been left to her. On 25 April 1885 two of the five members of the municipal commission reviewing the street-names of Louveciennes proposed rechristening the Grand-Rue the rue Vigée Le Brun. At that time it was still unthinkable to give a main street anywhere the name of a woman, even a famous one, and the recommendation was rejected. But twenty years later there was a minor consolation for the artist. On 11 June 1905 the rue de la Charbonnière became the rue Vigée Le Brun, a name it has kept to this day.

NOTES

Introduction

1. Sir George Beaumont, quoted in Joseph Farington, *Diary*, ed. James Greig, 8 vols (London, 1922–8), II (1802–4), 219.
2. She was christened Marie Louise Elisabeth, but never used the first and more commonly signed herself by the third than the second.
3. Elisabeth Vigée Le Brun, *Souvenirs*, ed. Claudine Herrmann, 2 vols (Paris, 1986), I.32.
4. See, e.g., Michael Levey, *Painting and Sculpture in France 1700–1789* (New Haven and London, 1993), p.280.

1

1. Jacques Hillairet, *Dictionnaire historique des rues de Paris*, 2 vols. (Paris, 1963), I.391.
2. *Souvenirs*, I.25.
3. ibid., I.30.
4. See John Goodman, 'Altar against Altar: The Colisée, Vauxhall Utopianism and Symbolic Politics in Paris (1769–77)', *Art History*, 15 (1992), pp.445–6; Jules Guiffrey, 'Histoire de l'Académie de Saint Luc', *Archives de l'art français*, nouvelle période, IX (1915).
5. *Souvenirs*, I.26.
6. ibid., p.28.
7. ibid., p.33.
8. See Carol Duncan, 'Happy Mothers and Other New Ideas in French Art', *Art Bulletin*, LV (1973), p.574; Simon Schama, *Citizens: A Chronicle of the French Revolution* (London, 1989), p.145.
9. See D. G. Charlton, *New Images of the Natural in France* (Cambridge, 1984).
10. *Souvenirs*, I.25.
11. Madame du Deffand, *Lettres à Voltaire, 1759-1775*, ed. M. de Lescure (Paris, 1994), p.64.
12. *Encyclopédie, ou Dictionnaire raisonné des sciences, des arts et des métiers*, ed. Denis Diderot and Jean Le Rond d'Alembert, 218 vols (Paris, 1751-1772). The article 'Femme (morale)' is by Desmahis.
13. *Souvenirs*, I.41.
14. Charles Augustin de Sainte-Beuve, *Causeries du Lundi*, 16 vols (Paris,

1926–42), II.309.

15. *Souvenirs*, I.37.

16. ibid., p.24.

17. See Joseph Baillio, 'Quelques peintures réattribuées à Vigée Le Brun', *Gazette des beaux-arts*, XCIX (1982), p.14.

18. See Papiers Tripier Le Franc, in Bibliothèque d'art et d'archéologie (Fondation Jacques Doucet), MfB XXXIII, 27635. It amounted to 35,339 *livres* 12 *sols*.

19. Louis Petit de Bachaumont, *Mémoires secrets pour servir à l'histoire de la République des Lettres en France depuis MDCCLXII jusqu'à nos jours*, 36 vols (London, 1780–89), XXIV.103.

20. Jean-Baptiste Pierre Le Brun, *Précis historique de la vie de la citoyenne Le Brun peintre* (Paris, 1793–4), p.5.

21. *Souvenirs*, I.36–7.

22. ibid., p.46.

23. Denis Diderot, *Le Neveu de Rameau*, ed. Jean Fabre (Geneva, 1963), p.3.

24. *Souvenirs*, I.33–4.

25. ibid., p.29.

26. See Virginie Ancelot, *Les Salons de Paris* (Paris, 1858), p.79, and Sophie Gay, *Salons célèbres* (Paris, 1882), p.73.

27. Jean-Jacques Rousseau, *Emile*, in *Oeuvres complètes*, ed. Marcel Raymond and Bernard Gagnebin, 4 vols (Paris, 1959–69), IV.319.

28. *Souvenirs*, I.34.

29. Denis Diderot, *Salons*, ed. Jean Seznec and Jean Adhémar, 4 vols (Oxford, 1957–67), III.335–6.

30. ibid., III.338.

31. In Laclos, *Oeuvres complètes*, ed. Laurent Versini (Paris, 1979), pp.392–434.

32. *Salons*, III, loc. cit.

33. Friedrich Schiller, *Über naive und sentimentalische Dichtung*, ed. W. F. Maitland (Oxford 1951).

34. *Salons*, II.58.

35. ibid., III.250.

36. Denis Diderot, *Correspondance*, ed. Georges Roth and Jean Varloot, 16 vols. (Paris, 1954–70), VII.98.

37. *Salons*, III.251.

38. ibid., p.252.

39. *Souvenirs*, I.35.

40. See Olivier Blanc, *Madame de Bonneuil, femme galante et agent secret* (Paris, 1987).

41. *Souvenirs*, I.49.

42. ibid., I.96-7.
43. Jean-Jacques Rousseau, *La Nouvelle Héloïse*, in *Oeuvres complètes*, II.23.
44. ibid., p.24.
45. *Souvenirs*, I.45.
46. ibid., p.38-9.

2

1. *Souvenirs*, I.50-1.
2. *Journal de l'inspecteur d'Hémery*, quoted in Benedetta Craveri, *Madame du Deffand and Her World*, trans. Teresa Waugh (London, 1994), p.93.
3. *Souvenirs*, I.56.
4. Quoted in Craveri, p.94.
5. ibid., p.96.
6. See Michel Gallet, 'La maison de Madame Vigée Le Brun rue du Gros-Chenet', *Gazette des beaux-arts*, LVI (1960), p.276.
7. *Souvenirs*, I.89.
8. ibid., p.53.
9. See Francis Haskell, *Rediscoveries in Art* (London, 1976), p.18.
10. See A. P. de Mirimonde, 'Les Opinions de M. Lebrun sur la peinture hollandaise', *Revue des arts* 6 (1956), p.209.
11. *Souvenirs*, I.53.
12. ibid., p.54.
13. See Edmond and Jules de Goncourt, *La femme au dix-huitième siècle* (Paris, 1862). p.187.
14. *Souvenirs*, I.93.
15. ibid., I.54.
16. Papiers Tripier Le Franc, MfB XXXIII.27853-5.
17. *Souvenirs*, I.54.
18. ibid., I.54-5.
19. Papiers Tripier Le Franc, MfB XXXIII.27246-7.
20. See Gilberte-Emile Mâle, 'Jean-Baptiste-Pierre Le Brun (1748-1813). Son rôle dans la restauration des tableaux du Louvre', *Mémoires de la Fédération des sociétés historiques et archéologiques de Paris et de l'île de France*, VIII (1956); also Colin B. Bailey, 'Lebrun et le commerce d'art pendant le Blocus continental', *Revue de l'art*, 63 (1984).
21. See Haskell, p.18.
22. See Gallet, p.284, n.18.
23. *Souvenirs*, I.78.
24. ibid., I.79.
25. ibid., I.90.

26. See, for example, *Lettre de Madame Lebrun à Monsieur de Calonne* (n.p., 1789) and *Réponse de Monsieur de Calonne à la dernière – lettre de Madame Lebrun* (n.p. 1789) – the second allegedly by Gorsas.
27. Le Brun, *Précis historique*, pp.12–13.
28. *Souvenirs*, I.93.
30. See comte Armand d'Allonville, *Mémoires secrets de 1770 à 1830*, 6 vols (Paris, 1838–45), I.123.
31. *Souvenirs*, I.90.
32. See Schama, *Citizens*, p.233; also Aileen Ribeiro, *The Art of Dress: Fashion in England and France, 1750-1800* (New Haven and London, 1995), p.50.
33. For both quotations, see Robert Lacour-Gayet, *Calonne, financier, réformateur, contre-révolutionnaire 1734–1802* (Paris, 1963), p.63.
34. ibid., p.92.
35. *Souvenirs*, I.91.
36. ibid., I.92.
37. ibid., I.93.
38. *Salons*, III.118.
39. See Philip Mansel, *The Court of France 1789–1830* (Cambridge, 1988).
40. *Souvenirs*, I.85–6.
41. ibid., p.88.
42. ibid., p.79.
43. See *Mémoires du prince de Talleyrand*, ed. duc de Broglie, 3 vols (Paris, 1891), I.49.
44. *Souvenirs*, I.79.
45. ibid., p.82–3.
46. ibid., p.83.
47. ibid., p.84.
48. ibid., p.83.
49. ibid., p.55.
50. Laclos, ed. cit., p.170.
51. *Souvenirs*, I.34.
52. Bachaumont, XXIV.103.
53. *Souvenirs*, II.315.
54. *Paradoxe sur le comédien* in *Oeuvres esthétiques*, ed. Paul Vernière (Paris, 1968), p.341.
55. ibid., pp.347–8.
56. *Souvenirs*, I.239.
57. ibid., p.240.
58. See P. J. B. Nougaret, *Anecdotes secrets du dix-huitième siècle*, 2 vols (Paris, 1808), II.284.
59. See A. de Montaigon ed., *Procès-verbaux de l'Académie royale de*

peinture et de sculpture, 10 vols (Paris, 1875–92), 154–6; Anne Marie Passez, *Adélaïde Labille-Guiard, 1749–1803* (Paris, 1973), p.18; Joseph Baillio, 'Marie-Antoinette et ses enfants par Madame Vigée Le Brun', *L'Oeil* 308 (1981), p.38.

60. *Souvenirs*, I.77.
61. ibid., p.76.
62. ibid., p.77.
63. ibid.
64. *Salons*, I.113.
65. ibid., p.208.
66. ibid., III.188.
67. See Marianne Roland Michel, *Anne Vallayer-Coster 1744–1818* (London, 1970), p.43.
68. See Mary D. Sheriff, *The Exceptional Woman* (Chicago, 1996), p.74.

3

1. See Danielle Rice, 'Vigée Le Brun vs. Labille-Guiard: A Rivalry in Context', *Proceedings of the 11th Annual Meeting of the Western Society for French History*, 3–5 November 1983 (Lawrence, Kansas, 1984).
2. *Souvenirs*, I.232.
3. Germaine Greer, *The Obstacle Race* (London, 1979), p.99.
4. *Souvenirs*, I.90.
5. See Charles Oulmont, *Les Femmes-peintres du XVIIIe siècle* (Paris, 1928), p.25.
6. *Souvenirs*, II.244.
7. Bachaumont, XXIV.4.
8. ibid., p.5.
9. *Année littéraire*, 1783, p.263.
10. *Observations de Monsieur le marquis de S . . . capitaine de cavalerie sur quelques tableaux exposés cette année au Salon* (MS., Collection Deloynes, Bibliothèque nationale, Paris, LI.1345), p.291–2.
11. Le Brun, *Précis historique*, p.8.
12. See Daniel and Guy Wildenstein, *Documents complémentaires au catalogue de l'oeuvre de Louis David* (Paris, 1973), p.23 (letter of 21 July 1787).
13. *Journal de Paris* (1785), p.788.
14. *Souvenirs*, I.89.
15. Rousseau, ed. cit., IV.768.
16. *Salons*, III.39.
17. See her *Histoire des salons de Paris*, 6 vols (Paris, 1837–8), VI.152ff.
18. ibid., p.185.
19. *Souvenirs*, I.40.

20. Chateaubriand, *Mémoires d'outre-tombe*, ed. Maurice Levaillant and Georges Molinier, 2 vols (Paris 1958), I.116–17.
21. Bachaumont, XXX.161; *Minos au Sallon* [*sic*] (Paris, 1785), p.22.
22. Baronne d'Oberkirch, *Mémoires sur la cour de Louis XVI*, quoted in the catalogue *Elisabeth Louise Vigée Le Brun 1755–1842* (exhibition at Kimbell Art Museum, Fort Worth, 1982), ed. Joseph Baillio, p.81.
23. *Souvenirs*, I.60.
24. See Mildred Archer, *India and British Portraiture 1770–1825* (London, 1989), p.75.
25. *Souvenirs*, I.61.
26. *Journal d'émigration*, ed. Ernest d'Hauterive (Paris, 1912), p.242.
27. *Le Deuxième Sexe*, 2 vols (Paris, 1949), II.550.
28. Madame de Genlis, *Mémoires*, 10 vols (Paris, 1825), II.29.
29. *Souvenirs*, I.298–9.
30. ibid., p.299.
31. *Mémoires sur la vie privée de Marie-Antoinette, suivis de Souvenirs et anecdotes*, ed. F. Barrière, 3 vols (Paris, 1822), I.138ff.
32. ibid., p.141.
33. D'Abrantès, I.275.
34. *Mémoires*, ed. Charles Nicoullaud, 4 vols (Paris, 1907–8), I.33.
35. *Histoire des salons de Paris*, I.11–12.
36. *Souvenirs*, I.128.
37. ibid., p.123–4.
38. ibid., p.124.
39. Gouverneur Morris, *Diary and Letters*, ed. Anne Cary Morris, 2 vols (London, 1889), I.79.
40. D'Espinchal, p.151.
41. *Souvenirs*, I.125.
42. ibid., loc. cit.
43. ibid., p.126.
44. ibid., p.124.
45. ibid., p.126.
46. ibid., p.127.
47. See Henning Bock, 'Ein Bildnis von Prinz Heinrich Lubormirski als Genius des Ruhms von Elisabeth Vigée Lebrun', *Niederdeutsche Beiträge zur Kunstgeschichte*, XVI (1977), p.87.
48. *Souvenirs*, I.102.
49. ibid., p.104.
50. ibid., p.106.
51. ibid., p.105.
52. See Baillio, 'Marie-Antoinette et ses enfants'.
53. *Mémoires sur la vie privée de Marie-Antoinette*, I.95–6.

54. Quoted in Madge Garland, 'Rose Bertin: Minister of Fashion', *Apollo* LXXXVII (1968), p.42.
55. Ribeiro, *The Art of Dress*, pp.70–1.
56. *Souvenirs*, I.66.
57. ibid., p.68.
58. ibid., p.66.
59. ibid., p.66.
59. ibid., p.69.
60. James Northcote, *The Life of Sir Joshua Reynolds*, 2 vols (London, 1819), II.100.
61. Honoré de Balzac, *Ursule Mirouët, La Comédie humaine*, ed. P.-G. Castex, 12 vols (Paris, 1976–81), III.810.
62. See Marcia Pointon, 'Portrait-painting as a Business Enterprise in London in the 1780s', *Art History*, 7 (1984), p.187.
63. Bachaumont, XXXVI.351.
64. ibid., pp.349 and 347.
65. *Souvenirs*, I.69.
66. See John Whitehead, *The French Interior in the Eighteenth Century* (London, 1992), p.15.
67. See Paula Rea Radisich, ' "Qui peut définir les femmes?": Vigée Le Brun's Portraits of an Artist', *Eighteenth-Century Studies*, 25 (1991–2), p.447.
68. *Souvenirs*, I.130.
69. ibid., p.131.
70. ibid., p.132.
71. ibid., p.133.
72. ibid., p.144.
73. ibid., p.139.
74. See Gallet, p.277.
75. ibid., p.280.
76. ibid., p.284.
77. *Souvenirs*, I.142.
78. ibid., p.141.
79. ibid., p.139.
80. ibid., II.248.
81. ibid., I.142.
82. Marquise de la Tour du Pin, *Journal d'une femme de cinquante ans*, 2 vols (Paris, 1924–5), I.174.
83. *Souvenirs*, II.259.
84. See Gabriel de Broglie, *Madame de Genlis* (Paris, 1985), p.128.
85. D'Espinchal, p.335.
86. *Souvenirs*, I.144.

87. ibid., p.148.
88. ibid., p.143.
89. ibid., p.145.
90. ibid., p.148.

4

1.   *Souvenirs*, I.147.
2.   Edmund Burke, *A Philosophical Enquiry into the Origin of Our Ideas on the Sublime and the Beautiful*, 2nd ed. (London, 1759; facsimile reprint Menston, 1970), p.58.
3.   *Souvenirs*, I.148.
4.   See Frank Brady and Frederick A. Pottle eds, *Boswell on the Grand Tour: Italy, Corsica and France 1765–6* (Melbourne, London and Toronto, 1955), p.23.
5.   Hester Piozzi, *Observations and Reflections Made in the Course of a Journey Through France, Italy and Germany*, 2 vols (London, 1789), I.36.
6.   Marie-Jeanne Roland, *Voyage en Suisse 1787* (Neuchâtel, 1937), p.110.
7.   Arthur Young, *Travels in France and Italy during the Years 1787, 1788 and 1789* (London, 1911), p.299.
8.   Chateaubriand, *Oeuvres romanesques et voyages*, ed. Maurice Regard, 2 vols (Paris, 1969), II.1433.
9.   Creuzé de Lesser, *Voyage en Italie et en Sicile* (Paris, 1806), pp.16–17.
10. Ed. cit., I.162.
11. *Souvenirs*, I.149.
12. ibid., p.36.
13. Young, p.233.
14. See, for example, Vincent Woodrow Beach, *Charles X of France: His Life and Times* (London, n.d.).
15. D'Espinchal, p.188.
16. ibid., p.163.
17. *Souvenirs*, I.149.
18. ibid., p.150.
19. ibid., p.261.
20. ibid., p.151.
21. ibid., p.152.
22. ibid., p.196.
23. *Correspondance de l'Académie de France à Rome*, ed. Jules Guiffrey, 18 vols (Paris, 1887–1912), XV.388.
24. *Souvenirs*, I.154.
25. ibid., p.248.
26. ibid., p.155.

27. ibid., p.157.
28. Geneviève Gennari, *Le Premier Voyage de Madame de Staël en Italie, et la genèse de 'Corinne'* (Paris, 1947), p.99.
29. *Souvenirs*, I.160.
30. Nathalie de Kourakine, *Souvenirs des voyages* (Moscow, 1903), p.245.
31. Jean Gigoux, *Causeries sur les artistes de mon temps* (Paris, 1885), p.102.
32. *Correspondance*, ed. Guiffrey, XV.401.
33. ibid., p.403.
34. Eugène Müntz, 'Lettres de Madame Le Brun relatives à son portrait de la galerie des Offices', *Nouvelles Archives de l'art français*, 1874–5, p.457.
35. See Radisich, p.461.
36. *Souvenirs*, I.162.
37. Madame de Staël, *Corinne, ou l'Italie*, ed. Simone Balayé (Paris, 1985), p.47.
38. *Oeuvres romanesques et voyages*, II.1476.
39. Piozzi, I.378.
40. *Souvenirs*, I.164.
41. ibid., p.165.
42. See Ghislain de Diesbach, *Histoire de l'émigration*, revised edition (Paris, 1984), p.438.
43. D'Espinchal, p.80.
44. *Correspondance*, ed. Guiffrey, XV.441.
45. ibid., p.367.
46. *Souvenirs*, I.168.
47. Winckelmann, 'Freundschaftliche Briefe', *Werke*, ed. Joseph Eiselein, 12 vols (Osnabrück, 1965), X.169.
48. *Souvenirs*, I.168.
49. ibid., p.169.
50. ibid., p.170.
51. *Souvenirs*, II.309.
52. ibid., I.187.
53. ibid., p.167.
54. Goethe, *Italienische Reise*, ed. Andreas Beyer and Norbert Miller, *Sämtliche Werke*, 20 vols (Munich, 1985–91), XV.467–8.
55. ibid., p.609.
56. See Peter Walch, 'Angelica Kauffman', Ph.D.thesis, Princeton University, 1968, p.1 ff.
57. See Boek, p.84.
58. See William S. Childe-Pemberton, *The Earl-Bishop*, 2 vols (London, 1924), I.419.

59. See *Civiltà del '700 a Napoli 1374–1799*, 2 vols (Naples, 1980), I.314.
60. *Souvenirs*, I.167.
61. See Joseph Govani, *Mémoires secrets et critiques des cours, des gouvernements et des moeurs des principaux états de l'Italie*, 3 vols (Paris, 1793), II.158.
62. Lady Anne Miller, *Letters from Italy in the Years 1770 and 1771*, 2 vols (London, 1776), II.193.
63. *Souvenirs*, I.171.
64. D'Espinchal, p.74.
65. John Moore, *A View of Society and Manners in Italy*, 5th ed., 2 vols (London, 1790), I.386.
66. *Bergeret et Fragonard: Journal inédit d'un voyage en Italie, 1773–4*, ed. A. Tornézy (Paris, 1895), entry of 10.12.73; d'Espinchal, p.75.
67. *Souvenirs*, I.176.
68. Piozzi, I.407.
69. *Souvenirs*, I.180.
70. D'Espinchal, p.80.
71. See Angela Rosenthal, 'Kauffman and Portraiture', in *Angelica Kauffman*, ed. Wendy Wassyng Roworth (Brighton, 1992), p.96.
72. *Souvenirs*, I.182.
73. ibid., p.184.
74. ibid., p.186.
75. 'Freundschaftliche Briefe', *Werke*, X.161.
76. See Childe-Pemberton, I.6.
77. *Souvenirs*, I.186.
78. ibid., loc. cit.
79. ibid., p.172.
80. Papiers Tripier Le Franc, MfB XXXIV.28618–25.
81. *Correspondance*, ed. Guiffrey, XV.413.

5

1. *Souvenirs*, I.196.
2. *Werke*, X.260.
3. Saint-Non, *Voyage pittoresque de Naples et de Sicile*, 5 vols (Paris, 1781–6), I.239.
4. *Corinne*, p.287; *Mme de Staël: Choix des Lettres*, ed. Georges Solovieff (Paris, 1970).
5. See Gennari, p.78.
6. Saint-Non, I.224–5.
7. *Souvenirs*, I.196.
8. ibid., p.197.
9. Comte de Ségur, *Mémoires, ou Souvenirs et anecdotes*, 3 vols

(Stuttgart, 1829), II.245; see also d'Oberkirch, p.152.

10. See Eleanor Tufts, 'Elisabeth Louise Vigée Le Brun', *Art Journal*, XLII (1982), p.337.

11. *Souvenirs*, I.197.

12. By Sotheby's.

13. Brady and Pottle, p.62.

14. *Souvenirs*, I.204.

15. *Correspondance*, ed. Guiffrey, XVI.9.

16. *Souvenirs*, I.217.

17. ibid., II.64.

18. See Childe-Pemberton, I.i.

19. See Carlo Knight, 'I Luogi di delizie di William Hamilton', *Napoli noblissima*, XX (1981).

20. *Souvenirs*, I.199.

21. See *The Hamilton and Nelson Papers*, ed. Alfred Morrison, 2 vols (London, 1893), I.49.

22. *Correspondance*, ed. Guiffrey, XV.436.

23. *Souvenirs*, I.199.

24. On all this, see Susan Sontag, *The Volcano Lover: A Romance* (London, 1992), pp.165–6.

25. *Souvenirs*, I.199.

26. ibid., p.200.

27. On this subject see Kirsten Gram Holström, *Monodrama, Attitudes, Tableaux Vivants* (Stockholm, 1967).

28. See Joseph Burke, *English Art 1714–1800* (Oxford, 1976), p.476f.

29. *Souvenirs*, I.201.

30. ibid., p.202.

31. ibid., p.201.

32. See Juliana de Krüdener, *Valérie (1803)*, ed. Michel Mercier (Paris, 1974), p.66.

33. See, for example, d'Espinchal, p.89.

34. *Diary and Letters*, I.453.

35. Dorothy Margaret Stuart, *Dearest Bess: The Life and Times of Lady Elizabeth Foster* (London, 1955), p.59.

36. *Souvenirs*, I.202.

37. Doyen's description of Grimod de la Reynière's wife: *Souvenirs*, II.263.

38. Boigne, I.114–15.

39. See Meyer, p.184f.

40. *Souvenirs*, I.209.

41. ibid., p.210.

42. *Oeuvres romanesques et voyages*, II.1469.

43. *Souvenirs*, I.212.
44. See *The Golden Age of Naples: Art and Civilisation under the Bourbons 1734–1805*, 2 vols (Detroit, 1981), I.1–3.
45. *Sämtliche Werke*, XV.408.
46. D'Espinchal, p.83.
47. *Souvenirs*, I.230.
48. ibid., p.231.
49. ibid., p.199.
50. ibid., p.231.
51. Quoted in Harold Acton, *The Bourbons of Naples (1734–1825)* (London, 1956), p.219.
52. *Observations and Reflections*, I.92.
53. *Correspondance*, ed. Guiffrey, XVI.36.
54. *Souvenirs*, I.219.
55. *Correspondance*, ed. Guiffrey, XVI.36.
56. Deloynes, XVII.442, p.10.
57. See Baillio, catalogue *Elisabeth Louise Vigée Le Brun*, p.95.
58. *Rome, Naples et Florence*, ed. Henri Martineau (Paris, 1950), p.40.
59. *Souvenirs*, I.216.
60. ibid., p.222.
61. ibid., p.226.
62. Quoted in Acton, p.187.
63. See Govani, I.31, 260.
64. *Souvenirs*, I.227.
65. Baronne du Montet, *Souvenirs 1785–1866* (Paris, 1904), p.98.
66. *Souvenirs*, I.228.
67. See Rice, p.134r.
68. *Souvenirs*, I.232.
69. ibid., p.241.
70. ibid., p.233.
71. See Gianni Guadalupi, *Elisabeth Vigée Le Brun: Dalla Corte di Versailles alla corte di Napoli, 1781–1790*, 2 vols (Milan, 1989), I.13.
72. See Leone Vicchi, *Les Français à Rome pendant la Convention [1792–1795)* (Paris, 1893), p.cxlviii.
73. D'Espinchal, p.81.
74. *Werke*, X.129.
75. ibid., p.155.
76. Young, p.256.
77. *Souvenirs*, I.202.
78. See Gennari, p.105.
79. *Corinne*, p.420.
80. See Judith Nowinski, 'Baronne Dominique Vivant Denon (1741–1825)'

Ph.D. thesis, Columbia University, 1968, *passim.*

81. *Souvenirs,* I.245–6.
82. ibid., p.246.
83. D'Espinchal, p.121.
84. *Souvenirs,* pp.246 and 249.
85. Vivant Denon, *L'Originale e il ritratto* (Bassano, 1792), p.x f.
86. *Souvenirs,* I.251.
87. ibid., p.248.
88. *Oeuvres Complètes,* ed. cit., Rousseau, I.315.
89. See *De l'amour* on the phenomenon of crystallisation.
90. *Souvenirs,* I.258.
91. ibid., p.264.

6

1. Du Montet, p.35.
2. *Correspondance intime du comte de Vaudreuil et du comte d'Artois,* ed. Léonce Pingaud, 2 vols (Paris, 1889), I.90.
3. See Stella Musulin, *Vienna in the Age of Metternich* (London, 1975), p.21.
4. *Souvenirs,* I.284.
5. ibid., p.266.
6. ibid., p.279.
7. See Ludwig Kohl, *Neue Bilder aus dem Leben der Musik und ihrer Meister* (Munich, 1870), p.130.
8. See Alexandre de Laborde, *Voyage pittoresque en Autriche,* 3 vols (Paris, 1821–2), II.38, 279.
9. See *Voyage de deux Français dans le nord de l'Europe,* 5 vols (Paris, 1796), V.95; also Soulavie, *Mémoires historiques et politiques du règne de Louis XVI,* 6 vols (Paris, 1801), VI.41.
10. See Ribeiro, *Dress in Eighteenth-Century Europe,* p.73.
11. Abbé Georgel, *Voyage à Saint-Pétersbourg en 1799–1800* (Paris, 1818), p.77.
12. *Souvenirs,* I.282.
13. ibid., pp. 282–3.
14. ibid., p.286.
15. ibid., p.277.
16. See Henry Swinburne, *The Courts of Europe at the Close of the Last Century,* ed. Charles White, 2 vols (London, 1841), I.345.
17. See Friedrich Nicolai, *Beschreibung einer Reise durch Deutschland und die Schweiz im Jahre 1781,* 8 vols Jacques Rambaud, second edition, 2 vols (Paris, 1912), II.24.
19. *Souvenirs,* I.267.

20. See Eduard Hanslick, *Geschichte des Concertwesens in Wien*, 2 vols (Vienna, 1869), I.47; Rudolph Procházka, *Mozart in Prag* (Prague, 1899), p.30ff (letter of 24 March 1786 to Leopold Mozart).

21. *Memoirs of the Courts of Berlin, Dresden, Warsaw and Vienna in the Years 1777, 1778 and 1789*, 2 vols (London 1799), II.241.

22. *Souvenirs*, I.267.

23. See Eduard Vehse, *Geschichte der deutschen Höfe seit der Reformation*, 34 vols (Hamburg, 1851–60), XV.22.

24. D'Espinchal, p.145.

25. Du Montet, p.235.

26. *Souvenirs*, I.268.

27. ibid., p.267.

28. ibid., p.270.

29. *Correspondance intime*, I.xv.

30. *Souvenirs*, I.271.

31. See, for example, Wraxhall, II.466.

32. See Jean Chatelus, *Peindre à Paris au xviiie siècle* (Nîmes, 1991), p.249.

33. *Souvenirs*, I.270.

34. ibid., p.279.

35. Hanslick, I.3, 46.

36. See Gräfin Lili Thürheim, *Mein Leben*, ed. René Van Rhyn (Munich, 1913), p.135.

37. See Alexandre Wassiltchikow, *Les Razoumovski*, trans. Alexandre Brückner, 3 vols (Halle, 1893–4), II.ii.79.

38. See Nicolai, V.248.

39. *Souvenirs*, I.281.

40. ibid., p.278.

41. See comte Fleury, *Souvenirs du congrès de Vienne* (Paris, 1901), p.36.

42. Comte d'Allonville, *Mémoires secrets de 1770 à 1830*, 6 vols (Paris, 1838–45), IV.78.

43. *Souvenirs*, I.273.

44. See Madame de Staël, *Correspondance générale*, ed. Béatrice Jasinski (Paris, 1960), VI (letter of 18 February 1806).

45. *Souvenirs d'un académicien*, ed. Dr Cabbarès, 2 vols (Paris, n.d.), I.169.

46. See d'Allonville, II.338.

47. Lovelace is the villain-hero in Samuel Richardson's *Clarissa* and Valmont his counterpart in Laclos's *Les Liaisons dangereuses*.

48. *Souvenirs*, I.285.

49. *Souvenirs*, II.11.

50. ibid., I.284–5.

51. ibid., p.281.
52. *Correspondance intime*, II.166.
53. ibid., p.174.
54. *Souvenirs*, I.286.
55. See *Nouveau Guide par Vienne* (Paris, 1792), p.196.
56. *Souvenirs*, I.280.
57. For example, *Panorama von Wiens Umgebung* (Vienna, 1807), p.278.
58. *Souvenirs*, I.281.
59. See Max Friedländer, *Landscape, Portrait, Still-Life: Their Origin and Development*, trans. R. F. C. Hull (Oxford, 1949), p.112.
60. *Souvenirs*, I.288.
61. *Correspondance intime*, II.223.
62. *Souvenirs*, I.287.
63. ibid., p.278.
64. *Correspondance intime*, II.189.
65. ibid., p.195.
66. *Souvenirs*, I.290.
67. ibid., p.291.
68. Fleury, p.10f.
69. Quoted in *Souvenirs*, II.293.
70. ibid., p.294.
71. See Maria Päwlik, 'Emigranten der französischen Revolution in Österreich (1789–1814)', Dokt. Diss. University of Vienna, 1967, p.137.
72. See Hans Danzmayr, *Der Kahlenberg* (Josefsdorf, 1978), p.15f.
73. *Souvenirs*, I.289.
74. ibid., p.290:

> For having robbed the empyrean
> As Prometheus did
> You deserve punishment…
> Forget your nation,
> Honoured by your genius,
> But now a land of desolation!
> May my mountain, fortunate
> In the proud possession
> Of the talents by which the earth is ravished, astonished,
> Be for ever celebrated in our songs!

7

1. *Souvenirs*, II.269.
2. ibid., p.301.
3. ibid., p.302.

4. ibid., p.303.
5. *Mémoires, ou souvenirs et anecdotes*, II.217.
6. See Gladys Scott Thompson, *Catherine the Great and the Expansion of Russia* (London, 1947), p.240.
7. *Mémoires et lettres*, new edition (Paris, 1923), p.292.
8. *Souvenirs*, I.343.
9. See Whitehead, p.31.
10. See Léonce Pingaud, *Les Français en Russie et les Russes en France* (Paris, 1886), p.196.
11. See *Vorontzov Archive*, ed. Petr Bartenev, 40 vols (Moscow, 1863–1917), VIII.130.
12. *Souvenirs*, I.343.
13. ibid., pp.309–10.
14. ibid., pp.305–6.
15. ibid., p.304.
16. ibid., p.305.
17. See *Russia under Western Eyes, 1517-1825*, ed. Anthony Cross (London, 1971), p.227.
18. *Souvenirs*, I.311.
19. See Emile Haumont, *La Culture française en Russie (1700–1900)*, second edition (Paris, 1913), p.70.
20. See Tamara Talbot Rice, 'Influences in Russian Art and Architecture', in *The Eighteenth Century in Russia*, ed. J. G. Garrard (Oxford, 1973), p.283.
21. See Scott Thompson, p.245.
22. *Souvenirs*, I.307.
23. ibid., p.306.
24. Prince de Ligne, *Oeuvres choisies*, ed. Gustave Charlier, 2nd ed. (Brussels, 1944), p.41.
25. See John T. Alexander, *Catherine the Great: Life and Legend* (New York and Oxford, 1989), p.324.
26. For example, F. C. P. Mason's *Mémoires of Catherine II and the court of St Petersburg*.
27. *Souvenirs*, I.306.
28. *Oeuvres choisies*, p.41.
29. See K. Waliszewski, *Le Roman d'une impératrice: Catherine II de Russie* (Paris, 1902), p.447.
30. *Oeuvres choisies*, p.42.
31. ibid., p.147.
32. See Lucien Perey, *Histoire d'une grande dame au XVIIIe siècle: la comtesse Hélène Potocka* (Paris, 1888), p.101f.
33. *Souvenirs*, II.22.

34. Prince de Ligne, *Mémoires, lettres et pensées*, ed. Chantal Thomas (Paris, 1989), p.99.
35. See G. P. Gooch, *Catherine the Great and Other Studies* (London, 1954), p.50.
36. See Alexander, p.202.
37. *Souvenirs*, II.19.
38. ibid., p.24.
39. *Mémoires*, IV.283.
40. Count Cobentzl to comte de Merry, St Petersburg 4.3.1793, in Frankreich Varia 1786–93, Karton 48, Vienna, Haus-, Hof-, und Staatsarchiv.
41. See Gooch, p.103.
42. *Mémoires 1771–1815*, ed. Alphonse Roserot, 2 vols (Paris, 1896), I.38.
43. *Souvenirs*, I.323.
44. See Perey, p.103f.
45. *Vorontzov Archive*, VIII.121.
46. Friedrich Melchior Grimm, *Correspondance artistique avec Catherine II*, ed. L. Réau (*Archives de l'art français*, nouvelle période, vol XVII (1932)), p.199.
47. ibid., p.200.
48. *Souvenirs*, p.305.
49. *Souvenirs*, ed. K. Waliszewski (Paris, 1910), pp.96–7.
50. *Souvenirs*, I.320.
51. *Vorontzov Archive*, VIII.113.
52. *Souvenirs*, I.319.
53. ibid., p.320.
54. ibid., p.345.
55. ibid., p.314.
56. See abbé Jean-François Georgel, *Voyage à St-Pétersbourg en 1799–1800* (Paris, 1818), p.196.
57. See catalogue *Elisabeth Louise Vigée Le Brun*, ed. Baillio, p.114.
58. *Souvenirs*, I.340.
59. See Nikolenko, p.93.
60. See Waliszewski, *Autour d'un Trône: Catherine II de Russie, ses collaborateurs, ses amis, ses favoris*, 8th ed. (Paris, 1905), p.418f.
61. See Scott Thompson, p.232.
62. Duchesse de Saulx-Tavanes, *Mémoires (1791–1806)*, ed. marquis de Valons (Paris, 1934), p.66.
63. See Erika Thiel, *Geschichte des Kostüms* (Berlin, 1963), p.490; Haumont, p.205.
64. Quoted in Alison Adburgham, *Shops and Shopping 1800–1914* (London, 1964), p.1.

65. *The Stranger in France, or A Tour from Devonshire to Paris* (London, 1803), p.88.
66. *Souvenirs*, I.333.
67. ibid., p.334.
68. ibid., pp.334–5.
69. *Mémoires, ou souvenirs et anecdotes*, II.239.
70. ibid., p.226.
71. See Cross, p.208.
72. *Souvenirs*, I.335.
73. See Book 12; also Haumont, p.214.
74. *Mémoires et lettres*, p.238.
75. See *La France et la Russie au siècle des Lumières* (Paris, 1986), p.438.
76. *Histoire et mémoires*, II.145f.
77. See Haumont, pp.116–17.
78. *Souvenirs*, I.345.
79. ibid., pp.330–1.
80. See *La France et la Russie*, p.440.
81. See Isabel de Madariaga, *Russia in the Age of Catherine the Great* (London, 1981), p.329.
82. *Correspondance artistique*, p.52 (letter of 16 April 1779).
83. ibid., p.135 (letter of 19 November 1779).
84. *Souvenirs*, II.8–9.
85. ibid., pp.9–11.
86. ibid., p.11.
87. ibid., p.16.

8

1. *Souvenirs*, II.23.
2. ibid., p.24.
3. ibid., p.25.
4. See Gooch, p.22.
5. *Souvenirs*, II.31.
6. ibid., p.30.
7. See Roderick E. McGrew, *Paul I of Russia 1754–1801* (Oxford, 1992), p.211.
8. *Souvenirs*, II.29.
9. ibid., p.34.
10. ibid., p.38.
11. ibid., p.38.
12. ibid., p.39.
13. ibid., p.43.
14. See Ségur, *Mémoires, ou Souvenirs et anecdotes*, II.153.

15. *Souvenirs*, II.44.
16. ibid., p.50.
17. ibid., p.51.
18. Papiers Tripier Le Franc, MfB XXXIV.28644–50.
19. *Souvenirs*, II.53.
20. *Lettres*, ed. Gérard-Gailly, 3 vols (Paris, 1953–7), II.325 (letter of 11 August 1677).
21. *Souvenirs*, II.53.
22. ibid., p.56.
23. ibid., pp.56–7.
24. *A la recherche du temps perdu*, general editor Jean-Yves Tadié, 4 vols (Paris, 1987–9), II.39.
25. *Souvenirs*, II.57.
26. See *Voyage de deux Français dans le nord de l'Europe*, III.270–1.
27. *Souvenirs*, II.62–3.
28. ibid., p.61.
29. ibid., p.66.
30. See Waliszewski, *Autour d'un trône*, p.20.
31. *Souvenirs*, II.68.
32. *Autour d'un trône*, pp.22–3.
33. *Souvenirs*, II.67.
34. ibid., p.68.
35. *Autour d'un trône*, pp.23–5.
36. See Charles Sterling, *Great French Paintings in the Hermitage* (New York, 1958), p.11.
37. *Souvenirs*, II.70.
38. 'They change their sky, not their minds,
    Those who hasten across the sea.'
39. *Souvenirs*, II.73.
40. ibid., p.79.
41. ibid., p.80.
42. ibid., p.81.

9

1. *Souvenirs*, II.81.
2. ibid., p.82.
3. ibid., pp.82–3.
4. ibid., p.84.
5. ibid., p.85.
6. ibid., p.86.
7. ibid., p.87.
8. *De l'Allemagne*, ed. comtesse Jean de Pange with Simone Balayé,

5 vols (Paris, 1958), I.236.

9.   *Souvenirs*, II.91.

10. ibid., p.92.

11. ibid., p.88.

12. ibid., p.90.

13. See Papiers Tripier Le Franc, MfB XXXIV.28610.

14. *Précis historique*, p.16.

15. ibid., p.17.

16. ibid., p.18.

17. ibid., p.22.

18. *Souvenirs*, II.90.

19. ibid., p.91.

20. ibid., p.94.

21. ibid., p.95.

22. Benjamin Constant, *Correspondance générale*, ed. C. P. Courtney (Tübingen, 1993–), I.50.

23. *Souvenirs*, II.95.

24. Staël, *Correspondance générale*, I.152.

25. ibid., p.166.

26. *Souvenirs*, II.97.

27. Staël, I.136–7.

28. *Souvenirs*, II.98.

29. ibid., p.99.

30. ibid., p.100.

31. ibid., p.101.

32. Brifaut, p.142.

33. *Causeries*, p.100.

34. *Souvenirs*, II.110.

35. *Mémoires*, I.336–7.

36. See Françoise Wagener, *Madame Récamier* (Paris, 1986), p.48.

37. ibid., p.111.

38. *Souvenirs*, II.102.

39. *Correspondance*, VII.98.

40. ed. cit., p.14.

41. *Souvenirs*, II.109.

42. See Thomas W. Gaehtgens and Jacques Lugand, *Joseph-Marie Vien peintre du roi (1716–1809)* (Paris, 1988), p.82.

43. *Souvenirs*, II.108.

44. *Mes Souvenirs* (Paris, 1853), p.68.

45. *Souvenirs*, II.109.

46. See Armand Dayot, *L'Image de la femme* (Paris, 1899), p.315.

47. See Wagener, p.11.

48. *Souvenirs*, II.110.
49. See Wagener, p.118.
50. ibid., p.119.
51. See Christina Colvin, *Maria Edgeworth in France and Switzerland* (Oxford, 1979), p.53.
52. D'Abrantès, IV.9.
53. *Journal: An Englishman in Paris, 1803*, ed. J. P. T. Bury and J. C. Barry (London, 1953), p.7.
54. See Wagener, p.83.
55. Greatheed, p.7.
56. ibid., p.126.
57. *Souvenirs*, II.106.
58. ibid., p.104.
59. ibid., p.112.
60. ibid., p.106.
61. ibid., p.113.
62. D'Abrantès, V.86.
63. ibid., p.266.
64. *Souvenirs*, II.104.
65. Greatheed, p.7.
66. 'Mémoires sur Napoléon', *Oeuvres complètes*, ed. Louis Royer, new ed., 50 vols (Paris, 1968–74), XL.65.
67. *Oeuvres complètes*, XXXIX.65.
68. See Philip Mansel, *The Court of France, 1789–1830* (Cambridge, 1988), p.10.
69. *Mémoires*, III.35.
70. *Souvenirs*, 107–8.
71. *Souvenirs*, II.115.
72. ibid., loc. cit.
73. Greatheed, p.27.
74. 13 October 1802.
75. *Lettre de Madame Vandeul, née Diderot, sur le Salon de l'an X.*
76. *Souvenirs*, II.115.

10

1. See Northcote, II.99–101; Farington, I.261.
2. *Souvenirs*, II.118.
3. See Baert, *Tableau de la Grande Bretagne*, 4 vols (Paris, 1800), IV.219.
4. See Weiner, p.96.
5. Baert, IV.218–9.
6. Lévis, *L'Angleterre*, p.93.
7. See H. Forneron, *Histoire générale des émigrés pendant la Révolution*

française, 3 vols (Paris, 1884–90), II.41.

8. *Mémoires pour servir à l'histoire des moeurs de la fin du dix-huitième siècle*, 3 vols (Paris, 1828), I.234.
9. See E. M. Wilkinson, 'The French Emigrés in England, 1789–1802', 2 vols B. Litt. thesis, University of Oxford, 1952, I.57.
10. See Diesbach, *Histoire de l'émigration*, p.264.
11. *Souvenirs*, II.124.
12. Boigne, I.136.
13. *Mémoires d'outre-tombe*, I.325; see also Forneron, II.48f.
14. See Langlade, pp.228, 248.
15. See Nouvion and Liez, p.189.
16. *Souvenirs*, II.129.
17. *Anecdotes of the Manners and Customs of London*, second edition, 2 vols (London, 1810), II.356.
18. See Roger Portalis, *Henry-Pierre Danloux, peintre de portraits, et son journal pendant l'émigration* (London, 1910), p.224.
19. *Survey of London* (London, 1900–), XXXIV.492.
20. *Souvenirs*, II.118.
21. Farington, II.106.
22. *Modern London* (London, 1804), p.392.
23. *Souvenirs*, II.135.
24. ibid., pp.135–6.
25. ibid., I.203.
26. See William Henry Helm, *Vigée-Lebrun: Her Life, Works and Friendships* (London, 1915), p.150.
27. *Souvenirs*, II.120.
28. *Londres et les Anglais*, 4 vols (Paris, 1804), I.14.
29. *Souvenirs*, II.121.
30. See Lévis, *L'Angleterre*, p.203.
31. *Souvenirs*, II.120.
32. See San Costante, III.78.
33. See Celina Fox, *London – World City 1800–1840* (New Haven/ London, 1992), p.26.
34. Papiers Tripier Le Franc, MfB XXXIII.27490.
35. *Souvenirs*, II.136.
36. See Baert, IV.262.
37. Phillips, p.142.
38. *Souvenirs*, II.131.
39. ibid., p.126.
40. ibid., p.130.
41. ibid., p.131.
42. See Marcia Pointon, 'Portrait-Painting as a Business Enterprise in

London in the 1780s', *Art History*, 7 (1984).

43. *Souvenirs*, II.125.
44. See John Hayes, *The Portrait in British Art* (London, 1991), p.18ff.
45. Baert, IV.181.
46. *Souvenirs*, II.122.
47. See Dan Cruickshank and Neil Burton, *Life in the Georgian City* (London, 1990), p.46.
48. See David Piper, *The English Face* (London, 1957), p.195.
49. *Souvenirs*, II.128.
50. See Ivy Leveson Gower, *The Face Without a Frown: Georgiana, Duchess of Devonshire* (London, 1944), p.173.
51. Tilly, II.16.
52. See Leveson Gower, p.34.
53. See *Georgiana: Extracts from Her Correspondence*, ed. Earl of Bessborough (London, 1953), p.5.
54. *Souvenirs*, II.129.
55. See Lévis, *L'Angleterre*, p.328.
56. See Roy Porter, *London: A Social History* (London, 1994), p.177.
57. *Souvenirs*, I.203.
58. ibid., II.126.
59. See, for example, Madame Sartori, *Petit Tableau de Paris*, 3 vols (Paris, 1818), II.73f.
60. See F. W. J. Hemmings, *Culture and Society in France 1789–1848* (Leicester, 1987), p.79.
61. *Souvenirs*, II.153.
62. ibid., p.122.
63. *The Stranger in France, or A Tour from Devonshire to Paris*, p.177.
64. *Journal*, p.9.
65. 'The English on Sunday', *Beyond Good and Evil*, ed. Oscar Levy, trans. Helen Zimmern (London, 1907), p.109.
66. *Souvenirs*, II.124.
67. ibid., p.138.
68. ibid., p.142.
69. For this and the following references, see Porter, p.97.
70. *Souvenirs*, II.151.
71. ibid., p.150.
72. *Journal d'une femme de cinquante ans*, II.188.
73. *Souvenirs*, II.148.
74. Diesbach, *Histoire de l'émigration*, p.287.
75. *Souvenirs*, II.149.
76. ibid., pp.149–50.
77. ibid., p.145.

78. San Costante, I.234.
79. ed. cit., II.557–8.
80. *Souvenirs*, II.149.
81. *Corinne*, p.363.
82. ibid., p.367.
83. *Souvenirs*, II.122.
84. ibid., p.146.
85. *Memoirs*, 2 vols (London, 1826), I.123.
86. ibid., II.88.
87. ibid., p.109.
88. *Souvenirs*, II.147.
89. ibid., p.148.
90. Baert, p.56.
91. *Souvenirs*, II.148.
92. V. Sackville-West, *Knole and the Sackvilles* (London, 1991), p.18.
93. Farington, II.107.
94. *Souvenirs*, II.140.
95. ibid., p.141.
96. *Northanger Abbey* (London, 1948), p.17.
97. *Souvenirs*, II.143–4.
98. ibid., p.142.
99. ibid., pp.142–3.
100. ibid., p.143.
101. *Northanger Abbey*, p.24.
102. On 24 August 1803.
103. *Court and Private Life in the Time of Queen Charlotte*, ed. Mrs V. Delves Broughton, 2 vols (London, 1887), II.253.
104. ibid., II.252.
105. *Souvenirs*, II.130.
106. ibid., p.131.
107. See Farington, II.35.
108. ibid., p.107.
109. ibid., p.219.
110. *Oriental Tales*, trans. John Hoppner (London, 1805), p. x.
111. ibid., p.xi.
112. ibid., p.dvi.
113. *Souvenirs*, II.134.
114. Hoppner, p.xviii.
115. Farington, II.107.
116. *Journal*, p.32.
117. *Les Salons de Paris*, p.22.
118. See Bailey, art. cit., p.37f.

119. See Sylvie Martin, 'Portraits anglais et français: un approche comparative à travers les textes du XVIIIe siècle', *Gazette des beaux-arts*, CXVII (1991), *passim*.
120. *Souvenirs*, II.123.
121. See Shawe-Taylor, p.7.
122. *Souvenirs*, II.132.
123. ibid., p.152.
124. ibid., p.155.

11

1. *Souvenirs*, II.158.
2. Note in the Tripier Le Franc papers.
3. *Souvenirs*, II.159.
4. See Jean Tulard, *Napoleon: The Myth of the Saviour*, trans. Teresa Waugh (London, 1984), p.253.
5. *Journal et Souvenirs*, p.51.
6. D'Abrantès, VI.135.
7. *Souvenirs*, II.156.
8. ibid., p.157.
9. For all these references, see Roland, p.15ff.
10. ibid., p.19.
11. ibid., p.192.
12. *Souvenirs*, II.162.
13. All this may have occurred on Louise's return trip to Switzerland in 1808: see Sandor Kuthy, 'Elisabeth Louise Vigée Le Brun und das Alphirtenfest in Unspunnen', *Zeitschrift für schweizerische Archäologie und Kunstsgeschichte*, 33 (1976), p.160.
14. *Rêveries du promeneur solitaire*, ed. cit., I.1040–41.
15. Mary Wollstonecraft, *A Vindication of the Rights of Woman*, ed. Sylvana Tomaselli (Cambridge, 1995), p.110f and *passim*.
16. *Souvenirs*, II.178.
17. ibid., p.179.
18. All these are mentioned in a MS. note in the Tripier Le Franc papers, MfB XXXIII.27960.
19. See Jean Aubert, 'Acquisitions recentes. Chambéry: Musée des Beaux-Arts', *Revue du Louvre et des musées de France* (1979), p.400.
20. *Souvenirs*, II.186–7.
21. ibid., p.165.
22. See Sabine Voigt, 'Das Bild einer Künstlerin: Elisabeth Vigée Le Brun', *Philosophicher Taschenkalender*, vol. 2 (1992–3), p.36.
23. *Souvenirs*, II.187.
24. ibid., p.189.

25. On 30.x.1807.
26. See Tripier Le Franc papers, MfB XXXIII.27525.
27. See Yvonne Bezard, *Madame de Staël d'après ses portraits* (Paris and Neuchâtel, 1938), p.7.
28. See marquis de Bombelles, *Journal*, ed. Jean Grassion and Frans Durif (Geneva, 1977–) II.135; Thürheim, p.235.
29. See Bezard, p.3.
30. *Souvenirs*, II.181.
31. See Mario Praz, *On Neoclassicism*, trans. Angus Davidson (London, 1969), p.258.
32. *Souvenirs*, II.181.
33. Damas, II.56.
34. D'Abrantès, V.54.
35. *Souvenirs*, II.184.
36. See Bezard, p.37.
37. Boigne, I.246–7.
38. See Bezard, p.15.
39. *Souvenirs*, II.181–2.
40. ibid., p.182.
41. Staël, *Correspondance*, VI.464.
42. Staël, *Choix de lettres*, p.345.
43. See Charles Eynard, *Madame de Krüdener*, 2 vols (Paris, 1849), I.105.
44. Alphonse de Lamartine, *Histoire de la Restauration*, 8 vols (Paris, 1851–2), II.419, 424.
45. *De l'Allemagne*, I.159–60.
46. ibid., p.161.
47. ibid., p.160.
48. See Marc Fumaroli, *Le genre des genres littéraires: la conversation* (Zaharoff Lecture 1990–1) (Oxford, 1992), p.30.
49. *Souvenirs*, II.184.
50. See Kuthy, p.158ff.
51. ibid., p.160.
52. *De l'Allemagne*, I.281.
53. ibid., p.284.
54. ibid., p.286.
55. *Souvenirs*, II.198.
56. ibid., p.201.
57. *De l'Allemagne*, I.286–7.
58. Quoted in Kuthy, p.161.
59. *Souvenirs*, XX.202.
60. On this and ff., see Kuthy.
61. *Souvenirs*, II.198.

62. See her own note to ibid., p.202.
63. *Souvenirs*, II.183.
64. ibid., p.203.
65. See Jacques and Monique Lay, *Louveciennes mon village* (n.d., n.p.), p.60.
66. *Souvenirs*, II.216–7.
67. ibid., p.204.
68. ibid., p.216.
69. ibid., p.203.
70. ibid., p.203.
71. ibid., p.205.
72. ibid., p.207.
73. ibid., p.208.
74. ibid., p.209.
75. ibid., p.211.
76. ibid., p.212.
77. ibid., I.71.
78. ibid., II.212.
79. See G. Bertier de Sauvigny, *La Restauration* (Paris, 1955), p.351.
80. *Souvenirs*, II.213.
81. See Mansel, *The Court of France*, p.191.

12

1. See G. Bertier de Sauvigny, *Nouvelle Histoire de Paris: La Restauration 1815–1830* (Paris, 1977), p.222.
2. See Brifaut, p.56.
3. *Histoire de la Restauration*, II.419–20.
4. Article 'Français'.
5. ed. cit., p.268.
6. ibid., p.181.
7. ibid., p.184.
8. *Causeries*, p.99.
9. ibid., p.100.
10. See Alfred Sensier, *Etude sur Georges Michel* (Paris, 1873), p.15.
11. Brifaut, p.142.
12. ibid., p.155.
13. Ancelot, p.147.
14. ibid., p.155.
15. Kourakine, p.53.
16. *Souvenirs*, II.317.
17. Brifaut, p.152.
18. Ancelot, p.43.

19. *Mémoires*, I.144.
20. *Souvenirs*, II.317.
21. Ancelot, p.15.
22. ibid., p.24.
23. ibid., p.33.
24. *Souvenirs*, II.311.
25. Ancelot, p.36.
26. See Francine-Dominique Liechtenhan, *Astolphe de Custine, voyageur et philosophe* (Paris & Geneva, 1990), p.10.
27. Ancelot, *Un Salon de Paris 1824 à 1864* (Paris, 1866), p.380.
28. id., *Les Salons de Paris*, p.38.
29. Kourakine, p.79.
30. ibid., p.84.
31. ibid., p.99.
32. See Louis Hautecoeur, *Madame Vigée-Lebrun* (Paris, n.d.), p.122.
33. See Hillairet, II.454.
34. Ancelot, *Les Salons*, p.38.
35. ibid., p.40.
36. Kourakine, p.85.
37. See Papiers Tripier Le Franc, MfB XXXIV.28629.
38. ibid., MfB XXXIV.28658.
39. *Souvenirs*, II.215.
40. Brifaut, p.142.
41. *Causeries*, p.99.
42. See *French Painting 1774–1830: The Age of Revolution* (Detroit and New York, 1975), p.665.
43. *Souvenirs*, II.220.
44. ibid., p.221.
45. ibid., p.223.
46. See Mâle, p.375.
47. See Bailey, pp.36–7.
48. See Papiers Tripier Le Franc, MfB XXXIII.27474ff.
49. ibid., MfB XXXIII.27345. Louise seems to have bought the house from her ex-husband's estate, though she managed to avoid taking over the loan secured on it.
50. ibid., MfB XXXIII.27475.
51. ibid., MfB XXXIII.27532.
52. *Souvenirs*, II.224.
53. Information passed on to me by Dr Joseph Baillio.
54. Papiers Tripier Le Franc, MfB XXXIII.27511–12.
55. ibid., MfB XXXIII.27723.
56. ibid., MfB XXXIII.27724.

57. ibid., MfB XXXIII.27725.
58. *Souvenirs*, II.224.
59. ibid., p.228.
60. ibid., p.225.
61. ibid., p.227.
62. ibid., p.226.
63. ibid., p.229.
64. ibid., p.231.
65. ibid., pp.231–2.
66. ibid., p.232.
67. Papiers Tripier Le Franc, MfB XXXIII.27496.
68. De Bawr, p.67.
69. Papiers Tripier Le Franc, MfB XXXIII.27555.
70. ibid., MfB XXXIV.28756.
71. ibid., MfB XXXIV.28836.
72. ibid., MfB XXXIII.27495.
73. Louvre *dossier* Vigée Le Brun, note of 19 July 1831.
74. Papiers Tripier Le Franc, MfB XXXIV.28732–46.
75. On all this, see MfB XXXIV.28755.
76. See MfB XXXIV.28757.
77. MfB XXXIII.27497–8.
78. See Albert Vuaflart, 'La tombe de Madame Vigée Le Brun à Louveciennes', *Bulletin de la Société de l'histoire de Paris*, 42 (1915), p.iii. Much of the following information on Louise's burial comes from him.
79. *Souvenirs*, I.26.
80. ibid., II.260.
81. De Bawr, pp.10–1.
82. See Papiers Tripier Le Franc, MfB XXXIV.28750.
83. See *Journal des débats* 1 April 1842.
84. *Souvenirs*, II.232.
85. See Papiers Tripier Le Franc, MfB XXXIV.28758ff.
86. MfBXXXIV.28759.
87. MfB XXXIV.28761.
88. MfB XXXIII.27495.

Conclusion

1. See Papiers Tripier Le Franc, MfB XXXIII.28209.
2. See Richard Wendorf, *The Elements of Life* (Oxford, 1991), p.68.
3. *Souvenirs*, I.72.
4. See Wendy Steiner, *Exact Resemblance to Exact Resemblance* (New Haven/London, 1978), p.4.
5. See Linda Nochlin, 'Why Have There Been No Great Women Artists?', *Women, Art and Power and Other Essays* (London, 1989), p.148f.
6. See Sister Wendy Beckett, *Sister Wendy's Odyssey* (London, 1993), p.64.
7. See Henry Lapauze ed., *Procès-verbaux de la Commune générale des arts et de la Société populaire et républicaine des arts* (Paris, 1903), xlix–l.
8. See Radisich, p.467.
9. See Voigt, p.30.
10. *Correspondance*, VI.304.
11. MS, University of Rochester Library, Department of Rare Books, Manuscripts and Archives, quoted in Baillio, *Elisabeth Louise Vigée Le Brun*, pp.129–30.
12. Comtesse de Genlis, *Mémoires*, 10 vols (Paris, 1825), VI.16.
13. P.-C. Lévesque, quoted in Donna Marie Hunter, 'Second Nature: Portraits by J.-L. David 1769–1792', Ph.D. thesis, Harvard University, 1988, p.24.
14. ibid., p.24, f.n.17.
15. *Souvenirs*, I.121.

BIBLIOGRAPHY

Manuscript Sources

Paris, Bibliothèque d'art et d'archéologie (Fondation Jacques Doucet), Papiers Tripier Le Franc.

Vienna, Haus-, Hof- und Staatsarchiv: Frankreich Varia Kartons 46, 47, 48; Stadtarchiv: Count Zinzendorf, *Tagebuch*.

Printed Sources

Léon Abensour, *La Femme et le féminisme avant la Révolution* (Paris, 1923).

Laure Junot, duchesse d'Abrantès, *Histoire des salons de Paris*, 6 vols (Paris, 1897–8).

    Mémoires, 10 vols (Paris, 1893).

Harold Acton, *The Bourbons of Naples (1734–1825)* (London, 1956).

Alison Adburgham, *Shops and Shopping 1800–1914* (London, 1964).

John T. Alexander, *Catherine the Great: Life and Legend* (New York and Oxford, 1989).

Armand, comte d'Allonville, *Mémoires secrets de 1770 à 1830*, 6 vols (Paris, 1838–45).

Virginie Ancelot, *Un Salon de Paris 1824 à 1864* (Paris, 1866).

    Les Salons de Paris (Paris, 1858).

Maurice Andrieux, *Daily Life in Papal Rome in the Eighteenth Century*, trans. Mary Fitton (London, 1968).

Elizabeth, Margravine of Anspach, *Memoirs*, 2 vols (London, 1826).

Frederick Antal, *Reflections on Classicism and Romanticism* (London, 1966).

Guy Arbellot, Bernard Lepetit and Jacques Bertrand (eds.), *Atlas de la Révolution française*, vol 1 (Paris, 1987).

Mildred Archer, *India and British Portraiture 1770–1825* (London, 1989).

Claude Arnaud, *Chamfort* (Paris, 1985).

C. Arnaud and B. Minoret, *Les Salons* (Paris, 1985).

Jean-Paul Aron, *Misérable et glorieuse, la femme du XIXe siècle* (Paris, 1980).

353

Jean Aubert, 'Acquisitions récentes. Chambéry: Musée des Beaux-Arts', *Revue du Louvre et des musées de France* (1979).

Louis Petit de Bachaumont, *Mémoires secrets pour servir à l'histoire de la République des Lettres en France depuis MDCCLXII jusqu'à nos jours*, 36 vols (London, 1780–89).

Elisabeth Badinter, *Emilie Emilie: L'Ambition féminine au XVIIIe siècle* (Paris, 1983).

Charles Alexandre, baron de Baert, *Tableau de la Grande-Bretagne*, 4 vols (Paris, 1800).

Colin B. Bailey, 'Lebrun et le commerce d'art pendant le Blocus continental', *Revue de l'art*, 63 (1984).

Joseph Baillio, 'Une Artiste méconnue: Rose Adélaïde Ducreux', *L'Oeil*, 399 (1988).

Catalogue 'Elisabeth Louise Vigée Le Brun 1755–1842' (exhibition at Kimbell Art Museum, Forth Worth, 1982).

'Identification de quelques portraits d'anonymes de Vigée Le Brun aux Etats-Unis', *Gazette des beaux-arts*, XCVI (1980).

'Marie-Antoinette et ses enfants par Mme Vigée Le Brun', *L'Oeil*, 308 and 310 (1981).

'Les Portraits du dauphin et de la dauphine par Greuze', *Gazette des beaux-arts*, CXXII (1993).

'Quelques Peintures réattribuées à Vigée Le Brun', *Gazette des beaux-arts*, XCIX (1982).

Elizabeth Baker and Thomas Hess, *Art and Sexual Politics* (New York, 1973).

Simone Balayé, *Les Carnets de voyage de Madame de Staël* (Geneva, 1971).

Honoré de Balzac, *Ursule Mirouët*, in *La Comédie humaine*, ed. Pierre-Georges Castex, 12 vols (Paris, 1976–81), III.

Jean-Bertrand Barrère, *L'Idée de goût de Pascal à Valéry* (Paris, 1972).

Christine Battersby, *Gender and Genius: Towards a Feminist Aesthetics* (London and Bloomington, 1989).

Sophie de Bawr, *Mes Souvenirs* (Paris, 1853).

Stephan Bayley, ed., *Commerce and Culture* (Penshurst, 1989).

Vincent Woodrow Beach, *Charles X of France: His Life and Times* (London, n.d.).

Simone de Beauvoir, *Le Deuxième Sexe*, 2 vols (Paris, 1949).

Sister Wendy Beckett, *Sister Wendy's Odyssey* (London, 1993).

Emile Bellier de la Chavignerie, 'Les Artistes français du XVIIIe siècle oubliés ou dédaignés', *Revue universelle des arts*, XIX (n.d.).

'Notes pour servir à l'histoire de l'exposition de la jeunesse à la Place Dauphine et sur le Pont Neuf', ibid.

John Berger, *Ways of Seeing* (London, 1972).

Oliver Bernier, catalogue, 'The Eighteenth-Century Woman' (exhibition at the Metropolitan Museum of Art, New York, 1981–2).

Mary Berry, *Social Life in England and France* (London, 1831).

G. de Bertier de Sauvigny, *Nouvelle Histoire de Paris: La Restauration 1815–1830* (Paris, 1977).
La Restauration (Paris, 1955).

Yvonne Bezard, *Madame de Staël d'après ses portraits* (Paris and Neuchâtel, 1938).

Ilse Bischoff, 'Madame Vigée Le Brun at the Court of Catherine the Great', *Russian Review*, 24 (1965).

Yvon Bizardel, 'Une Etude au pastel de Madame Vigée Le Brun pour le portrait d'Aniela Angélique Radziwill, princesse Czartoryska', *Bulletin du musée national de Varsovie* (1964).

Olivier Blanc, *Madame de Bonneuil, femme galante et agent secret* (Paris, 1987).

André Blum, *Madame Vigée-Lebrun, peintre des grandes dames du XVIIIe siècle* (Paris, 1920).

Henning Bock, 'Ein Bildnis von Prinz Heinrich Lubomirski als Genius des Ruhms von Elisabeth Vigée Lebrun', *Niederdeutsche Beiträge zur Kunstgeschichte*, XVI (1977).

Eléonore-Adèle, comtesse de Boigne, *Mémoires*, ed. Charles Nicoullaud, 4 vols (Paris, 1907–8).

Marc Marie, marquis de Bombelles, *Journal*, ed. Jean Grassion and Frans Durif (Geneva, 1977–), vols I & II.

Jean-Luc Bordeaux, 'Elisabeth Louise Vigée Lebrun,' *Art International* XXVI (1983).

Frank Brady and Frederick A. Pottle eds., *Boswell on the Grand Tour: Italy, Corsica and France 1765–6* (Melbourne, London and Toronto, 1955).

Ferdinand Boyer, *Le Monde des arts en Italie et la France de la Révolution et de l'Empire* (Turin, 1969).

Germain Brice, *Description de la ville de Paris*, 9th ed. (1752), ed. Pierre Codet (Geneva and Paris, 1971).

Charles Brifaut, *Souvenirs d'un Académicien sur la Révolution, le premier Empire et la Restauration*, ed. Dr Cabarrès, 2 vols (Paris, n.d.).

Richard Brilliant, *Portraiture* (London, 1991).

Gabriel de Broglie, *Madame de Genlis* (Paris, 1985).

Edmund Burke, *A Philosophical Enquiry into the Origin of Our Ideas on the Sublime and Beautiful*, 2nd ed. (London, 1759; facsimile reprint Menston, 1970).

Joseph Burke, *English Art 1714–1800* (Oxford, 1976).

J. Cailleux, 'Portrait de Madame Adélaïde de France', *Burlington Magazine*, CXI (1969).

The Sweetness of Life

Wesley D. Camp, *Marriage and the Family in France since the Revolution* (New York, 1961).

Jeanne-Louise-Henriette Campan, *Mémoires sur la vie privée de Marie-Antoinette, suivis de Souvenirs et anecdotes historiques sur les règnes de Louis XIV, de Louis XV et de Louis XVI*, ed. F. Barrière, 3 vols (Paris, 1822).

John Carr, *The Stranger in France, or A Tour from Devonshire to Paris* (London, 1803).

Giacomo Girolamo Casanova de Seingalt, *Mémoires*, 12 vols (Paris, 1924–35).

Catherine II, *Lettres au prince de Ligne*, ed. princesse Charles de Ligne (Brussels and Paris, 1924).

Whitney Chadwick, *Women, Art and Society* (London, 1990).

D. G. Charlton, *New Images of the Natural in France* (Cambridge, 1984).

R. Chartier, M.-M. Compère and D. Julia, *L'Education en France du XVIe au XVIIIe siècle* (Paris, 1976).

Victorine, comtesse de Chastenay, *Mémoires 1771–1815*, ed. Alphonse Roserot, 2 vols (Paris, 1896).

François-René, compte de Chateaubriand, *Mémoires d'outre-tombe*, ed. Maurice Levaillant and Georges Molinier, 2 vols (Paris, 1958).
Oeuvres romanesques et voyages, ed. Maurice Regard, 2 vols (Paris, 1969).

Jean Chatelus, *Peindre à Paris au XVIIIe siècle* (Nîmes, 1991).
'Quelques Réflexions sur les peintres et l'argent à Paris au XVIIIe siècle', in *La France d'Ancien Régime*, 2 vols (Paris, 1987), I.

Marcus Cheke, *The Cardinal de Bernis* (London, 1958).

William S. Childe-Pemberton, *The Earl-Bishop*, 2 vols (London, 1924).

Civiltà del '700 a Napoli 1374–1799, 2 vols (Naples, 1980).

Denis Cochin, *Louis-Philippe* (Paris, 1918).

Linda Colley, *Britons: Forging the Nation 1707–1837* (New York and London, 1992).

William Wilkie Collins, *The Moonstone* (Oxford, 1982).

Pierre du Colombier, *The Enchantment of Rome*, trans. Mary Fitton (London, 1970).

Christina Colvin ed., *Maria Edgeworth in France and Switzerland* (Oxford, 1979).

La Condition sociale de l'artiste XVIe–XXe siècles. Actes du groupe de chercheurs en histoire moderne et contemporaine du C.N.R.S. 12 octobre 1985 (St-Etienne, 1987).

Philip Conisbee, *Painting in Eighteenth-Century France* (Oxford, 1981).

Claire Constans, 'Un Portrait de Catherine Vassilievna Skavronskaia par Madame Vigée-Lebrun', *Revue du Louvre*, 4–5 (1967).

Benjamin Constant, *Correspondance générale*, ed. C. P. Courtney (Tübingen, 1993–).

Consulat, Empire, Restauration: Art in Early Nineteenth-Century France (New York, 1982).

Benedetta Craveri, *Madame du Deffand and Her World*, trans. Teresa Waugh (London, 1994).

Charles, baron de Crespy Le Prince, *Chroniques sur les cours de France*, 2 vols (Paris, 1843).

Auguste Creuzé de Lesser, *Voyage en Italie et en Sicile* (Paris, 1806).

Benedetto Croce, *History of the Kingdom of Naples*, ed. H. Stuart Hughes, trans. Frances Frenaye, 6th ed. (Chicago and London, 1970).

Anthony Cross, ed., *Russia under Western Eyes 1517–1825* (London, 1971).

Thomas E. Crow, *Painters and Public Life in Eighteenth-Century Paris* (New Haven and London, 1985).

Dan Cruickshank and Neil Burton, *Life in the Georgian City* (London, 1990).

Roger, comte de Damas, *Mémoires*, ed. Jacques Rambaud, 2nd ed., 2 vols (Paris, 1912).

Catherine Daschkoff, *Mémoires*, ed. Pascal Portremoli (Paris, 1989).

Armand Dayot, *L'Image de la femme* (Paris, 1899).

Deloynes, Collection, 63 vols (Bibliothèque nationale, Paris).

François Descotes, *La Révolution française vue de l'étranger* (Paris, 1897).

Georgiana, Duchess of Devonshire, *Georgiana: Extracts from her Correspondence*, ed. Earl of Bessborough (London, 1955).

Denis Diderot, *Correspondance*, ed. Georges Roth and Jean Varloot, 16 vols (Paris, 1955–70).

    Le Neveu de Rameau, ed. Jean Fabre (Geneva, 1963).

    Paradoxe sur le comédien, in *Oeuvres esthétiques*, ed. Paul Vernière (Paris, 1968).

    Salons, ed. Jean Seznec and Jean Adhémar, 4 vols (Oxford, 1957–67).

Denis Diderot and Jean le Rond d'Alembert (eds.), *Encyclopédie, ou Dictionnaire raisonné des sciences, des arts et des métiers*, 18 vols (Paris, 1751–72).

Ghislain de Diesbach, *Histoire de l'émigration*, revised ed. (Paris, 1984).

    Madame de Staël (Paris, 1983).

Elisabeth Divoff, *Journal et souvenirs*, ed. S. Kaznakoff (Paris, 1929).

'*La Douceur de vivre*': *Art, Style and Decoration in Eighteenth-Century France* (Wildenstein, London, June–July 1983).

H. T. Douwes-Dekker, 'A. Kaufmann imitatrice de madame Vigée-Lebrun', *Gazette des beaux-arts*, CIV (1984).

Victor Du Bled, *La Comédie de société au dix-huitième siècle* (Paris, 1893).

Dreissig Briefe über Galizien (Vienna and Leipzig, 1787).

Madame du Deffand, *Letters à Voltaire, 1759-1775*, ed. M. de Lescure (Paris, 1994).

Paule-Marie Duhet ed., *1789: Cahiers de doléance des femmes*, new ed. (Paris, 1989).

Carol Duncan, 'Happy Mothers and Other New Ideas in French Art', *Art Bulletin*, LV (1973).

Charles-Marguerite-Jean Dupaty, *Sentimental Letters on Italy (1785)*, 2 vols (London, 1789).

Louis-Etienne Dussieux, *Les Artistes français à l'étranger*, 3rd ed. (Paris, 1876).

Leon Edel, *Writing Lives* (New York and London, 1987).

Mary Ellman, *Thinking about Women* (New York, 1968).

Georges Engelbert, 'Une Grande Dame cosmopolite du XVIIIe siècle: la comtesse Charlotte de Thiennes de Rumbeke, née Cobenzl', *Jahrbuch des Vereines für Geschichte der Stadt Wien* (1993).

Thomas, comte d'Espinchal, *Journal d'émigration*, ed. Ernest d'Hauterive (Paris, 1912).

Valentin, comte Esterházy, *Lettres à sa femme, 1784–1792*, ed. Ernest Daudet (Paris, 1907).

Charles Eynard, *Madame de Krüdener*, 2 vols (Paris, 1849).

Joseph Farington, *Diary*, ed. James Greig, 8 vols (London, 1922–8), II (1802–4).

Rita Felski, *Beyond Feminist Aesthetics* (London, 1989).

Fleury, comte de, *Souvenirs du congrès de Vienne* (Paris, 1901).

Michal Florisoone, *Portraits français* (Paris, 1946).

J. E. Folkman, *Die gefürstete Linie Kinsky* (Prague, 1861).

Franklin L. Ford, *Europe 1780-1830* (London, 1970).

H. Forneron, *Histoire générale des émigrés pendant la Révolution française*, 3 vols (Paris, 1884–90).

Brian Fothergill, *Sir William Hamilton, Envoy Extraordinary* (London, 1964).

Celina Fox (ed.), *London – World City 1800–1840* (New Haven and London, 1992).

Londoners (London, 1987).

La France et la Russie au siècle des Lumières (Paris, 1986).

E. François, ed., *Sociabilité et société bourgeoise en France 1750–1850* (Paris, 1986).

Flora Fraser, *Beloved Emma: The Life of Emma Lady Hamilton* (London, 1986).

French Painting 1774–1830: The Age of Revolution (Detroit and New York, 1975).

Auguste-François de Frenilly, *Recollections* ed. Arthur Chuquet, trans.

Frederic Lees (London, 1909).

Bruno S. Frey and Werner W. Pommerehne, *Muses and Markets* (Oxford, 1989).

Max Friedländer, *Landscape, Portrait, Still Life: Their Origin and Development*, trans. R. F. C. Hull (Oxford, 1949).

Walter Friedländer, *David to Delacroix*, trans. Robert Goldwater (Cambridge, Mass., 1952).

Marc Fumaroli, *Le Genre des genres littéraires: la conversation* (Zaharoff Lecture 1990–91) (Oxford, 1992).

Herbert Furst, *Portrait Painting: Its Nature and Function* (London, 1927).

Thomas W. Gaehtgens and Jacques Lugaud, *Joseph-Marie Vien peintre du Roi (1716-1809)* (Paris, 1988).

Elise Gagne, *Madame de Bawr* (Paris, 1861).

Michel Gallet, 'La Maison de Madame Vigée-Lebrun rue du Gros-Chenet', *Gazette des beaux-arts*, LVI (1960).

Madge Garland, 'Rose Bertin: Minister of Fashion', *Apollo*, LXXXVII (1968).

Kenneth Garlick, *Sir Thomas Lawrence: Portraits of an Age 1790–1830* (Alexandria, Virginia, 1993).

J. G. Garrard, ed., *The Eighteenth Century in Russia* (Oxford, 1973).

Sophie Gay, *Salons célèbres* (Paris, 1882).

Stéphanie-Félicité, comtesse de Genlis, *Dictionnaire critique et raisonné des étiquettes de la cour et des usages du monde* (Paris, 1818).
Leçons d'une gouvernante (Paris, 1791).
Mémoires, 10 vols (Paris, 1825).

Geneviève Gennari, *Le Premier Voyage de Madame de Staël en Italie et la genèse de 'Corinne'* (Paris, 1947).

Abbé Jean-François Georgel, *Voyage à Saint-Pétersbourg en 1799–1800* (Paris, 1818).

Salomon Gessner 1730-1788, catalogue to exhibition at Herzog-August-Bibliothek, Zürich (Zürich, 1980).

Jean Gigoux, *Causeries sur les artistes de mon temps* (Paris, 1885).

Marguerite Glotz and Madeleine Maire, *Salons du XVIIIe siècle* (Paris, 1945).

Jacques Godechot, *The Counter-Revolution*, trans. Salvator Attanasio (London, 1972).

Johann Wolfgang von Goethe, *Briefe*, ed. Karl Robert Mandelkow and Bodo Morawe, 2nd ed., 4 vols (Munich, 1968–76).
Italienische Reise, ed. Andreas Beyer and Norbert Miller, *Sämtliche Werke*, 20 vols (Munich, 1985–91), XV.

The Golden Age of Naples: Art and Civilisation under the Bourbons 1734–1805, 2 vols (Detroit, 1981).

359

Barbe, comtesse Golovine, *Souvenirs*, ed. K. Waliszewski (Paris, 1910).

Edmond and Jules de Goncourt, *La Femme au dix-huitième siècle* (Paris, 1862).

Histoire de la sociéte française pendant la Révolution (Paris, 1845).

G. P. Gooch, *Catherine the Great and Other Studies* (London, 1954).

John Goodman, 'Altar against Altar: The Colisée, Vauxhall Utopianism and Symbolic Politics in Paris (1769–77)', *Art History*, 15 (1992).

Olympe de Gouges, *Oeuvres*, ed. Benoîte Groult (Paris, 1986).

J. G. Goulinat, 'Les Femmes peintres au XVIIIe siècle', *L'Art et les artistes*, 13 (1926).

Thalia Gouma-Peterson and Patricia Mathews, 'The Feminist Critique of Art History', *Art Bulletin* LXIX (1987).

Joseph Govani, *Mémoires secrets et critiques des cours, des gouvernements et des moeurs des principaux états de l'Italie*, 3 vols (Paris, 1793).

Bertie Greatheed, *Journal: An Englishman in Paris, 1803*, ed. J. P. T. Bury and J. C. Barry (London, 1953).

Donald Greer, *The Incidence of the Emigration during the French Revolution* (Cambridge, Mass., 1951).

Germaine Greer, *The Obstacle Race* (London, 1979).

Friedrich Melchior von Grimm, *Correspondance artistique avec Catherine II*, ed. Louis Réau (*Archives de l'art français*, nouvelle période, vol. XVII (1932).

Rees Howell Gronow, *Celebrities of London and Paris* (London, 1865).

Gianni Guadalupi, *Elisabeth Vigée Le Brun: Dalla corte di Versailles alla corte di Napoli, 1781–1790*, 2 vols (Milan, 1989).

Jules Guiffrey ed., *Correspondance de l'Académiè de France à Rome*, 18 vols (Paris, 1887–1912).

Histoire de l'Académie de St-Luc (*Archives de l'art français*, nouvelle période, vol IX, 1915).

Notes et documents inédits sur les expositions du XVIIIe siècle (Paris, 1873).

Eduard Hanslick, *Geschichte des Concertwesens in Wien*, 2 vols (Vienna, 1869).

Erica Harth, *Cartesian Women: Versions and Subversions of Rational Discourse in the Old Régime* (Ithaca and London, 1992).

Francis Haskell, *Rediscoveries in Art* (London, 1976).

Emile Haumont, *La Culture française en Russie (1700–1900)*, 2nd edition (Paris, 1913).

Louis Hautecoeur, *Madame Vigée-Lebrun* (Paris, n.d.).

Francis W. Hawcroft ed., *Travels in Italy 1776-83, Based on the Memoirs of Thomas Jones* (Manchester, 1988).

John Hayes, *The Portrait in British Art* (London, 1991).

George Heard Hamilton, *The Art and Architecture of Russia*, 3rd ed. (Harmondsworth, 1983).

J.-F. Heim, C. Béraud and P. Hein, *Les Salons de peinture de la Révolution française, 1789–1799* (Paris, 1989).

William Henry Helm, *Vigée-Lebrun: Her Life, Work and Friendships* (London, 1915).

F. W. J. Hemmings, *Culture and Society in France 1789–1848* (Leicester, 1987).

John Hibberd, *Salomon Gessner* (Cambridge, 1976).

Jacques Hillairet, *Dictionnaire historique des rues de Paris*, 2 vols (Paris, 1963).

Evocation du vieux Paris (Paris, 1953).

Eric Hobsbawm, *The Age of Revolution* (London, 1962).

Kirsten Gram Holmström, *Monodrama, Attitudes, Tableaux Vivants* (Stockholm, 1967).

Ann M. Hope, *The Theory and Practice of Neoclassicism in English Painting* (New York and London, 1988).

John Hoppner, trans., *Oriental Tales* (London, 1805).

T. E. B. Howarth, *Citizen King: The Life of Louis-Philippe, King of the French* (London, 1961).

Philippe Huisman and Marguerite Jallut, *Marie-Antoinette, l'impossible bonheur* (Lausanne, 1970).

Lynn Hunt, *The Family Romance of the French Revolution* (London, 1992).

Donna Marie Hunter, 'Second Nature: Portraits by J-L. David, 1769–1792', Ph.D thesis, Harvard University, 1988.

Guillaume Imbert, *La Chronique scandaleuse ou Mémoires pour servir à l'histoire de la génération présente*, 4 vols (Paris, 1788–9).

David Irwin, *English Neoclassical Art: Studies in Inspiration and Taste* (London, 1966).

Gervase Jackson-Stops, ed., *The Treasure-Houses of Britain* (New Haven and London, 1985).

Paul Jarry, 'Notes sur le Colisée', *Bulletin de la Société historique des VIIIᵉ et XVIIᵉ arrondissements* (1913).

Wend Graf Kalnein and Michael Levey, *Art and Architecture of the Eighteenth Century in France* (Harmondsworth, 1972).

Verena Keil-Budischowsky, *Die Theater Wiens* (Vienna and Hamburg, 1983).

Francis M. Kelly and Randolf Schnabe, *Historic Costume* (London, 1925).

Linda Kelly, *Women of the French Revolution* (London, 1987).

V. O. Kluchevsky, *A History of Russia*, trans. C. J. Hogarth, 5 vols (London 1911–31).

Carlo Knight, 'I Luoghi di delizie di William Hamilton', *Napoli nobilissima*,

XX (1981).

Ludwig Kohl, *Neue Bilder aus dem Leben der Musik und ihrer Meister* (Munich, 1870).

Natalie de Kourakine, *Souvenirs des voyages* (Moscow, 1903).

Juliana de Krüdener, *Valérie (1803)*, ed. Michel Mercier (Paris, 1974).

Edith Krull, *Women in Art* (London, 1989).

Sandor Kuthy, 'Elisabeth Louise Vigée-Lebrun und das Alphirtenfest in Unspunnen', *Zeitschrift für schweizerische Archäologie und Kunstgeschichte*, 33 (1976).

Alexandre, comte de Laborde, *Voyage pittoresque en Autriche*, 3 vols (Paris, 1821–2).

Pierre Choderlos de Laclos, *Oeuvres complètes*, ed. Laurent Versini (Paris, 1979).

Robert Lacour-Gayet, *Calonne, financier, réformateur, contre-révolutionnaire 1734-1802* (Paris, 1963).

Léon Lagrange, *Les Vernet: Joseph Vernet et la peinture au XVIIIᵉ siècle* (Paris, 1864).

Alphonse de Lamartine, *Histoire de la Restauration*, 8 vols (Paris, 1851–2).

Joan B. Landes, *Women and the Public Sphere in the Age of the French Revolution* (Ithaca and London, 1988).

Emile Langlade, *La Marchande de modes de Marie-Antoinette: Rose Bertin* (Paris, 1911).

Henry Lapauze ed., *Procès-verbaux de la Commune générale des arts et de la Société populaire et républicaine des arts* (Paris, 1903).

Charles de La Rivière, *Catherine II et la Révolution française* (Paris, 1895).

Henriette-Lucie, marquise de la Tour du Pin, *Journal d'une femme de cinquante ans*, 2 vols (Paris, 1924–5).

André Lebon, *L'Angleterre et l'émigration française de 1794 à 1801* (Paris, 1882).

Jean-Baptiste-Pierre Le Brun, *Précis historique de la vie de la citoyenne Le Brun peintre* (Paris, an II, 1793–4).

Charles A. LeGuinn, 'The Language of Portraiture', *Biography*, 6 (1983).

Gaston de Leiris, 'Les Femmes à l'Académie de peinture', *L'Art*, 45 (1888).

Jacques Lethève, *Daily Life of French Artists in the Nineteenth Century*, trans. Hilary E. Paddon (London, 1972).

Lettre de Madame Lebrun à Monsieur de Calonne (Paris, 1789).

Iris Leveson Gower, *The Face Without a Frown: Georgiana, Duchess of Devonshire* (London, 1944).

Michael Levey, *Painting and Sculpture in France 1700–1789* (New Haven and London, 1993).

Painting at Court (London, 1971).

Rococo to Revolution (London, 1966).

Gaston, duc de Lévis, *L'Angleterre au commencement du dix-neuvième siècle* (Paris, 1814).
  Souvenirs et portraits 1780–1789 (Paris, 1813).
Francine-Dominique Liechtenhan, *Astolphe de Custine, voyageur et philosophe* (Paris/Geneva, 1990).
Charles-Joseph, prince de Ligne, *Mémoires et lettres*, new ed. (Paris, 1923).
  Mémoires, lettres et pensées, ed. Chantal Thomas (Paris, 1989).
  Oeuvres choisies, ed. Gustave Chavlier, new ed. (Brussels, 1944).
David M. Lubin, *The Act of Portrayal* (New Haven, 1985).
J. Lucas-Dubreton, *La Restauration et la monarchie de juillet* (Paris, 1926).
Albert de Luppé, *Les Jeunes Filles dans l'aristocratie et la bourgeoisie à la fin du XVIIIe siècle* (Paris, 1924).
Roderick E. McGrew, *Paul I of Russia 1754–1801* (Oxford, 1992).
Isabel de Madariaga, *Russia in the Age of Catherine the Great* (London, 1981).
James Peller Malcolm, *Anecdotes of the Manners and Customs of London during the Eighteenth Century*, 2nd ed., 2 vols (London, 1810).
Gilberte-Emile Mâle, 'Jean-Baptiste-Pierre Le Brun (1748–1813). Son rôle dans l'histoire de la restauration des tableaux du Louvre', *Mémoires de la Fédération des sociétiés historiques et archéologiques de Paris et de l'île-de-France*, VIII (1956).
Claude Manceron, *Le Sang de la Bastille* (Paris, 1987).
'Reynolds Oil Sketches', *Burlington Magazine*, 133 (1991).
David Mannings, 'Shaftesbury, Reynolds and the Recovery of Portrait Painting in Eighteenth-Century England', *Zeitschrift für Kunstgeschichte*, 48 (1985).
Philip Mansel, *Charles-Joseph de Ligne (1735–1814): Le Charmeur de l'Europe*, trans. Françoise Adelstain (Paris, 1992).
  The Court of France 1789-1830 (Cambridge, 1988).
  The Eagle in Splendour: Napoleon I and his Court (London, 1987).
  Louis XVIII (London, 1981).
  'Monarchy, Uniform and the *Frac* 1760–1830', *Past and Present*, 96 (1982).
Sylvie Martin, 'Portraits anglais et français: un approche comparative à travers les textes du XVIIIe siècle', *Gazette des beaux-arts*, CXVII (1991).
André Masson, *Un Mécène bordelaise, Nicolas Beaujon 1718–86* (Bordeaux, 1937).
André Maurois, *La Conversation* (Paris, 1927).
Sara Melzer and Leslie Rabie eds., *Rebel Daughters: Women and the French Revolution* (Oxford, 1992).
Louis-Sébastien Mercier, *Parallèle de Paris et de Londres*, ed. Claude

Bruneteau and Bernard Cottret (Paris, 1982).

Le Tableau de Paris, ed. Jeffrey Kaplow (Paris, 1982).

Friedrich Johann Lorenz Meyer, *Les Tableaux d'Italie*, ed. and trans. Elisabeth Chevallier (Naples, 1980).

Grand-Duke Nicholas Mikhailovich, *Portraits russes des XVIIIe et XIXe siècles*, 5 vols (St Petersburg, 1905–9).

Lady Anne Miller, *Letters from Italy in the Years 1770 and 1771*, 2 vols (London, 1776).

A. P. de Mirimonde, 'Les Opinions de M. Lebrun sur la peinture hollandaise', *Revue des arts*, 6 (1956).

A. Molinier, 'A propos des Souvenirs de Madame Vigée-Lebrun', *L'Art, revue illustrée*, LXIV (1905).

A. de Montaiglon, *Procès-verbaux de l'Académie royale de peinture et de sculpture*, 10 vols (Paris, 1875–92).

Alexandrine Prévost, baronne du Montet, *Souvenirs 1785–1866* (Paris, 1904).

John Moore, *A View of Society and Manners in Italy*, 5th ed., 2 vols (London, 1790).

Lady Sydney Morgan, *France*, 2nd ed., 2 vols (London, 1817).

Edith J. Morley ed., *Crabb Robinson in Germany, 1800–1805* (London, 1929).

Gouverneur Morris, *Diary and Letters*, ed. Anne Cary Morris, 2 vols (London, 1889).

Alfred Morrison ed., *The Hamilton and Nelson Papers*, 2 vols (London, 1893).

H. V. Morton, *The Traveller in Southern Italy* (London, 1969).

Edgar Munhall, 'Vigée le Brun's Marie-Antoinette', *Art News*, 82 (1983).

Eugène Müntz, 'Lettres de Madame Le Brun relatives à son portrait de la galerie des Offices', *Nouvelles Archives de l'art français*, 1874–5.

Stella Musulin, *Vienna in the Age of Metternich* (London, 1975).

Ralph Nevill, *French Prints of the Eighteenth Century* (London, 1908).

Friedrich Nicolai, *Beschreibung einer Reise durch Deutschland und die Schweiz im Jahre 1781*, 8 vols (Berlin and Stettin, 1784–6).

Friedrich Nietzsche, 'The English on Sunday', *Beyond Good and Evil*, ed. Oscar Levy, trans. Helen Zimmern (London, 1907).

Lada Nikolenko, 'The Russian Portraits of Madame Vigée-Lebrun', *Gazette des beaux arts*, LXX (1967).

Linda Nochlin, 'Why Have There Been No Great Women Artists?', *Women, Art and Power and Other Essays* (London, 1989).

Pierre de Nolhac, *Madame Vigée Le Brun, peintre de Marie-Antoinette* (Paris, 1934) *Peintres français en Italie* (Paris, 1934).

James Northcote, *Life of Sir Joshia Reynolds*, 2 vols (London, 1819).

P. J. B. Nougaret, *Anecdotes secrets du dix-huitième siècle*, 2 vols (Paris, 1808).

Nouveau Guide par Vienne (Paris, 1792).

Pierre de Nouvion and Emile Liez, *Un Ministre de la mode sous Louis XVI* (Paris, 1911).

Judith Nowinski, 'Baron Dominique Vivant Denon (1747–1825): Hedonist and Scholar in a Period of Transition', Ph.D Thesis, Columbia University, 1968.

Henriette-Louise, baronne d'Oberkirch, *Mémoires sur la cour de Louis XVI et la société française avant 1789*, ed. Suzanne Burkard (Paris, 1970).

Vera Oravetz, *Les Impressions françaises de Vienne (1567–1850)* (Szeged, 1930).

Charles Oulmont, *Les Femmes-peintres du XVIIIᵉ siècle* (Paris, 1928).

Alan Palmer, *Alexander I: Tsar of War and Peace* (London, 1974).

Panorama von Wiens Umgebungen (Vienna, 1807).

Mrs Papendiek, *Court and Private Life in the Time of Queen Charlotte*, ed. Mrs V. Delves-Broughton, 2 vols (London, 1887).

Rozsika Parker and Griselda Pollock, *Old Mistresses: Women, Art and Ideology* (London, 1981).

Anne Marie Passez, *Adélaïde Labille-Guiard, 1749–1803: Biographie et catalogue raisonné de son oeuvre* (Paris, 1973).

Maria Pawlik, 'Emigranten der französischen Revolution in Österreich (1789–1814)', Dokt. Diss., University of Vienna, 1967.

Nicholas Penney, ed., Catalogue 'Reynolds' (exhibition at Royal Academy, London, 1986).

Lucien Perey, *Histoire d'une grande dame au XVIIIᵉ siècle: la princesse Hélène de Ligne* (Paris, 1887).
Histoire d'une grande dame au XVIIIᵉ siècle, 2: la comtesse Hélène Potocka (Paris, 1888).

Michelle Perrot, ed., *Une Histoire des femmes est-elle possible?* (Paris and Marseilles, 1984).

Karen Petersen and J. J. Wilson, *Women Artists: Recognition and Reappraisal from the Early Middle Ages to the Twentieth Century* (London, 1978).

E. G. Pettenegg, *Ludwig und Karl von Zinzendorf* (Vienna, 1879).

Richard Phillips, *Modern London* (London, 1804).

Caroline Pichler, *Denkwürdigkeiten aus meinem Leben*, 4 vols (Vienna, 1844).

Roger de Piles, *Cours de peinture par principes* (Paris, 1798).

Charles Pillet, *Madame Vigée-Le Brun* (Paris, 1890).

Léonce Pingaud ed., *Correspondance intime du comte de Vaudreuil et du comte d'Artois*, 2 vols (Paris, 1889).

Les Français en Russie et les Russes en France (Paris, 1886).

Hester Lynch Piozzi, *Observations and Reflections Made in the Course of a Journey through France, Italy and Germany,* 2 vols (London, 1789).

David Piper, *The English Face* (London, 1957).

Marcia Pointon, 'The Georgians: Eighteenth-Century Portraiture and Society', *Art History,* 14 (1991).

'Interior Portraits: Women, Philosophy and the Male Artist', *Feminist Review,* 22 (1986).

'Portrait-Painting as a Business Enterprise in London in the 1780s', *Art History,* 7 (1984).

Diane, comtesse de Polignac, *Mémoires sur la vie et le caractère de madame la duchesse de Polignac* (London, 1796).

Griselda Pollock, *Vision and Difference* (London and New York, 1988).

Roger, baron Portalis, *Henry-Pierre Danloux, peintre de portraits, et son journal pendant l'émigration* (London, 1910).

Roger, baron Portalis and Henri Béraldi, *Les Graviers du XVIIIe siècle,* 3 vols (Paris, 1880–2).

Hélène, countess Potocka, *Memoirs,* ed. Casimir Stryienski, trans. Lionel Strachey (London, 1901).

Mario Praz, *On Neoclassicism,* trans. Angus Davidson (London, 1969).

August, Graf Preysing, 'Das Familienbildnis der Grafen Fries', *Jahrbuch des Vereines für Geschichte der Stadt Wien* (1951).

Rudolph Procházka, *Mozart in Prag* (Prague, 1899).

Marcel Proust, *A la recherche du temps perdu,* gen. ed. Jean-Yves Tadié, 4 vols (Paris, 1987–9).

Auguste Racinet, *Le costume britannique,* 6 vols (Paris, 1888).

Paula Rea Radisich, ' "Qui peut définir les femmes?": Vigée Le Brun's Portraits of an Artist', *Eighteenth-Century Studies,* 25 (1991–2).

Agatha Ramm, *Europe in the Nineteenth Century* (Grant and Temperley's *Europe in the Nineteenth and Twentieth Centuries,* 7th ed.), 2 vols (London and New York, 1984).

Louis Réau, *L'Europe français au siècle des lumières* (Paris, 1938).

Johann Friedrich Reichardt, *Vertraute Briefe aus Paris* (1802–3); *Vertraute Briefe geschrieben auf einer Reise nach Wien,* ed. Gustav Gugitz, 2 vols (Munich, 1915).

G. A. H. de Reiset, ed., *Livre-journal de Madame Eloffe,* 2 vols (Paris, 1885).

Gerald Roberts Reitlinger, *The Economics of Taste* (London, 1961).

Esther Renfrew and Simone Balayé, 'Madame de Staël et la sibylle du Dominiquin', *Cahiers Staëliens,* new series, 2 (1964).

Réponse de M. de Calonne à la dernière lettre de Mme Le Brun (Paris, 1789).

Nicolas-Edme Restif de la Bretonne, *Les Parisiennes,* 4 vols (Neufchâtel, 1787).

Nicholas V. Riasnovsky, *A History of Russia*, 4th ed. (New York and Oxford, 1984).

Aileen Ribeiro, *The Art of Dress: Fashion in England and France, 1750–1800* (New Haven and London, 1995).
Dress in Eighteenth-Century Europe 1715–1789 (London, 1984).
Fashion in the French Revolution (London, 1988).

Danielle Rice 'Vigée Le Brun vs. Labille-Guiard: A Rivalry in Context', *Proceedings of the Eleventh Annual Meeting of the Western Society for French History, 3–5 November 1983* (Lawrence, Kansas, 1984).

P. L. Roederer, *Mémoire pour servir à l'histoire de la société polie en France* (Paris, 1835).

Marie-Jeanne Roland, *Mémoires*, ed. Paul de Roux (Paris, 1966).
Voyage en Suisse 1787 (Neuchâtel, 1937).

Marianne Roland Michel, *Le Dessin français au XVIIIe* (Fribourg, 1987).
'Un Portrait de Madame du Barry', *Revue de l'art*, 46 (1979).
Anne Vallayer-Coster 1744–1818 (London, 1970).

Annette Rosa, *Citoyennes: Les Femmes et la Révolution française* (Paris, 1988).

Pierre Rosenberg, 'A Drawing by Madame Vigée-Le Brun', *Burlington Magazine*, CXXIII (1981).

Robert Rosenblum, *Transformations in Late Eighteenth-Century Art* (Princeton, 1967).

Angela Rosenthal, 'Kauffman and Portraiture', in *Angelica Kauffman*, ed. Wendy Wassyng Roworth (Brighton, 1992).

Jean-André Rouquet, *Etat des arts en Angleterre* (Paris, 1755).

Jean-Jacques Rousseau, *Oeuvres complètes*, ed. Bernard Gagnebin and Marcel Raymond, 4 vols (Paris, 1959–69).

George Rudé, *Europe in the Eighteenth Century* (London, 1972).

Andrzey Ryskiewicz, 'Les Portraits polonais de Madame Vigée-Le Brun. Nouvelles Données pour servir à leur identification et histoire', *Bulletin du musée national de Varsovie*, XX (1979).

V. Sackville-West, *Knole and the Sackvilles* (London, 1991).

Charles Augustin de Sainte-Beuve, *Causeries du lundi*, 16 vols (Paris, 1826–42).

Richard de Saint-Non, *Voyage pittoresque de Naples et de Sicile*, 5 vols (Paris, 178–6).

St Petersburg um 1800 (catalogue to exhibition at Villa Hügel, Essen, 1990) (Recklinghausen, 1990).

J. L. Ferri di San Costante, *Londres et les Anglais*, 4 vols (Paris, 1804).

Madame de Sartory, *Petit Tableau de Paris*, 3 vols (Paris, 1818).

Aglaé-Marie-Louise, duchesse de Saulx-Tavanes, *Mémoires (1791–1806)*, ed. marquis de Valons (Paris, 1934).

Simon Schama, *Citizens: A Chronicle of the French Revolution* (London, 1989).

'The Domestication of Majesty: Royal Family Portraiture, 1500–1850', in *Art and History: Images and Their Meaning*, ed. Robert I. Rotberg and Theodore K. Rabb (Cambridge, 1988).

Edmond Scherer, *Etudes sur la littérature au XVIIIᵉ siècle* (Paris, 1891).

Friedrich von Schiller, *Über naive und sentimentalische Dichtung*, ed. W. F. Maitland (Oxford, 1951).

Justus Schmidt, 'Die Emigrantenkolonie in Wien', *Mitteilungen des Vereines für Geschichte der Stadt Wien* (1931).

K. Scott, 'Hierarchy, Liberty and Order: Languages of Art and Institutional Conflict in Paris (1766–1776)', *Oxford Art Journal*, 12 (1981).

Gladys Scott Thompson, *Catherine the Great and the Expansion of Russia* (London, 1947).

Alexandre, vicomte de Ségur, *Les Femmes, leur condition et leur influence dans l'ordre social*, 2 vols (Paris, 1820).

Louis-Philippe, comte de Ségur, *Histoire et mémoires*, 7 vols (Paris, 1873). *Mémoires, ou Souvenirs et anecdotes*, 3 vols (Stuttgart, 1829).

Pierre, marquis de Ségur, *Le Royaume de la rue St-Honoré*, 9th ed. (Paris, 1925).

Alfred Sensier, *Etude sur Georges Michel* (Paris, 1873).

Marie de Rabutin-Chantal, marquise de Sévigné, *Lettres*, ed. Gérard-Gailly, 3 vols (Paris, 1953–7).

Desmond Shawe-Taylor, *The Georgians: Eighteenth-Century Portraiture and Society* (London, 1990).

Mary D. Sheriff, 'Invention, Resemblance, and Fragonard's *Portraits de fantaisie*', *Art Bulletin*, LXIX (1987).

The Exceptional Woman: Elisabeth Vigée-Lebrun and the Cultural Politics of Art (Chicago and London, 1996).

G. Sievernich and H. Budde, eds., *Europa und der Orient 1800–1900* (Berlin, 1989).

Skizze von Wien, 6 vols (Vienna and Leipzig, 1789).

Alastair Smart, *Allan Ramsay* (New Haven and London, 1992).

Vincent A. Smith, *Oxford History of India*, ed. Percival Spear, 3rd ed. (Oxford, 1967).

Tobias Smollett, *Travels through France and Italy*, 2 vols (London, 1766).

Albert Soboul, *Précis d'histoire de la Révolution française* (Paris, 1962).

Susan Sontag, *The Volcano Lover: A Romance* (London, 1992).

Jean-Louis Soulavie, *Mémoires historiques et politiques du règne de Louis XVI*, 6 vols (Paris, 1801).

W. S. Sparrow, *Women Painters of the World* (New York, 1905).

Samia I. Spencer, ed., *French Women and the Age of the Enlightenment*

(Bloomington, 1984).

Paul Spencer-Longhurst, 'A Vigée-Le Brun for the Barber Institute', *Burlington Magazine*, CXXIII (1981).

Germaine de Staël, *Choix de lettres*, ed. Georges Solovieff (Paris, 1970).
Corinne, ou l'Italie, ed. Simone Balayé (Paris, 1985).
Correspondance générale, ed. Béatrice W. Jasinski (Paris, 1960–).
De l'Allemagne, ed. comtesse Jean de Pange with Simone Balayé, 5 vols (Paris, 1958).

Valerie Steele, *Paris Fashion* (New York and Oxford, 1988).

Wendy Steiner, *Exact Resemblance to Exact Resemblance* (New Haven and London, 1978).

Stendhal, 'Mémoires sur Napoléon', *Oeuvres complètes,* ed. Louis Royer, new ed., 50 vols (Paris, 1968–74), XXXIX and XL.
Promenades dans Rome, ed. V. Del Litto, 2 vols (Paris, 1980).
Rome, Naples et Florence en 1817, ed. Henri Martineau (Paris, 1950).

Charles Sterling, *Great French Painting in the Hermitage* (New York, 1958).

Frederick Leopold, Count Stolberg, *Travels through Germany, Switzerland, Italy and Sicily,* trans. Thomas Holcroft, 2 vols (London, 1796).

Casimir Stryienski, *Mesdames de France, filles de Louis XV,* 2nd ed. (Paris, 1911).

Dorothy Margaret Stuart, *Dearest Bess: The Life and Times of Lady Elizabeth Foster, Afterwards Duchess of Devonshire, from Her Unpublished Journals and Correspondence* (London, 1955).

The Survey of London (London, 1900–).

Ann Sutherland Harris and Linda Nochlin, *Women Artists 1550–1950* (Los Angeles and New York, 1978).

Denys Sutton, 'Madame Vigée Le Brun: A Survivor of the *Ancien Régime*', *Apollo,* CXXI (1982).
'Russian Francophiles of the *dix-huitième*', *Apollo,* CI (1975).

Henry Swinburne, *The Courts of Europe at the Close of the Last Century,* ed. Charles White, 2 vols (London, 1841).

Hippolyte Taine, *Les Origines de la France contemporaine,* 6 vols (Paris, 1876–94), I.

Prince de Talleyrand, *Mémoires,* ed. duc de Broglie, 3 vols (Paris, 1891).

J. L Talmon, *Romanticism and Revolt: Europe 1815–1848* (London, 1967).

Erika Thiel, *Geschichte des Kostüms* (Berlin, 1963).

J. M. Thompson, *Napoleon Bonaparte: His Rise and Fall* (Oxford, 1969).

Walter Thornbury, *Old and New London,* 6 vols (London, n.d.).

Lulu, Gräfin Thürheim, *Mein Leben,* ed. René Van Rhyn (Munich, 1913).

Tigers round the Throne: The Court of Tipu Sultan 1750–1799 (catalogue of exhibition at Zamana Gallery, London, 1990).

Alexandre, Comte de Tilly, *Mémoires pour servir à l'histoire des mœurs de la fin du dix-huitème siècle,* 3 vols (Paris, 1828).

Alexis de Tocqueville, *L'Ancien Régime et la Révolution,* ed. J. P. Mayer (London, 1967).

A. Tornézy, ed., *Bergeret et Fragonard: Journal inédit d'un voyage en Italie, 1773–4* (Paris, 1895).

Treasures of a Polish King: Stanislas Augustus as Patron and Collector (catalogue of exhibition at Dulwich Picture Gallery, London, 1992).

Raleigh Trevelyan, 'Robert Fagan: An Irish Bohemian in Italy', *Apollo,* 1972.

Justin Tripier Le Franc,
'Les Actes de mariage et de divorce de Madame Vigée-Le Brun', *Nouvelles Archives de l'art français* (1876).
'Notice sur la vie et les ouvrages de Madame Vigée-Le Brun', in *Journal dictionnarie de biographie* (Paris, 1828).

Henri Troyat, *Catherine the Great,* trans. Emily Read (London, 1993).

Nadia Tscherny, 'Reynolds' Streatham Portraits and the Art of Intimate Biography', *Burlington Magazine,* 128 (1986).

Herbert Tschulk, 'Franzosen in Wien', *Wiener Geschichtsblätter,* 39 (1984).

Alexandre Tuetey, 'L'Emigration de Madame Vigée-Le Brun', *Bulletin de la Société de l'histoire de l'art français,* 1911.

Eleanor Tufts, 'Elisabeth Louise Vigée Le Brun', *Art Journal,* XLII (1982).
Our Hidden Heritage: Five Centuries of Women Artists (New York, 1974).

Jean Tulard, *Napoleon: The Myth of the Saviour,* trans. Teresa Waugh (London, 1984).

J. Turquan, *Les femmes de l'émigration* (Paris, 1911).

Twilight of the Grand Tour: Catalogue of Drawings by James Hakewill in the British School at Rome Library (Rome, 1992).

Robert Upstone, *Sketchbooks of the Romantics* (Secaucus, New Jersey, 1991).

Pierre de Vaissière, *A Coblence* (Paris, 1924).

Eduard Vehse, *Geschichte der deutschen Höfe seit der Reformation,* 34 vols (Hamburg, 1851–60).

Leone Vicchi, *Les Français à Rome pendant la Convention (1792–1795)* (Paris, 1893).

Elisabeth Louise Vigée-Le Brun, 'Enoncé des différents bruits que j'ai eu à supporter jusqu'à ce moment', in Princesse N. Kourakine, *Souvenirs de voyage* (Moscow, 1903).
Souvenirs, ed. Claudine Herrmann, 2 vols (Paris, 1984).

Dominique Vivant Denon, *L'Originale e il ritratto* (Bassano, 1792).

Sabine Voigt, 'Das Bild einer Künstlerin: Elisabeth Vigée-Le Brun', *Philosophischer Taschenkalender,* vol. 2 (1992–3).

Vorontzov Archive, ed. Peter Bartenev, 40 vols (Moscow, 1863–1917).

Michel Vovelle, *La Chute de la monarchie 1787–1792* (Paris, 1972).

Voyage de deux François dans le nord de l'Europe, 5 vols (Paris, 1796).

Albert Vuaflart, 'La Tombe de Madame Vigée Le Brun à Louveciennes', *Bulletin de la Société de l'histoire de Paris,* 42 (1915).

Françoise Wagener, *Madame Récamier* (Paris, 1986).

Hans Wagner, 'Ligne und Österreich' in *Österreich in Geschichte und Literatur,* 6th Year (1962), vol. 8.

Peter Walch, 'Angelica Kauffman', Ph.D. Thesis, Princeton University, 1968.

K. Waliszewski, *Autour d'un trône: Catherine II de Russie, ses collaborateurs, ses amis, ses favoris,* 8th edition (Paris, 1905).

Le Roman d'une impératrice: Catherine II de Russie (Paris, 1902).

Margaret Waller, 'The Melancholy Man and the Lady with the Lyre: the Sexual Politics of Genius in Early Romantic Fiction and Painting', *Correspondences: Studies in Literature, History and the Arts in Nineteenth-Century France,* ed. Keith Busby (Amsterdam, 1993).

Martin Warnke, *The Court Artist,* trans. David McLintock (Cambridge, 1993).

Alexandre Wassiltchikow, *Les Razoumovski,* trans. Alexandre Brückner, 3 vols (Halle, 1893–4).

Wendy Wassyng Roworth, ed., *Angelica Kauffman: A Continental Artist in Georgian England* (catalogue to exhibition in Brighton Museum and Art Gallery, Brighton, 1992).

Margery Weiner, *The French Exiles, 1789–1815* (London, 1960).

Richard Wendorf, *The Elements of Life* (Oxford, 1991).

'Ut pictura biographia', in *Articulate Images,* ed. Richard Wendorf (Minnesota, 1983).

S. Weston, *A Slight Sketch of Paris in Its Improved State since 1802* (London, 1814).

Henry B. Wheatley, *London Past and Present,* 3 vols (London, 1891).

John Whitehead, *The French Interior in the Eighteenth Century* (London, 1992).

Beverly Whitney Kean, *All the Empty Palaces: The Merchant Patrons of Modern Art in Pre-Revolutionary Russia* (New York, 1983).

Wien von Maria Theresa bis zur Französenzeit: aus den Tagebüchern des Grafen Karl von Zinzendorf, ed. and trans. Hans Wagner (Vienna, 1972).

Daniel and Guy Wildenstein, *Documents complémentaires au catalogue de l'œuvre de Louis David* (Paris, 1973).

Stephanie Wiles, 'The Picturesque Landscape', in *Sketching at Home and Abroad: British Landscape Drawings, 1750–1850* (New York, 1992).

E. M. Wilkinson, 'French Emigrés in England, 1789–1802', 2 vols, B. Litt. thesis, University of Oxford, 1952.

H. M. Williams, *A Tour in Switzerland* (London, 1798).

Andrew Wilton and Ilaria Bignamini, eds., *Grand Tour: The Lure of Italy in the Eighteenth Century* (London, 1996).

Johann Joachim Winckelmann, 'Freundschaftliche Briefe', *Werke*, ed. Joseph Eiselein, 12 vols (Osnabrück, 1965), X.

Mary Wollstonecraft, *A Vindication of the Rights of Women*, ed. Sylvana Tomaselli (Cambridge, 1995).

N. W. Wraxhall, *Memoirs of the Courts of Berlin, Dresden, Warsaw and Vienna in the Years 1777, 1778 and 1992*, 2 vols (London, 1799).

Henry Redhead Yorke, *France in 1802*, ed J.A.C. Sykes (London, 1906).

Arthur Young, *Travels in France and Italy during the Years 1787, 1788 and 1789* (London, 1911).

INDEX